Losing an Enemy

Losing an Enemy

Obama, Iran, and
the Triumph of Diplomacy

TRITA PARSI

Yale UNIVERSITY PRESS/NEW HAVEN & LONDON

Yale University Press books may be purchased in quantity for
educational, business, or promotional use. For information,
please e-mail sales.press@yale.edu (U.S. office) or
sales@yaleup.co.uk (U.K. office).

Set in Minion type by Westchester Publishing Services
Printed in the United States of America

Library of Congress Control Number: 2016963576
ISBN 978-0-300-21816-9

A catalogue record for this book is available from
the British Library.

This paper meets the requirements of ANSI/NISO Z39.48-1992
(Permanence of Paper).

10 9 8 7 6 5 4 3 2 1

To the memory of my friend and teacher,
Ruhi Ramazani

Contents

Preface

Blessed are the peace makers.

Jesus of Nazareth, ca. AD 30

This book is focused on geopolitics and foreign policy and, more specifically, on how the leaders of Iran, the United States, the United Kingdom, France, Germany, Russia, and China avoided the twin dangers of war and a nuclear-armed Iran. It's the triangular story of an intertwined geopolitical battle primarily among the United States, Israel, and Iran. The security interests of the United States and Israel, which never fully coincided, increasingly diverged after the 2003 Iraq war, while the enmity of the United States and Iran was never complete either. The book seeks to document and explain how domestic and geopolitical factors—as well as luck—made diplomacy possible, and how the diplomats and negotiators made the nuclear deal achievable. It analyzes the decisions of the governments and actors involved, as well as factors that impacted the decision-making process, such as lack of information, mistrust of the other side's intentions, and domestic constraints on foreign policy maneuverability. Earlier chapters of the book are based on my two previous books on this matter, *Treacherous Alliance: The Secret Dealings of Israel, Iran, and the United States,* and *A Single Roll of the Dice: Obama's Diplomacy with Iran,* which explained the foundation for the geopolitical rivalry and documented the many missed chances to resolve tensions diplomatically, including over Iran's nuclear program. This book is in many ways the third part of a trilogy, and shows not only how the United States and Iran resolved the nuclear crisis, but also how the American policy of containing Iran and establishing a Middle East order without Iran's inclusion—which is at the center of the geopolitical tensions—finally came to an end.

This book is based predominantly on primary sources, that is, interviews with decision-makers from the United States, the European Union, Russia, Israel, and Iran. For the chapter dealing specifically with the nuclear negotiations after 2010, more than seventy interviews were conducted with top government officials and the actual negotiators, as well as with outside actors in Washington, DC, who were aiding President Obama's diplomatic strategy. Their accounts of the events have been cross-checked. Where information comes from just one or two testimonies, it is accompanied by appropriate caveats. The interviewees were selected on the basis of their direct role in the negotiations or in planning them.

Much of the book also comes from my personal observations as a witness and a minor actor in the process. As the president of the National Iranian American Council and a longtime advocate of diplomacy, I was consulted and briefed by the U.S. government throughout the negotiations and in their aftermath. Simultaneously, I maintained a close dialogue with the Iranian negotiators to better understand their perspective. It wasn't unusual for me to attend a briefing at the White House a few days before a round of negotiations and then have a two-hour conversation with the Iranian foreign minister in his private hotel room in the midst of the negotiations a few days later. My access to top decision-makers on both sides gave me a unique perspective, which I have tried to use to enrich this book and its analysis. Secondary sources, such as the writings of other analysts and news items, have also been utilized. The news items are primarily from English-language sources as well as from Iranian newspapers written in Persian.

Although it is not possible to list all the officials interviewed (and a number of them preferred to remain anonymous), some should be mentioned. Secretary of State John Kerry, Deputy Secretary of State William Burns, Deputy National Security Advisor Ben Rhodes, lead negotiator Wendy Sherman, as well as other key players in the U.S. negotiating team such as Jake Sullivan, Richard Nephew, and Rob Malley, among others, provided invaluable insights into the Obama administration's thinking and strategic considerations in regard to the negotiations as well as the broader geopolitical situation. Concerning the efforts to secure the deal in Congress, I am very grateful for the perspectives of Senators Tim Kaine and Dick Durbin and House members Nancy Pelosi, Jan Schakowsky, Keith Ellison, and David Price.

On the Iranian side, Foreign Minister Javad Zarif was enormously generous with his time and insights, as were Mohammad Nahavandian, President Hassan Rouhani's chief of staff, and Deputy Foreign Minister Majid Ravanchi. In addition, the high representative of the European Union for foreign affairs and security policy, Federica Mogherini, France's ambassador to the United States, Gérard Araud, Britain's ambassador to the United States, Peter Westmacott, Germany's ambassador to the United States, Peter Wittig, and Russia's deputy foreign minister, Sergey Ryabkov, provided contexts for and insights into the views and calculations of the other key players in these historic events.

The book begins with a geopolitical scene setter. Chapters 2–4 then go on to describe the roots of the rivalry among the United States, Israel, and Iran, as well as the roots of the disorder in the Middle East following the U.S. invasion of Iraq. Chapters 5 and 6 address President Obama's first attempt at diplomacy and how domestic political constraints led him to abandon it. In Chapters 7 and 8, I describe the effort to dramatically ramp up sanctions on Iran, as well as the tensions between Obama and the Israeli prime minister, which worsened due to Netanyahu's threats to take military action against Iran. In Chapters 9 and 10, I reveal previously unknown details about the groundbreaking secret negotiations between the United States and Iran hosted by the government of Oman, which eventually helped lay the foundation for the nuclear deal. Chapter 11, which focuses on the surprise election of Hassan Rouhani, analyzes how he managed to defeat his political rivals and considers the ways in which his victory significantly improved the prospects for a nuclear breakthrough. Chapters 12–15 tell the story of how the negotiators, after twenty months of painstaking talks, finally managed to secure the historic deal, while Chapter 16 gives an inside account of the subsequent fight in Congress where opponents of diplomacy made their last stand against Obama's nuclear deal.

The last chapter of the book analyzes why diplomacy succeeded and what we can learn from this episode in order to better use this tool of statecraft to resolve future international conflicts. It also provides a forward-thinking consideration of the threats to the durability of the nuclear deal, as well as asking whether the deal will enable the United States to lose an enemy in the Middle East—or whether the positive gains in U.S.-Iran relations will eventually be lost.

Acknowledgments

This project would never have been completed had it not been for the help and assistance of countless friends and colleagues. There is not enough room here to thank everyone who deserves credit, nor can I thank enough the ones I do mention. I would like to thank my agent, Deborah Grosvenor, for the invaluable help she has provided, and Chris Rogers and Seth Ditchik at Yale University Press for their patience and persistence. Stephen Heintz and the Rockefeller Brothers Fund offered generous support for the research behind the book. I must also thank the many talented research assistants who provided vital help in editing, information gathering, and research. I wish to thank first and foremost Erin Poll, who worked with me almost from the outset of this project and whose assistance went well beyond what was required of her. I also wish to thank Derya Corcor, Leila Gharagozlou, Maria Hardman, Parsa Ghahramani, Behbod Negahban, Sofia Jannati, Chiya Manuchery, Roksana Borzouei, Shervin Vahedi, Emily Salwen, Aylar Banafshe, Joseph Molnar, Karina Bakhshi-Azar, and Christian Jepsen.

Of course, I would like thank my family: my wife, Amina, who showed far more patience during the writing of this book than I deserved, my children, Darius, Jamil, and Yasmine, whose curiosity inspires me to remain young at heart, my parents, and my brother Rouzbeh.

But above all, I must thank my friend and mentor, the late Ruhi Ramazani, Dean of Iranian Foreign Policy Studies at the University of Virginia, who passed away only weeks before I completed this book. I could not have written it had it not been for his advice and friendship and, perhaps more important, the standards he set for the study of Iranian foreign policy.

Sadly, I never got the chance to let him know that I was planning to dedicate the book to him.

Losing an Enemy

Introduction

Where there is a will, there is a way.

Old English proverb

L ieutenant David Nartker and his nine sailors were frantically trying to revive the engine of one of their command boats. Their mission had gone astray halfway between Kuwait and Bahrain. They had left Kuwait three hours late, they didn't have enough fuel for their 240-nautical-mile journey, and on top of that, one of their boats had mechanical problems. They had no choice but to stop in the middle of the Persian Gulf to cannibalize parts from one of their boats to fix the other. They knew they were off course, but with a malfunctioning navigation system they could not tell how far.

They didn't know they were in Iranian waters.

Suddenly, two patrol boats belonging to the Iranian Revolutionary Guard Corps (IRGC)—the hardline Iranian military force that often put itself in the crosshairs of the United States in Iraq, Afghanistan, and the Persian Gulf—showed up, guns drawn. This was every U.S. sailor's worst nightmare: the Americans had superior firepower, but the hostility between the United States and Iran in the Persian Gulf could cause a small incident like this to escalate into full-blown war. While U.S. forces were strictly ordered to avoid any altercations with the Iranians— including through an unwritten rule stating not to shoot first—the IRGC Navy had a history of provoking the U.S. side with reckless maneuvers that on many occasions could easily have led to a military confrontation.

One of the Americans waved a wrench in the air to signal they were suffering mechanical problems and had no hostile intent. But the Iranians weren't that easily convinced. As they saw it, military boats with armed sailors from a hostile power had entered their waters unin- vited. Two more Iranian ships joined in, surrounding the Americans and ordering them to surrender. For a brief moment, Nartker consid- ered fighting his way out of the situation. He could have aimed his M4 assault rifle at one of the Iranians and taken him out, but he knew he couldn't get very far with a broken boat. "I am not going to kill this guy right now over a bullshit navigation mistake," he thought to himself. It wasn't just the immediate situation he worried about—it was the reper- cussions of his actions that frightened him. "I was not going to ignite a conflict over this," he later told the American news magazine *Foreign Policy*. "And I don't have the authority to start a war."[1]

The Americans thus handed over their weapons, kneeled down, and put their hands behind their heads. They were now prisoners of the Revolutionary Guard. It was January 12, 2016: in a few hours, President Barack Obama was scheduled to deliver his last State of the Union ad- dress to Congress, while in five days the United States was scheduled to lift sanctions against Iran as part of a historic nuclear deal.

The timing of the mechanical mishap could not have been worse.

Iran's energetic foreign minister, Javad Zarif, was leaving a theater in Tehran after watching a play about Amir Kabir, the nineteenth-century Persian prime minister widely known as "Iran's first reformer." It was nine o'clock in the evening, and he had to go to the Foreign Ministry for a call with U.S. Secretary of State John Kerry to discuss the final steps before "Implementation Day" and the scheduled lifting of U.S. and EU sanctions on Iran. As he left, his cell phone rang; Iran's deputy na- tional security advisor was calling to break the news to Zarif about the American sailors. Four hours had passed since the sailors were apprehended by the IRGC, and the Iranians had concluded that the Americans were telling the truth. The sailors had lost their way, and there had been no hostile intent, even though the timing was curious.

Zarif immediately worried that Obama would address the incident publicly before or during his State of the Union address. Since it was a mistake, the best scenario was for the sailors to be released as soon as possible. If Obama or other senior U.S. officials began commenting on the matter, particularly with threatening language, it would become drastically more difficult for Zarif to navigate the Iranian political system and secure the sailors' swift release. As Zarif likes to say, Iranians are allergic to threats. "Knowing the United States," Zarif told me, "the language they'd use would be 'Iran *must* release our guys.' And then Iran would take it as a threat. And then we would have responded, and then this whole thing would have taken a life of its own."[2]

Too much was at stake for it to be put at risk by a navigation error by some U.S. sailors. After years of threats, sanctions, and painstaking negotiations, Iran, the United States, and the permanent members of the UN Security Council plus Germany (P5 + 1) had found a compromise that satisfied all sides. The deal blocked all of Iran's paths to a nuclear bomb through a combination of technical restrictions, inspections, and transparency mechanisms. In turn, Iran kept an exclusively peaceful nuclear energy program that included uranium enrichment. Having been on the precipice of war, the United States and Iran had miraculously managed to make a move for peace.

While the deal was based on a groundbreaking scientific formula, the real challenge to the negotiations was not technical but human. After more than three decades of mutual demonization and intense geopolitical rivalry, trust between the United States and Iran was essentially nonexistent. Without trust, even the most brilliant and self-evident solution would be rejected by the overly suspicious parties. However, after 2003 and the turmoil following the invasion of Iraq, the geopolitical and domestic political stars in the United States and Iran slowly began to align, opening the path for a possible diplomatic solution. If, that is, the leaders in power had the political will and courage to invest in a process that might be geopolitically necessary, but dangerous from a domestic political standpoint. As luck would have it, both the United

States and Iran had leaders at the time—Barack Obama and Hassan Rouhani respectively—who were skeptical of military action and inclined to explore what diplomacy might bring to fruition.

Now, the fruits of their efforts were in jeopardy—not because of Prime Minister Netanyahu and his allies in Congress and Saudi Arabia, but because of ten lost U.S. sailors. It wasn't just the nuclear deal with its potential long-term benefits for U.S.-Iran relations that was at risk. For the past fourteen months, the United States and Iran had been secretly negotiating a prisoner swap that would secure the release of five Americans held in Iran and five Iranians held in the United States. The swap was scheduled to take place within a few days. If the sailor issue wasn't quickly resolved, it would be politically impossible for the United States to lift sanctions on Iran as it was obligated to do by the deal or release its Iranian prisoners for the Americans held in Iran. "It is hard for us to imagine being able to announce that we were gonna lift sanctions on Iran and go ahead with the implementation of the deal if they were holding some number of American sailors in an unresolved situation," a senior administration official told me. "Nothing would have moved." The Iranians had reached the same conclusion. "I was afraid that this would jeopardize everything, not just the implementation of the nuclear deal," Zarif said.[3]

Secretary of State John Kerry and Secretary of Defense Ash Carter were meeting with their Filipino counterparts on the eighth floor of the State Department when they were informed about the apprehension of the sailors. At first, Kerry and Carter operated in a fog: Were the sailors in Iranian or international waters? If the former, how did they end up there? Was this an accident or a deliberate effort by the IRGC Navy to sabotage the nuclear deal? As soon as it was clear that the error was on the American side, the Obama administration swiftly moved to deescalate the situation. Several U.S. agencies reviewed prior cases of sailor incidents and found they usually took two to three weeks of extensive diplomacy to resolve, if not longer. Had the incident taken place only two years earlier, U.S. diplomats would be scrambling for a plan. Now, thanks to the strong relationship Kerry and Zarif had developed over the course of the nuclear talks, Washington had one: talk to the

Iranians directly to sort things out. "Three years ago, we wouldn't have known who to call," Kerry explained to me.[4]

Zarif was waiting by the phone, since he and Kerry were scheduled to speak at 9:30 p.m. (his time), 1:00 p.m. (EST). "Do you know the story?" Kerry asked. "Had you not called, I would have called you," Zarif replied. Kerry explained the sailors were headed to Kuwait from Bahrain but got off course due to mechanical problems. They had not attempted to violate Iran's sovereign territory; America's priority, Kerry assured Zarif, was the sailors' release and well-being. He repeated several times to the Iranian foreign minister that if this issue was resolved quickly, it "could turn what is a very complicated situation into a story that is somewhat positive for both of us and demonstrate the ability to solve problems in a crisis." If it wasn't, however, this incident could derail everything from the prisoner swap, to implementation day, to any potential non-nuclear dividends that could follow the nuclear deal.

"I know what will happen if this doesn't get resolved," Zarif answered. "You don't need to threaten me. You've committed a grave mistake. So I think what you need to do right now is to say 'We made a mistake. We're sorry.'" If Kerry's message was "Don't let this unravel the nuclear deal," Zarif's argument was "We don't want the sailors, so don't force us to keep them by making threats." They decided to touch base again within an hour. Zarif made phone calls within the Iranian system to secure the release, while Kerry ensured that U.S. messaging and tone wouldn't aggravate the situation. The Pentagon quickly confirmed that the sailors were in Iranian waters and were being treated well. "In some ways this has been very professional," a Pentagon official told the press. It was noteworthy that the U.S. side admitted guilt and refrained from using language that could be perceived as threatening. Clearly, Zarif's advice had been taken to heart.[5]

The two spoke again an hour later, with Zarif giving a briefing on the state of the sailors. It was nighttime in Iran, so it would be better if the sailors were to be released at dawn the next morning, he said. As Zarif was speaking to Kerry, he heard on his other phone that IRGC commanders were reporting that U.S. Navy ships and helicopters were approaching the Iranian island where the sailors were kept. If they violated Iranian airspace, things could get ugly. "Please tell your navy not to get close," Zarif told Kerry, his tone revealing the urgency of the matter. "We don't want a military confrontation. But if your planes get close, we will have serious trouble." Kerry immediately hung up and called General Joseph Dunford, the chairman of the Joint Chiefs of Staff, to urge him to pull back. "We're risking potential escalation here," Kerry told the general. "They were giving us positive indications that they are gonna release these guys, so we should back off the helicopters for now and test if this is real." Dunford complied and a dangerous confrontation was avoided. To prove that the sailors were safe, Zarif later emailed a picture of them from his Gmail account to Kerry's State Department email.[6]

For Zarif, this was a damage control operation on two fronts. First, he had to make sure that the United States didn't make any threatening statements or raise the issue in the State of the Union address in a way that could turn the release of the sailors into a political problem in Iran. Second, he had to make sure other actors in the Iranian system didn't move the sailors to the Iranian port city of Bushehr, since that would have caused "all sorts of political tendencies to come to the surface" and transform it from a military to a political issue.[7]

Zarif and Kerry spoke to each other five times that day. Clearly, the Iranians were cooperating, and the channels of communication were open and effective. President Obama saw no value in raising the issue in the State of the Union address, even though the news had broken. By contrast, his critics "rushed to declare that it was the start of another hostage crisis" and portrayed him as weak, indecisive, and foolish, all the while blatantly ignoring the intrusion of the sailors into Iranian waters. "The fact that you have an active conversation going on diplomatically means you're not going to be talking about this," a White House official explained.[8]

Despite the detractors, the American sailors were released unharmed only sixteen hours after their apprehension. A crisis that could have jeopardized everything from the nuclear deal to the prisoner swap was resolved in less than a day thanks to the newly won ability for Iran and the United States to talk to each other directly. Had the incident taken place only a few years earlier, the United States would have been at a loss. "We would have called the Swiss. We would have called some other country and said, 'Can you help us?'" Kerry said at the Aspen Ideas Festival. "Enough time would have gone by, and there would have been sufficient level of enmity that those guys probably would have been hostages and we would have had another situation. But within thirty minutes I had my counterpart on the phone; within an hour and a half we had a deal." And had it not become dark outside by the time a deal had been secured, the sailors could have been released even sooner. "If we had not hit the night, it would have been resolved in less than [sixteen hours], because there was no reason to keep them," Zarif recalled.[9]

Something remarkable had happened. The "Great Satan" and the "foremost terror sponsor in the world" weren't acting like sworn enemies anymore. In the past, even small windows of opportunity to reduce tension had been sabotaged by hawkish elements in Iran or the United States. The domestic balance of power in the capitals of both countries had favored those addicted to enmity. Now the hawks couldn't even capitalize on a crisis. Although both Tehran and Washington had a clear interest in moving forward with the nuclear deal and the prisoner swap, the fact that hawks in Iran lacked the strength to throw a wrench in the wheels of diplomacy was indicative of the promise of a new relationship that could emerge in the aftermath of the nuclear deal. "They could have had people in their system arguing, 'This gives us a new bargaining chip, we should try to reopen the negotiations and get something for this,'" a White House official told me. In the end, though, the Iranians didn't even ask for additional concessions from the U.S. side.[10]

While the nuclear deal was never sold to the American public as a means of establishing a new relationship with Iran or to shift Iran's other policies, Obama and his team clearly hoped that the nuclear deal would open a path toward improved relations. "The idea of exploring a different relationship with Iran over the next fifteen years was attractive," a former National Security Council official said of the broader implications of the deal. The sailor incident was the first datapoint indicating that something dramatic had changed in the U.S.-Iran relationship. It had matured. A modicum of trust had been built. "The relationship is more resilient now and less fragile," a senior White House official told me. "The nuclear deal has helped create constraints on the degree of conflict and help compartmentalize the relationship."[11] The president did not shy away from crediting his nuclear diplomacy with the release of the sailors and the American prisoners in Iran:

> For decades, our differences with Iran meant that our governments almost never spoke to each other. Ultimately, that did not advance America's interests. Over the years, Iran moved closer and closer to having the ability to build a nuclear weapon. But from Presidents Franklin Roosevelt to John F. Kennedy to Ronald Reagan, the United States has never been afraid to pursue diplomacy with our adversaries. And as President, I decided that a strong, confident America could advance our national security by engaging directly with the Iranian government. . . . I want to also point out that by working with Iran on this nuclear deal, we were better able to address other issues. When our sailors in the Persian Gulf accidentally strayed into Iranian waters that could have sparked a major international incident.[12]

The hardliners did fight back, though they were reduced to scoring pitiful propaganda points rather than successfully sabotaging the release. For instance, after footage of the sailors' arrest was made public, the IRGC reenacted it in a parade, infuriating the United States. The U.S. Navy was deeply embarrassed by the entire episode, and six of the U.S. sailors were later reprimanded for having caused the incident in the first place. According to a Navy investigation, the sailors had committed almost every mistake possible. It "was a Three Stooges movie from beginning to end," a Pentagon official admitted.[13]

Still, the swift resolution of the crisis went beyond anyone's expectation. No one could suggest that the United States had gained a new friend in Iran, since tensions still remained on many fronts. But was the United States beginning to lose an enemy?

During President Obama's last term, diplomacy between the United States and Iran reached unprecedented levels, and, against all odds, a compromise on the nuclear issue was reached. Both the diplomacy that led to the deal and the deal itself flew in the face of conventional wisdom in the West. Iran was supposed to be an irrational actor, hell-bent on Israel's destruction and acquiring nuclear weapons, and so ideologically and geopolitically opposed to the United States that attempting to negotiate with Tehran was absurd. Instead, with the aid of its allies in the P5 + 1, the United States negotiated over the course of twenty months a historic deal that simultaneously evaded two potential disasters: a war with Iran and Tehran obtaining a nuclear weapons option.

But it would be erroneous to view these negotiations and the deal they produced solely as a nuclear matter. In essence, they formed the final chapter of a thirty-five-year battle over the geopolitical order in the region in general and Iran's place in that order in particular. After containing Iran for decades, the United States and the West had come to terms with the idea of Iran as a regional power. This was the primary reason why Saudi Arabia and Israel opposed the nuclear deal: it marked the end of U.S. efforts to uphold an order in the region based on Iran's exclusion on the one hand and Israel's and Saudi Arabia's primacy on the other. After all, pressure and containment had not shifted Iran's policies and conduct in the preferred direction. On the contrary, throughout this period, Iran had grown more powerful, its nuclear program had expanded, and it had become more capable of challenging Western interests.

Ultimately, the United States shifted its Iran policy for two reasons. First, the Middle East had begun losing strategic significance, leaving the United States overcommitted there and undercommitted in the region gaining greater geopolitical importance: East Asia. Second, the containment policy—and its nuclear subpolicy of sanctioning Iran—had been bringing the United States and Iran to the brink of war. The United States' ability to shift its focus east would have been decisively set back had the nuclear standoff ended in a military confrontation. For the sake of the United States' global geopolitical priorities, a peaceful solution to the Iranian conundrum had to be found.

Nevertheless, the United States could not simply acquiesce to an Iranian nuclear fait accompli. The problem had to be resolved in such a manner that Iran's paths toward a bomb would be blocked—otherwise the risk of war would quickly rise again, jeopardizing the United States' larger geopolitical objectives. Through secret negotiations in Oman, Obama enticed the Iranians with an offer to accept uranium enrichment on Iranian soil in return for restrictions on their program and intrusive inspections. With Iran's redline now accepted, Tehran finally showed flexibility and agreed to the limitations to its nuclear program that it had earlier refused. With that, Iran and the United States managed to chart a path toward peace from the depths of enmity. The question that remains is not only whether the nuclear deal will endure, but also whether it will pave the way for a broader opening between the United States and Iran. In other words, will the nuclear deal enable the United States to lose Iran as an enemy and usher in a new relationship?

I argue that it is critical to understand how and why diplomacy with Iran succeeded. The United States' ability to use the blueprint of the Iran deal to resolve future conflicts necessitates an accurate understanding of how the deal came about, from the geopolitical factors to the negotiation tactics. Indeed, in an increasingly tumultuous world, the debate in the U.S. foreign policy establishment will involve calibrating between pressure and inducements for years to come. I challenge the conventional wisdom in Washington, which tends to credit sanctions and pressure, and show that the sanctions regime placed on Iran ultimately proved only that sanctions do not work. Rather than bringing the parties closer to a deal, sanctions brought them closer to war. In the end, it was Obama's acceptance of Iran's redline—enrichment on Iranian soil—that elicited a softer Iranian stance, which, in turn, enabled a compromise. Absent this crucial shift, the United States would likely be at war with Iran right now.

Israel's Master Stroke

While the Iranian Revolution of 1979 turned the United States and Iran into bitter enemies almost overnight, the U.S.-Iran relationship still managed to take an additional turn for the worse after the 1991 Persian Gulf War and the collapse of the Soviet Union. These two geopolitical shocks—the defeat of Iraq in 1991, which decimated the most powerful Arab army in the world, and the transition toward a unipolar world following the defeat of the Soviet Union in the Cold War—dramatically altered the global balance of power. In the new world order, the United States was the sole, undisputed superpower of the world. The shifting balance was also significant regionally. With Iraq defeated and the Soviet Union no longer there to back the Arab bloc, Israel and Iran emerged out of the ashes of the old order as two of the most powerful states in the region. But unlike in previous decades, when common threats had prompted them to collaborate on shared geostrategic interests in spite of Iran's anti-Israeli posture, their geopolitical outlook started to dramatically diverge (even though Iran's revolutionary zeal was actually cooling). The common threats had evaporated. Israeli strategists began to argue that with no powerful Iraq to buffer Iran from Israel, the Islamic Republic now had the ability to pose a threat to Israel. Perhaps more important, the inevitable process of establishing a new regional equilibrium pitted Iran and Israel against each other, with Iran seeing the reordering of the region as an opportunity to break out of its isolation and regain a stronger standing, and Israel having more to lose than to gain from this geopolitical shock. But through a bold strategic move, Israel managed both to reclaim its centrality in the United States' strategic outlook for the Middle East and to convince Washington to establish a new order in the region based on Iran's prolonged isolation.

During the Cold War, Israel's alliance with the United States followed strong strategic logic. Israel was an important member of the Western camp and a buffer against Soviet penetration in the Middle East. In the post–Cold War world, however, the strategic logic of the U.S.-Israel relationship was put to test. The first sign of this came in the run-up to the Persian Gulf War. When Iraqi strongman Saddam Hussein invaded Kuwait in 1990 with the goal of annexing it, he failed to recognize that the weakness of the Soviet Union would limit its ability to frustrate any effort by the United States to seek UN Security Council action to challenge or reverse his annexation attempt. To Saddam Hussein's surprise, Moscow acquiesced to the United States' leadership, paving the way for the Security Council to authorize the use of force to repel Saddam's invading army.

President George H. W. Bush, however, saw that a mere international coalition to stop Saddam was insufficient. It had to have a strong Arab component in order to dispel any notion that the conflict was between the West and the Arab world, or that the United States was leading a campaign against Islam. But before the United States' Arab allies could join the coalition, Israel had to be kept out of the coalition. In what some have described as the end of Arab nationalism, the Arab states could stomach fighting another Arab country alongside the United States. But they could not stomach fighting another fellow Arab nation together with the United States *and* Israel.[1]

This was as unprecedented as it was worrisome for Israel: for the first time, the United States went out of its way to attract Arab states to join in a regional coalition while keeping Israel at arm's length. To make matters worse, Saddam tried to break up the Arab anti-Iraq alliance by linking Iraq's occupation of Kuwait with Israel's control over Palestinian territory. In an effort to win over the Arab publics (also referred to as the Arab streets), Saddam offered to leave Kuwait if Israel relinquished its hold on Palestinian land. Moreover, Saddam deliberately attacked Israel with thirty-four Scud missiles to incite Israeli retaliation, calculating that the moment Israel entered the war, the Arab anti-Iraq coalition would fall apart.

Saddam Hussein's maneuvering complicated the United States' challenge. On the one hand, Washington had to put unprecedented pressure on Israel in order to prevent it from retaliating against Iraqi Scud attacks and thus told Israel "in the strongest possible words" that it needed to keep itself out of the Iraq operation.[2] On the other hand, the Israeli doctrine of deterrence, which dictated that Arab attacks needed to be met with disproportionate force, made not responding at all an extremely difficult decision for Israeli Prime Minister Yitzhak Shamir. The image that Israel was relying on the United States for protection was hard for ordinary Israelis to accept. Many feared the decision to accommodate the United States "would cause irreparable damage to Israel's deterrent capabilities."[3]

Furthermore, in order to neutralize Saddam's linkage between Kuwait and Palestine, as well as to compel the Arabs to help push back against Iraqi occupation of Kuwaiti territory, Washington had to promise that after the military campaign against Iraq, it would host a major conference to address the Israeli occupation of Palestinian territory. The United States essentially used the promise of resolving the Arab-Israel conflict as a carrot to convince the Arab states to join the anti-Iraq coalition.

This new political dynamic—in which Israel was a liability rather than a strategic asset to the United States and in which Washington was perceived to be gravitating toward the Arab position on the Israeli-Palestinian conflict—was most worrisome to Tel Aviv, even though the destruction of Saddam's war machine greatly benefited Israel. In the new emerging order, Israeli leaders were worried that Israel had lost its strategic significance.[4] Indeed, some Western officials publicly argued that the value of the alliance with Israel had sharply declined. William Waldegrave, British minister of state at the Foreign Office, said in Parliament that in the new Middle East order, Israel had ceased to matter.

The United States, Waldegrave explained, should learn that a strategic alliance with Israel "was not particularly useful if it cannot be used in a crisis such as this. . . . Now the U.S. knows that an alliance with Israel that is of no use for this situation is useless."[5]

In the absence of a conventional Arab military, Israel's focus shifted to three new security challenges: the internal threat posed by an increasingly rebellious Palestinian population living under occupation, the spread of weapons of mass destruction, and the challenges to Israel's special relationship with Washington.[6] The most immediate threat was the Palestinian uprising—the Intifada. Israelis were taken aback by the Palestinians' resilience and ability to sustain their uprising. As a result, the cost of the occupation was becoming too high, while the disintegration of Palestinian society also posed a danger to Israel. During the talks between Israeli and Palestinian envoys in Norway, Israel's chief negotiator, Uri Savir, told his Palestinian counterpart, Abu Ala, that "the occupation is corrupting our youth. We want to free ourselves from it."[7]

The other main challenge was maintaining Israel's special relationship with Washington. Any shift in the regional order could undermine the Jewish State's strategic significance, which had previously been so considerable. The Persian Gulf War showed Israel that the Soviet collapse had given Washington much more leeway with the region's Arab states and that the demand for Israel's services as a reliable pro-Western ally in the muddy waters of Middle East politics had declined.[8] With U.S.-Arab relations already warming, decision-makers in Jerusalem feared that a breakthrough in U.S.-Iran relations could wipe out what little strategic significance Israel still retained. As Henry Kissinger had once quipped, "Iran is a crucial piece of strategic real estate."[9] It is strategically located right between the world's two largest reservoirs of oil and natural gas: the Persian Gulf and the Caspian Sea. Iran borders the landlocked central Asian states, which sit on major reserves of oil and natural gas. In the period following the dissolution of the Soviet Union, Iran had a population of more than sixty million and thus offered an economic market ten times larger than that of Israel. In the aftermath of the Persian Gulf War, Israel wrestled with the question of how to prove its strategic utility to the United States. Washington felt that an opportunity existed to resolve the Israeli-Palestinian issue—"It was time to seize the moment because . . . something potentially significant [was] stirring among the Arabs," Secretary of State James Baker wrote in his memoirs—and that the United States' newly won position as the sole superpower of the world necessitated American leadership on this issue.[10] For Israel, this was bad news, as Washington's desire to tackle the issue came at a time when it was already improving its relations with the Arab states. "There was a feeling that there was an inherent danger in this," said Efraim Halevy, the former head of the Israeli Mossad. "The United States might feel a necessity to tilt towards the Arabs. . . . The conditions of peace would be such that it would not be acceptable to Israel."[11]

But Yitzhak Shamir was in no mood for peacemaking with the Palestinians. He was expanding illegal settlements on Palestinian territories, despite promises to the Bush administration that the expansions would end. The Bush-Shamir relationship was fraught with tensions, and the resulting squabbles were often heated. At one point Secretary of State Baker even banned Israel's Deputy Foreign Minister Benjamin Netanyahu from the State Department after Netanyahu publicly accused the United States of "building its policy on a foundation of distortion and lies."[12] (Twenty-five years later, at the height of the congressional fight over the Iran nuclear deal, Baker blasted Netanyahu again, accusing him of "diplomatic missteps and political gamesmanship" in his all-out campaign against the deal. But there was added symbolism that few failed to note. The Republican former secretary of state chose the annual gala of J Street—a new, progressively oriented pro-Israel lobby that publicly opposed the Netanyahu government for its rejection of diplomacy with Iran and its continued occupation of Palestinian territories—to present his critique of Netanyahu.[13] The message was clear: Netanyahu had moved so far to the right—as had the Republican Party—that a Republican secretary of state could use the platform of a progressive organization to critique the Israeli premier.)

After another big fight over American loan guarantees to Israel and Shamir's refusal to negotiate with the leader of the Palestine Liberation Organization (PLO), Yasser Arafat, Washington's patience with the Shamir government was reaching a breaking point. During a heated telephone conversation between Bush and Shamir, Bush clarified that the United States was "not trying to force [Israel] to talk with the PLO. But we do wish there could be less delay in responding factually to us. . . . If you give us a positive response, then Israel and the U.S. can move forward together. If you don't respond, we have to interpret that you don't want to go forward. . . . I've just read the wire story quoting you about a confrontation with the United States. If you want that—fine." The tensions in U.S.-Israel relations were fittingly summed up by Baker's brusque public message to Israel: "When you're serious about peace, call us." Clearly, U.S.-Israel relations were at a low point.[14]

Tehran's Ticket Out of Isolation?

Where Israel saw threats, Iran saw opportunities. For more than a decade, the Arab states had viewed Iran as the greatest threat to their interests, to the extent that they funded Saddam Hussein's efforts against Iran during the Iran-Iraq war (1980–1988). But with Saddam now turning his guns against the very same Arab states that had paid for those guns, Tehran felt vindicated, as Saddam's actions demonstrated the Arabs' shortsightedness in previously supporting Iraq. Saddam's aggression against a fellow Arab state was nothing short of a moral victory for Tehran, which believed that Saddam's aggression proved that it was Iraq and not Iran that needed to be balanced.[15]

Perhaps more important, Saddam's recklessness provided Iran with an opportunity to make common cause with the United States. Officially, Iran remained neutral throughout the conflict, siding with neither Washington nor Baghdad. The Iranians called opposing Iraq's occupation while at the same time remaining outside the U.S. anti-Iraqi alliance a policy of "positive neutrality." In reality, however, the policy aided the Americans. "The Iraqis even came and begged for our support," explained Mahmoud Vaezi, Iran's deputy foreign minister at the time, "but we declared that our policy was neutral in the war, which in reality meant that it was a policy against Iraq."[16] Privately, Iran permitted the U.S. Air Force to use Iranian airspace and denied Iraqi requests for support. A special channel of communications with Washington was set up in order to avoid any misunderstandings. Iran also kept a check on the millions of Iraqi refugees who fled to Iran and Turkey after the end of the war, as well as refusing to return Iraqi jets that Iraq had flown to Iran for safekeeping.[17]

Iran's most consequential step was to refrain from aiding the uprising of Iraq's Shia population against Saddam at the end of the war, thereby helping to prevent Iraq from disintegrating into sectarian civil war. These measures were so valuable to Washington that in an unprecedented move, then secretary of state James Baker publicly praised Iran.[18] Yet this appreciation did not translate into a new Iran policy. Nor did the United States become less of a threat in Iran's view—on the contrary. As a result of the Persian Gulf War, the United States had established a major military presence in the gulf. The United States was now inside Iran's sphere of influence with forces that could topple the regime in Tehran. "The U.S. managed to portray Iran as a greater threat to the Arabs than even Israel," said Mohammad Reza Tajik, an advisor to former Iranian president Mohammad Khatami. "This had a crucial impact on our thinking. The U.S. sold more weapons to the Arabs as a result and became the hegemon of the Persian Gulf. Consequently, Iran came under direct U.S. threat."[19]

Yet, the threat from the United States was still overshadowed by the continued danger posed by Saddam's regime in Iraq. Even after its crushing defeat by the United States, Iraq still remained the only country in the region able to threaten Iran's territorial integrity.[20] The psychological scars of the Iran-Iraq war—during which Saddam systematically used chemical weapons against Iranian troops and civilians alike, and with tacit support from the West—were simply too deep for Iran to shift its focus elsewhere as long as Saddam remained in power.[21] As long as Saddam remained in power, Iran had little choice but to focus on the Iraqi threat. "I never had the confidence that [the Iraqis] would miss an opportunity to destroy Iran. And they gave me every reason to further believe that," Iran's then UN ambassador and current foreign minister Javad Zarif told me in 2004.[22]

And it was precisely because of the continued Iraqi threat that Tehran restarted its dormant nuclear program, which later almost brought Israel and the United States to war with Iran (Ayatollah Khomeini had suspended the program in the 1980s on the basis that nuclear

weapons were "un-Islamic"[23]). The end of the Iran-Iraq war did not
bring about a stable peace. On the contrary, both sides were convinced
that the fragile armistice was untenable and that in the first phase of the
inevitable next war, the other side would use weapons of mass destruction, because neither side could afford another lengthy conflict.[24] "We
knew that as long as Saddam was in power, he would do all he could
to seek revenge," said then deputy foreign minister Mahmoud Vaezi.[25]
Later interrogations of Saddam Hussein while in U.S. captivity revealed the Iraqi dictator's obsession with Iran, even in the wake of a
looming U.S. attack on his country. Saddam "was more concerned
about Iran discovering Iraq's weaknesses and vulnerabilities than the
repercussions of the United States for his refusal to allow U.N. inspectors back into Iraq." The interrogations also unveiled the depth of
Washington's misreading of Iraq, prompting one of the Americans involved to describe the United States' understanding of Iraq in 2003 as
"cartoonish."[26]

While Tehran continued to focus on Iraq as its main threat, it did
not discard its central objective of regaining the leadership role it had
lost as a result of the excesses of the revolution and the damage from its
war with Iraq. Iran remained convinced that because of its size and
power, it was destined to be the preeminent state in the Persian Gulf. To
Tehran, the time had come for Washington to recognize this power and
accept Iran as a regional leader. Officials in Iran believed that Iran was
needed in order to establish stability in the region. Hashemi Rafsanjani,
president of Iran from 1989 to 1997, said as much himself: "There is only
one power that can provide the peace and stability of the Persian Gulf,
and that is Iran's power."[27]

But the Iranians did recognize that they needed to change their
strategy. Anti–status quo policies and ideological rigidity would not
bring Iran closer to its geopolitical goals concluded Rafsanjani's centrist
government. Rather, the path toward regional acceptance and leadership was improved relations with the United States and the Arab states
in the Persian Gulf. Iran's policy of positive neutrality during the Persian Gulf War had been well received by the Gulf Cooperation Council
(GCC) states, and old grievances had been set aside, at least for the time
being. Even Saudi Arabia, which Khomeini three years earlier had de-

clared an enemy of Islam, recognized Iran's new pragmatism and extended an invitation to Rafsanjani to visit the kingdom.[28]

Moreover, Rafsanjani coupled the thaw in its relations with its Arab neighbors with a policy of "development first, rearmament second," meaning that Iran significantly cut its arms spending. Its military forces shrank from 654,000 in 1988 to an average size of 480,000 in the 1990–1999 period, and its military expenditure dwindled from $9.9 billion in 1990 to $5.3 billion in 1995. Notably, as a result of this policy, Iran's armed forces were only slightly larger than those of Iraq *after* Saddam's defeat. This policy went beyond the demobilization that often follows war; it was a strategic decision made despite the lack of a final peace agreement between Iran and Iraq. According to General Brent Scowcroft, who served as President George H. W. Bush's national security advisor, Washington did notice Iran's new orientation, but failed to appreciate the full extent of Tehran's new pragmatism.[29]

Iran's objective was to collaborate with the GCC and to create a new security architecture in the Persian Gulf that would balance Iraq and help make the Arab states less dependent on the United States. Washington, however, had a different order in mind. American pressure presented another option for the GCC—to seek either a Middle East order with Iran or an Arab order with the United States. In the end, Iran did not stand much of a chance. Washington preempted a common Persian Gulf security arrangement and managed to continue Iran's exclusion from regional decision-making, cutting the Arab-Iranian honeymoon short.[30] Iran would soon realize that neither Washington nor Tel Aviv was eager to see it come in from the cold.

The Missed Opportunity of Madrid

By October 1991, Shamir had run out of excuses, and Washington managed to drag the Israelis to the peace summit in Madrid. Bush had declared that all peoples of the region would have a say in the formation of the new order of the Middle East, and Baker worked extensively to ensure that regional states had a stake in the process, so that it wouldn't be "easy to walk away from it." Washington's success in ensuring the participation of Israel, Syria, and the Palestinians alike reflected its new position of strength. Almost every nation in the region was invited with one noted exception—Iran.[31]

The Madrid conference of October 1991 was a celebration of the United States' new global position as the sole superpower. While the Soviet Union was still a few months away from crumbling, the writing was on the wall. The great powers co-chaired the conference, but from the very outset, it was clear who was calling the shots. One track of the conference addressed the Israeli-Palestinian conflict; a second, less highlighted one focused on building the Middle East of the future, addressing everything from water, to the environment, arms control, refugees, economic development, and regional security. Altogether, participants in the multilateral talks included forty-three nations, of which fifteen were regional states. At a time when Tehran believed that its opportunity had come to be accepted as a regional power and be included in Middle East decision-making, Washington dashed Iran's hopes by refusing to invite it to the conference. To make matters worse, it was not just that the United States failed to appreciate Tehran's new pragmatism.[32] More important was that Washington did not view Iran as being particularly relevant any longer, partly because it had little to no influence over the Palestinian Authority. "Iran simply had nothing to contribute. It had no leverage over the Arabs, so how could it help the peace process?" then national security advisor General Scowcroft argued.[33] (A few years later, however, both Israel and the United States would blame the failure of the peace process on Iran's influence over the Palestinians.)

Iran wasn't just irrelevant to the Israeli-Palestinian conflict in the minds of Washington's decision-makers; it was irrelevant period. Tehran reacted bitterly to Washington's snub, particularly after the helpful role it felt it had played in indirectly aiding the U.S.-led war against Iraq. Madrid, after all, was not merely a conference on the Israeli-Palestinian conflict; it was the defining moment in forming the new Middle East order—one in which Tehran hoped to play a role commensurate with its geopolitical weight.[34] "It definitely insulted Iran, there is no doubt about that," former deputy foreign minister Hadi Nejad-Hosseinian recalled.[35]

Washington's failure to reciprocate Iran's gestures—even though Tehran's expectations may have been exaggerated—strengthened the hands of Iranian rejectionists, who argued that Washington would never come to terms with Iran voluntarily. Slowly Rafsanjani's policy of moderating Iran's foreign policy and drawing it closer to the Western bloc began to collapse.[36] Convinced that Washington wouldn't grant Iran its legitimate role in the region, Tehran concluded that it was left with no choice but to make U.S. nonrecognition as costly as possible by sabotaging its policies.[37] This conviction "prompted Iran to turn to Palestinian and Lebanese groups that shared the Iranian outlook," noted Ali Reza Alavi Tabar, a prominent Iranian reformist.[38] The Israeli-Palestinian situation was one of the few in which Iran could undermine the United States. Rafsanjani began adopting a sharper position on Israel and departed from his original line of accepting the wishes of the Palestinian Authority.[39]

As soon as it became clear that an invitation to the conference wasn't forthcoming, Iran's supreme leader, Ayatollah Seyyed Ali Khamenei, gave a green light to Ali Akbar Mohtashamipour—one of the cofounders of the Lebanese Hezbollah, who had lobbied Ayatollah Khomeini to actively confront Israel during the 1980s—to organize a conference in opposition to that of Madrid.[40] This was a watershed moment, in that for the first time Iran started to seriously reach out to rejectionist Palestinian groups, in spite of the Shia-Sunni divide and their enmity, which dated back to the Iran-Iraq war, as well as because only a year earlier Iran had begun to reduce its financial support to Hezbollah in Lebanon.[41]

Moreover, this was a critical inflection point, as Iran now began to oppose not only U.S. policies in the region, but the very U.S.-led order in the region. While Iran had pursued an anti–status quo policy for more than a decade, the order in the region prior to the end of the Cold War was a balance between the Western and Eastern blocs. It was not a U.S.-led order. Now that had changed, and Iran's anti–status quo policy directly targeted the United States' leadership. For the next two decades, the underlying conflict between the United States and Iran—manifested in many ways, including through the nuclear issue—was rooted in the struggle for control of the order in the region. In hindsight, Dennis Ross, President Bush's Middle East envoy, recognized that excluding Iran from Madrid was of greater significance than many thought at the time.[42]

Israel's U-Turn

Israel's confrontation with the United States was untenable. The United States was Israel's closest ally, and its support was essential for Israel's security. And the United States was now also enjoying its unipolar moment. In terms of other superpower protectors Israel could turn to, there simply was no other game in town. Furthermore, with the shifting threat picture in the region and with the Arab states no longer capable of mustering a conventional military threat to Israel, Iran was gaining influence, and the toll of the occupation was becoming taxing. In effect, the Shamir government's line was simply contradicting Israel's geopolitical interests. By June 1992, the Israeli public had reached a similar conclusion. Running on a platform of making amends with the United States, sacrificing some of the settlements, and diverting resources to better absorb the influx of Soviet Jews, the Labor Party sought to deal with Israel's real security threat—the so-called battle of the bedrooms, or the demographic discrepancy between the fast-growing Palestinian population and the stalling Israeli population. That year, the Israeli public handed the Labor Party its biggest electoral victory yet.[43] "The Madrid process had been launched and clearly the Shamir government wasn't going places with it. We needed to fix the relationship with the Bush-Baker administration, which had been spoiled by the Shamir-Sharon team," explained Itamar Rabinovich, a close advisor to Labor's Yitzhak Rabin, who became prime minister following the 1992 election.[44] Labor won a landslide victory and—for the first time in fifteen years—managed to completely exclude the hardline Likud party from power.[45]

With the clear backing of the electorate, Rabin and Peres's Labor Party believed it could turn the dangers of the Intifada and Israel's troubled relations with Washington into an opportunity. Labor recognized that Israel's internal threats and external problems—particularly its falling from grace in Washington—were closely linked. Addressing one without tackling the other would leave both unsolved. The old order no longer existed, and Israel would have no future in the new order unless it could find a rationale for Washington to continue the strategic relationship.[46] Israel wasn't strong enough to reverse these trends. It could remain passive and watch its rivals lead the creation of a new order tilted in their favor, or it could take the initiative and shape a Middle East that suited Israeli interests. In this regional game, however, Israel's competition was no longer the Arabs—it was Iran. Israel was convinced that Iran, which emerged as one of the winners of the Persian Gulf War, would seek to impose its own order on the Middle East—particularly if it came to terms with the United States.[47] The drastic shift in Labor's view of Iran—only six years earlier, it was the same leaders of the Labor Party who were pushing the Reagan administration to talk to Iran, sell arms to Iran, and not to pay attention to Iran's venomous rhetoric on Israel—"stemmed from the fact that [Tehran] could aspire to [the] regional hegemony to which Israel aspires."[48] In this new rivalry for the future of the region, Labor viewed every Iranian gain as a loss for Israel.[49]

Labor's strategy boiled down to two critical and mutually reinforcing components: make peace with the Palestinians and depict Iran as a threat to the world to ensure its prolonged isolation. Israel's cards vis-à-vis the Palestinians were strong, as the PLO under Arafat was significantly weakened for several reasons, including Arafat's political isolation by the Arab world after he had sided with Saddam Hussein during the Persian Gulf War. By the summer of 1993, the PLO was near collapse. In its hour of desperation, it simply had to make a deal with Israel.[50] "If they didn't we would overrun them entirely," asserted Israel's former Mossad chief, Efraim Halevy.[51]

Moving toward making a deal was an unprecedented shift in Israel's geopolitical outlook. It completely contradicted what had been the very heart of Israel's guiding strategy since the days of David Ben-Gurion, the founder of Israel: the Periphery Doctrine, that is, the idea that Israel should balance the threat from the Arab states in its vicinity by creating alliances with the non-Arab states in the region's periphery. By seeking peace with the Arab states in Israel's vicinity and portraying the key peripheral state, Iran, as a threat, Rabin and Peres turned the Periphery Doctrine on its head. Now it was the Persian periphery that could pose a threat to the Jewish State, not the Arab vicinity.[52] After all, the role Peres had in mind for Israel in the new Middle East came at the expense of Iran; in order for Israel to take center stage in the new Middle

East, Iran would have to remain on the political fringe of the region and continue to be denied the role to which it believed it was entitled.[53] "There's no doubt that when the prospects for peace with the inner circle emerged, [the depiction of Iran as a threat] started," explained David Makovsky, an expert on Israeli foreign policy.[54]

Already in late 1991, arguments for this shift had begun to appear in Israeli newspapers, defying the traditional view of Iran as a strategic non-Arab ally and depicting it as Israel's greatest strategic threat. For instance, the *Jerusalem Post* wrote in November 1991 that the "Iraqi decline has created a power vacuum that Iran, motivated by Pan-Islamic and hegemonic inclinations, was eager to fill. A massive Iranian military buildup complemented the newly found political objectives. Both may be enhanced by a nuclear plan supported by India and China." As a result, the Israeli daily argued, "Iran looms as the next strategic challenge facing Israel. In a sense, Iran has become a mirror image of what Iraq hoped to become five years ago."[55] Only a few months after Labor's election victory, Peres and Rabin launched a global campaign to secure a regional order based on Iran's exclusion by convincing the United States and the European Union that Iran was a global threat. The duo began mirroring Iran's inflammatory rhetoric. Peres accused Iran of "fanning all the flames in the Middle East," implying that the failure to resolve the Israeli-Palestinian conflict was rooted in Iran's meddling rather than in the shortcomings of Israel and the Palestinians.[56] Rabin accused Iran of having "megalomaniac tendencies" and said that it sought to become the "leading power in the region."[57] He told the Knesset in December 1992 that Israel's "struggle against murderous Islamic terror" was "meant to awaken the world which is lying in slumber" to the dangers of Shia fundamentalism. "Death is at our doorstep," Rabin concluded, even though only a few years earlier he had called Iran a strategic ally.[58]

The Israeli shift was as intense as it was unexpected. What today often is misunderstood as a conflict that began with the Islamic revolution in 1979, actually began in 1992 as a result of the struggle for the Middle East order after the defeat of Saddam Hussein and the collapse of the Soviet Union. "Suddenly this thing just appeared. They were all over with this; this was a campaign," recalled Gary Sick, who served on the National Security Council during the Carter and Reagan administrations.[59] Only days after the 1992 U.S. presidential elections, the Rabin government sought to convince the incoming Bill Clinton administration to focus not on Iraq as the menace, but on Iran. "Iran has to be identified as Enemy No. 1," Yossi Alpher, who served at the time as an advisor to Rabin, told the *New York Times* four days after Clinton's election victory.[60] Rabin repeatedly presented this message to U.S. officials in order to pressure Washington to take action against Iran. According to Israeli academic Israel Shahak, Labor's strategy was "to push the U.S. and other Western powers into a confrontation with Iran." Israel could not confront Iran itself, because it would risk turning the affair into an Israeli-Islamic conflict. To forestall this danger, the Israelis put forward a message that Iran wasn't a danger just to Israel, but to the entire Western world.[61]

Israel's case was based on two key allegations that continued to define the debate in Washington and reached their crescendo during the debate on the nuclear deal during the summer of 2015: that Iran was seeking both nuclear weapons and regional hegemony. In a TV interview in 1992, Peres warned that Iran would be armed with a nuclear bomb by 1999, a clearly outlandishly alarmist prediction. "Iran is the greatest threat [to peace] and greatest problem in the Middle East . . . because it seeks the nuclear option while holding a highly dangerous stance of extreme religious militantism," he argued, adding that you can't deter a fanatic terrorist state with nuclear weapons.[62] Moreover, in terms that foreshadowed the nuclear debate, the Labor government argued that the nature of the Iranian regime, with its anti-Israel ideology, made it a threat in and of itself. Coexistence with such an irredeemable regime was impossible. Iran was simply "insane," Peres and Rabin declared; a decade later, neoconservative, pro-Likud circles in Washington took the same view.[63] The veteran Israeli politicians "never missed an opportunity to blame Iran," Makovsky noted. Rabin repeated his mantra on Khomeinism in "every single speech he gave when he traveled . . . I think he said it a thousand times."[64]

Israel Baffles Washington

Israel's sudden change of heart raised eyebrows in the United States. After all, Iran had used even viler rhetoric against Israel a decade earlier, at a time when Israel was violating an American arms embargo by selling arms to Iran.[65] At first, Washington was skeptical. The notion that Iran was the new threat to the region and to the United States' position in the Middle East was, as the *Washington Post* put it, "a controversial idea" with little credibility.[66] The *New York Times* concurred. "Why the Israelis waited until fairly recently to sound a strong alarm about Iran is a perplexity," it said. In the same article, Israeli officials were quoted as linking Israel's wariness of Iran with the peace process and with the need for "sound relations with the new American Administration."[67]

Beyond skepticism, the Israeli line simply did not connect with the geopolitical analysis of the administration of newly elected president Bill Clinton—at least not at first. The Clinton White House was focused on Iraq, not Iran. Israel was once again going in the opposite direction of the United States—in the 1980s, it had courted Iran and pushed Washington to move closer to Tehran, while the Reagan administration was a de facto ally of Iraq in the Iran-Iraq war. Now, when the United States had come around to the earlier Israeli position and viewed Iraq as the main threat to the region, Israel had shifted once again and begun depicting Iran as the primary danger while sending feelers out to the Iraqi regime. "After the Iraq war, when it would make sense for us to talk to Tehran, the Israelis did not come and make the argument. Instead, they started to reach out to the Iraqis," said Martin Indyk, Clinton's special assistant for Near East and South Asian Affairs at the National Security Council.[68]

The widespread feeling inside the Clinton administration that the Peres-Rabin government exaggerated the Iranian threat also stemmed from the fact that Israel's campaign against Iran came at a time when Tehran was lowering its profile on the Palestinian issue. This was recognized privately by decision-makers in both Tel Aviv and Washington.[69] "At that time, there were Iranian attempts to rhetorically soften the radical language of Khomeini," explained Keith Weissman of the American Israel Public Affairs Committee (AIPAC). "No doubt about it, there was a famous Rafsanjani interview . . . where he said that if it's okay with the Palestinians, it's okay with us."[70]

However passionately Peres and Rabin spoke against Iran, few believed that Iran overnight had turned into a major threat. The reality

was not that Iran had changed; everyone else had. Iran was more prominent on the Israeli radar not because it had become more antagonis-
tic toward Israel, but because all previous threats had more or less
evaporated.[71] "Nothing special happened with Iran, but because Iraq
was removed, Iran started to play a greater role in the threat perception of Israel," recalled Shlomo Brom, a member of the Israeli government's Iran Committee.[72] The defeat of Iraq and the disappearance
of the dreaded "eastern front" caused Israel's eyes to turn to Iran.
"Iran became the major threat because the eastern front disintegrated.
There was no longer that coalition that always presented an existential
threat because of the expeditionary forces from Iraq and the long-range
missiles that Iraq has. After 1991, that front disintegrated," said Ranaan
Gissin, who was a spokesperson for Ariel Sharon when he was Israel's
prime minister.[73] Even the asymmetrical threat Iran could pose was
limited at the time. Iran was active with Hezbollah in Lebanon, but it
had no presence in the Palestinian territories, explained Halevi.[74] A few
years later, this changed. By 1995, Iran had become a major backer of
Palestinian rejectionist groups. In 1992, when Rabin and Peres launched
their campaign against Iran, Israeli alarmism preceded the threat.

But Rabin and Peres's sudden campaign against Iran made political sense. Even though most Israelis yearned for peace, convincing the
public that Arafat and the Palestinians were no longer terrorists but
partners for peace was a monumental task. Just as Labor had done with
the Arab states and Iran, it needed to present a more ominous danger
looming on the horizon to convince a skeptical Israeli public to accept
this dramatic strategic shift.[75] "Rabin played the Iranian threat more
than it was deserved in order to sell the peace process," noted Efraim
Inbar of the conservative Begin-Sadat Center in Jerusalem.[76] Iran became "a convenient argument" in the Israeli domestic discourse, used
by the Labor Party to induce Israeli public opinion to favor bold steps
for negotiating peace with the neighboring Arabs.[77]

Perhaps most important, the alarm over Iran reinforced the message that Washington needed Israel and that Iran needed to be contained. The strategic importance Israel had enjoyed during the Cold
War could be regained by emphasizing the threat of Iran and Islamic
fundamentalism: instead of being a friendly bulwark against Soviet

expansionism, Israel would now be a friendly bulwark against Iran's regional ambitions in a unipolar world.[78] This necessitated a new order in the region, one centered on a U.S.-Israel relationship that was unified in perceiving Iran as a threat. "There was a feeling in Israel that because of the end of the Cold War, relations with the U.S. were cooling and we needed some new glue for the alliance," Inbar said. "And the new glue . . . was radical Islam. And Iran was radical Islam."[79]

It didn't take long before the new glue started to stick. Only a few months into Clinton's first term, Washington adopted the policy of Dual Containment.[80] The policy was a major shift in the United States' approach to the region. Traditionally, Washington had sought to balance Iran and Iraq against each other to maintain a degree of stability. Now, the Clinton White House argued, the United States' strength had reached such levels that it did not need to balance the two against each other; it could balance both without relying on either. According to Kenneth Pollack, who then served as an Iran analyst with the CIA, the policy was "designed to reassure Israel that the U.S. would keep Iran in check while Jerusalem embarked on the risky process of peacemaking."[81]

Washington Baffles Tehran

Israel's swift offensive to isolate Iran took Tehran by surprise. As far as the Iranians were concerned, the unspoken understanding between Israel and Iran should still have been honored. Iran would remain nothing more than an armchair critic of Israel; it would continue to issue colorful diatribes against Israel while paying lip service to the Palestinian cause. Israel, in turn, would turn a deaf ear to Iran's rhetoric and remember that Tehran's slogans did not reflect its real policy. But Rabin and Peres's campaign indicated that times had changed. Slowly, Tehran began to realize that Israel was becoming its key rival in the formation of a new Middle East order.

To the Iranians, no Israeli accusation revealed Israel's real objectives more than its claim that Iran wanted to establish hegemony over the Middle East. Tehran believed that seeking to isolate Iran would ensure only continued conflict. Iran's isolation was unnatural, unjust, and untenable, Tehran insisted.[82] The failure of the 1991 Madrid conference should have taught Washington a valuable lesson that no major change in the region could take place without Iran's cooperation. "There is no doubt that Iran wanted and felt that it was its right to play the role of a regional power," explained Hadi Nejad-Hosseinian, who served in the cabinet of Iranian President Hashemi Rafsanjani in the 1990s. "We should be the greatest power in the region and play a role accordingly. We have the potential and we should actualize it."[83] But leadership wasn't the same as hegemony, Tehran maintained. The concept of political role (*naqsh*), in the minds of the Iranians, wasn't about domination, but rather an indication of diplomatic inclusion for defensive purposes. Naqsh is what "makes other actors listen to you and consult with you" so that you can "inhibit processes if they harm your interest," explained Mahmoud Sariolghalam, who served as an advisor to Hassan Rouhani prior to his becoming Iran's president.[84]

Iran and Israel were among the few countries in the region that were powerful enough to shape the new Middle East order. With drastically different interests, a refusal to accept each other as legitimate players in the region, and a zero-sum view of their competition, the two were soon embroiled in an explosive rivalry to define the region. As long as an Israeli-Palestinian deal was out of reach, Tehran was reluctant to act too openly against Israel. But all of this changed on September 13, 1993. It was at this point that Tehran began cultivating serious relationships with Palestinian rejectionist groups with which it historically had had poor relations, including Hamas, which had supported Saddam Hussein during the Iran-Iraq war.

Israel's Master Stroke

In August 1993, a historic agreement was reached between Israel and the PLO based on the principle of "land for peace": by returning occupied land to the Palestinians, Israel would obtain peace. A month later, with much fanfare, the Declaration of Principles was signed, and the two former enemies, Yasser Arafat and Yitzhak Rabin, nervously shook hands at a White House ceremony. Against all odds and in complete secrecy, the Israelis and Palestinians had succeeded in brokering a peace deal that could push Iran to the fringes of regional politics in a way that

Madrid never could have done. Iran reacted swiftly and harshly. It showed that its elevated opposition to Israel had become an important policy by increasing its rhetorical opposition to Israel and announcing in the hardline newspaper *Ettelaat* that Iran would offer limitless support to the opponents of the Oslo agreement.[85] Almost overnight, the cold peace that had reigned between Israel and Iran in the 1980s turned into a cold war.[86]

A day after the ceremonies on the White House lawn, Rafsanjani accused Arafat of having "committed treason against the Palestinian people."[87] While calls for Israel's destruction had been made in the past, their frequency now increased.[88] In March 1994, a slight majority of Iran's 270 parliamentarians signed a statement "stressing the need for the annihilation of Israel from the world map," arguing that the Palestinian issue would not be settled except through armed struggle against Israel.[89] Peace between the Arabs and the Israelis was not a threat to Iran per se. Only when combined with the Israeli-American effort to isolate Iran—to depict it as a threat and exclude it from regional decision-making—did peace make Tehran nervous. If Oslo was successful, and the Arabs rushed to make peace with Israel, Iran would be left in a state of prolonged isolation, Rafsanjani feared.[90] In the new Israel-centric order that would be created, Israel would lead while Tehran would be prevented from "playing a role equal to its capacity and power."[91]

But if Iran was included in the political process, the Iranians maintained that an entirely different picture could emerge. The Rafsanjani government, which prior to Madrid had reduced Iran's profile on the Palestinian issue and signaled that it wouldn't stand in the way of a peace agreement, would have been willing to go along with an Israeli-Palestinian accord, if the United States had accepted Iran's leading role in the region in return and ended the policy of isolating Tehran. By being included in the political process, Iran could both ensure that the peace treaty wouldn't undermine its interests and demonstrate its ability to be a positive and stabilizing force in the region.[92]

It was at this point, and not following the Islamic Revolution of 1979, that Iran began to translate its anti-Israel rhetoric into operational policy. Contrary to the dictum of Ayatollah Khomeini, who had declared that Iran should provide only ideological support for the Palestinians and avoid any direct entanglement with Israel, Iran would now become a front-line state against Israel, because from Tehran's vantage point, the weakest link in the Israeli-American strategy to isolate it was the Oslo process. If Oslo failed, so would the efforts to create a new regional order on the back of Iran's isolation. Ironically, because of Rafsanjani's new foreign policy orientation, Iran's support for Hezbollah had in the preceding years waned considerably, making many Shia leaders in Lebanon feel abandoned.[93] Now, however, Tehran's focus turned back to Hezbollah and other Islamist groups. Iran's vocal stand against Israel and the United States would strengthen its standing with the Arab masses, Tehran reasoned, which in turn would make it more difficult for Israel to form an Arab-Israel front against Iran.[94] Just as it had done at the beginning of the revolution, Iran appealed to the Arab street to undermine pro-Western Arab governments from below by making them look soft on Israel. The aim was to "create a situation in which the Israelis couldn't reach the deal," explained an Iranian political figure. "Because the more messy the situation, the better off we are, because it wins us time."[95]

By 1994, Iranian actions against Israel seemed to justify the Rabin government's previous allegations of the Iranian threat. Privately, the Israelis recognized that despite Iran's support of Palestinian rejectionist groups such as Hamas and the Islamic jihad, Iran wasn't the primary cause of the terror that Israel endured. "Whatever Iran was doing against Israel through terror," said David Menashri, a Tel Aviv University professor, "the Palestinians did a better job at it themselves."[96] This posed a significant political problem for the Rabin government. If Israel put the blame squarely on the Palestinians, it would undermine the very basis of the peace process—the idea that the Palestinians were partners in peace and not enemies. Iran, however, was a convenient—and partially responsible—target. Though exaggerated, "the threat was real, it wasn't invented," Rabinovich told me.[97] And the exaggeration of the threat reinforced Israel's other objectives: it undermined any warm-up in U.S.-Iran relations, it compelled Washington to take stronger measures against Iran, it turned many pro-Western Arab states against Iran, and it became "the greatest threat to [Iran's] goal of regional dominance."[98] If Israel hadn't painted Iran as the main threat to peace and stability in the region and beyond, the international community and the United States would not have sought to contain and isolate it.[99]

As Rabin and Peres had predicted, the Oslo process helped end Israel's diplomatic isolation. After the signing of the accords, Israel established diplomatic relations with a record number of states, including several Arab governments.[100] The normalization of relations with heavyweights China and India was the most radical change in Israel's international status since 1948 and boosted its bid to retain strategic significance in the Middle East—and in Washington.[101] Israel had outsmarted and outmaneuvered Iran in the Middle East. Now, it would do so in the United States as well.

Writing Iran's Isolation into Law

Having outsmarted Iran in the region, Israel moved to lock in its win by writing the isolation of Iran into law in the United States. It was a remarkable shift for Israel, which only a few years earlier was the unlikely defender of and apologist for Iran in Washington, taking great risks to pressure the Reagan administration to open up channels of communication with Iran. Now, Israel did the opposite. Israel wanted the United States to put Iran under economic and political siege.[102] While some questioned the wisdom of this shift, the prevailing view in the Israeli government was that a U.S.-Iran dialogue would not benefit Israel, because Iran was interested only in reducing tensions with Washington—not with Israel.[103] "What the Iranians want is to have the U.S. recognize them as a regional superpower in the Middle East," Israeli General Amos Gilad argued.[104]

Any indication of Iran moderating its behavior toward Israel would be nothing but a tactical maneuver aimed solely at reducing U.S. pressure on Tehran and having no strategic implications.[105] Once that happened, it would be very difficult for Israel to compel Washington to reinstate the pressure. So negotiations were nothing short of a slippery slope toward Iran's political rehabilitation.[106] As soon as the U.S. pressure eased, Iran would betray the Jewish State, Israel believed.[107] And even worse, if the Iranians didn't betray Israel, the United States could. Two decades later, this very logic still guided Israel's opposition to diplomacy with Tehran. Apprehension that Washington would "sell Israel out" and pursue its own interests in a U.S.-Iran dialogue weighed heavily on the minds of Israeli strategists in 2013 during the nuclear talks as they did in 1994.[108] Because Israel viewed a U.S.-Iran dialogue as a greater threat than that of Iran itself, the optimal strategy was to prevent such a dialogue from developing in the first place.[109]

This provided the American Israel Public Affairs Committee (AIPAC), the most potent pro-Israeli lobby group in the United States, with a new cause. For AIPAC, this cause was heaven sent, since the peace process had deprived AIPAC of its previous key rallying call—the Arab and Palestinian threat to Israel's existence. Now that the Palestinians were peace partners, not enemies, a critical part of the organization's raison d'être—countering Arab influence in Washington—had become obsolete.[110] Iran was the savior. AIPAC needed a new issue, and Israel needed help in turning Washington against Iran. It was a win-win situation.

By mid-1994, Israel and AIPAC turned the full force of their diplomatic and lobbying powers against Iran. Rabin held a teleconference with U.S. Jewish leaders in September 1994 to coordinate the strategy. His message was clear: Iran was the greatest threat to Middle East peace. "Behind [the Palestinian rejectionists] there is an Islamic country, Iran, that . . . tries to develop in the coming seven to fifteen years nuclear weapons and ground-to-ground missiles that can reach every part of the Middle East," he said.[111] At the behest of the Israeli government, AIPAC drafted and circulated a seventy-four-page paper in Washington arguing that Iran was a threat not only to Israel, but also to the United States and the West.[112]

What eventually made Israel successful was the Clinton White House's policy focus on a peace process. Washington had invested heavily in Oslo and in the creation of a new order in the Middle East. The Clinton administration was willing to go to great lengths to convince the Israelis and Palestinians to remain on the path of peace, even if it meant escalating tensions with Iran. According to Kenneth Pollack, who served in the Clinton White House, "It was simply a matter of, 'What do we need to do to get you guys to move down this road, tell us what you require and we'll do it.' And look, we didn't like Iran anyway."[113] By October 1994, Washington had started to adopt the Is-raeli line on Iran. U.S. Secretary of State Warren Christopher told an au-dience at Georgetown University in October 1994 that "Iran is the world's most significant sponsor of terrorism and the most ardent opponent of the Middle East peace process. . . . The evidence is overwhelming: Iran is intent on projecting terror and extremism across the Middle East and beyond. Only a concerted international effort can stop it."[114] Months later, Christopher went on to declare that "wherever you look, you find the evil hand of Iran in this region," while former assistant secretary of state Martin Indyk defined Iran as a threat to Israel, Arabs, and the West—a position that Washington had refused to take only two years earlier.[115]

In practical terms, Israel and its allies were demanding that eco-nomic sanctions be placed on Iran. "The Right, AIPAC, the Israelis were all screaming for new sanctions," Pollack explained, adding that the Clinton administration saw Iran only through the prism of the Israeli-Palestinian conflict.[116] The push for sanctions came at a time when Iran had prepared an economic olive branch for Washington. Because a direct political rapprochement with the United States remained un-likely, Rafsanjani chose to use Iran's economic ties with Washington to create areas of common interest that could later pave the way for such a rapprochement.[117] Thus, the Rafsanjani government offered the American oil company Conoco a lucrative oil deal in 1995. The symbolism of this move was significant. The nationalization of the oil industry played a central role in the Iranian Revolution as well as in the coun-try's economic and political development earlier in the twentieth century. Iran opened bidding for production agreements for two of its offshore oil fields to international companies in 1994. The first oil contract after the revolution, worth $1 billion, was expected to go to the French-owned Total. However, after having negotiated with Conoco, Iran announced on March 6, 1995, that the contract would go to the Americans.[118] To ensure the blessing of the White House, Conoco had kept the U.S. gov-ernment closely informed of its negotiations. The State Department had repeatedly reassured Conoco that the White House would approve the deal.[119]

The Conoco deal quickly became the target of AIPAC. In a report released on April 2, 1995, titled "Comprehensive U.S. Sanctions Against Iran: A Plan for Action," AIPAC argued that Iran must be punished for its actions against Israel. Pressured by Congress, AIPAC, and the Israelis, President Bill Clinton swiftly scrapped the deal by issuing two executive orders that effectively prohibited all trade with Iran.[120] The decision was announced on April 30 by Clinton in a speech before the World Jewish Congress.[121] Targeting the Conoco deal—which was a result of Tehran's eagerness to improve relations with the United States— was "a major demonstration of [American] support for Israel."[122] Immediately, speculation in the U.S. media began on "where U.S. foreign policy ends and Israeli interests begin."[123] But politically, the decision to scuttle the Conoco deal had no cost, as there was no organized political campaign in favor of a U.S.-Iran rapprochement in Washington. "From a political standpoint, nobody pays a price to be tough on Iran," Dennis Ross explained.[124]

But the initial sanctions weren't enough to satisfy the anti-Iran camp. Although Clinton had with the stroke of a pen eliminated billions of dollars' worth of U.S.-Iran trade, he could easily lift the orders and reinstate the trade. If sanctions were imposed by Congress, however, the president's—any president's—maneuverability would be limited. Working with Senator Alfonse D'Amato of New York and the Israelis, AIPAC helped push for the passage of the Iran Libya Sanctions Act (ILSA) by Congress in 1996.[125] ILSA not only barred American companies from investing in Iran's energy sector, but also sanctioned non-U.S. companies active in the Iranian energy sector. The Clinton administration balked, but it was no match for AIPAC's influence in Congress. The bill passed the House of Representatives by 415 votes to 0 and was reluctantly signed into law by Clinton in August 1996.[126] ILSA was a major success for AIPAC and Israel—but not because it forced a change in Iranian foreign policy—it never did. Rather, it was a success because it created an almost irremovable political obstacle to any effort at improving U.S.-Iran relations—a critical Israeli objective. "We were against it [U.S.-Iran dialogue] . . . because the interest of the U.S. did not coincide with ours," then–Israeli deputy defense minister Ephraim Sneh admitted.[127]

The Clinton administration might not have taken into account the full implications of these decisions. By adopting the Israeli line on Iran and turning the isolation of that country into American law through the sanctions regime and the Dual Containment policy, Washington opted for a U.S.-led order in the region with Israel and Saudi Arabia at its center, and with Iraq and Iran isolated and excluded from regional decision-making. It was an unnatural order, because it could not stand on its own legs. Neither Saudi Arabia nor Israel—nor any other U.S. ally in the region, for that matter—had the capacity or the political will to uphold the order on its own. That order could be upheld only by American blood and money; there was no other way to exclude two powerful states such as Iraq and Iran. It was an order that required full American commitment with all that that implied. But it also meant that the two main benefactors of this order—Israel and Saudi Arabia—had an interest in tying the United States down in the region and extending the United States' commitment to the order beyond its own interest. But before the United States sought to reduce its presence in the region due to the heavy cost of Pax Americana, it first made a turn toward an even stronger American hegemonic role in the Middle East.

The Epic Mistake

T he inherent weakness of the U.S.-led order based on Dual Containment was concealed by the United States' unrivaled strength in the 1990s. However, underneath the surface, tensions were mounting, although not in the manner Washington had expected. The Clinton administration was worried that Dual Containment would push Iran and Iraq closer together and compel them to form an alliance to counter the United States. "We were much more focused, at the time, on a breakout strategy in which our Dual Containment would lead [Iran] to a rapprochement with Iraq," observed Martin Indyk, the main author of the Dual Containment policy in the Clinton White House. The idea that Iran would turn to terror wasn't something Washington considered likely, even though the accusation of Iranian support for terror was used to justify isolating Iran. "What the Iranians did was to outsmart us by taking on the peace process.... And they became very aggressive supporters of Palestinian terrorism and not just Hezbollah."[1]

In time, Washington began to understand the critical strategic flaw in its policy of Dual Containment: by rejecting Tehran's overtures and aiming to create a new order in the Middle East based on excluding Iran, the United States was giving Iran strong incentives to sabotage the weakest link in the policy, the fragile Israeli-Palestinian talks. According to Indyk,

[The Iranians] had every incentive to oppose [the peace pro-
cess]. Our strategy was to, on one hand, use the engine of
peacemaking to transform the region and on the other hand
contain the [Iranians] through sanctions and isolation. The
two were symbiotic. The more we succeeded in making
peace, the more isolated [they] would become. The more we
succeeded in containing [the Iranians], the more possible it
would be to make peace. So they had an incentive to do us in
on the peace process in order to defeat our policy of containment and isolation. And therefore, they took aim at the peace
process.[2]

   As Iran turned its anti-Israel rhetoric into actual policy, critics
in Israel began to worry that the Peres-Rabin government's focus on Iran
had helped turn it from a distant threat into an immediate enemy. A committee consisting of representatives of the Mossad, the Foreign Ministry, the Defense Ministry, and the Israeli National Security Council
was set up inside the Israeli government to review its Iran policy.[3] The
committee argued that although Labor's aggressive campaign had succeeded in putting international pressure on Iran, Israel had little to gain
by making itself Iran's primary enemy. Labor's inflammatory rhetoric
had only attracted Iran's attention and strengthened Iran's perception of
an Israeli threat, which in turn had made Israel less, not more, secure.
Moreover, Israel had to tread carefully to put Iran on the international
agenda while avoiding making Iran an "Israeli issue." For Israel's strategy to work, the international community had to conclude that Iran
and its nuclear program were a global threat, not just a threat to Israel.
In the end, the Peres-Rabin government ignored the committee's recommendations, although over the course of the next two decades, both
the Likud and Labor governments did occasionally try to tone down the
anti-Iran rhetoric. However, the more Israel portrayed itself as an
enemy of Iran, the more fearful it became of the United States and Iran
initiating negotiations. The risk that such a dialogue would come at
Israel's expense only grew with heightened Israeli-Iranian tensions.[4]

   As the peace process suffered a slow death—beginning with the
assassination of Yitzhak Rabin in 1996—the Dual Containment policy

also began to be criticized more and more in Washington. While the policy had contained Iran and Iraq, it had done little to encourage political change in those countries. On the contrary, critics maintained, it had sustained a status quo in which both Saddam and the clerical regime in Tehran remained in power. In short, the United States was expending significant resources to maintain an order that carried increasingly limited benefits for the United States: it had not brought peace between Israel and the Palestinians, and it had not neutralized the potential threats from Iraq and Iran. Furthermore, after the election of Iran's reformist president Mohammad Khatami in 1997, the Arab states' frustration with the stalling peace process pushed them closer to Tehran. Even the European Union had a rapprochement with Iran during the Khatami years, notwithstanding Iran's continuous efforts to challenge the United States in the region. This made a mockery of the American policy of isolating Iran. Two decades later, senior American officials admitted that the United States' bilateral sanctions on Iran had not had an effect on Iranian behavior.[5]

As the American people went to cast their votes in the 2000 elections, both Iran and Israel believed that a Republican victory could bring about a significant change in Washington's Middle East policy. In both capitals, it was thought that if Democrat Al Gore and his vice-presidential pick, Joe Lieberman, prevailed, they would continue the Clinton administration's Middle East line: strong support for Israel and the Middle East peace process, along with significant pressure to sanction and isolate Iran. A Bush-Cheney White House, on the other hand, could bring back the foreign policy approach of the elder George Bush: pressure on Israel to withdraw from Palestinian territories, greater sensitivity to the interests of Washington's Arab allies, and an energy policy that wouldn't cut off American oil businesses from major markets such as Iran. After all, as the former CEO of Halliburton and George W. Bush's vice-presidential running mate, Dick Cheney had severely criticized the Clinton administration's economic sanctions on Iran. There was little doubt over who Israel and Iran were rooting for as they anxiously watched the ballots in Florida being counted and recounted.

When the U.S. Supreme Court gave the presidency to George W. Bush on December 9, 2000, Israel and its allies quickly moved to preempt

any attempt by the new administration to soften the United States'
stance on Iran by easing economic sanctions or narrowing its efforts
to block Tehran's nuclear program. AIPAC built up support on Capitol
Hill to renew some of the sanctions on Iran. By March 2001, only weeks
after Bush entered office, AIPAC had already secured the support of
more than three hundred cosponsors in the House (the bill needed
only 218 votes to pass). But Israel's worries proved unfounded. On September 11, 2001, nineteen members of the Sunni terrorist group al-Qaeda
pulled off the single deadliest terrorist attack on U.S. soil. The Bush administration used the attack as an opportunity both to significantly increase the United States' military presence in the Middle East and to
reshape the balance of power in the region by overthrowing the hostile
regimes of Afghanistan and Iraq, while keeping a watchful eye on Iran.
The world didn't change on September 11, but the United States did.
Washington's response to the cataclysmic terror attack would eventually bring more turmoil to the Arab and Muslim world and help give
rise to one of the worst terrorist organizations that the world has seen
thus far—the Islamic State (ISIS).[6]

That evening, Secretary of State Colin Powell ordered a small
group of his top staffers to work through the night in order to produce
a strategy for assembling an international coalition to take out Osama
bin Laden, the mastermind behind the attacks. The plan became the
blueprint for the diplomatic strategy of "Operation Enduring Freedom"—
the United States' war against the Taliban and al-Qaeda in Afghanistan. To win against the Taliban, the United States needed more than the
support of its traditional allies—it needed the specific support of Iran,
Afghanistan's neighbor and a bitter enemy of the Taliban. Throughout
the 1990s, Iran had been the primary sponsor of the anti-Taliban force
in Afghanistan, the Northern Alliance. Iran served as the primary
backer of the alliance at a time when the United States was turning a
blind eye to the Taliban's abuse and support for terror. Having a
staunchly anti-Iranian and anti-Shia government in Afghanistan had
hardly undermined the Clinton administration's overarching goal of
isolating Iran. A few years later, that policy was coming back to haunt
the United States. Now, the Iranians were eager to offer their help to
Washington and show the United States the strategic benefits of coop-

eration with Iran. "The Iranians had real contacts with important players in Afghanistan and were prepared to use their influence in constructive ways in coordination with the United States," recalled Flynt Leverett, who at the time was serving as the senior director for Middle East Affairs in the National Security Council. The plan that had been prepared by Powell called for using cooperation with Iran as a platform for persuading Tehran to terminate its involvement with anti-Israeli terrorist groups in return for a positive strategic relationship with Washington.[7]

The plan incensed Israel. Suddenly, much as they had after the end of the Cold War, events in the Middle East had the potential to make Israel a burden rather than an asset to the United States, while giving Iran a chance to prove its value to the United States and get back in from the cold. The crisis of September 11 shook the foundations of the status quo in the Middle East and forced all states to reassess their position and role. If a U.S.-Iran dialogue was initiated, there would be "a lot of concern in Israel," Yossi Alpher, an advisor to Israeli Prime Minister Ehud Barak, told me. "Where are we [Israel] in this dialogue? Will the U.S. consult with us about our needs and fears? Will we be part of some package deal with Iran and if so, what part?" Alpher's questions reflected Israelis' inherent fear about Israel's relations with the United States: Would the United States betray Israel's interest if it deemed a U.S.-Iran rapprochement to be in *the United States'* interest? With Britain as the go-between, Washington secretly courted Iran while it kept Israel at arm's length. And just as the British government had done in 1991 with regard to the Persian Gulf War, British Foreign Secretary Jack Straw suggested that Israel was partly to blame for the attacks. In a statement that the Israelis called an "obscenity" and a "stab in the back," Straw implied that terrorism and the festering Israeli-Palestinian dispute might be linked to the events of 9/11.[8]

Israeli and American neoconservatives, who had found their way back to the corridors of power after Bush's election, had a different plan in mind: the United States should put on notice all the actors it accused of supporting terror—particularly Iran and the Palestinian Authority. Forty-one prominent neoconservatives urged Bush in a letter to target not only al-Qaeda, but also Hezbollah, Iran, and Syria, as well as to "consider appropriate measures of retaliation against these known state sponsors of terrorism." Starting a war with Iran and Syria could over-extend the United States, but it would also put the United States and Israel on the same side in the war and increase—rather than decrease—the United States' need for Israel. The neoconservatives' push to expand the war to also target Israel's rivals in the region was initially in vain, as the strategy to take out the Taliban secretly already included Iran. State Department and National Security Council officials began clandestine meetings with Iranian diplomats in Paris and Geneva in October 2001. The discussions focused on how to effectively unseat the Taliban and then set up a new Afghan government. Iran's help was extensive. The Iranians offered their airbases to the United States; volunteered to perform search-and-rescue missions for downed American pilots; and served as a bridge between the United States and the Northern Alliance. Iran also used U.S. information to find and kill fleeing al-Qaeda leaders.[9]

The height of U.S.-Iran collaboration occurred during the Bonn Conference on December 10, 2001, when a new governing plan for Afghanistan was decided. The United States and Iran had carefully laid the groundwork for the conference weeks in advance. Iran's political clout with the various warring Afghan groups proved to be crucial. It was Iran's influence over the Afghans, not the United States' threats and promises, that moved the negotiations forward. Curiously enough, the instructions of the U.S. negotiating team contained nothing about democracy in Afghanistan. It was the Iranian delegation—and not the U.S. delegation—that pointed out that the draft of the Bonn Declaration contained no language on democracy or any commitment on behalf of Afghanistan to help fight international terrorism.

The Iranian delegation was led by Tehran's then UN ambassador, Javad Zarif, who twelve years later spearheaded the Iranian delegation at the nuclear talks. It was during the negotiations over Afghanistan that the American diplomatic corps developed their respect for Zarif's skills and acumen. By the last night of the conference, an interim constitution had been agreed upon and all other issues had been resolved except the toughest one: Who was to govern Afghanistan? The Northern Alliance insisted that, as the winner of the war, the spoils should be its own. Although it represented about 40 percent of the country, it wanted to occupy eighteen of the twenty-four ministries. Around 2 a.m., the lead American diplomat, Ambassador Jim Dobbins, gathered the Afghan parties, the Iranians, the Russians, the Indians, the Germans, and Ambassador Lakhdar Brahimi of the United Nations in order to resolve this final sticking point. For two hours, the different delegations took turns trying to convince Yunus Qanooni, the representative of the Northern Alliance, to accept a lower number of ministries, but to no avail. Finally, Zarif took Qanooni aside and began whispering to him in Persian. A few minutes later, they returned to the table, and the Afghan conceded. "Okay, I give up," he said. "The other factions can have two more ministries." This was a critical turning point, because the efforts by other states to convince Qanooni had all failed. "It wasn't until Zarif took him aside that it was settled," Dobbins admitted in retrospect. "We might have had a situation like we had in Iraq, where we were never able to settle on a single leader and government." The next morning, the historic Bonn Agreement was signed. The United States had not only won the war, but, thanks to Iran, it had also won the peace.[10]

For the Iranians, this was a moment of triumph. Not only had a major enemy of Iran—the Taliban—been defeated, but Iran had also demonstrated both how it could help stabilize the region and how the United States could benefit from a better relationship with Tehran. Iran even offered to help rebuild the Afghan army—under U.S. leadership— in order to strengthen the Afghan government vis-à-vis the various warlords who still controlled parts of the country. "We're prepared to house, pay, clothe, arm, and train up to twenty thousand troops in a broader program under your leadership," the Iranians told Dobbins during one of the meetings in Geneva. But the Bush administration wasn't interested. "I saw no glimmer of interest outside of State" for a strategic discussion with the Iranians, Dobbins recalled. It was 1991 all over again: there was no appreciation for Iran's strategic interest in a stable Middle East or for the possibility that Tehran wanted to patch up relations with the United States.[11]

Predictably, Israel was incensed by Washington's collaboration with Tehran. In an unusually harsh rebuke of Bush, Israeli Prime

Minister Ariel Sharon publicly suggested that Bush was acting like British Prime Minister Neville Chamberlain (1937–1940), selling out Israel the way Chamberlain had sold out the Czechs by refusing to confront Adolf Hitler. The comments enraged the American president, and White House press secretary Ari Fleischer called Sharon's remarks "unacceptable." However, much to Israel's satisfaction, the U.S.-Iran flirtations came to an abrupt end only weeks after the success in Bonn. Dobbins returned to Washington to brief key administration officials on the unprecedented Iranian offer, which he had concluded was intended as a friendly gesture. Nevertheless, Dobbins ran into a brick wall at the Pentagon. He briefed Secretary of Defense Donald Rumsfeld on the proposal, but throughout the entire meeting the secretary did not utter a word. Staring intently at Dobbins, he took a few notes but never showed any real interest in the proposal. Right there, the proposal died. "To my knowledge, there was never a response," Dobbins said. "There was a disposition not to take Iranian offers seriously and not to give them any broader meaning." Moreover, Dobbins, argued, the administration was not interested in a broader strategic opening "because Washington largely focused on Iran's behavior towards Israel" rather than on its behavior toward the United States.[12]

Three Words in a Speech

On January 29, 2002, in his first State of the Union address, Bush lumped Iran together with Iraq and North Korea as regimes that with "their terrorist allies, constituted an axis of evil, arming to threaten the peace of the world by seeking weapons of mass destruction." Bush said these regimes posed "a grave and growing danger." Tehran was shocked. Khatami's policy of détente and the help Iran provided the United States in Afghanistan had been for naught. Khatami had seen his domestic agenda fall apart, and now his international standing was dealt a blow. He had stuck out his neck and argued against hardliners in Tehran, whose skepticism about the United States' trustworthiness appeared to have been proven right. "'Axis of Evil' was a fiasco for the Khatami government," said Farideh Farhi, an Iran expert at the University of Hawaii. "That was used by the hardliners, who said, 'If you give in, if you help from a position of weakness, then you get negative results.'" Beyond weakening the moderates in Tehran, the three infamous words in Bush's State of the Union address closed the window of opportunity for continued U.S.-Iran cooperation and improved relations. "The chance for a serious dialogue that might actually have led somewhere pretty much ended with 'axis of evil,'" said Ambassador Ryan Crocker, who served as an American envoy to Iraq, Afghanistan, and other countries in the region. "In a matter of a few days, a policy of cooperation was transformed into a policy of confrontation," Zarif explained to me in 2004.[13]

The Geneva channel—the diplomatic venue where the United States and Iran discussed Afghan matters—was closed soon thereafter. Only one meeting took place after the "axis of evil" speech. The Iranians protested against President Bush's policy of putting Iran in the same category as Iraq and North Korea. Dobbins explained that the United States still had many disagreements with Tehran, including how to resolve the Israeli-Palestinian conflict, and that the cooperation in Afghanistan, while very helpful, did not change that reality. On most issues, the United States and Iran were still at odds, he pointed out. The Iranian response crystalized the opportunity that the "axis of evil" comment likely had squandered. "We would have liked to have discussed those matters too," the Iranians said, unveiling to Dobbins Tehran's intention to resolve outstanding issues between itself and the United States by continuing the cooperative relationship the two countries had enjoyed while working together in Afghanistan.[14] But even if the Geneva track had remained open, it is unclear if the U.S.-Iran collaboration could have been expanded. What the Iranians did not know was that the Bush administration had never intended to reward Iran for its cooperation—or allow relations to improve. Rules had been set up to regulate how Washington should interact with rogue states such as Iran. The regulations—known as the "Hadley Rules" after Deputy National Security Advisor Stephen Hadley—determined that tactical collaboration with rogue states such as Iran was permissible within the context of the so-called War on Terror, but that this tactical collaboration could never be permitted to translate into a change in the strategic nature of the United States' relations with these states. In other words, regardless of how fruitful U.S.-Iran collaboration in Afghanistan could be, it simply would not change the definition of Iran as a mortal enemy of the United States.[15]

Unbeknownst to Iran, the Bush administration already had a plan in mind for the Middle East, and it entailed far stronger U.S. dominance over the region through military confrontation with the United States' main rivals. Already in September 2000, a year before the explosive 9/11 terrorist attacks, Dick Cheney, Donald Rumsfeld, Paul Wolfowitz, Florida Governor Jeb Bush, and Cheney aide Lewis Libby had prepared a paper spelling out their vision of the United States' role in the Middle East, which included an attack on Iraq.[16] Called "Rebuilding America's Defenses: Strategies, Forces, and Resources for a New Century," the report argued that the United States must have a permanent military presence in the Persian Gulf, and that although "the unresolved conflict with Iraq provides the immediate justification [for an Iraqi invasion], the need for a substantial American force presence in the Gulf transcends the issue of the regime of Saddam Hussein." With the invasion of Iraq, the Bush administration scrapped the Dual Containment policy. But they weren't planning to replace it with a security arrangement that would end Iran's estrangement. Rather, the new order would, at a minimum, continue Iran's isolation and at a maximum, force a change in the regime in Tehran. Prior to Washington taking on Iran, though, it needed first to put the final nail in the coffin of Saddam Hussein's rule.[17]

Handing Iraq to Iran on a Silver Platter

The Iraq war—or the "liberation of Iraq" as Bush administration officials preferred to call it—was promised to be a "cakewalk." Militarily, Saddam's forces were no match for the U.S Army. Within three weeks of fighting, Baghdad had fallen, and Saddam and his inner circle were all fugitives. However, winning the war and winning the peace proved to be two different matters. Regardless of whether the error of the endeavor lay in its inception or in its implementation, the end result was undeniable: the Iraq war was the single most destabilizing event in the Middle East of the past two decades. For the United States, it was a strategic mistake of unparalleled proportions.[18]

Suspecting that the invasion of Iraq was just a stepping stone toward a U.S.-Iran confrontation, the Iranians opposed the war, despite their own animosity toward Saddam. Iraq was already severely weakened and isolated; it simply did not pose a significant threat to Iran in the short term. The danger of a hostile but powerless Saddam was preferable to the danger posed by the installation of a pro-Western client government in Iraq with hostile intentions toward Tehran. Strategists in Tehran feared that a Baghdad regime with a Western tilt would complete the United States' encirclement of Iran.

But the United States' pending invasion of Iraq could also serve as an opportunity for Iran. Iran knew that, as in Afghanistan, it held strong cards in Iraq and could be of great help to Washington—perhaps even to the point of convincing the Bush administration to reevaluate their relations. One of these cards was Iran's superior intelligence on and familiarity with Iraq. Due to the eight-year Iran-Iraq war in the 1980s, the Iranians, unlike the Americans, understood the complex Iraqi tribal social networks and knew how to navigate them. Washington would need such knowledge, Tehran figured. Without a channel of communication, misunderstandings could occur, which would benefit Iran's regional rivals, including Israel and the Sunni Arab states. After all, the Iranians needed a channel to understand and influence American decisions on Iraq, and the Americans needed Iran to not complicate the United States' plans. So by late spring 2002, the State Department approached the Iranians, and the Geneva channel was resurrected. According to Kenneth Pollack of the Brookings Institution, Iran ended up playing a very helpful role in the invasion of Iraq, particularly in the reconstruction phase immediately following the collapse of the Iraqi army. Among other things, Iran instructed its influential Shia proxy groups in Iraq to participate in reconstruction after the war, rather than resist the American occupation. Iran could have created havoc for the United States, and it chose not to. "If the Iranians wanted to create chaos in Iraq [after Saddam's fall], they could have easily done so in the darkest days after the war, and the United States was fortunate that they did not," Pollack wrote.[19]

The swiftness with which the United States defeated the strongest standing Arab army—one that the Iranians had failed to defeat throughout eight bloody years of warfare—sent tremors down the spines of the United States' foes in the region and beyond. During the entirety of their twenty-four-year reign, the Iranian clerics had seldom felt so vulnerable. Only days before Bush's May 1 declaration of "Mission Accomplished," Tehran made one last attempt to reach out to the United States. Figuring that the regime's very existence could be at stake, the Iranians put everything on the table—Hezbollah; the Israeli-Palestinian conflict, including Hamas and Islamic jihad; and Iran's nuclear program.

The Iranians prepared a comprehensive proposal, addressing all points of contention between the two countries and spelling out the contours of a potential grand bargain between them. The first draft of the proposal was written by Sadegh Kharrazi, Iran's ambassador to France at the time and the nephew of the then Iranian foreign minister. The draft went to Iran's supreme leader for approval, who asked Iran's UN ambassador, Zarif, to review it and make final edits before it was sent to the Americans. In addition, the Iranians consulted Tim Guldimann, the Swiss ambassador to Iran, who would eventually deliver the proposal to Washington. The proposal stunned the Americans. It was an astonishing—and authoritative—document. "The Iranians acknowledged that WMD [Weapons of Mass Destruction] and support for terror were serious causes of concern for us, and they were willing to negotiate," said Leverett. "The message had been approved by all the highest levels of authority." Unlike in the past, when the Iranians had at times been hesitant to negotiate with the United States, Tehran was now putting all its cards on the table, declaring what it wanted from the United States, and what it was willing to offer in return. "That letter went to the Americans to say that we are ready to talk, we are ready to address our issues," said Mohammad Hossein Adeli, who was then a deputy foreign minister in Iran.[20]

Iran was seeking a dialogue of "mutual respect," wherein the United States and Iran would engage each other as equals. Within that dialogue, the Iranians offered to end their support to Hamas and Islamic jihad and pressure them to cease attacks on Israel. On Hezbollah, Iran's closest partner in the Arab world, Iran offered to support the disarmament of the Lebanese militia and transform it into a purely political party. On terrorism, Tehran offered full cooperation against all terrorist organizations—above all, al-Qaeda, which only two years earlier had attacked the American homeland. On Iraq, Iran offered to actively work with the United States to support political stabilization, establishment of democratic institutions, and—most importantly—the creation of a nonreligious government, just as it had in Afghanistan. The Iranians included an olive branch to Israel, offering to accept the Beirut Declaration of the Arab League—that is, the Saudi peace plan from March 2002, in which the Arab states offered to make peace collectively with Israel, recognizing and normalizing relations with the Jewish State in return for Israeli agreement to withdraw from all occupied territories and accept a fully independent Palestinian state. Through this step, Iran would formally recognize the two-state solution and consider itself at peace with Israel. This was an unprecedented concession by Tehran.

The proposal also included some very critical measures on the nuclear issue. At a time when Iran had less than two hundred centrifuges and a very limited knowledge about the fuel cycle, Tehran offered to completely open up the Iranian nuclear program to intrusive international inspections in order to alleviate any fears of Iranian weaponization. The Iranians would sign the Additional Protocol to the Non-Proliferation Treaty, and they also offered extensive American involvement in the program as a further guarantee and goodwill gesture. (A decade later, by which time Iran had 22,000 centrifuges, thousands of kilograms of low enriched uranium, and a much more sophisticated nuclear program, Washington negotiated to convince Tehran to agree to some of these very measures.) In return, Tehran sought a long-term understanding with the United States including having the United States put a halt to hostile behavior, such as the "axis of evil" rhetoric and interference in Iran's domestic affairs; end all sanctions against Iran; support Iranian national interests in Iraq and Iranian demands for war reparations; respect Iran's right to full access to nuclear, biological, and chemical technology; and finally, recognize Iran's legitimate security interests in the region. The document also spelled out a procedure for step-by-step negotiations toward a mutually acceptable agreement.[21]

The proposal was delivered to the United States by the Swiss ambassador to Tehran, since Switzerland was the caretaker of U.S. interests in Iran in the absence of a U.S. embassy. Official messages between the United States and Iran were usually sent through the Swiss from 1990 onward, after the channel was established to avoid any misunderstandings between the United States and Iran during the first Persian Gulf War. "I got the clear impression that there is a strong will of the regime to tackle the problem with the U.S. now and to try it with this initiative," Guldimann wrote in the cover letter to the proposal. Washington, however, was not in the mood for reconciliation.[22]

For many in the State Department, the proposal was a no-brainer. The State Department recognized that it was an authentic document approved by the highest levels in Iran and offering major concessions in return for an end to the sanctions policy. Secretary Powell and his deputy, Richard Armitage, favored a positive response. Together with National Security Advisor Condoleezza Rice, they approached the president about the proposal, but instead of instigating a lively debate on the details of a potential American response, they found Cheney and Rumsfeld quickly putting the matter to an end. Their argument was simple but devastating. "We don't speak to evil," they said. Not even a single interagency meeting was set up to discuss the proposal. "In the end," Wilkerson said, in a harsh reference to the neoconservatives led by Cheney and Rumsfeld, "the secret cabal got what it wanted: no negotiations with Tehran." Once again, Iran's belief that it could resolve its tensions with Washington proved frustratingly naive.[23]

Just as in 1991, when the United States chose not to invite Iran to the Madrid conference, negotiating with the Iranians was low on the White House's agenda. Iran made this offer only because it was weak and desperate, hardliners in the Bush administration argued. These officials opposed a deal with Iran no matter what the ayatollahs offered, because, they said, the United States could get what it wanted for free simply by removing the regime in Tehran. Negotiating with Iran, however, and striking a deal with the clerical regime would signal the United States' acceptance of Iran's role and interest in the region. Mindful of the fact that the Bush administration's objective was to strengthen the United States' control over the region, giving space to a country like Iran, which challenged the Pax Americana, was simply unacceptable. Instead, the United States should dictate terms from a position of strength and force Iran into submission. Israeli-born

Middle East specialist Meyrav Wurmser (whose husband served as a senior advisor to Dick Cheney) spelled out the logic of the Bush administration as follows: "Our fight against Iraq was only one battle in a long war," Wurmser said. "It would be ill-conceived to think that we can deal with Iraq alone. . . . We must move on, and faster. . . . Rather than coming as victors who should be feared and respected rather than loved, we are still engaged in old diplomacy, in the kind of politics that led to the attacks of September 11." After all, the logic went, the swift success in Iraq showed that taking on Iran would not be too complicated. Only a month earlier, Undersecretary of Defense for Policy Douglas Feith had briefed Defense and State Department officials on how the war in Iraq could be continued into Iran and Syria in order to replace the regimes there. The plans were quite extensive and far reaching. "It was much more than just a contingency plan," Wilkerson recalled.[24]

To make their rejection of any accommodation with Iran crystal clear, rebuffing the proposal was not enough. Insult needed to be added to injury: the Bush administration decided to punish the Swiss for having delivered the proposal in the first place. Only a few days after its delivery, Washington rebuked Guldimann and the Swiss government for having overstepped their diplomatic mandate. "It was the most shameful thing," Wilkerson confessed. But the message to Tehran was unmistakable: not only would the Bush administration refuse Iran the courtesy of a reply; it would also punish those who sought to convey messages between the two.[25]

An opportunity for a major breakthrough had been willfully wasted. Many former Bush administration officials admit that the nonresponse was a mistake. The proposal had come at an opportune time. Tehran did not have a functioning nuclear program, and they were not swimming in oil revenues from soaring energy demand. Richard Haass, head of policy planning at the State Department at the time and now head of the Council on Foreign Relations, pointed out that the proposal was at least worth exploring. "To use an oil analogy, we could have drilled a dry hole," he said. "I didn't see what we had to lose." To those in the administration opposed to the neoconservative agenda, it was difficult to fathom how such an opportunity could have been dismissed. "In my mind it was one of those things you throw up in the air and say, 'I can't believe we did this,'" Wilkerson said.[26]

Once again, the United States had humiliated the moderates in Iran who wanted to reach out to the United States. Just as in the 1991–1993 period, after Iran was shunned from the Madrid conference and the United States intensified its efforts to isolate Iran following Iran's help in the first Persian Gulf War, Washington's decision strengthened the hands of those in Tehran who argued that the United States could be compelled to come to the negotiating table only if a cost was imposed on it when it refused to do so. The Bush administration would agree to deal with Iran on an equal basis, the clerics reasoned, only if it were deprived of all other options. The balance in Iran thus tilted in favor of the hardliners, and, as before, the diplomats involved in the overture to the United States paid a price for taking the risk. "The failure is not just for the idea, but also for the group who were pursuing the idea," Iran's Ambassador to the United Kingdom Seyyed Mohammad Hossein Adeli said.[27]

Rejecting the Iranian negotiation proposal was a missed opportunity not just in terms of the opening that Iran had offered, but also in terms of the privileged position the United States enjoyed at that moment—which it erroneously assumed would be long-lasting. Only months after the defeat of Saddam, an insurgency erupted in Iraq that yet again turned the tables on Iran and the United States. The liberation of Iraq quickly turned into the quagmire of Iraq. While the United States was running into the inevitable problems of governing a country whose state institutions had either been destroyed or dismantled, Iran was enjoying the maneuverability provided by its ties to Shia and Kurdish factions and its experience in navigating the complex Iraqi tribal landscape. Rather than cornering Iran, Washington found itself trapped in its strategy to encircle Iran. It wasn't Iran that was the sitting duck; it was the U.S. military in Iraq. The glee on then deputy oil minister Hadi Nejad-Hosseinian's face was obvious as he explained how the United States, through its intent to control the region and isolate Iran, had actually inadvertently strengthened Tehran. Washington had unchained Iran by defeating its two main rivals, Saddam and the Taliban, all the while getting itself bogged down in Mesopotamia. "Iraq couldn't have turned out better for us," he told me, smiling.[28]

Among U.S. allies that benefited from the American order in the region after Saddam was expelled from Iraq and whose interest lay in Iran's continued isolation, there was a sense of betrayal. "The Americans handed over Iraq to Iran on a silver platter," a Saudi intellectual close to the government in Riyadh told me bitterly in 2010.

American Disorder

I n 547 BC, the Lydian king Croesus sent an envoy to the Oracle at Delphi to inquire whether he should attack the rising Persian Empire to the east. The oracle famously replied, "If Croesus goes to war, he will destroy a great empire." Failing to recognize the ambiguity in the oracle's answer, Croesus launched an attack on Persia only to suffer a crushing defeat and see his own empire destroyed.

Two thousand five hundred years later, President George W. Bush did not have Croesus's oracle, but shared his faith in entering a war of choice. Also like Croesus, his militarism ultimately destroyed much of the power and influence of his own empire. By invading Iraq in 2003, President Bush did not just end the reign of Saddam Hussein. He also set in motion a series of events that eventually ended the American-led order in the Middle East. For Iran—which had opposed the old order and sought to free itself from American containment for decades— President Bush's aggression turned out to be a blessing in disguise precisely because it failed so miserably. The Middle East had lost a hegemon powerful enough to enforce stability and a clear set of rules of engagement. As a result, its geopolitical chess game not only changed, but began to fall apart, testing existing friendships and enmities alike. As powers rose and fell, new alliances were forged and new rivalries were created. Although geopolitical forces first pushed the United States and

Iran toward a military confrontation, the changing game ultimately helped bring about an unprecedented convergence toward diplomacy.

The Iraqi army was no match for the United States. Governing Iraq, however, proved a task beyond the U.S. military's capability. Its problems began once the war ended and the responsibility to uphold security and rebuild the state and society fell on U.S. servicemen and women. A president who in the election campaign had promised that the U.S. army would no longer be used for nation-building had now entangled the United States in one of the most extensive and challenging nation-building projects in modern times. The United States was hopelessly unprepared and unfit for this task.[1] The costs of the occupation were astronomical not just for the Americans: between 2003 and 2011 more than 250,000 Iraqis were killed and 1.4 million were displaced. "We will be lucky if Iraq even exists as a country in a few years," a former senior Iraqi official told me in 2013, while expressing regret for his earlier support for the U.S. invasion. Despite nearly 5,000 U.S. soldiers killed and an estimated $3 trillion spent on nation-building, Iraq today is neither safe, nor stable, nor a successful democracy.

The war and the Bush administration's rejection of diplomacy in general—arguing it was a sign of weakness and legitimized the United States' foes—profoundly weakened the country's standing and maneuverability internationally. Undoubtedly, the United States remained the most powerful country in the world, but it was now far removed from the position it enjoyed after the collapse of the Soviet Union. Bush's war had squandered its privileged position by overextending the U.S. military, making the American public reluctant to use military force in the future, and making the United States' allies in the region question its intentions and competence. At least in the Middle East, the United States was now a limping giant.

By 2005, half of the American public had turned against the Iraq war, up from 22 percent only two years earlier. Active support for the war dropped from 72 percent in 2003 to 47 percent in 2005, and became increasingly partisan. In 2006, 68 percent of Republicans still viewed the decision to go to war in Iraq favorably, while 88 percent of Democrats viewed it unfavorably or very unfavorably. In the military, morale took a huge hit as public support for the war waned and rationales for it, such as destroying Saddam's "weapons of mass destruction" and bringing democracy to Iraq, proved false. Suicide rates within the military skyrocketed: between 2001 and 2013, the number of active duty servicemen who committed suicide more than tripled.[2]

By 2011, more U.S. servicemen in Iraq and Afghanistan were taking their own lives per year than were killed in battle. Among veterans of the Iraq and Afghanistan wars, the numbers were even more staggering. A record 6,500 former military personnel killed themselves in 2012 alone—roughly equivalent to the total number of U.S. personnel killed in the Iraq and Afghanistan wars combined. To make matters worse, recruitment numbers dropped, forcing the military to extend soldiers' deployments from twelve to fifteen months and require many to do repeated deployments in combat zones. Once deployments were extended beyond twelve months, many soldiers missed important family occasions, such as the birthdays of their children, two years in a row. All in all, the wars were breaking the U.S. military.[3]

It wasn't just the war in Iraq and the instability that it fomented that damaged the United States' standing internationally. It was also the Bush administration's disregard for international law and the perspectives of its allies and friends. "Going it alone" was a virtue for the Bush administration, not a path it chose out of necessity. The United States' moral position became more and more looked down upon by international players. Not only were many of its European allies opposed to the Iraq invasion; they were infuriated by Bush's squandering of opportunities to resolve the tensions with Iran diplomatically.[4]

With Bush never missing an opportunity to remind Iran that the United States' military option was still on the table, the European Union feared the United States would eventually declare yet another war. And since Bush showed no inclination to engage Iran diplomatically, the United Kingdom, France, and Germany began their own negotiations with Iran, aimed at limiting its nuclear program and depriving Washington of a pretext to attack. "The neocons were on 'a high,'" explained Alastair Crooke, who served as an advisor to Javier Solana, the EU foreign policy chief at the time. "They literally were levitating off the ground in pure excitement, and planning all the next Middle Eastern dominoes that needed to be toppled over. I recall worried Europeans at the time returning from Washington, shaking their heads, and saying that the neocons kept repeating that 'it was only the wimps that went to Baghdad; "real men" were going to Tehran.' In this heightened context, I recall a very senior EU official saying that the need for EU involvement in the nuclear issue was not so much to contain Iran, but to contain America."[5]

The Bush administration's rejection of diplomacy was not limited to the nuclear issue. Opportunities for U.S.-Iran diplomacy also existed in Iraq, with U.S. ambassador Zalmay Khalilzad working to open a channel to Tehran to find common ground on how to stabilize Iraq. Through Iraqi interlocutors, Khalilzad managed to reach Tehran and get Ayatollah Khamenei's approval for a U.S.-Iran dialogue. But as soon as the channel had been set up, the Bush administration did an about face and closed it down, much to Khalilzad's frustration. In retrospect, Khalilzad considers the failure to keep a channel to Iran continuously open one of the great missed opportunities of the Iraq war. "I am convinced that if we had combined diplomatic engagement with forcible actions, we could have shaped Iran's conduct."[6]

By the end of Bush's second term, his unpopularity at home and abroad, combined with the unmitigated disasters his foreign policy had brought about, had created a favorable situation for Tehran. Distrust in the United States' intentions had enabled Tehran to create divisions within the international community about its nuclear program. The United States' ability to create a strong alliance against Iran was limited precisely because Washington had skirted so many diplomatic openings. In the eyes of many states, the United States was at fault when it came to the festering nuclear crisis, not Iran. The next occupant of the White House recognized that reversing this belief necessitated proving to the world that the United States was open to diplomacy.[7]

Pivot to Asia

By the time then senator Barack Obama announced his bid for the presidency, support for the Iraq war had dropped to an all-time low of 38 percent. Clearly, political winds in the United States were blowing in favor of those opposing the Iraq war and preferring diplomacy to military adventures. Already in 2006, the congressionally appointed bipartisan Iraq Study Group recommended direct U.S. dialogue with Iran regarding Iraq and the situation in the Middle East. Two months before the U.S. presidential elections in 2008, five former secretaries of state—Madeleine Albright, Colin Powell, Warren Christopher, Henry A. Kissinger, and James A. Baker III—called on the United States to talk to Iran.[8]

Then senator Obama took the unusual step of making engagement with U.S. adversaries a central part of his foreign policy platform during the 2008 presidential election. Under normal electoral circumstances, this would have been considered political suicide. Obama boldly declared that it was "critical" that the United States "talk to the Syrians and the Iranians," and that those saying that the United States "shouldn't be talking to them ignore our own history." The Illinois senator was scorned by his Republican rival, Senator John McCain, who called his position "misguided." Even his Democratic opponent Senator Hillary Clinton dismissed his call for diplomacy as "irresponsible and frankly naive." However, the American public sided with Obama and not with his more hawkish contestants.[9]

Still, any diplomatic engagement with foes of the United States needed to fit into a larger, more global strategy. Even before he took office, Obama gathered his national security team and tasked them with re-examining the United States' global presence and priorities. His national security advisor, Tom Donilon, explained the process in an address to the Asia Society in March 2013: "We asked what the U.S. footprint and face to the world was and what it ought to be. We set out to identify the key national security interests that we needed to pursue. We looked around the world and asked: Where are we overweighted? Where are we underweighted?" The review concluded that "the lion's share of the political and economic history of the 21st century will be written in the Asia-Pacific region." This created a challenge for the United States, since so many of its resources were devoted to the Middle East, where there were two seemingly unending wars and a potential third one, if the nuclear stand-off with Iran wasn't resolved. "It was clear that there was an imbalance in the projection and focus of U.S. power," Donilon explained. "It was the President's judgment that we were overweighted in some areas and regions, including our military actions in the Middle East. At the same time, we were underweighted in other regions, such as the Asia-Pacific."[10]

The United States needed a strategic pivot to Asia, away from the Middle East. The unstated message of the "pivot to Asia" was that the real challenger to the United States' global standing would not be a Middle Eastern country, but an East Asian one—China, to be precise. To be able to meet that challenge, the United States could no longer allow itself to be drained and weakened by strategically marginal conflicts in the Middle East. It needed to end the wars in Iraq and Afghanistan and avoid unwise military engagements in the region, which would redirect focus away from the challenge that China could pose. Obama had to change the United States' course, Deputy National Security Advisor Ben Rhodes explained, because it was ensnared in "a completely unsustainable resource allocation in Iraq and Afghanistan, two countries that frankly [were] not going to dictate the course of the 21st century."[11]

To Obama, who, according to aides, entered the White House with a clear idea about the limits of American power, this was as much about meeting the challenge of twenty-first century as it was about ending the United States' otherwise endless wars. In an address to the Australian parliament, Obama described the two objectives as being intrinsically linked:

> For the United States, this reflects a broader shift. After a decade in which we fought two wars that cost us dearly, in blood and treasure, the United States is turning our attention to the vast potential of the Asia Pacific region. In just a few weeks, after nearly nine years, the last American troops will leave Iraq and our war there will be over. In Afghanistan, we've begun a transition—a responsible transition—so Afghans can take responsibility for their future and so coalition forces can begin to draw down. . . . So make no mistake, the tide of war is receding, and America is looking ahead to the future that we must build.[12]

Throughout his presidency, this broader global objective—the pivot to Asia—took a central role in Obama's calculations. Particularly as tensions in the Middle East continued to flare up, Obama remained consistent about avoiding major military escapades there, despite mounting criticisms of his foreign policy in Washington. As his secretary of defense, Ashton Carter, said, Obama believes that Asia "is the part of the world of greatest consequence to the American future, and that no president can take his eye off of this. . . . He consistently asks, even in the midst of everything else that's going on, 'Where are we in the Asia-Pacific rebalance? Where are we in terms of resources?' He's been extremely consistent about that, even in times of Middle East tension."[13]

Iran—and finding a diplomatic solution to the nuclear issue—fit perfectly with Obama's pivot to Asia. By preventing a nuclear-armed Iran through diplomacy, the United States would eliminate the most significant risk that could drag it back into another prolonged military endeavor in the Middle East, according to Deputy National Security Advisor Ben Rhodes. Phil Gordon, former coordinator for the Middle East at the National Security Council, also commented: "Absent the nuclear deal, Iran would continue its progress towards a nuclear weapons capability, leaving us a potential choice between acquiescence or the use of force." Either outcome ran counter to Obama's overall goal of not getting bogged down in the Middle East. Even short of conflict, "all out containment" of Iran was sucking up U.S. energy in and of itself while positioning the United States on the edge of warfare. Containment simply wasn't a stable policy—the risk of its deteriorating into a military confrontation was ever-present. Further, containment enabled American allies with their grudges against Iran to utilize U.S. power against it in ways that could counter the United States' interests. This was particularly true for Saudi Arabia, which wanted to enlist the United States as a full participant in its sectarian conflict with Iran—something that would go completely counter to the United States' interest to pivot to Asia. After all, Obama believed that some of these Sunni allies of the United States actually engaged in more destabilizing activities than Iran.[14]

The Arabs Rise Up

Not getting bogged down in the Middle East is easier said than done, particularly for a superpower that does not recognize limits to its power, whose policy elites obsess about the country not "coming across as weak," and whose population impulsively wants to intervene in every flare-up across the planet. "Our foreign policy establishment becomes deeply uncomfortable when they are aware that we're recognizing American limits," Rhodes said. "That's not in the career manual for a foreign policy commentator or thinker," he quipped. Nor did it help that the political situation in the Middle East wasn't conducive to Obama's pivot to Asia. Just as Washington was hoping to wind down the wars in Afghanistan and Iraq, a new wave of instability engulfed the region and threatened Obama's strategic rebalancing. The Arab uprisings were also a clear sign that the U.S.-led order in the region had collapsed. The United States was no longer capable of establishing and underwriting the security of the Middle East, nor was it inclined to do so.[15]

It is not entirely clear what caused twenty-six-year-old Mohamed Bouazizi to snap on December 17, 2010. Was it the public humiliation he endured that morning, when the local police officer confiscated his vegetable cart, or was it the years of humiliation he and his impoverished family endured while living under the repressive Tunisian dictatorship? We may never know, but there is little doubt that he himself never expected that his actions that morning would light the fire of revolution throughout the region. A struggling street vendor, Bouazizi set himself on fire in protest against the government. His desperate act struck a chord with thousands of other Tunisians who poured into the streets. Within weeks, the protests had spread to Egypt, the most populous Arab country.

At first, the West paid little attention to the Tunisian riots. Few realized that years of corruption, mismanagement, youth unemployment, the weakening of their Western guardians, and a general loss of hope for the future had made Tunisia and its Arab neighbors ripe for revolution. France, which later took a leading role in ousting the Libyan dictator Muammar Qaddafi, initially offered the Tunisian dictator, Zine al-Abidine Ben Ali, assistance in clamping down on the protesters. Nor did anyone expect that tiny Tunisia would be the birthplace of an event that would shake the Arab world at its very foundation. Within a few weeks, the uprisings had spread to Jordan, Algeria, and Oman. When protesters started to gather at Tahrir Square in Cairo, Egypt, the world realized that these were no ordinary riots.[16]

The administration had not seen this coming. President Obama was angered by the U.S. intelligence community's failure to predict the riots and their misjudgment of how quickly the unrest in Tunisia would unseat the Ben Ali regime. "It has taken not just us, but many people, by surprise," Chairman of the Joint Chiefs of Staff Admiral Mike Mullen admitted. Obama was taken off guard by an earth-shattering event that pitted the United States' commitment to its authoritarian Arab allies against its stated commitment to democracy and universal values such as human rights. After all, the strategic importance of Egypt lay in its role as the cornerstone of American policy in the Middle East, where it was the largest and most militarily powerful Arab country and the first one to make peace with Israel. While unquestionably authoritarian and undemocratic, Egypt had for decades delivered a relatively stable and predictable region. "We got what we needed," said Steven Cook at the Council on Foreign Relations. Moreover, there were strategic implications for siding with the losers in the struggle between the Arab populations and their repressive dictators. Not surprisingly, the Obama administration sent mixed signals that befuddled friends and foes alike in the chaos and confusion of the embryonic revolution. More than anything, the uprisings revealed that the United States was no longer in command. Its ability to drive events on the ground and impact the course of history was not what it once was.[17]

The Obama administration first sought to convince Egyptian president Hosni Mubarak to quietly step down and pave the way for an orderly transition. Mubarak refused, however, and took an uncompromising stance against the protesters as their numbers grew and their passion intensified. Within the administration, some argued that the protesters would prevail and that the United States must stand for democracy, while others feared that too rapid a transition would lead to chaos. The former worried that "the U.S. preoccupation with stability could put a historic president on the wrong side of history." The latter worried Egypt would fall from the control of longtime allies like Mubarak into the hands of elements hostile to the United States. The administration's public statements were seldom ahead of events, but rather in reaction to developments on the ground. At first, the administration refrained from publicly criticizing the Mubarak government. It didn't call for new and open elections, but rather urged the Egyptian government to refrain from using violence against protesters. Obama even praised Mubarak as a "patriot" who cared deeply about his country, and his envoy to the Egyptian president, Ambassador Frank Wisner, publicly stated that Mubarak was indispensable to Egypt's democratic transition.[18]

A turning point came seven days into the uprising during a telephone conversation between Obama and Mubarak. Obama had watched the Egyptian strongman give a defiant speech on television and called him to dispel any notion he had that he could avoid reform. But Mubarak wasn't budging and told Obama that he knew the Egyptian people better. After the call, Obama instructed his White House to toughen its public position, yet still did not call for Mubarak to step down. "We're not picking between those on the street and those in the government," Obama's Press Secretary Robert Gibbs told the press. It wasn't until the pro-democracy demonstrators eventually won that the United States took their side.[19]

After three weeks of protests and violent crackdowns, one of the longest serving dictators in the Arab world was forced to resign. On February 11, Mubarak handed over power to the armed forces. The announcement was received with a roar of approval from a crowd of hundreds of thousands at Tahrir Square. Mohamed ElBaradei, the former head of the International Atomic Energy Agency–turned opposition leader, hailed the moment as the "greatest day of my life" because "the country has been liberated after decades of repression." At this point Obama explicitly supported the protesters, and the debate within the administration was moot. The more important challenge now was to ensure that the United States was seen as having been on the right side of history. President Obama congratulated the protesters and declared that "Egypt will never be the same."[20]

The White House's initially cautious approach to the protests shifted to treating the largely peaceful uprisings as a model for political change. Having failed to impact the events, the Obama White House sought to encourage Arab leaders to heed the demands of their restive populations. "You have a young, vibrant generation within the Middle East that is looking for greater opportunity," Obama said. "And if you are governing these countries, you've got to get out ahead of change. You can't be behind the curve. . . . You can't maintain power through coercion. At some level in any society, there has to be consent."[21]

For many of the protesters, Obama was late to the game. He lent his support to the pro-democracy protesters at the last possible moment, in their view. "Obama has disappointed the Egyptian people by not having a clear point of view during the revolution," said Gameela Ismail, a founding member of the Al-Dostour Party. "He waited a long time to announce a clear opinion so he did not lose any of the parties. He never really supported the rights and freedom of the Egyptian people." At the same time, Saudi Arabia and Israel were incensed by what they regarded as Obama's betrayal of an old and loyal ally. If Washington could abandon Mubarak, how seriously could Riyadh take the United States' commitment to Saudi Arabia's security? Israel was equally enraged. While Prime Minister Benjamin Netanyahu instructed his cabinet not to criticize Obama publicly, Israeli president Shimon Peres did not mince his words in public in accusing Obama of "betraying" Mubarak.[22]

These allies—incidentally the main benefactors of the American-led order in the region—had an understandable interest in sustaining the United States' commitment to the regional order in general and to their security in particular. If the United States were to shift its focus toward Asia because of overextension in the Middle East, Mubarak's fate could become the norm for the region's state leaders. In the future, loyal U.S. allies and pivotal security partners would no longer be able to count on the United States to come to their aid against internal or external security threats. This could catapult Islamist movements into power throughout the Arab world and unleash ambitious new regimes similar to Iran's. Whereas the United States had concluded the status quo in the region was untenable, and that a new order must be struck between the governments and populations of the Middle East, the Israeli and Saudi view was that the status quo was sustainable, and that it was the United States' responsibility to maintain it.[23]

Nonetheless, Washington's waning influence was a key reason why it believed the old order was unsalvageable. When Washington had the ability to support the status quo, it did so—with little regard for the state of democracy (or lack thereof) in the Arab world. Egyptians had risen up against Mubarak on several earlier occasions without receiving any support—or even platitudes—from Washington. When the United States did publicly criticize Mubarak and call on him to allow for greater reform, those views were never translated into any meaningful support for the pro-democracy opposition. Thus, for example, in June 2005, in an address at Cairo University, then secretary of state Condoleezza Rice assailed the Mubarak government for its massive human rights abuses. "For 60 years," she said, "my country, the United States, pursued stability at the expense of democracy in this region, here in the Middle East, and we achieved neither. Now we are taking a different course. We are supporting the democratic aspirations of all people." She continued to list several measures the Mubarak government had to take, from holding free elections to respecting human rights. Mubarak never forgave the Bush administration for this public humiliation, but it had little to no effect on broader U.S.-Egyptian relations. In the end, this speech consisted of only empty promises as pragmatic priorities triumphed over lofty rhetoric about American and universal values. Several months later, when Egyptian protesters who took to the streets over election fraud were met with lethal force, Washington sided with Mubarak just as it had previously. Standing next to Egypt's foreign minister, Ahmed Aboul Gheit, Rice struck a very different note. "We can't judge Egypt," she said. "We can't tell Egypt what its course can be or should be."[24]

By 2011, it wasn't just a change of administration that prompted a different American attitude toward the plight of democracy in Egypt—it was also the inability of the United States to sustain its allies. The power to tilt the scale in favor of Mubarak in a manner that shaped the outcome in Egypt simply no longer existed. "We can't control what happens in Egypt this week," Jon Alterman, director of the Middle East program at the Center for Strategic and International Studies, commented at the time. "In the longer term, this could be the beginning of a cascading series of profound challenges, but there's nothing the U.S.

can do right now to either prevent or steer those challenges." As a result of Washington's waning power following the invasion of Iraq, the United States was now an irrelevant superpower. Pax Americana was something of the past. If the Bush administration intended to spread democracy to the Middle East, then the irony is that in some sense it could deserve some credit for inadvertently doing so: by weakening the United States through the unwise invasion of Iraq, Washington no longer had the capacity to protect its authoritarian Arab allies in the region. Once American support for these dictatorships was gone, the long-existing societal factors that all pointed in the direction of change (but had been largely stymied by Washington's backing of the autocrats) came to the forefront and rendered these states ripe for revolution—though not for democracy. Unfortunately for the proponents of democracy, the revolutions that at first had been popularized as an Arab spring quickly turned into a cold and bitter Arab winter.[25]

American Order, American Disorder

As a rule, revolutions rarely breed democracies, and those in the Middle East proved no exception. The swift ousting of Mubarak in Egypt proved to be an outlier. Elsewhere, the euphoria of the Arab masses turned into despair as protests escalated into armed conflicts and protracted civil wars. Instead of building better governments and institutions, the Arab uprisings resulted in failed states, plunging the region further into instability. The American order had disintegrated into the American disorder.

The Arab spring clearly demonstrated that the United States lacked the ability to steer developments in the region. These new limits made the burden of Pax Americana in the Middle East even more unappealing and the pivot to Asia only more attractive. The cost of sustaining order in the region had already skyrocketed, courtesy of the Iraq war, while the dividends of hegemony were plummeting. Now sustaining the order entailed not only maintaining stable relations among states, but also rebuilding collapsed and collapsing states. The United States would become even more overextended in the Middle East just to maintain the level of disorder predating the Arab spring.

For U.S.-Iran diplomacy, however, the chaos of the Arab winter arguably did more good than harm. Throughout this period, the nuclear issue was becoming more pressing as Iran's nuclear program advanced and Israeli threats of military action escalated. Yet for several reasons, a deal with Iran was now emerging as one of the lowest hanging diplomatic fruits in the Middle East.

A New Year's Greeting

By the time the uprisings swept the Arab world, diplomacy with Iran had already been tried—and abandoned. Immediately after taking office, however, Obama instructed his administration to chart a path for a new Iran policy that would be centered on engagement. One of the first steps was to change the United States' vocabulary on Iran. In order to create an atmosphere conducive to diplomacy, the U.S. government had to employ a language that reflected that desire. The tough talk of the Bush administration had been confrontational, with the "axis of evil" speech and Bush's insistence on repeating at every given opportunity that "all options remain on the table"—a not-so-veiled threat of military action—having been the clearest examples of the kind of rhetoric that spoiled opportunities for diplomatic openings.

But there were also more subtle phrases that poisoned the atmosphere, many times unbeknownst to the United States. For instance, U.S. officials explaining the logic of the Obama administration's engagement strategy often spoke of eliciting a change in Iranian behavior using "carrots and sticks," a rather innocent expression in the American political mind. But the term translated poorly into Persian, both linguistically and culturally. To Iranian ears, it portrayed Iran as a donkey that the United States would either lure or coerce into submission. It was the opposite of the "mutual respect" the Iranians were seeking. It also signaled that the United States viewed the negotiations as a zero-sum exercise. Conceptually, a negotiation based on carrots and sticks seemed to preclude the very existence of a win-win outcome. For the weaker party, a negotiation within that framework was understandably unappealing. As soon as the Obama administration became aware of how the Iranians interpreted this phrase, it was eradicated from the State Department's talking points.[1]

A Message from the United States

Obama's revamping of the United States' Iran posture went beyond just discarding unhelpful terminology. The most important step was his effort to avoid being trapped in the baggage of his predecessors and to instead send bold, positive messages to Tehran about his desire to resolve their tensions diplomatically. The first signal came just twelve minutes into his inaugural address. "To the Muslim world, we seek a new way forward, based on mutual interest and mutual respect. . . . We will extend a hand if you are willing to unclench your fist," Obama said in his address to the 1.5-million-strong crowd on the Washington mall. The phrase "mutual respect" was specifically intended for Iran. Over the past decades, the Iranians had insisted that they would agree to talks with the United States only if Washington accepted Iran as an equal and engaged with it with "mutual respect." While the American analysis of the U.S.-Iran conflict focused on Washington's and Tehran's clashing policy differences, what the Iranians sought was to emancipate themselves from an uneven relationship—one in which Iran had to submit itself to the United States by virtue of the United States' superiority in terms of hard power. The phrase "mutual respect" is so critical to Tehran that the Iranians even included it in their 2003 negotiation offer to the Bush administration.[2]

Only two months after his inaugural address, Obama went even further. On the eve of the Iranian New Year (Norouz) in March 2009, Obama taped a three-and-a-half-minute statement congratulating the Iranians and expressing his wish for a better future for the two nations. "I would like to speak directly to the people and leaders of the Islamic

Republic of Iran," he said, as he praised the contributions of the Iranian nation to art, music, and literature over the centuries:

> My administration is now committed to diplomacy that addresses the full range of issues before us, and to pursuing constructive ties among the United States, Iran, and the international community. This process will not be advanced by threats. We seek instead engagement that is honest and grounded in mutual respect. . . . You, too, have a choice. The United States wants the Islamic Republic of Iran to take its rightful place in the community of nations. You have that right—but it comes with real responsibilities, and that place cannot be reached through terror or arms, but rather through peaceful actions that demonstrate the true greatness of the Iranian people and civilization. And the measure of that greatness is not the capacity to destroy, it is your demonstrated ability to build and create.

Recognizing how revered poets are in Iranian culture, Obama quoted one of Iran's most famous to emphasize the common humanity between Iran and the United States. "There are those who insist that we be defined by our differences," he said. "But let us remember the words that were written by the poet Saadi, so many years ago: 'The children of Adam are limbs to each other, having been created of one essence.'"[3]

Everything about Obama's message was extraordinary: the respectful tone, the thoughtful message, the modern medium (the White House posted it on YouTube with Persian subtitles), as well as the very idea of speaking directly to the Iranian people and government. The video immediately went viral in Iran, and it largely achieved its principal objective: signaling to the Iranian government that Washington's desire to change the dynamic between Iran and the United States was sincere. More than anything, that came through thanks to Obama refraining from using the message to drive a wedge between the people and government of Iran. For the Iranian clergy, ever so paranoid about the United States seeking regime change in Iran, this was a prerequisite. Obama's using the official name of Iran—the Islamic Republic of

Iran—further reinforced his movement away from the standard rhetoric assumed by American politicians with regard to Iran. And by rejecting the idea that the growing problems between the United States and Iran could be resolved through threats, Obama conveyed that the trigger-happy days of the Bush administration were over. The most revealing phrase in the address, however, was Obama's indication that the United States wanted Iran to "take its rightful place in the community of nations." This phrase signified Obama's conditional openness to a new regional order where Iran would assume a greater role—a key demand of the Iranians, who were deeply frustrated by their belief that the role in regional affairs that had been delegated to them by the international community was not proportionate to their geopolitical weight. Obama's statement was in direct contradiction of the policy of Dual Containment, the Bush administration's isolation of Iran, as well as Israel and Saudi Arabia's aim to keep Iran permanently contained in the region.[4]

The Iranian government was caught off guard. It had not been given prior notice of the video message. But the reaction of Iran's supreme leader, Ayatollah Ali Khamenei, was swift. He responded to Obama during his own Norouz speech in his hometown of Mashhad. In an address that otherwise focused mostly on domestic issues, Khamenei devoted roughly twenty minutes to Obama's message. His response was typical: he presented a laundry list of Iranian grievances and offered only a small opening toward the end of his speech. To the untrained ear, the address would come across as an outright rejection of Obama's overture. Khamenei covered Iranian suffering due to sanctions and the freezing of assets; American support for Iranian opposition groups; and his belief that Washington gave Saddam Hussein the green light to invade Iran in 1980 and that it supported the Baluchi terrorist and secessionist group Jundollah. He did not call for an apology, however, and cited these grievances not as reasons why dialogue with the United States should be shunned, but rather to reinforce his skepticism about the Obama administration and justify why a change of tone and vocabulary wasn't enough to reconcile the differences between the two countries.[5]

Khamenei expressed his doubts about Obama's ability to change the United States' approach to Iran ("I do not know who makes decisions

for America, the president, the congress, behind the scene elements?");
he rejected the idea that Iran would respond to a policy of dialogue and
pressure (carrots and sticks); and he questioned the sincerity of the
Obama White House by arguing that in practice, beyond a change in
tone and words, nothing in the United States' policy toward Iran had
changed. "What has changed?" Khamenei asked. "Has your enmity
toward the Iranian nation changed? What signs are there to support
this? Have you released the possessions of the Iranian nation? Have you
removed the cruel sanctions? Have you stopped the insults, accusations
and negative propaganda against this great nation and its officials?
Have you stopped unconditional support for the Zionist regime?" Real
change could not be a mere change of tactics while pursuing the same
old strategic aim, Khamenei continued. "This is not a change. This is
deceit," he declared soberly.[6]

But Khamenei also offered a small and cautious opening to the
United States. Admitting that the Obama administration did not carry
the baggage of previous administrations when dealing with Iran,
Khamenei proclaimed that Iran would change its policy toward the
United States, if Obama followed through with his promise and delivered real change in the United States' approach to Iran. "You change and
we will change as well," Khamenei said. But the United States had to
take the first step, the supreme leader signaled. From Washington's perspective, the Iranian government essentially put a precondition on engagement taking place. The Iranian government famously said during
the Bush presidency that they had only one precondition for diplomacy,
and that was that there should be no preconditions. Now, as Washington dropped its precondition, Iran seemingly adopted its own.

Clearly, a change in language or tone was not enough to bring
about a diplomatic breakthrough. Obama had underestimated the depth
of Iran's suspicion of the United States. But the first obstacle to diplomacy turned out not to be Tehran's skepticism but Israel's intransigence.

Bibi and Barack: A Match Made in Hell

Senator Obama and Benjamin Netanyahu first met in a small office
in the administrative area of Ronald Reagan National Airport in

March 2007. Both leaders were in the minority parties of their respective countries at the time—Obama as a Democratic senator during the Republican reign of George W. Bush and Netanyahu as the leader of the opposition to the Kadima government in Israel. It would prove to be one of their best meetings—and from that point it was pretty much downhill in a personal relationship that, at a minimum, came to complicate growing tensions between Israel and the United States. Obama was not unique in failing to get along with the Israeli politician, who is known for his arrogance and impoliteness. Netanyahu had famously been declared persona non grata by Secretary James Baker in the early 1990s, and even President Clinton, who got along with virtually everyone, grew to loathe him. When the opportunity was given in 1999, the Clinton White House worked hard to have the incumbent Netanyahu lose the election. Bibi was simply an "Israeli politician who had shown himself totally unwilling to defer to the United States as the larger power in this bent relationship," explained Peter Beinart, a prominent expert in U.S.-Israel relations. In fact, tensions between Netanyahu and the Clinton teams were so high that when Obama clinched the presidency and made Hillary Clinton secretary of state and Rahm Emanuel—who had served in the Clinton White House and often sparred with Netanyahu—his chief of staff, the Netanyahu team's main concern was not Obama, but Clinton and Emanuel, who they feared "would poison Obama against Bibi."[7]

Netanyahu was on his way back to Israel when he took the time to meet Obama at the airport in 2007. He sensed that Obama had a shot at winning the Democratic nomination the following year, and he wanted to meet and size up the up-and-coming Illinois senator with a Muslim first and middle name. Obama was less excited about the meeting, but his forward-looking staff convinced him to go. The meeting lasted thirty minutes, with Iran topping the agenda. Netanyahu did most of the talking; Obama did the listening. Netanyahu, who had come to personify the Israeli mantra that Iran was an existential threat, could have given the speech in his sleep: Iran was irrational, suicidal, and hell-bent on the destruction of the Jewish State. Consequently, its nuclear program was "the world's greatest danger to peace." Obama did not express any disagreement at that meeting, but once in office he clearly questioned many of Netanyahu's declarations about Iran—particularly that Tehran was irrational and suicidal, and thus immune to a dialogue based on incentives and disincentives. Netanyahu elicited a sufficient amount of agreement and sympathy from Obama to report back to the Israeli embassy that it "was a very good meeting." To his wife, Netanyahu went even further: "I just met a man who is going to be president of the United States," he told her.[8]

The next time Barack and Bibi met on U.S. soil was in May 2009 in the Oval Office. Obama was now the United States' first black president. Netanyahu was prime minister in a coalition government with the Labor Party. The meeting was nothing short of a disaster. Obama's ambitions were not in line with Netanyahu's. He wanted to reach a peace accord between Israel and Palestine and create a Palestinian state. Netanyahu wanted to uphold his campaign promise not to demolish any Israeli settlements on Palestinian territory. Obama wanted to rebuild the United States' standing in the Islamic world, which necessitated creating a bit of a distance between it and Israel. Netanyahu wanted the United States to remain committed to a "clash of civilizations" worldview that pitted the United States, Israel, and the West against the world of Islam. Netanyahu wanted the United States to eliminate Iran's nuclear program, while Obama wanted to reach a diplomatic deal that prevented Iran from building a nuclear warhead and allowed for a peaceful nuclear program. Going up against the American president would be a dangerous gambit. Obama was an immensely popular president who continued to enjoy the political latitude American presidents usually experience only during their first year in office. The Democrats controlled not only the Executive, but also the Senate, where they held a supermajority, and the House of Representatives. Clashing with Obama under these circumstances could be very damaging. Still, that was the path Netanyahu chose.[9]

Obama and Netanyahu met alone in the Oval Office. After the routine pleasantries, they shifted to the Palestinian issue. Netanyahu was in for a shock. Obama demanded a complete settlement freeze— essentially insisting that Netanyahu break his campaign promise to his right-wing base. The Israeli premier felt ambushed, he later told his aides. The U.S. side had not given any hints that the president would make this demand. That was a deliberate move by the Obama White House, which feared that the Israelis would leak any such notification in order to torpedo the U.S. idea. After two hours, the topic turned to Iran, and aides of the president and prime minister joined the conversation. But even Iran—which was supposed to be an issue where the two sides differed less—proved difficult.[10]

Only two months earlier, the Israelis had tried to undermine Obama's Norouz message to Iran. After learning of Obama's unprecedented outreach, Israeli president Shimon Peres quickly released his own video. It was his first-ever direct video message to the Iranian people. Predictably, Peres's message stood in stark contrast to Obama's. Praising the Iranian people, he subtly urged them to overthrow their leaders. The press picked up on the contrast between the two messages. "While the Americans are actively seeking a way to start a dialogue, Israel is preaching confrontation and the toppling of the government in Tehran," a *Haaretz* editorial said. "It is clearly in Israel's interest to halt Iran's nuclear program, but it is no less in our interests to have close ties and a coordinated policy with the United States. The new government should give Obama's diplomatic initiative a chance." A former Israeli peace negotiator called Peres's message a "sabotage attempt." Recognizing the diluting effect Peres's statement could have on Obama's message, the White House quickly clarified that there had been no coordination between the United States and Israel on this matter.[11]

The Israelis had a well-prepared strategy to sabotage Obama's diplomacy. It centered on imposing impossible demands while simultaneously pushing for measures that would poison the atmosphere against diplomacy. First, Israel wanted the Obama administration to remain committed to the zero-enrichment redline adopted under the Bush administration. This meant that the United States could not accept any solution that entailed Iran enriching any uranium or spinning a single centrifuge—even if the enrichment was at levels that had no military utility. Earlier diplomatic endeavors had failed precisely because of this demand: while preventing Iran from enriching uranium made it next to impossible for Tehran to build a nuclear bomb, the Iranians categorically rejected the demand and refused to engage in a diplomatic process if zero enrichment was a possible negotiation outcome.

Some have called Iran's uncompromising stance on enrichment a matter of pride. But to the leaders of the clerical regime, it involved much more than that. For them, the issue was related to the very heart of the revolution—its effort to restore the country's dignity and independence, which could be achieved, they argued, only through the establishment of an Islamic republic. In their narrative, the revolution saved the country from the shah's policy of subjugation to the West. The centrality of the idea of independence as a tenet of the revolution cannot be underestimated. The "identity-marker of the Iranian revolution" became the slogan "Estiqlal, Azadi, Jomhuri-ye Eslami!" (Independence, Freedom, Islamic Republic!), a "pivotal yet broad demand" that decorated almost every banner and placard in revolutionary Iran. Ayatollah Khamenei brought this up in his reply to Obama's Norouz message in 2009: "Before the revolution, Iran was in the hands of the United States, its vital resources were in the hands of the United States, its political decision-making centers were in the hands of the United States, decisions to appoint and depose its vital centers were in the hands of the United States, and [the country] was like a field for the United States, the U.S. military, and others on which to graze. Well, this was taken away from them."[12]

In any negotiation with the United States, the litmus test for the Islamic Republic would be if it could uphold the promise of independence and an end to its perceived submission to the West. Over time, retaining Iran's ability to enrich uranium with the same freedoms and limitations that other parties to the Non-Proliferation Treaty were held to became the benchmark of that goal. Since the United States had supported Iran's nuclear program during the time of the shah, for the Islamic Republic to negotiate away what it had enjoyed during the era when Iran "was like a field for the United States, the U.S. military, and others on which to graze" would mean its crushing failure. In the Iranian press, losing enrichment capability was likened to the Treaty of Turkmenchay of 1828, one of Iran's greatest humiliations in modern history, when the Persian Empire ceded much of its territory in the Caucasus and Central Asia to Russia—the implication being that if Iran were to give up enrichment through negotiations, it too would be eternally forfeited. Later, when the nuclear deal was being finalized, hardline clerics lauded the deal precisely because Tehran had won the West's acceptance on the enrichment issue. Ayatollah Ahmad Khatami pointed out that "whenever a war took place against the country over the past two hundred years, its end marked the loss of parts of this country." But now, with the nuclear deal negotiated by the Islamic Republic, "the country has not been sold, is not sold, and will not be sold." By 2009, few analysts in the West viewed Netanyahu's zero-enrichment objective as realistic. Insisting on it was tantamount to pushing the talks toward failure.[13]

A second part of the Israeli sabotage policy involved the Israelis and their allies on Capitol Hill pressing for additional sanctions to be imposed on Iran prior to the start of negotiations. They argued that additional pressure would both strengthen the United States' bargaining position and further incentivize Iran to agree to talks. The Obama administration disagreed, fearing that additional sanctions would poison the atmosphere and make it harder to get talks started.[14]

Third, Netanyahu insisted that the United States should continue to adopt a very strong military posture and continue to repeat the mantra that "all options remain on the table." Iran would respond to diplomacy only if faced with a credible military threat. Diplomacy without a military component was futile, the Israelis maintained. The Obama White House, however, was skeptical about using such language, partly because it was redundant—the military option is always on the table, regardless of whether the president of the United States refers to it on a regular basis or not—and partly because reiterating the phrase would undermine the credibility of Obama's diplomatic outreach and fuel Iranian suspicions. A disconnect between the three states, their strategies, and their leaders seemed almost complete. "There's a three-way race going on here," one of Obama's strategists told the *New York Times*. "We're racing to make diplomatic progress. The Iranians are racing to make their nuclear capability a fait accompli. And the Israelis, of course, are racing to come up with a convincing military alternative that could plausibly set back the Iranian program."[15]

The last element of the Israeli strategy to undermine Obama's diplomacy was to demand a tight deadline of only eight to twelve weeks be set for diplomacy. If an acceptable outcome had not been achieved by then, diplomatic efforts had to be declared exhausted and failed, and the United States would consequently have to return to sanctions

and other forms of coercion. "It is important that the dialogue with
Iran be limited in duration and that if after three months it will be clear
that the Iranians are playing for time and not ceasing their nuclear
program, then the international community will have to take practical
measures," Israel's foreign minister, Avigdor Lieberman, said. Throughout the spring of 2009, recurring rumors surfaced regarding various
deadlines for the talks, and each time the Obama administration resisted committing itself to any deadline.[16]

Obama and Netanyahu publicly clashed over these issues at their
May meeting at the White House. After their tense conversation in the
Oval Office, they held an even more uncomfortable news conference.
Because of their deep-seated differences, they could not come to an
agreement on a joint statement summarizing their discussions. As if
that wasn't enough, their awkward body language virtually yelled out
their discord. With Netanyahu at his side clearly showing disagreement,
Obama explained the rationale for diplomacy and why it needed time
to succeed:

> We didn't expect—and I don't think anybody in the interna-
> tional community or anybody in the Middle East, for that
> matter—would expect that 30 years of antagonism and sus-
> picion between Iran and the United States would be resolved
> in four months. So we think it's very important for us to give
> this a chance. . . . The approach that we've been taking, which
> is no diplomacy, obviously has not worked. Nobody disagrees
> with that. Hamas and Hezbollah have gotten stronger. Iran
> has been pursuing its nuclear capabilities undiminished.
> And so not talking—that clearly hasn't worked. That's what's
> been tried. And so what we're going to do is try something
> new, which is actually engaging and reaching out to the
> Iranians.[17]

Obama refused to commit to an arbitrary deadline but accepted
that a timetable was needed in order to prevent talks from proceeding
indefinitely. "It is important for us, I think, without having set an artificial deadline, to be mindful of the fact that we're not going to have

talks forever. We're not going to create a situation in which talks become an excuse for inaction while Iran proceeds with developing a nuclear—and deploying a nuclear weapon." Once it was Netanyahu's turn to speak, he exacted revenge for Obama's surprise demand for a settlement freeze. During their conversation prior to the news conference, Obama had told the Israeli prime minister that the success or failure of diplomacy would be determined by the end of the year and that the military option remained on the table, according to leaked State Department cables.[18]

At the press conference, however, Obama deliberately did not utter a word about the military option. So instead, on the spot, Netanyahu decided to publicly reveal what the president had told him in their closed meeting. "I very much appreciate, Mr. President, your firm commitment to ensure that Iran does not develop nuclear military capability, and also your statement that you're leaving all options on the table," Netanyahu told Obama in front of the reporters. But Obama had made no such statement during the press conference. If Obama had ambushed Netanyahu in their closed meeting, Netanyahu chose to ambush Obama in public. It was difficult to interpret Netanyahu's audacious move as anything but a naked attempt to undermine Obama's strategy with Iran.[19]

This, however, was just the opening salvo. Subsequently, Netanyahu constantly sought to undermine Obama's diplomacy with Iran and—at least according to the Obama camp—even to oust Obama from the White House in 2012. By the summer of 2015, the conflict would escalate into "an all gloves off" showdown. But Israel was not the only actor that stood in the way of Obama's outreach to Iran. The Islamic Republic itself presented even greater challenges.[20]

Mousavi versus Ahmadinejad

Elections in Iran are neither free nor fair. Despite being competitive and highly consequential, Iranian elections are marred by unmistakable undemocratic elements, from candidates being vetted by the Guardian Council—an unelected body of twelve clergymen and jurists who decide which candidates are permitted to run—to other restrictions based on gender and religion. Still, what happened in the summer of 2009 was unprecedented.

Few presidents in Iran have been as polarizing as Mahmoud Ahmadinejad, the five-foot-two traffic engineer turned politician who was elected president of Iran in 2005. While he is infamous in the West for his Holocaust denial and combative rhetoric, he is better known in Iran for his incompetence and mismanagement. Ahmadinejad's entrance into national politics in Iran was accidental—the Iranian public cast their votes for him in the 2005 presidential elections precisely because he was unknown and thus, considered to be not part of the establishment. By 2009, however, they had gotten to know him. And for many, there wasn't much to like. Despite record-high oil revenues, the economy was suffering from incredible and unprecedented mismanagement. Between unsustainable cash-out programs to closing the government's Planning and Budget Organization, a nonpolitical body that oversaw national economic projects, the Ahmadinejad government had brought the Iranian economy to its knees long before Iran was hit with some of the most crippling sanctions in history.[21]

By spring 2009, Iran was ripe for change. Three candidates were permitted by the Guardian Council to run against Ahmadinejad—all of them insiders of the Islamic Republic: Mehdi Karroubi, the former speaker of the parliament who ran on a reformist platform; Mohsen Rezaii, the former head of the Iranian Revolutionary Guard Corps; and former Prime Minister Mir Hossein Mousavi. The candidate who would steal most of the limelight and pose the greatest challenge to Ahmadinejad was Mousavi, whose followers made up what became known as the Green movement that rocked the foundations of the country. His campaign had a slow start, but about two to three weeks before the election, a sudden groundswell of support for Mousavi emerged, beginning on university campuses and then spreading like wildfire. Ahmadinejad, who many Western governments thought would be comfortably re-elected, was in trouble, as his many critics were energized and had found a candidate around whom they could rally.

From the American perspective, the main benefit from a Mousavi victory was that he would bring a much-welcomed change in rhetoric and persona. Washington knew that Mousavi "was not going to revolutionize the dynamic," an American diplomat told me. "He would just make it easier, he was digestible." On the hot-button issues that had made Ahmadinejad so politically toxic in Washington, Mousavi offered a very different approach. He condemned the killing of Jews in the Holocaust, while Ahmadinejad called the Holocaust a myth. He resented the manner in which Ahmadinejad's confrontational foreign policy had raised tensions without bringing Iran any dividends, while Ahmadinejad seemed to view tensions as a dividend per se. On diplomacy with the United States, Mousavi expressed greater openness, but also some skepticism. "Holding talks with America is not a taboo for me. If America practically changes its Iran policy, then we will surely hold talks with them," Mousavi said two weeks before the election.[22]

Mousavi had praised Obama's New Year's greeting but also expressed reservations based on Iran's past experience with the United States. "Despite America's meddling in our affairs, whenever working with America was in our interest, like in the case of Afghanistan, we did it," he said. "However, as soon as these incidents are over, America returns to its old rhetoric and once again we've fallen down the same path. Of course, Obama's language differs from Bush's language. If he [Obama] effects real change, we will definitely negotiate with America. Otherwise, we will not." On Iran's key redlines, Mousavi did not stray away from the Islamic Republic's official position—that enrichment was Iran's inalienable right. "It is our right and we have no right to backpedal or there will be dire consequences," the candidate said, insisting Iran was not aiming to produce nuclear weapons. "I don't think he would have under any circumstances given up Iranian enrichment," one of Mousavi's advisors told me. "We would keep our enrichment capability, however, with safeguards and enough credible inspection regimes that would make it difficult for diversion [toward military use]."[23]

In the end, none of this came to matter. Higher forces within the Islamic Republic had decided that Mousavi would not be permitted to become president, regardless of the outcome of the election.

Fraud

The Ahmadinejad camp had a plan. Three days before the election, his Interior Ministry secretly issued arrest warrants for key people within the Mousavi and Karroubi campaigns. On the afternoon of election day, security officers stormed the headquarters of the Mousavi campaign in northern Tehran twice, arresting Mousavi's campaign officials and shutting down their access to the Internet. The polls had not even closed yet, but Ahmadinejad was clearly assuming power. Within forty-eight hours, most of the first and second circle of officials around Mousavi and Karroubi were arrested. Those who escaped arrest went into hiding. By arresting the mid- and top-level officials of the Mousavi campaign, the Ahmadinejad camp managed to disconnect Mousavi from his grassroots supporters. This was a devastating—and perhaps decisive—blow to his ability to lead and direct his movement.[24]

While the Mousavi campaign anticipated some level of foul play—and even warned about it publicly—they never expected that their headquarters would be ransacked on election day, or that campaign officials would be arrested en masse. But just as the reformists had underestimated the extent to which the Ahmadinejad camp was willing to go to retain power, the hardliners underestimated the Iranian people's determination to have their votes make an impact.

According to the official count, Ahmadinejad had won a landslide victory, securing 62.63 percent of the vote, with Mousavi gaining only 33.75 percent. But the election was rife with irregularities, and the results were immediately contested. Millions of Iranians, dressed in green to support Mousavi, spontaneously took to the streets and demanded an answer to their question: Where is my vote? But Iran's supreme leader would not budge. On June 14, two days after the election, he endorsed the results and gave his blessings to Ahmadinejad. The next day, up to three million Iranians came out to rally in support of Mousavi—the largest demonstration in Iran since the 1979 revolution. The Ahmadinejad government showed no mercy, unleashing both riot police and the Basij, an armed paramilitary group, on the protesters. Using cell phones and video cameras, demonstrators documented the brutality of the Iranian security forces. The videos were promptly uploaded onto Facebook and other social media websites and quickly reached international audiences. Moreover, hundreds of Western journalists who had traveled to cover the election were now caught in the midst of the demonstrations and were thus able to report on the election fraud and the Iranian government's brutal reaction to the protests. By the fourth day, the Iranian authorities restricted all journalists working for foreign media from reporting what was happening on the streets. But every protester with a cell phone had already morphed into a citizen journalist, and the footage and eyewitness accounts continued to slip out of Iran.[25]

After a week of protests, Khamenei delivered a televised sermon during the Friday prayers, which was watched by millions of Iranians. Many hoped he would opt for reconciliation and help find a compromise. Instead, he reiterated his endorsement of Ahmadinejad, rejected any notion of fraud, and warned against continued demonstrations. At this point, any continued demonstrations would be an act of direct defiance against the supreme leader. Khamenei had raised the stakes, but the protesters refused to back down. The next day, the protests continued, and the level of violence sharply increased, with police killing ten protesters. The intense divisions within the Iranian political class were out in the open, with Khamenei backing Ahmadinejad and endorsing a violent clampdown against the protesters, Mousavi urging his supporters to continue demanding their rights peacefully, and Ali Larijani, the powerful speaker of the Iranian parliament (Majles), declaring that insofar as enough people believed the election was fraudulent that their opinion should be respected. Reports of massive human rights abuse, including rape and killings in Iran's overcrowded jails, began to surface. Even children of senior Iranian officials were listed among the dead. The Iranian power establishment was literally at war with itself.[26]

By August, this war reached a level of intensity that had never been seen before. The protests continued, the clampdown became more ruthless, the death toll grew, and the human rights abuses became more extreme and widespread. The Iranian regime had never been so shaken. At the outset, the protests were not a revolt against the system but a simple demand that the votes be recounted, so that the results of the election would reflect the will of the people. Those who sought to overthrow the system did not cast their votes—rather, they routinely advocated boycotting the polls. But as the brutality of the Ahmadinejad government grew, the demands of the protesters on the streets changed. The slogan of "Where is my vote?" morphed into "Down with the dictator" and finally to "Down with Khamenei" and "Down with the Islamic Republic." With Mousavi and Karroubi—the figureheads of the Green movement—under house arrest, the Green movement was losing its central control, and the ideas of its leadership and the ideas of its grassroots were moving in different directions.

The United States Caught off Guard

The U.S. government has contingency plans for almost any scenario. But it had no plan for how to react to massive fraud followed by months of demonstrations, violent clampdown, and a virtual civil war within the Iranian elite. Washington's public reaction was initially timid. The Obama administration carefully evaded taking sides, aiming, instead, to keep the United States from becoming an issue in the election dispute. "There was a real calculation that said the less we say, the better because this is an issue . . . between the Iranian people and their government," explained Michael Ratney of the U.S. State Department's Near East Affairs Bureau. "This is not about the United States. This is not about U.S.-Iranian relations." Obama addressed the concerns of the protesters and framed them as a human rights issue, but stopped short of condemning the government-sponsored violence against the demonstrators. "For those people who put so much hope and energy and optimism into the political process, I would say to them the world is watching and inspired by their participation regardless of what the ultimate outcome of the election was," Obama said during a June 15 Oval Office meeting with Italy's prime minister, Silvio Berlusconi.[27]

The administration's critics on the Republican side derided Obama's reaction, calling for the president to side squarely with the protesters. Senator John McCain, Obama's rival in the 2008 election, said that the United States should make clear that it backs anti-Ahmadinejad demonstrators in their battle against "an oppressive, repressive regime." On June 19, 2009, the House of Representatives voted 405–1 to condemn Tehran's crackdown on demonstrators and the government's interference with Internet and cell phone communications. Despite the fact that the Democrats controlled Congress, Republicans were able to initiate and pass the nonbinding resolution as a veiled criticism of Obama.[28]

The Washington debate was taking place in a parallel universe, as far as leaders of the Green movement were concerned. None of the critics of the Obama administration who called for direct support of the Green movement had asked the leaders of the pro-democracy forces in Iran whether they would welcome such support. Perhaps most striking is that neither the United States nor Obama specifically was a major factor in the deliberations of the Mousavi camp. "There was rarely ever, I would say, talk of what is Obama thinking of, what is Obama going to do. We were thinking about how are we going to save ourselves," one of Mousavi's advisors told me. Washington's sway over developments in Iran was minimal: with neither trade relations, diplomatic relations, nor an embassy on the ground, the United States had few avenues of influence in Iran. And to the extent the United States did figure in their calculations, the leaders of the Green movement did not want American support, did not trust it, and did not view it as helpful. After thirty years of mutual demonization and enmity, American endorsement of an Iranian politician would be as damaging in Iran's political landscape as an Iranian endorsement of a U.S. politician would be in the United States' political world. "We had hoped he would say nothing actually," a Mousavi strategist explained. "We were worried that [the Obama administration] might say something stupid. That they would make life more miserable for us."[29]

On the contrary, much evidence suggests that Obama's more cautious approach had been directly helpful, at least up to a point. For eight years, President Bush had sought to destabilize Iran and bring about regime change through isolation, threats, and financial support for anti-Tehran groups. Despite all of his labors, the opposite occurred: the Iranian elite closed ranks, and hardliners used the perceived threat from the United States to clamp down on human rights defenders and pro-democracy activists. Obama's outreach and removal of this perceived threat did not necessarily create fissures among the Iranian elite in and of itself, but it did weaken the glue that united Iran's many political factions. If the Bush administration were still in power and continuing to provoke confrontation with Iran, Mousavi would probably not have disputed the voter fraud and called for street protests. Due to the perceived national security threat of American intervention, Mousavi probably would have swallowed his pride and anger and would have asked his followers to do the same. The absence of an external threat enabled existing internal differences to come to the surface and bring about an unprecedented political standoff. Internally driven political change would not have been initiated or come about under the shadow of an American military threat. If the United States' posture under Obama had been similar to that of the Bush administration, the forces of fear and ultranationalism might have swiftly quelled these indigenous forces for change. Still, Obama's reluctance to condemn the violence and human rights abuses more decisively—which would have been different from taking sides on the election dispute—eventually elicited both anger and disappointment from parts of the grassroots of the Green movement.[30]

But Obama's reluctance to raise the United States' profile any further was rooted in his investment in diplomacy. Earlier that spring, in complete secrecy, Obama had established a channel of communication with Iran's supreme leader. He had sent two letters to Khamenei via the Swiss embassy in Tehran—the caretakers of American interests in Iran in the absence of a U.S. embassy there. The first letter had spelled out U.S. interest in direct dialogue with Iran on a broad range of issues, with the aim of establishing a qualitatively different relationship between the two countries. Within two weeks, Khamenei had replied. According to several Obama administration officials, the response was mixed but sufficiently positive to warrant a second letter from Obama. But there would be no second reply from Khamenei, as the correspondence between the two was cut off by the election crisis. Still, the unprecedented exchanges raised the expectations in the White House that a substantive dialogue could begin after the election, addressing not only the nuclear issue, but also regional security, Iraq, and Afghanistan.[31]

By early June, the White House was ready to prepare for diplomacy with Iran—not deal with Iran's election fraud and human rights abuses. "They were caught flat-footed by the way [the Iranian] elections turned out. . . . They thought they had a game plan and suddenly they realized everything we prepared for is completely upended," a Senate ally of the White House commented. The Obama administration did not want to discount or betray the pro-democracy movement, but it grew increasingly doubtful of the Green movement's ability to topple the Ahmadinejad government. But the sympathy and momentum the

Obama administration's approach enjoyed on Capitol Hill, at least among Democratic lawmakers, quickly evaporated once the Iranian government began clamping down on the protests. By early July, the momentum was with the supporters of sanctions. Obama's honeymoon with Congress on Iran was over. From this point onward, holding back sanctions required significant effort from the administration. But for Obama, this was well worth the effort, as something unexpected had happened that showed him the real potential for a breakthrough with the Iranians. A week before the Iranian elections, Tehran had sent a letter to the International Atomic Energy Agency (IAEA) with a request that could create the best window of opportunity for diplomacy in more than a decade. Fraudulent elections or not, clearly Obama didn't want this unexpected opportunity to slip through his fingers.[32]

A Single Roll of the Dice

From the very first day Obama came into office, his administration sought ways to slow down Iran's nuclear program. The farther Iran was from having the know-how and the material to build a nuclear bomb, the more time there would be for diplomacy. Moreover, there would be less pressure from Israel, the Republicans, and the Saudis to take military action against Iran. Adding time to the clock was critical as Iran's nuclear advances were continuing, and in the absence of a game-changer, Washington would soon be faced with two bad options: to acquiesce to Iran's nuclear fait accompli or to take military action.

Time could be added to the clock in many different ways. The United Nations had already levied sanctions limiting Iran's ability to access nuclear hardware, and the United States was ensuring stringent enforcement of these restrictions. In addition, by the request of former president George W. Bush, Obama had continued and even expanded an unprecedented cyber warfare operation in conjunction with Israel. The program, called Olympic Games, planted computer viruses inside the Iranian nuclear program's Siemens operating computers, causing the centrifuges to self-destruct. But imploding centrifuges did little to undo the stockpile of enriched uranium the

Iranians had already amassed over the years. For that, diplomacy was needed.[1]

In 2005, Iran ended the voluntary suspension of its enrichment program. The termination of this measure came as a result of the European Union demanding that Iran abandon enrichment altogether—the zero-enrichment objective that was unacceptable to Iran. The Iranians felt duped. From their perspective, they had suspended enrichment in order to negotiate a final deal that limited but did not abolish enrichment on Iranian soil. Instead of acknowledging this in any significant way, the European Union tried to convert the suspension into a complete cessation. Once it broke the suspension, Tehran began amassing low-enriched uranium (LEU, at 3.5 percent). LEU can be converted into high-enriched uranium (HEU, at 85 percent or higher), which can be used to build a nuclear warhead. A simple nuclear warhead can be manufactured from approximately 25–50 kilograms of HEU, requiring the re-enrichment of approximately 1,300 kilograms of LEU. By summer 2009, Iran had amassed more than 1,500 kilograms of LEU.[2]

High-level officials in the State Department's Nonproliferation Bureau and their counterparts at the National Security Council began brainstorming ways to persuade the Iranians to ship their LEU out of the country. Demanding that Iran once again suspend its enrichment activities had proven to be a nonstarter, the only outcome having been that the Iranians had continued their nuclear activities and gotten closer to nuclear weapons capability. So instead, the focus turned to smaller, confidence-building measures that would be useful to the United States and acceptable to Iran. "We wanted to break the ice," a senior State Department official explained. "We had a whole variety of ideas, a dozen or so ways of breaking the ice, establishing some basis of trust and mutual confidence." Most of these ideas centered on the Iranian LEU stockpile.[3]

In the middle of developing some of these ideas, the United States was given what seemed like a gift from heaven. On June 2, 2009, the Iranian ambassador to the International Atomic Energy Agency (IAEA), Ali Asghar Soltanieh, sent a letter to the agency requesting to buy fuel pads for the Tehran Research Reactor (TRR), a medical research reactor.

The forty-year-old U.S.-supplied nuclear reactor produces medical iso-topes for an estimated 850,000 kidney, heart, and cancer patients. Fuel for the reactor was estimated to run out by the end of 2010. With a sig-nificant shortage of medical isotopes on the international market, the patients who relied on the TRR would face severe—even lethal—risks once domestic production dried up.[4]

The Obama administration immediately saw an opportunity. "All of a sudden the IAEA comes to us with this letter and said the Iranians need fuel for the Tehran Research Reactor. And we said, 'Hey, this is similar to an idea we've been working on,'" a senior State Department official explained. Iran was requesting fuel, which made it easier to pro-pose a swap: the supplier countries could use Iran's own LEU to pro-duce the fuel pads. The Obama administration devised a plan in which 1,200 kilograms of Iranian LEU would be shipped out to a supplier coun-try, where it would be reprocessed to 19.75 percent enriched uranium and subsequently turned into fuel pads. The swap would be advantageous for both the United States and Iran: Iran would get fuel for its research reactor before running out of medical isotopes, and the United States would get the LEU out of Iran, thereby reducing the pressure for mili-tary action and creating a window of opportunity for more serious ne-gotiations. "Getting 1,200 kilograms [of LEU] out would get you six months of time, and a lot of political space. We could tell the Israelis and [the] Congress to relax," a State Department nonproliferation offi-cial told me.[5]

There was also a clear and heavy cost to missing this opportunity. If no one in the international market sold Iran the fuel it was asking for, they could begin enriching the LEU to 19.75 percent themselves and, in doing so, creep closer to mastering the nuclear fuel cycle. "If we don't respond to this, somehow they're going to use this as a pretext to enrich to 20 percent. And that was a big issue," a European diplomat explained. (The Iranians argued that the request to purchase the fuel pads showed that Iran did not have the intention to enrich at 20 percent.) Critics maintained, however, that the swap provided de facto accep-tance of Iran's enrichment activities and thus sidestepped UN Security Council Resolution 1696, which demanded that Iran suspend its ura-nium enrichment program. Israel and other players feared that the proposal would eventually lead to an acceptance of Iranian enrichment. From the administration's perspective, however, making demands and issuing ultimatums had gotten the United States nowhere. To make a deal work, it had to work for both sides. "We tried very hard to think of a win-win," a senior Obama administration official said. "Not because we wanted to do Iran a favor, but because there was no other way to get a deal."[6]

By September, Washington had reached out to Russia to get its buy-in for the swap proposal. A month later, ElBaradei met privately with the head of the Iranian Atomic Energy Organization, Ali Akbar Salehi. ElBaradei gave the Iranians a one-page description of the U.S.-Russia visualization of the swap. Its key point was that Iran would receive the fuel pads it requested, if it gave up 1,200 kilograms of its LEU. The details of the deal would be worked out, Russia and the United States proposed, through direct negotiations. ElBaradei told the Iranians that they had until the end of the month to respond to the offer.[7]

The Obama administration had decided to proceed with their attempt at diplomacy despite the domestic turmoil in Iran, as U.S. intelligence assessments had concluded that the Iranian government was not likely to fall. And even if it did, an Iranian nuclear program and LEU stockpile would still exist and would still have to be addressed. But Iran's willingness to talk and its actual capability to do so were two wholly different matters. Even if the government was not about to fall, it was arguably still incapacitated by the intense infighting among political elites. But time was running out, political pressure against diplomacy was growing rapidly in the U.S. Congress, and some in the White House felt "it had a leg up" precisely because of the internal crisis in Iran.[8]

Iran and the United States Meet

On October 1, 2009, representatives of the American and Iranian governments finally met face to face. Officials from Iran and the P5 + 1, along with the high representative for the common foreign and security policy of the European Union, Javier Solana, held a daylong meeting in Geneva. William Burns, Bob Einhorn, and Puneet Talwar led the

American delegation. On the other side of the table sat Saeed Jalili and his deputy, Ali Bagheri. This meeting was significant not just because of the potential to solve the fuel swap, but because it was also the first opportunity for the Obama administration to directly test Iran's interest in the swap proposal and diplomacy.

The atmosphere of the Geneva talks was surprisingly positive. The morning session began with relatively short opening speeches—a good sign considering that Jalili was well known in diplomatic circles for his tendency to hold long monologues addressing the many injustices Iran had suffered at the hand of Western powers (a propensity that had earned him a reputation of being an "unbearable person"). As the parties broke for lunch, Burns approached Jalili and suggested that the U.S. and Iranian delegations engage in a private discussion. Jalili assented, and Burns, Talwar, Einhorn, Jalili, and Bagheri went aside for a bilateral session. It was the first direct and public encounter between U.S. and Iranian diplomats in three decades. Burns opened by presenting the Obama administration's novel approach and its genuine desire for a better relationship with Iran. Common interests existed between the two countries, Burns explained, and, while those should be explored, the nuclear issue was a major concern for the United States that needed to be addressed as well. The United States had ideas about a number of long-term solutions to the problem but believed that starting the process with the fuel swap would be an important confidence-building step.[9]

The U.S. delegation went over the swap concept with the Iranians: 1,200 kilograms of Iranian LEU would be shipped to Russia for reprocessing and then sent to a third country to be turned into fuel pads, after which the fuel would be sent to Iran for the Tehran Research Reactor. Jalili responded that, in principle, the Iranians agreed to the concept and were open to discussing it in greater detail. The United States then moved on to other issues, including the fate of three Americans who had been apprehended by the Iranian Revolutionary Guard Corps on the Iraq-Iran border. The meeting lasted less than an hour but was viewed as a success since an understanding had been reached on three critical points: that a second meeting would be held by the end of October to finalize the swap; that through the swap Iran would hand over 1,200 kilograms of its LEU; and that Iran would fully cooperate with the IAEA and grant access to the Fordo nuclear facility. Both sides were cordial and played it fair, according to a top Obama administration official.[10]

Diplomacy was off to a promising start. If the swap were accepted, it would be a major accomplishment that would set back Iran's breakout capability while creating more space for additional diplomacy. "At the end of the Geneva meeting, everybody thought that maybe we were at a turning point, maybe this was the beginning of a new process," an EU diplomat involved in the talks said. But the optimism lasted only a few days. By the start of the second round of negotiations, which were held under the auspices of the IAEA in Vienna on October 19, 2009, expectations had already been dampened. Technical meetings with the Iranians prior to the Vienna session exhibited several worrying signs, and the U.S. Congress kept pushing for new sanctions, a move that proponents of diplomacy feared could alienate Iran.[11]

ElBaradei led the second round of negotiations with focus and determination, knowing full well that this would be his last chance to find a solution to the Iranian nuclear challenge, as his final term as director general of the IAEA was to come to an end in November 2009. The meetings started with a more detailed presentation on the swap proposal. Though it differed from the U.S.-Russia proposal from September only in its level of detail, it had now been adopted by ElBaradei and was referred to as the "ElBaradei Proposal"—a development that did not please the Iranians. The additional details specified that 1,200 kilograms of Iranian LEU would be transferred to Russia in one shipment. The Russians would enrich the uranium to 19.75 percent, after which it would be sent to France for fuel production. After approximately nine to twelve months, the first batch of fuel pads would be delivered to Iran. The full amount of fuel would not be delivered until two years after Iran had handed its LEU over to Russia. Whether the LEU would be shipped in one or more batches had not been specified in Geneva, nor had the exact timeline for the delivery of fuel been set. According to the United States, however, Jalili had understood in Geneva that Washington was looking for the LEU to be shipped out of Iran in a single batch, even though this was not explicitly specified.[12]

In their opening remarks, the Iranians questioned the very principle of the swap proposal, casting it as unfair. Iran had purchased fuel for the reactor on the international market before, so there was no basis for forcing Iran to pay for the fuel with its own LEU, they argued. Tehran's core concern, however, was its need for a guarantee that if it handed over the LEU, Iran's counterparts would live up to their end of the bargain and deliver the fuel pads. Since Tehran would make the first move and give up its strategic asset—the LEU—it wanted guarantees that the Vienna group—the IAEA, the United States, France, and Russia—would reciprocate. "From the outset, Iran was ready to ship out the LEU, granted that a guarantee for delivery of the fuel pads was given," an Iranian negotiator said.[13]

The Iranians requested a mechanism for guaranteeing delivery and also offered several ideas of their own. The United States had suggested that the LEU could be held in the custody of the IAEA, which would guarantee that no country could confiscate it. The Iranians countered that if IAEA custody was acceptable to the West, then the LEU could be put under IAEA custody while remaining on Iranian soil. Moreover, instead of sending out the LEU in one shipment, the risk would be mitigated if it were divided into two or three shipments. For each shipment, Iran would simultaneously receive fuel pads. This way, neither side would find value in violating the agreement. But these proposals were not acceptable to the United States, Russia, and France. "The confidence-building value in our view was getting fuel out of Iran right away," one of the American negotiators explained. The political time and space the Obama administration sought from the deal could be achieved only if the Iranian LEU stockpile was drastically reduced in one fell swoop. And just as the Iranians did not trust that IAEA custody of the LEU would prevent the West from confiscating the material if it chose to do so, the United States had little faith that the Iranians would not take back the LEU from the IAEA if it remained on Iranian soil. "If Iran wants to take it, it takes it. It takes the wire cutters and cuts the seals and that's that," the American negotiator said. Similarly, the American offer to guarantee the delivery of fuel pads by signing a contract with Iran or by committing to the deal publicly did not impress the Iranians. The mistrust was just too deep.[14]

By the third day, there were clear signs that the talks were heading toward failure, though the atmosphere remained respectful and constructive. The Iranians did offer a key concession—they agreed to ship out the LEU instead of conducting the swap on Iranian soil—but they still insisted on guarantees for delivery. But at the end of the day, neither side had moved significantly from its original position. Two proposals remained on the table at the end of the talks: the Iranian one and the Russian-American one as presented by ElBaradei, and neither had gone through any major revisions. The Iranian proposal specified that Tehran was ready to buy and pay for the fuel pads. It would also accept shipping out the LEU, but only if Iran was simultaneously offered the fuel. The Russian-American proposal specified that the 1,200 kilograms of LEU would be transferred in one shipment, but the fuel would be delivered to Iran at a later date. No important revisions had been made to that plan either. Instead, the United States and its partners sought to pressure Iran to accept the proposal unamended. It was made abundantly clear to the Iranians that failure to accept this proposal would lead to a new round of UN Security Council sanctions. "At that point we were saying, 'Look, do you accept ElBaradei's proposal or not?'" a senior State Department official recalled.[15]

Both sides were deeply frustrated with each other, and both concluded that the other had come to the talks with instructions not to strike a deal based on a compromise. "Iran had compromised, but unfortunately they did not compromise," Soltanieh complained, referring to the Iranian agreement to ship out the fuel. The Americans, in turn, complained about what they perceived to be Soltanieh's instructions. "[Soltanieh] came there on the 19th of October, I think, instructed not to accept this," said one of the American negotiators. Neither side accepted the other's proposal, nor could they come to terms on a compromise. The message from Washington was clear: take it or leave it. "This is a pivotal moment for Iran. We urge Iran to accept the agreement as proposed and we will not alter it and we will not wait forever," Secretary of State Hillary Clinton told reporters in Washington. Obama's first attempt at diplomacy had failed; both sides engaged more in an exchange of ultimatums than true negotiations.[16]

The initial optimism from the first meeting in October had turned into deep disappointment by the first week of November. With the unofficial self-imposed deadline for diplomacy only two months away, time was running out for diplomacy, while pressure for sanctions and military action was growing. Disappointment among the permanent members of the UN Security Council plus Germany (P5 + 1) was widespread, and it was clear whom they saw as the party at fault. The frustration was particularly deep because in the years during which the Europeans conducted the negotiations without any U.S. presence at the talks, it had been widely believed that the absence of the United States explained the lack of progress. The Iranians were looking for a deal not with the European Union but with Washington, and as a result, it was believed, it would run against their interest to make any major concessions to the EU. Important compromises would be offered only in a deal with the United States. But now that the United States had been a full and active partner at the negotiating table for the first time and a diplomatic breakthrough had still not been achieved, this rationale seems to have been mistaken. The United States was at the table, and, in the words of ElBaradei, "Barack Obama is stretching backward, frankly, to engage Iran. And I have been saying to the Iranian leadership privately and publicly, 'Make use of that opportunity.' "[17]

Paralysis in Iran

But Tehran was paralyzed. Whatever objections Iran had to the U.S.-Russia proposal, the political chaos and infighting in the aftermath of the election dispute rendered these objections all the more insurmountable. Iran's decision-making process, which had already been taxing and slow, experienced unprecedented levels of deadlock. Even if Iranian officials wanted to engage, they were hamstrung because of the protests. "It is the internal crisis that really worries our leaders. They can't speak with one voice in the international community at this point," said reformist politician Mashallah Shamsolvaezin. Despite having first praised the swap concept, several high-profile political opponents of Ahmadinejad came out against the deal after the Vienna meeting. This created an awkward political situation for the Obama administration in which Ahmadinejad was more favorable toward the deal than his political opponents, with whom Washington preferred to deal.[18]

Almost all political factions within Iran criticized the deal and deliberately increased the political cost for Ahmadinejad to pursue it. The political nature of the criticism was often evident. Mousavi, for instance, cleverly positioned Ahmadinejad in a no-win situation by declaring, "If [the swap is] put in place, all the efforts of thousands of scientists will go to the wind. If [it is] not put in place, the foundations will be laid for wide-ranging sanctions against Iran, and this is the result of a confrontational stance in foreign policy and the neglect of national interests and principles." The combination of pressure from conservatives and reformists alike prompted Supreme Leader Khamenei to withdraw his initial support for the proposal, according to a former Iranian diplomat.[19]

The argument that Iran was unjustifiably putting its trust in the hands of the West was powerful; no Iranian politician wanted to come across as soft or naïve when dealing with the West. Accordingly, even the proponents of the deal refrained from defending it in public. But while Ahmadinejad's opponents blasted the deal on its merits, it is not clear whether their intent was to scuttle it or simply to make its acceptance as costly as possible for Ahmadinejad. "No one wanted Ahmadinejad to get credit, particularly if this was a good deal for Iran," a senior State Department official said. Emotions were running high. After all, Iran's political elite was literally at war with itself. "They were so angry. They were so mad," one of Mousavi's advisors said of Ahmadinejad's rivals. "I mean, their kids were in jail, their brothers were in jail."[20]

Under other circumstances, Iran might have accepted the fuel swap proposal. This point was not lost on the White House, which recognized that Tehran "was not in a position to accept" the deal since it had become "a victim of internal politics." According to David Miliband, then foreign secretary of the United Kingdom, "The bilateral outreach the Americans made fell victim to internal Iranian politics." This was a wake-up call for the White House. While it was aware of the complicating role Iran's domestic politics could play, it had not fully appreciated the extent to which domestic politics could impact prospective diplomacy. "It became clear to us then," Einhorn told me, "the domestic political problems that any Iranian regime would face in negotiating with us." The entire episode left all involved parties with a bitter taste. And

because of the actions—or inactions—of both sides, a deal that was supposed to build confidence between Iran and the international community ended up doing the opposite. "I think it turned out to be a
confidence-eroding measure," one of the key architects of the swap at the
State Department complained.[21]

The Second Track

Obama's first attempt at diplomacy lasted only a few weeks and amounted
to no more than two disappointing face-to-face meetings with the Iranians. After this initial failure, Obama activated the pressure track—
that is, he shifted focus from diplomacy to sanctions. Already on
October 7, 2009, before the Vienna meeting, Obama had gathered like-
minded states for a meeting in Washington to prepare the ground
for sanctions. Some senior officials at the State Department and the
White House had spent most of 2009 developing various sanctions
strategies in anticipation of the collapse of diplomacy. By late November 2009, weeks before his official deadline for progress on diplomacy,
President Obama gave a green light to the sanctions track. It was not
a sudden shift, but rather a gradual realization that the initial attempt
at dialogue had not yielded results. Diplomacy was not dead; it was
abandoned.[22]

Some suspected that the diplomatic gambit was actually intended
to pave the way for sanctions. The Bush administration had so hurt the
United States' credibility that the ability to assemble a coalition of states
to sanction Iran was wanting. Only by trying diplomacy could the
United States shift the blame for the stand-off to Iran, a prerequisite for
getting international buy-in for an effective sanctions regime. The administration itself was hesitant to defend its diplomacy, arguing instead
that its diplomatic efforts had helped win support for sanctions. Ultimately, this was a defensive posture that signaled vulnerability by emphasizing the unintended side effect of the policy. While technically
correct, the argument was the equivalent of defending one's love for
drinking wine, not because of its taste, but because of the pleasure of
the hangover. Even politically, the administration was abandoning
rather than standing by its diplomacy.[23]

But White House insiders argue that the president's aim with diplomacy was genuinely to reach a deal rather than pave the way for sanctions. The administration stumbled into the sanctions strategy, they argue. "The president thought an initiative to talk about the bomb with Iran would work, and then he found it would not. And the U.S. had no Plan B," a British diplomat told Seymour Hersh of the *New Yorker*. Obama was coerced into sanctions by Congress, by Israel, and by a lack of alternatives. The Obama team took office confident that because it was not the Bush administration, and because it was willing to directly engage with the Iranians, it could reach an interim agreement fairly quickly. When that didn't happen, Obama was stuck—and sanctions were the default option. Later, however, he found himself trapped in the sanctions policy.[24]

Yet others argue that there is less than meets the eye here: Obama was genuine about diplomacy, but he also calculated that if diplomacy failed, it would be easier to convince the international community to impose new sanctions precisely because Washington could argue that diplomacy had failed. "In the president's mind I think there was a clear strategy of testing Iran's intentions as well as capacity to engage in a serious negotiation," former deputy secretary of state Bill Burns explained. "That was what was behind the TRR initiative in the fall of '09. But that was also an investment in building a broader coalition, and wider leverage, and greater sanctions pressure, if the Iranians, at least in that first test, proved either unwilling or unable to engage." Ultimately, from Obama's perspective, the offer of diplomacy and its subsequent failure reversed a dynamic in which Iran was in the right, and the Bush administration and the United States were in the wrong.[25]

The administration did not pursue this policy with much confidence. Senior officials ranging from CIA Director Leon E. Panetta to Chairman of the Joint Chiefs of Staff Admiral Mike Mullen had publicly stated their skepticism about the ability of sanctions to force Iran to give up the major elements of its nuclear program. When Panetta asked himself aloud in a television interview whether the sanctions would deter Iran's "ambitions with regard to nuclear capacity," his answer came back with full clarity: "Probably not." The British government was so pessimistic about the likelihood of sanctions succeeding that "everything in London is now about containment and the notion that if the Iranians get a bomb, we'll have to live with it," according to a British diplomat.[26]

Still, the administration strongly believed that it was a proposition worth exploring, because all other options suffered from even greater uncertainty, particularly compared to the military option. Neither the political leadership in the Obama administration nor the military leadership felt that military action could provide a durable solution to the nuclear stand-off. While the United States had the military capacity to push back Iran's nuclear program perhaps by as many as four years, there was little doubt that Iran's determination to obtain a nuclear deterrence would grow in the aftermath of such an attack. In fact, the intelligence services of the United States, Europe, and Israel all agreed that Iran had not yet made the political decision to build a nuclear weapon. That assessment was shared by the IAEA, whose head, ElBaradei, often pointed out that while Tehran's lack of transparency justified caution and suspicion, evidence of an ongoing weapons program was lacking. "During my time at the agency," ElBaradei said, "we haven't seen a shred of evidence that Iran has been weaponizing, in terms of building nuclear-weapons facilities and using enriched materials."[27]

A military attack against its facilities, however, could push Tehran to make a decision that it had otherwise avoided. As such, a military strike had a greater likelihood of ensuring an Iranian nuclear weapon than preventing it.[28] Even the G. W. Bush administration had reached that conclusion. "When we talked about this in the government, the consensus was that [attacking Iran] would guarantee that which we are trying to prevent—an Iran that will spare nothing to build a nuclear weapon and that would build it in secret," former CIA and National Security Agency (NSA) chief, General Michael Hayden, said at an event hosted by the Center for the National Interest. Convinced that military action was likely counterproductive and that the absence of more pressure would render diplomacy futile, the Obama administration concluded that it had no other option than to pivot to sanctions despite its uncertainties. "It was an untested strategy in the sense that there weren't a lot of other examples where sanctions in and of themselves were able to resolve such a big problem," a member of the U.S. negotiation team told me.[29]

Once the sanctions track was activated, it became the only track, despite the Obama White House's argument that sanctions could work only when combined with diplomacy. According to a European diplomat, more than 90 percent of the West's focus was on marshaling sanctions once the Obama administration moved to the pressure track. "Basically the sanctions sucked all the air out of the room," a senior State Department official said. The Israelis, who had told the Obama administration that they could accept diplomacy as long as Washington expected it would fail, pushed the United States to quickly impose "crippling sanctions" of its own, rather than impose UN Security Council sanctions first. If the world "is serious about stopping Iran, then what it needs to do is not watered-down sanctions, moderate sanctions . . . but effective, biting sanctions that curtail the import and export of oil into Iran," Israeli Prime Minister Benjamin Netanyahu argued. "And if this cannot pass in the Security Council, then it should be done outside the Security Council, but immediately."[30]

This quickly became the new battle line: the White House's effort to secure UN Security Council sanctions first in order to build strong international consensus for the sanctions regime versus Congress and Israel's initiative to quickly hit the Iranian energy sector with escalating unilateral measures. From Congress's perspective, their push for unilateral sanctions was also, if not mainly, aimed at putting fire under the feet of the Obama White House on the sanctions front. "The whole pressure track and the whole sanctions effort at the UN was driven in large part by Congress," a senior Senate staffer told me. "If you had taken that away, I'm not sure that we would have gone down this track at all." On December 15, 2009, the House of Representatives passed legislation sanctioning Iran's gasoline imports. Unlike the Chinese, who viewed sanctions as a pathway to war, the sponsor of the sanctions bill, House Foreign Affairs Committee Chairman Howard Berman (D-CA), presented sanctions as the only way to prevent war.[31]

While the White House worried about Congress coming out ahead of it and thus undermining the opportunity to impose UN Security Council sanctions, it did not want a public fight with Congress about Iran sanctions. The health care reform bill topped the president's legislative agenda, and his legislative bandwidth was limited, to say the least. The choice between health care and sanctions on Iran was easy from a political standpoint, because health care "was potentially an existential issue for the White House," a senior Senate staffer explained. So Obama's pushback was limited and focused more on the timing of sanctions rather than on their substance. And though there were a handful of lawmakers who opposed sanctions based on the experiences of Cuba and Iraq, for instance, or who worried that such punitive measures would render negotiations down the road all the more unlikely, the political upside of opposing sanctions on Iran was simply nonexistent. There was no political cost for lawmakers to vote in favor of Iran sanctions, regardless of their impact or lack thereof. On January 29, 2010, the Senate passed gasoline sanctions on Iran after seven senators had written to Obama saying that they had had enough of waiting for the pressure-track activities to begin and arguing that because Obama's December deadline for diplomacy had long passed, sanctions were now the option that should be pursued. "Now that this deadline has passed, we believe that it is imperative to put into action your pledge of increased, meaningful pressure against the Iranian regime—what Clinton called 'crippling sanctions,'" the letter said. Now, it was only a matter of time before the sanctions bill reached the president's desk. If it did so before the administration could manage to secure a Security Council resolution, it could unravel the White House's diplomatic efforts at the UN. At the same time, however, the existence of a ready piece of legislation awaiting the president's signature served to pressure the Security Council to move sooner rather than later.[32]

China Resists

If Congress and Israel were the main forces behind the push for sanctions, China was the main obstacle. Because China holds a veto in the UN Security Council, no agreement could go into effect if the Chinese were not onboard. Even the Russians, who traditionally were skeptical of sanctions, did not take as hard of a stance as the Chinese did.[33]

But once again, the Iranians themselves helped unite the great powers against them. On February 7, the Iranian government informed the IAEA that because of the failure of the Vienna group to respond positively to Iran's proposal for a fuel swap, Iran had no choice but to begin indigenously enriching uranium at the 19.75 percent level, in order to produce the fuel pads for its research reactor. "Until now, we have not received any response to our positive logical and technical proposal," Ambassador Ali Asghar Soltanieh told the Associated Press. "We cannot leave hospitals and patients desperately waiting for radioisotopes" to be produced at the Tehran reactor for use in cancer treatment, he added. To the United States and its EU allies, the Iranian move was a provocation and escalation. The United States had sought to reduce the Iranian LEU stockpile and prevent Iran from increasing its enrichment levels. Now, instead, the LEU stockpile continued to grow, and the Iranians also expanded their level of enrichment activities.[34]

Though Iran was unable to produce the needed nuclear fuel in time to ensure the uninterrupted production of medical isotopes by its research reactor, its refusal to purchase the radioisotopes from the international market fueled suspicions that Tehran indeed sought to build nuclear weapons. "The Iranians did us a great favor," explained Obama's nonproliferation tsar, Gary Samore. "They behaved so obnoxiously, and so intransigently, and so blatantly [that] it was much easier to convince the Europeans, and even the Russians and the Chinese that we had no alternative but to go back to pressure both to make the diplomacy effective and to avoid war. In a letter to the IAEA dated February 12, France, Russia, and the United States argued that the Iranian move was "wholly unjustified, contrary to the UN Security Council resolutions, and represents a further step toward a capability to produce highly enriched uranium." In a moment of frustration, two days after the Iranian announcement, Obama told reporters that he had "bent over backwards to say to the Islamic Republic of Iran that we are willing to have a constructive conversation" about issues between the two countries. "They have made their choice so far."[35]

Iran had many enemies, and some of them helped convince the Chinese. The Saudis had historically competed with Iran for regional power and feared that Obama's diplomacy would eventually enable Iran to find an escape from its international isolation. For that very reason, Obama turned to the Saudis to get the Chinese to come around on sanctions. The Saudis offered to alleviate Beijing's primary concern—that sanctions would impede China's access to oil—by offering to guarantee Beijing's demand for energy on the condition that China would support sanctions. The Saudis justified the sanctions move by arguing that it offered an alternative to military action. By March, both Saudi Arabia and the United Arab Emirates had boosted their exports to China as part of this pressure campaign. Shipments increased from about 50,000 barrels per day in 2009 to 120,000, with a goal of up to 200,000 barrels per day by the end of 2010.[36]

The Israeli Wild Card

Congress's preempting the UN Security Council was not the only pressure Obama had to fend off. More than anything, the wild card was Israel and whether it would take unilateral military action against Iran—especially as it became clear that the sanctions process would not be expeditious—and set off a regional war. Originally, the Obama administration had promised to secure a resolution by the end of February, when the French held the rotating presidency at the UN. That was later changed to March, and then it was postponed to April. The sanctions process moved forward much more slowly than the United States had anticipated—much to Israel's discomfort. And as Israel became more and more uncomfortable, the White House became more and more nervous, knowing it could not afford any Israeli adventurism with Iran.

By April, questions began to arise over whether the sanctions could be passed at all; the Russian and Chinese resistance was surprisingly firm. Rather than wait for the sanctions process to result in failure, the United States should circumvent the United Nations and impose "crippling sanctions" right away, Netanyahu demanded publicly and with increased frequency. Meanwhile, Russia and China were doing their own shuttle diplomacy with Tehran, seeking to elicit any flexibility in Iran's position in order to fend off the UN sanctions. But after a few meetings, including a trip by Iran's lead nuclear negotiator, Saeed

Jalili, to Beijing, Russia and China both began to acknowledge the futility of their efforts. Russia's UN ambassador, Vitaly Churkin, voiced his country's frustration with Iran. "I don't think any of us wants to impose sanctions; what we want is to have a diplomatic solution," he said. But "if Iran wants to negotiate, it should start negotiating." Shortly thereafter, on March 30, the Chinese finally agreed to engage substantively in sanctions negotiations. But while Washington was focused on Moscow and Beijing, two American allies in the Security Council—Turkey and Brazil—turned victory bitter.[37]

The Tehran Declaration

After months of diplomatic wrangling with hostile and friendly actors and states alike, the Obama administration was finally on the verge of passing a UN Security Council resolution sanctioning Iran. Concessions had been given to the Russians and Chinese; pressure from Israel, Saudi Arabia, and Congress had been heeded; Iranian maneuvers to influence the vote had been countered; and a plan of action with the European Union had been agreed upon. All that remained were the formalities.

But in that last moment, Washington miscalculated the diplomatic skills of two rising states—Brazil and Turkey—and their desire to demonstrate their ability to take on diplomatic challenges usually reserved for the great powers. Both had played a peripheral role in the diplomatic efforts in the fall of 2009. At first, they had been encouraged to help. But by the time Washington's focus shifted to the sanctions track, their involvement became a nuisance for the Obama administration, which feared that the Iranians would use Brazil and Turkey to split the Security Council. On May 15, 2010, Brazilian president Luiz Inácio Lula da Silva traveled to Iran with an entourage of some three hundred Brazilian businessmen. It was his first visit there, and he sought Iran's agreement over the nuclear fuel swap in what the Obama administration and French president Nicolas Sarkozy described as the "last big shot at engagement." Soon thereafter, Turkish Prime Minister Recep Tayyip Erdogan and his foreign minister, Ahmet Davutoglu, joined Lula in an effort to convince Iran to ship out its low-enriched uranium (LEU). Two days later, Lula and Erdogan stunned the United States and the world: they had a deal.[38]

Contrary to expectations, and arguably to the hopes of some, they had succeeded in convincing the Iranian government to agree to a deal based on the American benchmarks—that 1,200 kilograms of Iranian LEU would be sent out in one shipment, and Iran would receive fuel pads for the Tehran Research Reactor roughly twelve months later. For a moment, it looked as if diplomacy had succeeded after all. But what could have been viewed as a diplomatic breakthrough—with Iran blinking first and then succumbing to American demands—was instead treated as an effort to sabotage the new and higher objective of imposing sanctions. The twisted dance of hostility and missed opportunities between the United States and Iran that Obama hoped to end had just come full circle—and all within the first sixteen months of his presidency.

Brazil and Turkey had their own separate motivations for pushing for diplomacy, but both also strongly feared that sanctions were a stepping stone toward a military conflict. Their apprehensions about what sanctions could lead to were not entirely unfounded. According to a State Department official who led the efforts to secure UN Security Council sanctions during the Bush administration, the effort was intended "to get us either aggressive autonomous sanctions or get us military action."[39]

Moreover, Brazil had its own nuclear program, and it feared that UN action on the Iranian nuclear file would set a precedent that defined enrichment of uranium as a military activity. The Brazilians also worried that sanctions would cause a repeat of the Iraq disaster, in which UN sanctions contributed to the death of 500,000 Iraqi children in 1990–2000 (by causing both food and medicine shortages) and were followed by an American invasion of that country. Turkey had a more complicated history with Iran but shared Brazil's perspective on how to deal with its neighbor to the east. Turkish Prime Minister Erdogan offered to mediate between the United States and Iran immediately after Obama's presidential win in 2008. Whether from sanctions, war, or both, Turkey had already suffered extensively from U.S. policies in the region. The UN sanctions on Iraq in the 1990s had cut Turkey off from one of its key trading partners and laid the groundwork for the establishment of an autonomous Kurdish state adjacent to Turkey's border. The U.S. invasion of Iraq in 2003 had spread instability and fanaticism in the region while strengthening both the Kurds and Turkey's historical rival, Iran. Another war in the region or a continuation of policies centered on isolating Iran could derail the projected growth of Turkey's economy (which aimed to become one of the ten largest economies in the world by 2023) while further destabilizing the region.[40]

In January 2010, Turkey and Brazil joined the UN Security Council as nonpermanent members, enabling them to coordinate their efforts to give new life to diplomacy. For them, the fight for diplomacy was a race against sanctions. The United States gave Turkey and Brazil a double message: efforts to convince Tehran to agree to the fuel swap were encouraged, but it was also important to impose new sanctions on Iran. And, according to the Obama administration, sanctions would actually help get the Iranians to agree to the fuel swap.[41]

On April 12 and 13, world leaders gathered in Washington for a nuclear summit led by Obama. During the gathering, a three-way meeting was held between Lula, Erdogan, and Obama. Clinton, Amorim, Davutoglu, and a few advisors also joined the conversation. The meeting, which lasted no more than fifteen minutes, was tense and testy. Echoing the words his own political opponents had spoken when he championed diplomacy a year earlier, Obama dismissed the prospects of diplomacy and signaled that Iran no longer preoccupied much of his time. There was nothing wrong with diplomacy, but the Iranians simply could not be relied upon, Obama argued. But Erdogan and Lula insisted that they could convince Tehran to agree to the fuel swap. At the end of the meeting, neither side was satisfied. And the mixed messages from Washington continued; Obama was skeptical of diplomacy, yet softly encouraged Turkey and Brazil's efforts. After the summit, both the French and the Americans framed Lula's upcoming state visit to Iran as the last chance for diplomacy. "I'm not criticizing President Lula, but we've agreed with President Lula that this is the last chance, last-resort and last-chance initiative, and it has to happen very swiftly," Sarkozy told reporters.[42]

Gary Samore, special assistant to the president on nonproliferation, expressed confidence that sanctions would be imposed "unless

Iran does something significant," which he found unlikely because Iran, in his view, had no serious interest in a nuclear deal. Consequently, Brazilian and Turkish mediation was bound to fail, he maintained. Samore did, however, make clear that the 2009 swap offer was still on the table if the Iranians were willing to accept it. "The Iranians have frankly not been prepared to accept that offer, it's pretty clear to anybody," Samore said. "And Turkey will soon satisfy themselves of that."[43]

Lula and the Brazilians arrived in Tehran on May 15. The visit had been preceded by a frenzy of diplomatic activities, with Turkish and Brazilian diplomats shuttling in and out of Iran. Davutoglu joined them shortly thereafter. Foreign Minister Manuchehr Mottaki and the head of the Iranian Atomic Energy Organization, Ali Akbar Salehi, led Iran's negotiating team, with the head of the National Security Council, Saeed Jalili, as the principal. Davutoglu headed the Turkish delegation and had with him five aides. On the Brazilian side was Amorim and his two advisors.[44]

The discussions were difficult, and privately neither the Turks nor the Brazilians had high hopes for a breakthrough. But by the end of the second day of talks, an agreement was within reach. The Turks and Brazilians had succeeded in convincing Iran to hand over 1,200 kilograms of LEU in one shipment in order to receive fuel pads for its research reactor within the next twelve months—the same parameters Tehran had rejected eight months earlier in Vienna. The LEU, however, would not go to Russia or France. Instead, it would be put in Turkey under IAEA seal, and, if the West violated the terms of the agreement, Iran could take its LEU back. This arrangement, Turkey and Brazil reasoned, would alleviate Iran's fear of undue exposure while putting the bulk of its trust in its neighbor, Turkey, rather than its adversary, Washington. The trilateral agreement between Brazil, Turkey, and Iran—only two pages long— became known as the "Tehran Declaration." Against all odds, Turkey and Brazil had achieved in a few months, through intensive diplomacy, what the Western powers had failed to do in several years.[45]

Shortly after the agreement was struck, the three states held a press conference in Tehran announcing the breakthrough. The mood was jubilant, and a picture of Lula, Erdogan, and Ahmadinejad jointly raising their hands in a victorious gesture immediately went viral. Davutoglu

called the fuel swap deal a "historic turning point," and Erdogan and
Lula both declared that the world no longer needed to consider further
sanctions against Iran. Once the agreement was announced, Mohammad ElBaradei, now the former director general of the IAEA, immediately gave it his blessing, calling the deal a "good agreement" that
indicated that Iran is "changing its hand." UN Secretary-General Ban
Ki-moon said the agreement was "an important initiative in resolving
international tensions over Iran's nuclear program by peaceful means."
Perhaps more important was that the Iranian political elite came out in
support of the deal, as they had not in the Vienna negotiations in the
fall. Two days after the agreement was struck, 234 out of the Iranian
parliament's 290 members, including the speaker of the parliament—
and Ahmadinejad's bitter enemy—Larijani, issued a public statement
supporting the fuel swap. In addition, key Green movement figures such
as Ataollah Mohajerani also extended their blessing to the deal. Considering the divisions within Iran's political elite, which by no means
had been resolved, the widespread support for the deal in Iran was noteworthy.[46]

Obama Doesn't Take Yes for an Answer

Enthusiasm for the Tehran Declaration did not extend to Washington.
Unbeknownst to Turkey and Brazil, the Obama administration had secured final approval for the sanctions resolution from Russia and China
only a day before Lula arrived in Tehran. A series of concessions had been
made to Russia and China since early April to secure their Security Council votes for the sanctions, starting with the signing of a new nuclear disarmament treaty (START) on April 8. Immediately thereafter, Moscow
signaled its support for sanctions in principle. As the deliberations at the
United Nations continued, additional concessions were made, including
the lifting of American sanctions against the Russian military complex;
an end to NATO expansion; and the scrapping of the proposed missile
defense shield in Europe; on their side, the Russians conceded to the demand that they cancel the sale of the S-300 anti-aircraft missiles to Iran.[47]

While the Turks and Brazilians characterized the Tehran Declaration as a breakthrough, the U.S. Department of State was "skeptical"

and did not believe it represented "anything fundamentally new." State Department spokesperson P. J. Crowley derided the deal for having failed to address suspension of Iran's enrichment activities—something the swap agreement from the fall meetings had not intended to do either. A day later, Clinton herself sounded the death knell for the deal in prepared remarks to the Senate while declaring that an agreement on a sanctions resolution at the United Nations had been reached. The choice of venue was not a coincidence. Between instituting sanctions and getting one bomb's worth of LEU out of Iran, Washington had chosen the former, and Congress had made that choice a reality. "We have reached agreement on a strong draft with the cooperation of both Russia and China," Clinton told a Senate committee. "We plan to circulate that draft resolution to the entire Security Council today. And let me say, Mr. Chairman, I think this announcement is as convincing an answer to the efforts undertaken in Tehran over the last few days as any we could provide." That same day, Obama met with a group of thirty-seven Jewish Democratic members of Congress for an hour and a half to assure them of his commitment to sanctions. A week later, Clinton raised the rhetorical volume even further, claiming that Turkey and Brazil's efforts had made "the world more dangerous."[48]

Washington was surprised by Turkey and Brazil's success. They were expected to fail and, in doing so, be forced to join the P5+1 in pushing for sanctions. At a White House meeting a week before Lula's trip to Tehran, an Obama administration official had raised the question of "What if Iran agrees?" But the likelihood was deemed so low that the issue was dismissed, and no further discussions preparing the United States for that scenario were held.[49]

The other P5+1 states were also dismissive of the Tehran Declaration, stating clearly that the agreement would not affect the march toward sanctions. The British viewed it as a "distraction." The French, who at best had been lukewarm about the fuel swap idea, took the opportunity to shoot down the entire concept. "Let us not deceive ourselves, a solution to the [fuel] question, if it happens, would do nothing to settle the problem posed by the Iranian nuclear program," spokesperson Bernard Valero said in a statement. Both EU and Israeli officials believed Turkey and Brazil had been taken for a ride, and that the Iranians were engaging with them only in order to split the Security Council on the issue of sanctions. "It was a blatant ploy by the Iranians," Israel's deputy foreign minister told me. "Unfortunately there were some in the international community that fell into the trap, namely here Brazil and Turkey. . . . It was just a measure of deceit and procrastination by Iran." Even the Russians and the Chinese rejected it, mainly because the Tehran Declaration would jeopardize all the concessions they had been offered by Washington in return for an approval of sanctions.[50]

Washington publicly presented a mixture of arguments against the deal, ranging from distrust of Iran and deficiencies in the deal to the introduction of completely new demands, such as requiring that Iran suspend all enrichment. On the technical side, the Obama administration pointed out that 1,200 kilograms of LEU constituted roughly 75 percent of Iran's total stockpile in October 2009. If the swap had taken place at that time, Iran's stockpile would have been less than the amount needed for a single bomb, which would have granted the White House valuable time and political space. By May 2010, however, 1,200 kilograms of LEU constituted only about 50 percent of Iran's LEU, and even with the fuel swap, Iran would maintain enough uranium for one bomb. As a result of this stockpiling, the benefits of the swap had been significantly reduced. In the words of one Obama administration official, Turkey and Brazil had "missed the sell-by date" for the deal, since the relative value in terms of nonproliferation and confidence-building had declined. Moreover, the Iranians had begun enriching to 19.75 percent in February 2010. An implicit component of the original 2009 swap deal was that Iranian enrichment would be recognized or accepted in return for limiting it to below 5 percent, meaning Iran would not engage in any higher enrichment (in other words, 19.75 percent) but the Tehran Declaration did not address this issue.[51]

Brazil and Turkey were stunned by Washington's fierce rejection of the deal. Lula had called Sarkozy from Tehran immediately after the agreement had been reached. The second person the Brazilians spoke to was Clinton: Amorim called her during a stopover while flying back to Brasilia immediately following the press conference in Tehran. Only five hours had passed since the declaration had been announced, but the secretary of state made it absolutely clear to Amorim that the United

States would continue pursuing sanctions. "So we were really taken aback not by the fact that they were negotiating sanctions, but that they wanted to make so clear the point that there was no room for negotiation," one of Lula's senior advisors told me. Brazil and Turkey fiercely defended their deal and attacked Obama for paying lip service to diplomacy. "What is the true meaning of engagement with Iran? Where is the engagement? There is no engagement. U.S. should do and deliver on what they say. . . . Obama has only changed America's conduct in words," a senior Turkish diplomat told me.[52]

Washington's public posture gave the impression that Turkey and Brazil had pursued their diplomatic intervention with Iran without consultations with the United States and without being diligent in assuring that the negotiated outcome would meet Washington's minimum requirements. What the public was not aware of was that on April 20—a week after their tense meeting with Obama in DC—the U.S. president had sent both Lula and Erdogan a letter, meant to remain private, spelling out the benchmarks of a deal that the United States believed would be feasible. The contents of the letter were stunning, given the Obama administration's basis for rejecting the Tehran Declaration—that taking 1,200 kilograms of LEU was not enough, and that the deal did not address Iran's enrichment at the 19.75 percent levels.

Obama's letter clarified that the purpose of the swap was "for both sides to gain trust and confidence." He spelled out the important markers that any agreement would have to meet to be acceptable to the United States. "For us, Iran's agreement to transfer 1,200kg of Iran's low enriched uranium (LEU) out of the country would build confidence and reduce regional tensions by substantially reducing Iran's LEU stockpile. I want to underscore that this element is of fundamental importance for the United States," the letter said. Obama also presented a compromise mechanism that the United States had floated back in November 2009—the idea that the Iranian LEU could be held in Turkey in "escrow" until the fuel was delivered to Iran: "I would urge Brazil to impress upon Iran the opportunity presented by this offer to 'escrow' its uranium in Turkey while the nuclear fuel is being produced."[53]

The letter spelled out three substantive points related to the questions of quantity (1,200 kilograms), timing (shipped out immediately, with the fuel rods delivered a year later), and place (an escrow in Turkey). On every point, Turkey and Brazil had delivered on Obama's requirements "sentence by sentence." At one crucial point in the negotiations, the Turks even pulled out the letter and showed it to the Iranians to assure them that they had Washington's commitment to the deal in writing. This proved decisive in convincing Tehran to agree to the American parameters of the swap deal.[54]

Moreover, the letter was silent on the issue of 19.75 percent enrichment—it made no mention of it at all. When Clinton objected to the deal by citing Iran's move to enrich at the 19.75 percent level in her conversation with Amorim immediately after the Tehran Declaration was announced, Amorim replied by saying that "these points are not part of President Obama's letter." A long silence followed, as Clinton had no response. All of the Obama administration's public objections to the Tehran Declaration were contradicted by Obama's own letter to Lula and Erdogan.[55]

The letter, however, was not public. Visibly angered by the Obama administration's treatment, the Brazilians leaked the letter to a local newspaper. Within hours, the U.S. media picked it up. The administration immediately shot back at Brazil and Turkey, saying that the letter only summarized Washington's position on the fall 2009 episode and was not a conclusive description of the Obama administration's position, nor was it a guideline or a set of instructions for talks with Iran. But the embarrassment was unmistakable—guidelines or not, it was difficult to interpret Obama's letter as anything but an encouragement for Brazil and Turkey to secure a yes from Iran. In reality, Washington was not interested in Iran's acceptance of the swap deal. Internally, the Obama administration concluded that the swap deal had expired already in January 2010, but it was kept on the table because there was a fear that if it was withdrawn, Washington would come across as the intransigent party that was unwilling to negotiate. The very concept of a dual-track approach would have been defeated if Washington admitted that diplomacy had been deactivated. "We wanted to sound reasonable to the Turks and Brazilians, but we never thought Iran would agree," a former State Department official told me years later. "We were not interested in a yes by that time."[56]

Obama Gets His Sanctions

Three weeks later, on June 9, 2010, the Obama administration finally got its sanctions on Iran accepted at the UN Security Council. But the victory was bittersweet. The debacle around the Tehran Declaration cost Obama a united council: Brazil and Turkey—two staunch U.S. allies—voted against resolution 1929, and Lebanon abstained. Of all the sanctions passed against Iran at the UN, this resolution had the weakest support. Obama's predecessor had, with no effort to engage the Iranians diplomatically, imposed three sets of UN sanctions on Iran; two were unanimously adopted, and one suffered an abstention. Now, for the first time, negative votes had been cast against a sanctions resolution on Iran. However, this did not deter Congress from passing gasoline sanctions on Iran with an overwhelming majority—408–8 in the House and 99–0 in the Senate—two weeks later. Obama signed the bill into law at a ceremony in the White House on July 1.

A year and a half into his presidency, Obama was celebrating not the diplomatic victory he had been seeking, but rather the imposition of sanctions he had hoped to avoid. The reality was that the Obama administration was not going to abandon the sanctions push for a nuclear deal at that point, primarily for reasons that had little to do with either the technical details of the Tehran Declaration or the substance of the Iranian nuclear file per se. "There was nothing that the Iranians could do to stop the sanctions push," a former State Department official said.[57]

A mixture of political factors, management of relations with other permanent members of the council, and a desire to maintain prestige made serious diplomacy a non-option by the time Washington had committed itself to the sanctions track. Forsaking sanctions—even for a diplomatic opening—would be seen as defeat for Obama and victory for Iran. Moreover, the political investment in the sanctions track was immense, including acts such as personal calls from Obama to other world leaders and high-level visits. Many agreements and trade-offs secured through that outreach, primarily between the United States, Russia, and China, all depended on the sanctions resolution passing. The imposition of sanctions on Iran had essentially become the organizing principle for alliance management within the P5 + 1, as well as with U.S.

allies in the region, such as Israel and some of the Sunni monarchies. A diplomatic breakthrough with Iran was simply a threat to the higher priority of passing sanctions.[58]

Most importantly, the Obama administration had run out of political space domestically to accept the Tehran Declaration. Congress was coming at the Obama administration like a steamroller, and the White House did not believe that investing capital in expanding the political space for the deal would be a politically wise move. The political maneuverability Obama enjoyed on Iran when he first took office had been completely eaten away by pressure from Israel and Congress, the fallout from the June 2009 Iranian presidential election, and Iran's refusal to accept the Russian-American swap proposal in October 2009. U.S. diplomats had even raised this as an argument for sanctions in the Security Council, making the case that sanctions were needed in order for the United States to be able to gain space for diplomacy down the road. "The impression, right or wrong, that was created was that we could not take yes for an answer," a former senior Obama administration official told me. "That was not what I would call a triumph of public diplomacy."[59]

Obama had entered the White House without any baggage on Iran. Because of his very persona—as America's first African American president, the son of a Muslim, and someone who was elected on a platform of ending the United States' wars in the Middle East—he had a unique opportunity to renew diplomacy and take a decisive step toward not only resolving the nuclear issue, but also ending the enmity between the United States and Iran. Yet, Obama found himself stuck in the same confrontational relationship with Iran as other American presidents had before him. In the end, he invested far more resources and time in diplomacy with the United States' allies to secure their support for sanctions than in diplomacy with Iran. But having embarked on a sanctions path that ultimately could lead to confrontation, Obama now faced the same challenges as previous administrations had: once on the path of pressure and confrontation, how could the United States find its way back to the negotiation table, reinvigorate diplomacy, and ensure that the escalation didn't lead to war?

All-Out Escalation

A lthough securing UN Security Council sanctions on Iran was a major triumph for the Obama administration, the United States still had no clear path to victory. Increasing the pressure was the easy part. Translating it into a change in Iran's calculations and policy was a far more complex process—and one that the United States had neither much insight into nor control over. Moreover, while the United States sought to force Iran into submission by crippling its economy, Tehran sought to do the same to Washington by aggressively expanding its nuclear program. Whether the escalation would lead to both sides finding their way back to serious negotiations or whether it would lead to war remained unclear to all, including the Obama administration.

Obama's diplomatic endeavor had clear benchmarks and even a timeline, though Obama was loath to share it publicly. Diplomacy had to yield some results—primarily Iran demonstrating "seriousness" by accepting the U.S.-Russia swap proposal—before the end of 2009. Failure to do so would indicate the end of diplomacy.

However, the sanctions track was not burdened with such limitations. Whereas diplomacy was given only twelve months to show results, sanctions were essentially an open-ended policy. This disparity was particularly noteworthy since the deadline for diplomacy was justified by the fear that Iran's growing stockpile of low-enriched uranium (LEU) would put it dangerously close to a nuclear weapon. There was a near obsession in the U.S. media about Iran's menacing LEU count, driven by the Obama administration's own frequent references to this metric as a justification for the life-and-death urgency of the deadline for diplomacy. Once Washington shifted toward sanctions, however, the Obama administration stopped referring to the LEU count, and the media stopped reporting on it. Inexplicably, the urgency had faded away.[1]

There was a logical reason, however, as to why Obama deliberately did not give sanctions a deadline: if sanctions were to fail, the two sides would not return to diplomacy. The United States would have to choose between going to war or accepting Iran as a de facto nuclear power. "Obama was not going to set any deadlines," his nonproliferation tsar, Gary Samore, explained to me, "because if sanctions didn't work by a certain date, then the only alternative left was war, which Obama wanted to avoid. So that was very deliberate and conscious." The absence of a deadline, however, made having a means for assessing the progress of the policy all the more important. Yet no clear benchmarks existed—at best, the policy was improvised, with a learn-as-you-go quality. "It was absolutely not scientific," explained France's Ambassador Gerard Araud, one of the most fervent champions of the sanctions policy. Rather, the Western powers applied whatever pressure they could to the Iranian economy without disrupting global markets.[2]

Although the sanctions policy was not "precisely calibrated"—it had no clear indicator of when their desired effect on Iran's nuclear calculations would kick in—the administration kept an eye on a few variables. First, and perhaps easiest, was the performance of the Iranian economy—such as its GDP, oil sales, and unemployment rates. While it was "impossible" to measure the political impact of sanctions, the U.S. government could "at least tell what the monetary impact was." The monitoring of these indicators was intense, with the U.S. intelligence community briefing the White House on developments in the Iranian economy on a weekly basis.[3]

Second, the United States closely followed developments in the Iranian nuclear program. This was a critical variable since it would "affect how much time we could allow for sanctions to create a window for diplomacy," said Ben Rhodes, deputy national security advisor to President Obama. Much to Washington's dismay, the Iranians accelerated their nuclear activities after the failure to agree on a fuel swap. Tehran installed more centrifuges at the underground, bombproof facility at Fordo and increased the level of uranium enrichment from 3 percent to 19.75 percent, with hints of going up to 60 percent. All the while, Iran invested heavily in developing newer and more efficient centrifuges. Together, these factors reduced Iran's breakout capability and brought it closer to a weapons option. Iran's decision to expand its nuclear activities this aggressively was a direct response to Washington's sanctions. The United States calculated that halting Iran's nuclear growth would force Tehran to reconsider its strategy. Instead, Tehran reckoned that expanding the nuclear program would prove to Washington that sanctions weren't working and force Obama to come back to the negotiating table with a more flexible approach to the nuclear program in general and to the matter of enrichment in particular. "Our strategy was to break the mentality of the other side by showing them that pressure wouldn't work," President Hassan Rouhani's chief of staff, Mohammad Nahavandian, explained to me while on a visit to the UN in New York. "So we escalated our nuclear activities to show what pressure would produce. Perhaps we really didn't need some of the nuclear facilities and activities we engaged in, but we deemed it necessary for breaking the mentality of the other side."[4]

The third variable was Israel. The Obama administration took the Israeli threat of unilateral military action against Iran very seriously, to the extent that much of the United States' Iran policy was just an extension of its Israel policy. Despite extensive conversations with Israel about the dangers of an Israeli attack against Iran, the Pentagon believed that Israel would not give the United States any meaningful forewarning if it attacked. The U.S. military was deeply frustrated by the limited impact Washington had on Israel's decision-making, since an Israeli attack would likely drag the United States into the ensuing war against its will. The fear of a surprise Israeli attack was so significant that a senior Pentagon official asked to have the moon cycle included in his daily intelligence brief. Chairman of the Joint Chiefs of Staff, Admiral

Mike Mullen lamented publicly about how "extremely concerned" he was about the possible repercussions of such a strike.[5]

The Israeli wild card also forced the United States to increase its military assets in the Persian Gulf to protect U.S. troops from repercussion in case Israel attacked Iran. The increased military presence also served another function: avoiding any unintended escalation in a potential conflict with Iran. With a heavy presence in place, the United States could not be perceived as escalating because of its already heavy presence, whereas adding military assets to the Middle East theater in the aftermath of an Israeli attack could be perceived as an escalation and generate additional military moves by Iran. Washington was racing to have its sanctions clock outpace both Iran's nuclear clock and Israel's military clock, all the while hoping the sanctions pressure would bring about new negotiations.[6]

However, the psychological blow of Iran's increased isolation and the impact of sanctions on Iran's nuclear policy could not be measured or observed unless a parallel negotiation process existed to continuously test Iran's willingness to limit its nuclear activities. "With respect to the sanctions," explained Jake Sullivan, a senior advisor to Secretary of State Hillary Clinton and Vice President Joe Biden, "the real metric for us was not so much an economic metric, but the metric of whether the Iranians would begin to seriously talk about the kind of constraints on their program which would be necessary." Slowly but surely, the pressure would wear the clerical regime down and make it understand that its very survival was at risk. Once this reality dawned on Tehran, it would begin negotiating in earnest, the logic went. "From the beginning, the idea of the sanctions were to convince the regime that when you make an analysis of cost benefit, at some point they considered that the nuclear program was too costly for the survival of the regime," Gerard Araud added. "So our calculation was to get the regime to come to the conclusion that for political reasons eventually it's too costly, so we have to negotiate." There were no precise indicators of when this shift would occur, however. Iran's internal politics remained a black box for the Western powers, and sanctions were at best a low-precision instrument. "Sanctions was always a conundrum," Germany's ambassador to the United States, Peter Wittig, commented. "Do the sanctions work, do they not work? We could never really tell." Like diplomacy, sanctions were an art, not a science.[7]

The Race for Sanctions

The UN sanctions legitimized the additional unilateral sanctions Washington wanted its allies to impose on Iran, and the Obama administration escalated its sanctions push immediately after their adoption. If the UN sanctions were the floor, Washington wanted to know how far it could go before it reached the sanctions ceiling. The United States wanted sanctions just below the point where political resistance to new ones would grow too strong, or where they would disrupt international energy markets.

At first, the sanctions policy resembled the George W. Bush administration's "shock and awe campaign" against Iraq: a whole slew of new measures were quickly adopted and implemented, leaving Tehran aghast. Airports in Europe and the UAE—one of Iran's greatest trading partners—began refusing to refuel Iranian passenger planes, hampering the movement of people between Iran and the outside world. The European Union and Canada imposed new oil and gas sanctions, going well beyond what the UN sanctions mandated. In what was to become a familiar theme, EU Foreign Affairs Chief Catherine Ashton explained the move as an effort to reinvigorate diplomacy. "Our objective remains, as I have always said, to persuade Iranian leaders that their interest is served by a return to the table. Sanctions are not an end in themselves," she said after the EU foreign ministers met in Brussels. By August, ships carrying Iranian oil started to face problems at UAE ports due to the U.S. Treasury's campaign to impose greater scrutiny on all trade hubs Iranian goods might pass through. At the same time, UAE banks curtailed their dealings with Iranian banks, drying up one of Iran's most important financial lifelines.[8]

Next, the United States turned its focus to Asian powers that had always shielded their economic ties with Iran from political turbulence. "In 2011, every bilateral meeting that the president had with an important country, Iran sanctions were the top issue," Deputy National Security Advisor Ben Rhodes explained. "This was extraordinary." Compelling them to adopt their own unilateral sanctions against Iran would have the twin effect of tightening the sanctions regime while dealing Tehran a massive psychological blow. South Korea and Japan, two American allies that also enjoyed strong and historic trade ties with Iran, were the main targets. Tehran was Seoul's biggest trading partner in the Middle East, with an annual trade of $10 billion in 2009, while Tokyo was loath to lose its stake in the Iranian energy sector to China. Nonetheless, South Korea also desperately needed American support to deter North Korea. Similarly, Japan depended heavily on Washington's support against Beijing and Pyongyang. Touting the growing international consensus against Iran, Obama was immeasurably helped by Ahmadinejad's divisive and belligerent rhetoric. At the same time, Obama subtly threatened that if Japan and South Korea did not comply with the United States, they themselves would be subjected to U.S. sanctions. Obama ultimately succeeded where Bush had failed abysmally: Seoul and Tokyo agreed to impose unilateral sanctions against Iran mirroring those by the European Union and Canada. Tokyo even took the agonizing step of pulling out of developing Iran's massive Azadegan oilfield.[9]

By October 2010, Obama had pushed four major oil companies—Statoil, Eni, Royal Dutch Shell, and Total—out of Iran under the threat of U.S. sanctions. Total's surrender to American pressure was particularly noteworthy. After the Clinton administration scuttled Conoco's groundbreaking deal with the Rafsanjani government in 1995, France's Total took over that lucrative contract. Ever since, Total had taken much pride in its share in the Iranian energy sector, and it had successfully resisted American pressure and deflected congressional threats—until, that is, the Obama administration's offer of diplomacy reversed a dynamic in which Iran was seen to be in the right and the United States was perceived to be in the wrong.[10]

Despite these blows, Iran remained defiant. It responded by doubling down on its nuclear stance, threatening to boycott countries adopting sanctions on Iran, and recommitting itself to diplomacy without pressure while rejecting any further dialogue with the United States. "Sanctions have no impact on the Iranian nation's will," Ahmad Avaei of the Iranian Majles noted. "Sanctions are nothing new, we have become accustomed to sanctions ever since the victory of the Islamic Revolution." The Iranian narrative on sanctions portrayed them as an unjust tool used by Western powers to subjugate Iran and deprive it of scientific progress. Sanctions had little to do with Iran's actions and everything to do with the West's desire to prevent Iran from living up to its full potential and assuming its rightful role in the region. A change in Iranian policies would not elicit the end of sanctions, the narrative claimed. "It is wrong to think that being soft in front of the enemy would lead to less pressure by them," Ahmadinejad commented. Negotiations could take place, he insisted, "but not if you think you can impose force on us and say negotiations mean that we have to accept whatever you say. Be aware that no such a thing will ever happen." The Green movement rejected the sanctions as well, pointing to the negative impact the economic pressure would have on the opposition movement and the general public. Sanctions pressure negatively impacted the Iranian people, the Greens argued, not the clerical government, while also providing the Ahmadinejad government with a pretext for cracking down further on the political opposition by equating it to Iran's foreign "enemies."[11]

Much like the United States and its allies, Iran was careful not to close the door on negotiations, but it vehemently rejected that negotiations and sanctions could go hand in hand. The very premise of a dual-track policy would "close all doors to the diplomatic solution of Iran's nuclear issue." Negotiations should not be another method of pressure, Tehran maintained, but rather a means to find a mutually acceptable solution. Painfully aware that it was the weaker party in the equation, it refused to continue negotiations if the talks were just a façade for strong-arming Iran. Ayatollah Khamenei stated as much in one of his sermons: "If superpowers want to threaten and put pressure and impose sanctions and show an iron hand and, on the other hand, seek to sit at the negotiating table, this is not a negotiation and we will not have this kind of negotiation with anyone," he said.[12]

Moreover, Khamenei rejected any direct negotiations with the United States unless sanctions and military threats were lifted, thereby rebuffing Obama's attempts to establish a direct channel to the Iranian leader. If the United States were to end its sanctions regime and its threats to bomb Iran, Khamenei crucially added, direct negotiations could be considered. "If these conditions are implemented, as I announced some years ago, we haven't sworn not to negotiate forever."[13]

At this point, the name of the game for the foreseeable future was becoming clear as both sides adopted a dual-track policy with an overwhelming focus on the first track, pressure. The United States and its allies were shock-and-aweing Iran with massive pressure in order to soften Iran's nuclear stance. Iran, in turn, was expanding its program and rejecting direct talks with the United States in order to compel the West to adopt greater flexibility. Negotiations would be pursued, but mostly to inquire whether the other side was ready to yield, not to engage in a proper search for a compromise. It was a contest of resilience, determination, and perseverance. It was a race between several clocks, in which the United States needed its sanctions clock to tick faster than both Iran's nuclear clock and Israel's pressure for military action. In his typical bombastic style, Ahmadinejad signaled Iran's defiance. "Whatever the heck you want to do in the next two years, do it now so we see what you are capable of," he said in a speech broadcast live on state television. As Washington would find out at the first opportunity for diplomacy after the 2009 failed fuel swap talks, the Iranian president was not bluffing.[14]

Debacle in Istanbul

The P5+1 and Iran were not to meet until months later in Geneva (December 2010) and Istanbul (January 2011), when the dual-track policy dictated that Washington had to raise the stakes. The United States and the European Union prepared a new package to present to Iran, which had tougher conditions than the package Iran had previously rejected. Rather than requesting that Iran ship out 1,200 kilograms of LEU, Obama now wanted Iran to hand over 2,000 kilograms of its enriched uranium. Iran would also have to halt enrichment at the 19.75 percent level. "This will be a first sounding about whether the Iranians still think they can tough it out or are ready to negotiate," a senior American official told the *New York Times*. "We have to convince them that life will get worse, not better, if they don't begin to move."[15]

Still, the United States was sending conciliatory signals ahead of the talks. In an interview with the BBC, Secretary of State Hillary Clinton said that Iran "can enrich uranium at some future date once they have demonstrated that they can do so in a responsible manner in accordance with international obligations." However vague, this was the clearest public signal yet that Washington could accept Iranian enrichment. The next day, Clinton ran into Iranian Foreign Minister Manuchehr Mottaki at a security conference in Bahrain. She recounted the story to American journalists on her plane back to Washington. "He saw me and he stopped and began to turn away and I said, 'Hello, minister.' He just turned away."[16]

Mottaki's cold shoulder foretold the difficulties Obama would have in getting the Iranians to engage directly with the United States again. When the talks began in Geneva on December 6, 2010, the Iranians choreographed the meeting to leave no room for any chance encounters between U.S. and Iranian diplomats. The Iranians insisted that all the diplomats from the P5+1 states be seated at the negotiating table before the Iranian delegation would march into the room and take their seats. When the meeting ended, the Iranians had to exit the room before the P5+1 diplomats were permitted to rise from their chairs. This became a pattern that repeated itself as long as the Ahmadinejad government remained in power. The meetings themselves were also void of any real interaction. Rather than negotiating, the two sides kept on talking past each other, with prepared statements laying out rehearsed and well-known positions. "We simply just gave competing speeches," a White House official complained.[17]

There were many diplomats in Istanbul but very little diplomacy. The United States and its partners in the P5+1 came with a revised swap proposal that few believed was realistic. The Iranians would not even discuss the proposal. They listened but asked no questions. The lead Iranian negotiator, Saeed Jalili, would not even promise to raise the proposals in Tehran and report back to the P5+1. Instead, he insisted that the West must first agree on a framework that respected Iran's rights as a signatory of the Non-Proliferation Treaty (NPT) to enrich for peaceful purposes and remove punitive economic measures. "I don't say these are preconditions," Jalili noted at the Istanbul press conference. "These are prerequisites."[18]

"The Iranians just took a totally outrageous position," U.S. negotiator Robert Einhorn recalled. "'We're not prepared to talk substance with you until you remove sanctions and explicitly recognize the right to enrich.' Even the Chinese and Russians thought it was ridiculous." Moreover, the Iranians refused to meet directly with the American delegation, despite pressure from the European Union that a bilateral meeting be held. While the United States and its allies were frustrated by Iran's insistence that sanctions be lifted before real negotiations could begin, Jalili complained about what he called "dictation, not dialogue" by Western powers. Without a common logic and framework, he said, "it's no longer a dialogue but just a set of special orders and specifications." After two frustrating days of talking past each other, not only did the talks collapse, but EU High Representative Catherine Ashton announced that she wouldn't be scheduling another meeting until the Iranians would agree to engage seriously. She wasn't closing the door on diplomacy, she insisted; the ball was simply in Iran's court. "Our proposals remain on the table," she said. "Our door remains open. Our telephone lines remain open."[19]

While there was little doubt that sanctions had hit the Iranian economy hard, the Istanbul round left the Obama administration with no choice but to concede that "while Iran's leaders are feeling the pressure, the sanctions have not yet produced a change in Iran's strategic thinking about its nuclear program." In reality, however, it is not clear whether the Western alliance wanted talks to begin this soon after the sanctions track had been activated. If the logic was that Iran would be at the height of flexibility when the sanctions pain was peaking, then it is not inconceivable that the P5+1's nonstarter proposal in Istanbul was meant to be rejected in order to give the sanctions track more time to gather steam and pressure. Iran may have subscribed to the same logic, deliberately delaying the diplomatic process while adopting nonstarter positions and rapidly expanding its nuclear program in order to wear down the United States and its allies' relative diplomatic power. Whether these tactics were deliberate or not, the next two years would see the two sides engage in all-out escalation while getting dangerously close to war.[20]

Game of Chicken

The Obama administration presented the sanctions and pressure policy as a component of diplomacy. In reality, the United States and its allies were engaged in a secret, behind-the-scenes war targeting Iran with sabotage, cyber warfare, efforts to delegitimize it in international forums, containing its influence in the Middle East following the Arab spring, and sanctions. Obama had inherited some of this policy from the G. W. Bush administration, which had asked Congress to approve $400 million for a program of support for rebel ethnic groups, as well as intelligence gathering and sabotage of Iran's nuclear program. One area the United States was not involved in, however, was the assassination of Iranian nuclear scientists. Still, the killing of Iran's scientists became very much a part of the larger picture of using pressure to slow down the Iranian nuclear program while attempting to decimate Iran's will to resist.[21]

Between 2009 and 2012, assassins on motorbikes in Tehran executed or tried to execute—in broad daylight—several individuals connected to Iran's nuclear program. Most were killed using remote-controlled bombs attached to their cars. Some were shot from behind as the assassins rode by them. Some of the victims, such as Fereydoon Abbasi, were important players in the Iranian nuclear program. (Abbasi survived the attempt on his life in November 2010 and went on to become the head of the Atomic Energy Organization of Iran.) Others, like thirty-two-year-old Mostafa Ahmadi Roshan, were not high-value assets to the Iranian nuclear program, and their assassinations hardly slowed down Iran's nuclear advances. In many cases, family members or colleagues of the target of the assassination were also killed or injured. One of the scientists was killed right in front of his young daughter.[22]

Iran's ballistic missile program was also subject to mysterious explosions and accidents. In one instance, a huge blast ripped through a Revolutionary Guards military base just west of Tehran. Dozens were killed, including the "father" of Iran's missile development project, General Tehrani-Moqaddam. Embarrassed that a foreign power could inflict such damage inside of Iran, Iranian officials often denied that anything had happened, only to admit later that an "accident" had occurred. But the sheer number of such accidents belied the fact that something far more sinister was taking place and that Tehran was—at first—at a loss as to how to stop it.[23]

The assassinations were conducted by the Israeli Mossad together with the Mujahedeen-e-Khalq (MEK), an Iranian terrorist organization opposed to the clerical regime in Tehran, according to current and former U.S. intelligence officials. "The MEK is being used as the assassination arm of Israel's Mossad intelligence service," said Vince Cannistraro, former head of the CIA's counterterrorism division. Israel made only lukewarm attempts at denying its role in the assassinations. When asked whether God had carried out the recent operations in Iran—a hint to operation "Wrath of God," Mossad's assassination of the Black September members behind the 1972 Munich Olympics—then Mossad head, Meir Dagan, smilingly said yes. In what perhaps gave a hint of Israel's plans, Israel's military chief of staff, Lieutenant General Benny Gantz, warned Iran on the day before one of the assassinations that 2012 would be a critical year for Iran because of "things which happen to them [the Iranians] in an unnatural way." Moreover, when asked in a CNN interview if Israel was involved, Israeli president Shimon Peres gave an unconvincing answer: "Not to the best of my knowledge." In the words of Israeli columnist Yossi Melman, "The war is under way, though no one declared it and no one will confirm it. This is the secret war against Iran's nuclear project. It did not start this week or last month. It has been under way for years, but only faint echoes have reached the public."[24]

Rejecting the idea that Israel could have undertaken these sophisticated operations against Iran without U.S. support or approval, Tehran pinned the blame on both Washington and Tel Aviv. Speaker of the Majlis, Ali Larijani, called one of the assassinations an "American-Zionist act of terror." Ahmadinejad told a press conference that "undoubtedly, the hand of the Zionist regime and Western governments is involved in the assassination," while vowing not to back down from Iran's nuclear goals. Iran's then foreign minister Ali Akbar Salehi directly accused the United States of giving the assassinations a green light. "We have all the information that it was the Zionist regime," he said. "But there is—there was—a tacit, we think, agreement from the United States as well, unfortunately." The Iranians were particularly infuriated that one of the scientists assassinated was the author of a confidential report Tehran had submitted to the IAEA in response to questions the agency had raised about Iran's nuclear activities. Iran believed that the IAEA had leaked the paper to the Mossad, which then decided to assassinate one of the scientists behind the report.[25]

Washington categorically rejected any involvement in the assassinations and condemned the killings. While the Obama administration may have found the assassinations a useful addition to the plethora of efforts to set back the Iranian program without resorting to war, the attacks also risked escalating matters to the point of a much more open confrontation. The Israelis may not have seen that as a negative side effect; in fact, the timing and target of some of the assassinations raised suspicions that Israel may have been more focused on undermining the prospects of diplomacy and eliciting Iranian escalation. One of the killings took place just weeks before a new round of negotiations was scheduled, prompting Secretary of State Hillary Clinton to take the unusual step of going to the podium to condemn the assassination.[26]

Iran then took the matter to the UN Security Council, urging it to take action against the perpetrators of the attacks, but Iranian hardliners wanted much more. The conservative newspaper *Kayhan* urged Tehran to retaliate in kind: "It is legal under international law to retaliate for the killing of the nuclear scientist," the daily said. "The Islamic Republic has gathered much experience in 32 years, thus assassinations of Israeli officials and military members are achievable," it added. Much indicates that this is exactly what Tehran chose to do, but with little success. Israeli diplomats and officials were attacked in failed assassination attempts in Kenya, Azerbaijan, Thailand, Georgia, and India. In several cases, Iranian nationals were arrested and convicted for the crimes. The direct connection to the Iranian government, however, could not always be proven. What was surprising, though, was the amateurish execution of these assassination attempts. Mindful of Iran's extensive experience in assassinations on foreign soil, Western intelligence services were perplexed.[27]

To a certain extent, the failed assassination attempts may simply have been due to the Israeli officials' impenetrable security apparatus. That may be why an Israeli tour bus in Bulgaria was blown up in July 2012, killing seven Israeli tourists and injuring scores more: while Israeli diplomats and officials are protected by layers of security, Israeli tourists are not. They are soft targets, much like Iran's scientists, who

never enjoyed the same protection other Iranian officials did. Netanyahu wasted no time pinning the blame of the bus bombing on Iran.
And while no evidence was presented at the time, Netanyahu might not
have been mistaken. The government in Tehran was a very likely suspect, precisely because of the Israeli assassination of Iranian scientists
and Iran's failure to strike back at Israeli officials. Six months later, in
February 2013, the Bulgarian government implicated Hezbollah in the
July 2012 bombing. The U.S. government supported the view that Iran
was also behind the bombing, based on intercepted communications.
Whether it was Iran or not, one thing is clear: since the Bulgarian bus
bombing, no more Iranian scientists have been assassinated.[28]

Iran reciprocated not only assassinations and sabotage, but also
cyberattacks on its nuclear program. Despite the sophistication of the
U.S.-Israel computer worms installed at Iran's nuclear facilities—which
damaged an estimated 5,000 centrifuges—Iran quickly bounced back
within a few months. "They have been able to quickly replace broken
machines," a Western diplomat with access to confidential IAEA reports told the media. Despite the setbacks, "The Iranians appeared to
be working hard to maintain a constant, stable output" of low-enriched
uranium, the diplomat continued. Once it had recovered, Iran struck
back: in August 2012, Iran launched three waves of cyberattacks against
American banks, as well as a massive assault on the Saudi Aramco oil
company, in which data on tens of thousands of computers were erased.
Defense Secretary Leon Panetta called these cyberattacks "probably the
most destructive attack the private sector has seen to date."[29]

Washington was taken aback by Iran's cyber skills. It had not
predicted how aggressive and sophisticated Iran's retaliatory measures
would be. Experts within the field cautioned the Obama administration
not to underestimate Tehran. "Iranians are unusually talented in cyberwarfare for reasons we don't fully understand," Google Executive
Chairman Eric Schmidt cautioned, following the attacks. While Washington's cyber capabilities were superior to Tehran's, the difference between the United States' and Iran's relative military power was simply
overwhelming. These relative disparities, combined with the United States'
infrastructural vulnerabilities, made cyberspace the arena where Tehran
would likely prefer to confront the United States. Moreover, the use of

cyberwarfare created a conundrum: Was the United States legitimizing cyberattacks as a measure short of war, which its rivals such as
China could use against the United States in the future? These were
questions the Obama administration wrestled with, given that cyberwarfare was an unchartered territory with no established precedents
and no laws guiding it. Iran's retaliation showed that even short of war,
cyber escalation carried great risks and costs. In fact, had the roles been
reversed, with Iran making the first move and attacking the United
States with the Stuxnet computer virus, the U.S. military would have
considered that an act of force, the legal equivalent of the political term
"act of war."[30]

There were other situations in which matters risked escalating out
of control. On September 29, 2011, an Iranian American was arrested at
John F. Kennedy Airport in New York for conspiring with the Iranian
Revolutionary Guard Corps (IRGC) to assassinate the Saudi ambassador to the United States at a popular Washington restaurant. It was a
stunning turn of events, not just because an assassination of an Arab
diplomat on U.S. soil would have been an unprecedented escalation, but
because the plot was so farcical and amateurish. In fact, many experts
in Washington doubted the Obama administration's narrative regarding the plot because it didn't fit with the assessment of Iran and its ally
Hezbollah as the "A-team of terrorist organizations." Nonetheless,
Obama stuck to his story and accused elements of Iran's government of
being behind the plot, but stopped short of implicating its top leadership. "We believe that even if at the highest levels there was not detailed
operational knowledge, there has to be accountability with respect to
anybody in the Iranian government engaging in this kind of activity,"
Obama said. "The important thing is for Iran to answer the international community why anybody in their government is engaging in
these kinds of activities?"[31]

Defending its accusation against Iran to a skeptical press corps
and experts community, Obama insisted the "facts are there for all to
see." "We would not be bringing forward a case unless we knew exactly
how to support all the allegations that are contained in the indictment,"
he added. The alleged plot was part of a pattern of "dangerous and reckless behavior by the Iranian government," Obama continued, while

promising to apply "the toughest sanctions" and to "continue to mobilize the international community to make sure that Iran is further and further isolated and that it pays a price for this kind of behavior." Obama's message was that if Tehran would escalate, so would Washington. Sure enough, the United States and Saudi Arabia took the matter to the UN General Assembly, which adopted a resolution by a vote of 106 in favor, 9 opposed, and 40 abstentions, deploring the plot and calling upon Iran to comply with all of its obligations under international law.[32] The plot, along with the crushing defeat in the UN General Assembly, were a huge embarrassment to Iran—and one that further reinforced Tehran's status as an international pariah. In turn, Iranian leaders denied any involvement in the plot, accusing the United States of concocting this "shameful allegation" to sow discord between Tehran and its Arab neighbors.[33]

While the cartoonish characteristics of the alleged plot were befuddling—"What we're seeing would be inconsistent with the high standards we've seen in the past," a senior U.S. official said—the U.S. intelligence community eventually reached the conclusion that the plot might have been deliberately botched. Rather than actually trying to assassinate the Saudi ambassador, the botched campaign was aimed at signaling Washington that in response to assassinations and U.S. sabotage on Iranian soil, Tehran was ready to escalate matters and hit American targets on U.S. soil. Director of National Intelligence James R. Clapper Jr. told the U.S. Congress that the thwarted plot "shows that some Iranian officials—probably including Supreme Leader Ali Khamenei—have changed their calculus and are now more willing to conduct an attack in the United States in response to real or perceived U.S. actions that threaten the regime." Iran had crossed a threshold in its adversarial relationship with the United States. Rather than softening Iran, American pressure had brought the two closer to war. Visibly worried about the trajectory of the situation, Senator Dianne Feinstein, an ardent supporter of diplomacy with Iran and the head of the Senate Intelligence Committee at the time, warned that the United States and an "increasingly hostile" Iran were on a "collision course."[34]

The tensions were further inflamed by a U-turn made by the IAEA on its assessment of the potential military dimensions of the Iranian nuclear program. With a new head of the agency, a Japanese diplomat named Yukiya Amano, who, secret U.S. government documents revealed, was "solidly in the U.S. court on every key strategic decision" including Iran, the IAEA adopted a new tone toward Tehran. At a meeting I attended at the White House in early 2011, hints were given that a new IAEA report would come out that would further increase the pressure on Iran. A key objective was to cut Iran off from a few key developing countries—India, Indonesia, South Africa, Brazil, and Egypt—which had resisted American efforts to put pressure on Iran via international organizations. The report came out a few weeks later. For the first time, it suggested that Iran might have an ongoing nuclear weapons program—directly contradicting earlier IAEA assessments as well as the 2007 U.S. National Intelligence estimate that asserted that Iranian weaponization efforts had ceased in 2003. Now, the IAEA said, there were indications that the alleged work in Iran "may have continued beyond 2004."[35]

The United States and Western powers immediately pointed to the report as new evidence that tougher measures against Iran were warranted. French Foreign Minister Alain Juppe said France and its allies were prepared to impose "unprecedented sanctions" on Iran. "We cannot accept this situation, which is a threat," he said in a radio interview. Britain's foreign secretary, William Hague, told the House of Commons that "no option is off the table" concerning Iran penalties, and that he would work on persuading Russia and China to view Iran more critically. Israeli Prime Minister Netanyahu saw the report as a vindication of Israel's long-standing suspicions. "The IAEA report confirms both the international community and Israel's claim that Iran is developing a nuclear weapon," he said.[36]

Others were unconvinced. Russian officials complained of a "well-orchestrated media campaign" against Iran's nuclear program being aimed at escalating matters. "We very much regret the IAEA has been drawn into the campaign. It is impossible not to see that this campaign over the director-general's report plays into the hands of those forces that would like to obstruct a diplomatic solution of the Iranian issue," Russian Ambassador Grigory Berdennikov observed. In Moscow's view, the report was "neither professional nor objective." Moreover, Moscow was infuriated that the report had been leaked to media without the IAEA Board of Governors giving its approval. Similarly, the Non-Aligned Movement (NAM), a group of 120 states that are not formally aligned with or against any major power bloc, expressed its deep dissatisfaction and concern over the "selective release" of the IAEA report.[37]

The main critics of the report, however, were former IAEA officials who deplored the new methodology Amano had adopted. The agency stated that the report was based on new information, but IAEA critics argued that the information was neither verified nor vetted. It was irresponsible for the agency to issue a report containing such harsh accusations and speculation without properly checking the information, they maintained. Robert Kelley, a former U.S. weapons scientist who ran the IAEA action team on Iraq at the time of the U.S.-led invasion, drew parallels to the G. W. Bush administration's use of unvetted information to make the case to invade Iraq. "Amano is falling into the Cheney trap. What we learned back in 2002 and 2003, when we were in the run-up to the war, was that peer review was very important, and that the analysis should not be left to a small group of people," Kelley said. "So what have we learned since then? Absolutely nothing. Just like Dick Cheney, Amano is relying on a very small group of people and those opinions are not being checked." Even Hans Blix, the former IAEA director general, took the unusual step of criticizing the agency. "There is a distinction between information and evidence, and if you are a responsible agency you have to make sure that you ask questions and do not base conclusions on information that has not been verified," he said.[38]

Mindful of the contentious election of Amano and the revelation of his proximity to Washington, the release of the controversial report served only to raise the temperature: Washington, the EU, and Israel insisted that the report necessitated additional pressure, while for Iran, the report reinforced the narrative that the nuclear issue was a concocted pretext, used by the United States and Israel to pressure and isolate Iran. Ultimately, the pressure on Iran was increasing, but so was skepticism about Obama's end goal.

Arab Spring, Arab Winter

The Arab uprisings erupted in the middle of the United States' and Iran's nuclear game of chicken. While this geopolitical shock did not directly impact the nuclear issue, it did change the context in which the U.S.-Iran rivalry played out and indirectly affected their calculations in several ways. First and foremost, it became another arena for the United States and Iran to wear each other down.

While Washington initially saw the Arab uprisings as a challenge, because some of its allied regimes were falling and could be replaced by anti-American governments, Tehran viewed the ouster of the Hosni Mubarak government in Egypt as the fruition of one of its long-standing predictions: that the pro-American Arab regimes in the region lacked legitimacy and would eventually fall in popular uprisings. For Tehran, this was an opportunity to extend its influence in the region and neutralize Washington's attempts to isolate Iran globally. From Tehran's perspective, whoever would take power in Egypt could not possibly be worse than Mubarak. The triumphant mood in Tehran—brought on by the collapse of pro-American governments in the Middle East in the midst of Washington's attempts to break the clerical regime in Iran—was unmistakable. "In my opinion, the Islamic Republic of Iran should see these events without exception in a positive light," said a leading conservative, Mohammad-Javad Larijani. For Iran, the Arab spring was the emergence of a "new Middle East, without the Zionist regime and U.S. interference."[39]

But Iran did not just welcome the Arab spring—it took credit for it. The Iranians started referring to the uprisings as an "Islamic awakening," indicating that the Arabs were following the path of Iran's 1979 Islamic Revolution. "This widespread awakening of nations, which is directed toward Islamic goals, will definitely become victorious," Khamenei declared in his 2011 New Year's message. If the new Arab regimes were independent of Washington and Islamist in their orientation, Tehran calculated, the effect would be a triple victory for Tehran: Iran's standing would improve, the United States would be on the defensive in the region, and the campaign to sanction and isolate Iran would be dealt a huge blow. Tehran saw an opportunity to turn the

Arab spring not only into a victory for Iran, but also into a defeat for Washington.[40]

If Iran was jubilant, the United States was nervous. Within a month after the fall of the Mubarak government, and for the first time since its 1979 revolution, the Iranian navy sent two warships through the Suez Canal with the permission of Egypt's new military leaders. Annoyed, President Obama pointed out the glaring contradiction in the Iranian position. While Tehran was celebrating the Arab uprisings, it had itself only two years earlier brutally suppressed the Iranian people's desire for greater freedom. And once the uprisings reached Syria, where Iran chose to stay loyal to its ally in Damascus, the hypocrisy in Iran's praise for the "Islamic awakening" could not be any starker. "I find it ironic that you've got the Iranian regime pretending to celebrate what happened in Egypt when, in fact, they have acted in direct contrast to what happened in Egypt by gunning down and beating people who were trying to express themselves peacefully in Iran," Obama said.[41]

In the end, no one won the Arab spring. Iran's hopes to improve its standing in the region came to naught after its support for the Syrian government's grip on power left hundreds of thousands dead and helped fuel the winds of sectarianism, which boosted Saudi Arabia's efforts to turn Arab states and publics alike against Shia Iran. The Arab uprisings did, however, catapult the rivalry and enmity between Iran and Saudi Arabia onto a whole new level, which came to trouble Washington later, when it sought to find a diplomatic solution to the nuclear deal. Riyadh, more so than Washington, feared that the Arab spring would open the door for Iran to spread its influence in what Riyadh regarded as its domain: the Sunni Arab world. Realizing that Washington would not protect its allies from domestic uprisings, Saudi Arabia decided to take matters into its own hands.[42]

When Washington began mediating between the Bahraini royal family and its Shia-dominated opposition, Saudi Arabia invaded the country with 2,000 troops and quelled the protests with force—against President Obama's explicit request. The king's message to Obama was simple: "Saudi Arabia will never allow Shia rule in Bahrain—never." Saudi Arabia abandoned its more cautious foreign policy, in which it often hid behind the United States, and embarked on a new and more aggressive posture vis-à-vis Iran. One of its main instruments was fanning the flames of sectarianism: if the regional conflict was framed as a Sunni versus Shiite struggle, then the vast majority of the Muslim states would automatically fall in the Saudi camp. Moreover, Iran's claim to regional leadership would take a huge hit if the Sunni public viewed Shias as enemies. While Saudi Arabia had tried to use this instrument in the past, it was Iran's own actions that made it successful in the post–Arab spring era. Iran's support for Bashar al-Assad's brutal repression of the Syrian uprising, which tended to be Sunni-dominated, as well as its arming and training of Shia militias in Iraq, made Sunni audiences significantly more receptive to Saudi Arabia's sectarian push against Iran. Within two years after the fall of Mubarak, Iran's standing in the Arab world was at its lowest point since the 1980s, and its hope to break out of America's encirclement and isolation had fallen flat. "We have more soft power in Latin America than we do in our own neighborhood right now," a senior Iranian official admitted to me.[43]

Sanctions Versus Centrifuges

The center of the escalation game, however, was Washington's and Brussels's sanctions versus Tehran's centrifuges. With global opinion shifting so strongly against Iran, Washington had, for the first time, the opportunity to use the oil weapon against Iran and even exclude it from global financial networks. Never before had such sanctions been imposed on a country that the United States was not formally at war with. But it was a strategy fraught with risk. The task was to break the Iranian economy without wreaking havoc in the global oil market, which could push the entire world into a recession. Moreover, as tensions with Iran heightened and the fear of war increased, the risk premium on oil shot up. Iran might sell less oil as a result of sanctions, but sanctions could also push up oil prices, mitigating the pain felt in Iran's coffers. Finding the right balance was a tricky process, as Congress wanted more sanctions than the White House believed the international markets could handle, and certainly more than what Washington's partners in the P5 + 1 would agree to. "We didn't want a trade war with China [from pushing sanctions too hard]," a former White House official explained. The fear that sanctions could drive the global economy into a deep recession was "very real," according to Richard Nephew, who was then responsible for the sanctions portfolio at the White House. "No one knew at the time we had shale gas revolution under way. No one knew at the time that demand in China was gonna slow down.... We were thinking that going into 2012 that we were going to have oil shortages if we forced Iran to exit from the legitimate oil market altogether."[44]

The uncertainty around the global markets' potential reaction to the sanctions compelled the administration to target investments in Iran's oil and energy industry, as well as its sales of petrochemical products instead. "Rather than go for a headshot, we were gonna go for leg shots," Nephew explained. Yet Congress and Israel wanted more: no sanctions policy could really be effective unless they went for the jugular—that is, Iran's oil income and its access to global financial markets. Despite the White House's resistance and caution, a unanimous Senate adopted sanctions on Iran's Central Bank in December 2011. Obama reluctantly signed the sanctions bill into law two months later, knowing very well its potential impact on the global energy markets and that the designers of the sanctions in Congress did not intend for them to be used as leverage in a future negotiation or to boost diplomacy. Rather, their aim was to permanently contain and isolate Iran, at least until the sanctions pressure would cause the clerical regime in Tehran to fall. Congress had even toyed with the idea of outlawing any contact with Iranian diplomats, which effectively would have made diplomacy with Iran illegal. This critical difference between Congress and the White House had little impact at the time. Two years later, however, it would catapult Congress's opposition to Obama's diplomacy to even higher levels.[45]

Under the terms of the sanctions legislation, any public or private financial institution that engaged in oil or non-oil transactions through the Central Bank of Iran would be denied access to the United States. The law effectively cut off the Iranian Central Bank from global markets. This was nothing short of a declaration of economic war, one that was forced upon Obama by Congress. "We had been mulling various ways to go after Iran's oil exports, but had not found a solution to the global supply problem. Politics forced us to come up with a solution," Nephew said.[46]

That same month, just a day before the EU ministers were to meet to discuss a potential oil embargo on Iran, Iranian hardliners sacked the British embassy and ratcheted up the confrontation between the West and Iran. The demonstrations had been organized by hardline groups on university campuses and Islamic seminaries, and while the Iranian government never claimed responsibility for the attack, few doubted that it could have occurred without a green light from the authorities in Tehran. The mob trashed rooms, damaged furniture, scrawled graffiti, and tore up a portrait of the Queen of England. "We had no idea how it was going to end," the British ambassador to Iran, Dominick Chilcott, said. "It felt like very spiteful."[47]

The attack checkmated the EU countries that had planned to push back against new sanctions at the scheduled meeting of the EU ministers. I met with the Swedish foreign minister, Carl Bildt—the most outspoken of the ministers within the anti-sanctions block in the European Union—the day after the attack on the British Embassy, and it was clear from our conversation that he knew that he was now championing a lost cause, since an attack on the British Embassy was an attack on all of the EU. "After the Brits were ransacked, the EU has no other choice but to stand up against Iran," a Tehran-based Western diplomat said. Decision-makers in Washington could hardly conceal their pleasure with Iran's action. "Iran has given the international community a condemnable act to rally around," an Obama administration official explained. "Anyone who might have been squishy on sanctions before now has reasons to act," he added. Sure enough, on January 23, 2012, the foreign ministers of the European Union agreed to ban all purchases of Iranian crude oil, effective July 1, 2012. A month later, the Society for Worldwide Interbank Financial Telecommunication (SWIFT), a Belgium-based organization that provides a network that enables financial institutions to send and receive information about financial transactions, removed Iran from its network.[48]

Iran had been dealt three massive blows in as many months. Tehran had grossly miscalculated; the world believed it could live without Iranian oil. Steps that were inconceivable only a few years earlier had become reality. The immediate impact on the Iranian economy was devastating: the Iranian currency dropped almost 30 percent in two days, plummeting to its lowest value against the dollar in decades. A sense of panic was taking hold among the Iranian public, yet Iran's leaders remained defiant. Ahmadinejad claimed that the oil embargo would backfire on Europe and that "Iran won't suffer." But while Foreign Minister Ali Akbar Salehi said Iran will "weather the storm," citing Iran's history of withstanding pressure from the outside, Minister of Economy Shamseddin Hosseini likened the ban to "economic war." Tehran renewed its attempts to convince Saudi Arabia not to make up for any oil lost as a result of the embargo on Iranian oil, but to no avail. The Iranian leaders also renewed their threats to close the strategically vital Strait of Hormuz in an attempt to increase the political risk and push up oil prices.[49]

Tehran calculated that higher oil prices would not only mitigate the impact of sanctions on Iran, but also push the global economy toward recession and force Washington to take its foot off of the gas pedal when it came to sanctions. The Iranians even warned Washington that it would take action if an American aircraft carrier that had left the Persian Gulf were to return. But while the turmoil did cause a sharp rise in oil prices, the markets did not tank, and the global economy did not slide into a recession. The Obama administration had been overly cautious in its assessment of what the global economy could handle in terms of taking Iranian oil off of the market, while underestimating their allies' discipline around the sanctions regime. "I was amazed at how effective we were," Gary Samore told me. "When we started, I could not imagine that we would be able to convince countries to reduce their purchases of Iranian oil to the point that they did."[50]

But it wasn't just the tolerance of the global oil markets that had been underestimated. The Obama administration had also miscalculated the resilience of the Iranian government in the face of economic downturn. Iran took huge hits, and its population endured tremendous pain and pressure, particularly in the healthcare sector, since Tehran's difficulties paying for the medical drugs it sought to import led to medicine shortages. Despite these problems, however, the government in Tehran never lost control. U.S. intelligence services had predicted that mass demonstrations and riots would occur within months after the imposition of sanctions. When the Iranian rial lost another 40 percent of its value over one week, sporadic protests erupted in Tehran, but within two days the government was back in charge. What some in Washington had hoped would ignite a larger protest turned out to be just a spark that fizzled out. "For a moment, I thought that October 2012 was the beginning of our Tunisia," Nephew told me, "when we saw that the currency lost about two-thirds of its value in a day. But then they regained control. In less than a day and a half . . . I was disappointed. Because I thought it was gonna really lead to some real internal problems for Iran and force them to negotiate a way out of the sanctions." To Washington's surprise, while Iran suffered, it remained calm. In one calendar year, GDP per capita declined by nearly 8 percent; inflation increased by over 10 percent; unemployment inched close to 20 percent; and Iran's crude oil export revenues fell by about 40 percent. Iran was hurt, but it wouldn't break, so the escalation continued.[51]

Between November 2008 and February 2013, Iran's stockpile of low-enriched uranium (LEU) grew from 839 to 8,271 kilograms—a near tenfold increase of the very variable that the Obama administration treated as a measurement of Iran's proximity to a bomb. In 2009, Obama had sought to keep Iran's LEU count below 400 kilograms as part of the failed fuel swap proposal. By 2013, Iran sat on more than twenty times that amount of LEU. Moreover, Tehran dramatically increased its IR-1 centrifuges from 7,100 in April 2009 to 12,669 by the end of February 2013, while also installing 180 of its more advanced IR-2m centrifuges. Even more worrisome was Iran's growing stockpile of enriched uranium at the 19.75 percent level (MEU). By February 2013, Iran had produced 280 kilograms of MEU, though 100 kilograms were used to produce fuel plates for the Tehran Research Reactor. This was a doubling of the MEU stockpile in just three months. Earlier, the White House had scoffed at Iran's claims that it would produce fuel pads for its reactors on its own. "We do not believe they have the capability," White House Press Secretary Robert Gibbs had told reporters. Iran had not only succeeded with that task—it was now going well beyond that measure.[52]

Tehran was meeting pressure with pressure. It counterescalated by raising the cost for the West's alleged refusal to deescalate the conflict. The expansion of the nuclear program brought Iran closer to a nuclear breakout capability, which in turn put Washington in a more compromised position. "Iran is under unprecedented sanctions, a barrage of physical sabotage, assassinations, and cyber war," a Tehran-based analyst close to the government said. "Yet it still manages to not only continue its nuclear program but to expand it. Under these circumstances, its counter pressure is to continue its nuclear program. That is a huge achievement." By deliberately doubling down on nuclear activities opposed by the West, Tehran sought to convince the international community that the sanctions path was futile. "The mere continuation of the nuclear program shows that sanctions aren't working," the analyst continued. And Tehran threatened to escalate matters even further. "Iran is willing to begin enriching uranium to 60–90 percent just to show that the sanctions don't work," a former Iranian nuclear negotiator added.[53]

In this game of chicken, Tehran's and Washington's policies were mirror images of each other. If sanctions were aimed at wrecking the Iranian economy and creating internal fissures that would ultimately lead Tehran to conclude that continuing on the nuclear path was too costly, the clerical regime's strategy was to raise the stakes even further by advancing the nuclear program beyond Iran's actual needs in order to ruin the confidence of the P5+1 that the sanctions strategy would elicit Iranian flexibility. And if sanctions did not lead to a softer Iranian position, the United States and its allies would be forced to choose between either escalating the matter to war or backing down. "This was a leverage game, and their [Iran's] endgame was to convince the other side that sanctions would not get them anywhere," Political Science Professor Farideh Farhi explained. "It would actually end up escalating the situation, ultimately leading the other side to contemplate the alternatives."[54]

When Director of National Intelligence James Clapper testified in the U.S. Senate in February 2012, his message was grim. "We see a disturbing confluence of events: an Iran that is increasingly rigid, autocratic, dependent on coercion to maintain control and defiant toward the West, and an Iran that continues to advance its uranium enrichment capabilities along with what appears to be the scientific, technical, and industrial capacity to produce nuclear weapons if its leaders choose to do so," he said, adding that "sanctions as imposed so far have not caused them to change their behavior or their policy."[55] While the sanctions were often lauded in the U.S. media for the pain they had caused to the Iranian economy, the failure to translate that pain into a slowdown of the nuclear program did not go unnoticed. The criticism came both from those arguing that sanctions had proven ineffective and that military action had to be contemplated and from those arguing that the excessive focus on sanctions at the expense of diplomacy only increased the risk of war. Not surprisingly, the Israelis fell in the former camp. "We are pleased to see increasing sanctions but so far they have not been deterred from their course," Israeli Foreign Minister Avigdor Lieberman said of the Iranian leaders while calling for tougher measures. The *Washington Post* editorial pages noted what it called a "stubborn reality: There has been no change in Iran's drive for nuclear weapons or in its aggressive efforts to drive the United States out of the Middle East. If anything, Tehran has recently grown bolder. . . . The bottom line is that the threat from Iran is not diminishing but growing. Where is the policy to reverse that alarming trend?"[56]

On the other side, some security and nonproliferation experts cautioned about the increasing risk of war as a result of the game of chicken. "[We] were concerned that sanctions were—that the United States was going to try continuing ratcheting up sort of the sanctions pressure without realistically pursuing diplomatic options," said Kelsey Davenport of the Arms Control Association, a key Washington, DC–based nonproliferation organization. The British newspaper the *Guardian* warned that in the escalation, "A negotiated climb-down by both sides is the least likely option" and that instead war was becoming increasingly likely. Its columnist Simon Jenkins put it in even starker terms: "This saber-rattling—in the midst of a recession—is beyond stupid. . . . The danger is that [sanctions] encourage militarist lobbies to escalate the steps that lead to open conflict," he wrote. "Britain is out of Iraq and desperate to get out of Afghanistan. So why gird ourselves for a fight with Iran, a proud country of 75 million people with whom we cannot go to war without taking leave of our senses? Do any of Britain's leaders really think further economic sanctions will stop Iran's nuclear programme? I cannot believe it."[57]

There were murmurs of dissent within the P5 + 1 as well. Neither the Chinese nor the Russians supported the unilateral sanctions imposed on Iran. "We don't think sanctions can solve the issue fundamentally," the Chinese Foreign Ministry spokesman said in October 2012. "They can only complicate the issue and escalate the tensions." Similarly, while the Russians had supported the UN sanctions on Iran, they strongly objected to the unilateral sanctions the United States and its allies imposed, regarding them as "unacceptable and contradictory to international law." According to Moscow, Tehran was likely to perceive the sanctions onslaught as an attempt to achieve regime change in Iran, which would be counterproductive since it would eliminate Iran's incentives to compromise. "We differed strongly in terms of the actual nature of the Iranian threat," Russia's Deputy Foreign Minister Sergei Ryabkov told me. "We also differed on the effects; we didn't believe in the effectiveness of sanctions." Echoing Iranian talking points, Russian Foreign Ministry spokesman Alexander Lukashevich even told Iranian media that "we are now witnessing that the previous sanctions against Iran were all futile."[58]

The Non-Negotiations

Contrary to what Washington had hoped for, sanctions not only failed to cause Iran to become more flexible, but also made it difficult for the diplomatic track to be fruitful, precisely because the Obama administration was unwilling to stop squeezing Iran before having first explored how much pressure the international community was willing to muster. According to this line of thinking, loosening the sanctions prematurely was the equivalent of willfully losing leverage, in terms of the prediction that Iran would show flexibility only once the sanctions pain had become unbearable. "Iran doesn't respond to pressure," the Obama administration said privately. "It only responds to *a lot of* pressure." This logic, however, also demonstrated that the two tracks were not equal. Sanctions were at the center of Obama's Iran policy, and diplomacy was primarily used to test and investigate if the sanctions bite had softened the Iranians' stance. This imbalance became even more evident when the parties finally returned to the negotiating table in early 2012.

BACK TO ISTANBUL

After fifteen months of diplomatic hiatus, the P5 + 1 and Iran reconvened in the Turkish city of Istanbul in April 2012. Contrary to their stance during the encounter in Istanbul one year earlier, the Iranians now agreed to discuss the nuclear program, though they continued to insist that Iran's right to enrichment was untouchable. Four key developments occurred in Istanbul. First, both sides struck a positive tone, and though there was still more sermonizing than bargaining occurring, at least the Iranians agreed to discuss the nuclear issue. "For the first time, the Iranians did not beat around the bush, and agreed to talk directly about their nuclear program," said one senior European official. The second key development was that according to the joint press statement by the P5 + 1 and Iran following the talks, the parties had agreed "that the NPT forms a key basis for what must be serious engagement, to ensure all the obligations under the NPT are met by Iran while fully respecting Iran's right to the peaceful use of nuclear energy."[59]

The Iranians argued that agreeing to conduct the talks within the framework of the NPT was tantamount to accepting Iran's right to enrich. "EU Reaffirms Tehran's Nuclear Rights," the government-run English-language *Iran Daily* said on its front page. When I spoke to one of the Iranian negotiators shortly after the Istanbul session, he made no secret of Iran's satisfaction and was confident that the crucial matter of enrichment would be further solidified in the next round of talks. EU diplomats, however, flatly rejected the Iranian interpretation and pointed out that the text referred to the NPT as *a* key basis for the talks, not *the* basis.[60]

Behind the smiles, there were other significant tensions. After the press conference, EU Foreign Policy Chief Cathy Ashton and Saeed Jalili, the lead Iranian negotiator, retreated to the Turkish foreign minister's private office, where they met for about ninety minutes. There, the smiles and politeness were gone. Despite the Iranians' bombastic dismissal of the sanctions, Jalili "relentlessly" pressed Ashton for a delay in the EU oil sanctions that were set to go into effect by July 1, 2012, Laura Rozen of *Al Monitor* reported. "During the Ashton bilateral, it was Jalili of old," an EU diplomat told Rozen. "He asked 100 times" for a delay in the oil sanctions.[61]

The talks did recover from that meeting, but the Iranians rebuffed all requests for bilateral meetings, except with the Chinese. The Turks reportedly tried to arrange a U.S.-Iran bilateral session, but the Iranians refused. Crucially, however, the Iranians did agree to schedule another round of talks only a month later and to begin a more regular series of meetings. But they still threw in a wrench: they made the venue of the next round a contentious issue, insisting that it had to be in a country that had not imposed unilateral sanctions on Iran. At first, the Iranians insisted on Kabul, Afghanistan, despite its perilous security situation. The parties eventually settled for Baghdad, Iraq, which, although not much of a haven of stability either, was not as unsafe as Kabul. "After first suggesting Kabul, Baghdad sounded fantastic to us," a White House official quipped. The final, and perhaps most crucial, development in Istanbul was the establishment of a step-by-step process guided by the principles of reciprocity and proportionality. This meant that if the United States were to offer an irreversible concession to Tehran, the Iranians would have to reciprocate by offering a proportionate and irreversible concession of their own. As diplomacy grew more serious, these principles became increasingly important.[62]

While all parties praised the talks, despite the behind scenes drama, one country blasted diplomacy: Israel. By "letting" Iran continue enriching for another five weeks until the Baghdad meeting, Tehran had been given a "freebie" by the West, Israeli Prime Minister Netanyahu lamented. Netanyahu's comments strongly irritated Obama administration officials. After all, getting Iran to suspend enrichment wasn't even on the agenda in Istanbul, which the Israeli prime minister knew very well, since the Israelis had had detailed discussions with the Americans in the weeks running up to the Istanbul meeting.[63]

FROM BAGHDAD TO MOSCOW

The tough nonbargaining continued in the subsequent meetings in Baghdad and Moscow, in May and June 2012, respectively. Washington entered the Baghdad meeting with considerable confidence. Sanctions had clearly negatively impacted the Iranian economy, and despite Tehran's public bravado, Jalili had pressed hard in Istanbul for the European

Union not to implement the oil embargo. The more Iran asked for sanctions relief, the greater the West's confidence that sanctions would eventually force Iran to back down—as long as the pressure wasn't eased. With only one month left until the embargo was to come into effect, neither Washington nor Brussels was in the mood to compromise. "They're nervous enough to talk," said a senior administration official. "Whether they're nervous enough to act, we don't know yet." The Associated Press reported ahead of the meeting that "Washington has shown little willingness to bargain."[64]

The morning session on May 23 was tense. Washington introduced a new package aimed at halting Iran's enrichment at the 19.75 percent level. It included no significant sanctions relief, only the easing of restrictions on airplane parts and on technical assistance to Iran's energy industry. Broader sanctions relief, Washington insisted, would come only when a more comprehensive agreement had been reached. Jalili did not just reject the proposal—he ignored it. "He did not even give the proposal a passing glance when it was handed over," said a participant at the Baghdad talks, and even refused to commit to passing it onward to Tehran.[65]

The Iranians countered with their own proposal, a five-point package that included broadening the focus of the talks to incorporate the escalating conflict in Syria as well as up-front sanctions relief for any Iranian concessions on 19.75 percent enrichment. To the West, not only was the sanctions relief demand unacceptable, but also the expansion of the agenda was viewed as a transparent attempt by Tehran, which was mindful of the severe differences within the Security Council on Syria, to split the P5 + 1.[66]

Both sides accused the other of being unrealistic. Western officials complained that the Iranians should not be "deluding themselves they are going to get sanctions relief now," attributing Iran's "maximalist" position to its isolation and disconnection from the international community. The Iranians in turn accused the West of presenting unbalanced proposals that did not offer Iran anything of value. Hossein Mousavian, a former member of Iran's negotiating team, told CNN that "the world powers are asking Iran for diamonds, in the form of ceasing to enrich uranium to 20 percent, and all they are offering in return is peanuts, in the form of spare parts for Iranian airline planes." The Iranians had also hoped that Baghdad would further firm up what Tehran had interpreted as the P5 + 1's acceptance of enrichment on Iranian soil by putting it explicitly in writing. But Washington was not ready to play the enrichment card. So, the Iranians interpreted the Baghdad meeting as the United States backtracking from what it had put forward in Istanbul.[67]

Not everyone in the P5 + 1 was comfortable with Washington's hard bargain. The Russians floated a "step-by-step" proposal asking for Iran to stop adding new centrifuges in return for the West refraining from imposing new sanctions. However, this proposal was a nonstarter for the Western powers, because it would abort the oil embargo that was scheduled to begin only one month later. Whatever flexibility Iran would show in Baghdad, the reasoning went, it would be even more flexible once the oil sanctions had slashed Tehran's oil revenue.[68]

By the time the parties reconvened in Moscow on June 17, 2012, diplomacy hung by a thread. The Iranians had threatened to cancel the meeting, and if confidence had characterized the P5 + 1 prior to Baghdad, it was uncertainty that clouded the mood before Moscow. Feeling that Washington had backtracked on the enrichment question, the Iranians once again made that the centerpiece of their demands: any deal would have to entail recognition of Iran's right to enrich, they insisted. They also repeated their demand to expand the agenda to include regional issues such as the Syrian war. Washington, in turn, also hardened its position. It now wanted Iran to fulfill all three demands of its "stop, shut, and ship" proposal—that is, to curtail enrichment of uranium to 19.75 percent purity, shut the underground facility at Fordo, and ship out 100 kilograms of its MEU. "Earlier, the U.S. had implied that they were ready to address the three E3 + 3 [P5 + 1] demands . . . separately," the *Al-Monitor* website revealed. "However, this position had changed in Moscow," where the United States insisted "that the three demands should be treated inseparably, as a package." And even if Iran agreed to all three demands, no substantive sanctions relief would be offered in return. The Iranians bitterly complained that at best, the P5 + 1 offered a vague promise of "thinking [about] finding a way for removal of unilateral sanctions."[69]

Moscow was a "dialogue of the deaf," with the two sides trading proposals that were miles apart. After five draining sessions, the talks ended in stalemate. The Iranians said there was no use negotiating since Washington was only months away from its presidential elections, leaving Obama with no political space to offer any meaningful sanctions relief. But then fearing that an admission that the talks had collapsed could trigger an Israeli military attack against Iran, the two sides agreed to schedule technical discussions in July 2012. Publicly, the two sides put on a brave face in order to not give away that diplomacy was now on life support.[70]

The hard bargaining did not pass without criticism. The *Guardian* pointed out that "for sanctions to work they not only have to be credible but also stoppable. At the moment they are neither." If the idea was that the sanctions pain would force Iran to cut back its nuclear activities, why would it do so if this wouldn't lead to sanctions being lifted? But stopping the sanctions was not on the menu in Moscow, the *Guardian* continued, pointing out that Iran had only been offered "token" incentives. This criticism was also echoed by former top CIA analyst Paul Pillar, who described it as the "Nothing-But-Pressure Fallacy": with no sanctions relief on the table, the Iranians were "left to believe that heavy pressure, including sanctions, will continue no matter what they do at the negotiating table, and that means no incentive to make more concessions."[71]

But the public pressure the Obama administration seemed most concerned about—only months before the presidential elections—came not from the advocates of diplomacy, but rather from the proponents of sanctions. Ahead of the Moscow session, forty-four U.S. senators wrote a letter to Obama, calling on him to abandon the talks in absence of a tangible agreement and focus on increasing pressure instead. At a minimum, they wrote, any agreement would have to include "shutting down the Fordo nuclear facility, freezing enrichment above 5 percent, and shipping all uranium enriched above 5 percent out of the country." Charles Robb of the Bipartisan Policy Center (BPC), told the House Armed Services Committee on the day of the talks that the dual-track approach had failed and that a third track had to be added: "credible and visible preparations for a military option." Senator Robb's testimony echoed the talking points of the Israeli government, which only weeks earlier had urged for a "three-pronged strategy," with "enhancing the threat perception" constituting the third prong.[72]

The tragedy of Moscow was that domestic politics in the United States meant that success would be failure, and failure would be success. Since the political cost of a small deal was deemed higher than the political cost of no deal, failing in Moscow would translate to success in Washington. By hardening his position, Obama could assert that he offered no compromise and no sanctions relief—which caused failure in Moscow but was well received in Washington. Indeed, the talks failed to produce an agreement—and no one in Washington complained. There were no sustained attacks from the Republicans. No complaints from Netanyahu. Democrats in Congress stayed silent. Instead, Obama was praised for having stood firm—and refusing to reach a compromise.[73]

But while Washington and Tehran continued to press each other with maximalist goals at the bargaining table, another crisis was reaching a boiling point. After years of unfulfilled threats, the White House was terrified that Netanyahu finally was about to go through with his threat to bomb Iran and pull an October surprise on Obama—right before the U.S. presidential elections.

Obama and the Mossad
Against Netanyahu

Israeli threats to bomb Iran's nuclear facilities were nothing new. Since the mid-1990s, various Israeli officials had, almost like clockwork, issued veiled and unveiled threats to take military action against Iran. Several Iranian officials had, in turn, used their own vile rhetoric against Israel, from questioning the Holocaust to praising terrorist attacks against the Jewish State. But throughout the Obama presidency, Israeli Prime Minister Benjamin Netanyahu drastically increased the volume and intensity of the threats. Whereas many had earlier suspected that Israel was bluffing and issued threats only to force the West to impose new sanctions on Iran or to sabotage diplomacy, the credibility of the Israeli threat was growing. The Obama White House soon came to the conclusion that it simply could not afford to assume that Israel was merely bluffing.[1]

From Point of No Return to Zone of Immunity

In September 2010, the *Atlantic* published an article by Jeffrey Goldberg warning that Israel was on the verge of bombing Iran. The Iranians, the article claimed, were reaching a technical "point of no return," after which an Iranian bomb was virtually inevitable. This magical point would be reached by March 2011, which meant that if by that date sanctions had not ground the nuclear program to a halt, or if the United States had not chosen to bomb Iran, Israel would have no choice but to take matters into its own hands. Goldberg argued that there was more than a 50 percent chance that Israel would strike Iran before July 2011. "If the choice is between allowing Iran to go nuclear, or trying for our-selves what Obama won't try, then we probably have to try," an unnamed Israeli official told Goldberg. Israel will not be asking for permission, because it will be too late to ask for permission, the article claimed.[2]

Goldberg uncritically recounted the arguments as to why the Israe-lis weren't bluffing, which included everything from the idea that Iran was an existential threat, to past daring military actions by Israel, to Netan-yahu's "deep sense of his role in Jewish history." Unsurprisingly, the article made waves in Washington. It framed the issue not as a question of war and peace, but rather as a question of who would start the war—Obama or Netanyahu? The Israelis accused Obama of being weak and indecisive. They lacked confidence in his courage and ability to be an effective world leader. If he failed to take command of the situation with Iran, he would force Israel to act, even though its ability to get the job done was far infe-rior to that of the United States. Goldberg's message was exactly the narra-tive the Obama administration did not want taking hold in Washington.

However, the article was deeply flawed. Although Goldberg had interviewed roughly forty current and past Israeli decision-makers and tested what he called a "consensus" by speaking to multiple sources, he somehow managed to miss the inescapable truth: Israel was deeply di-vided on Iran. And not just as to whether Iran constituted an existen-tial threat or a mere danger, but also to whether a military campaign was advisable. While the political leadership around Netanyahu toed his line and had a political incentive to point Goldberg in a certain di-rection, the security establishment deeply disagreed with Netanyahu's logic—and would soon make its dissent public. What the article did not get wrong, however, was that Netanyahu wasn't necessarily bluffing.

Netanyahu was not the only one finding utility in the threat of war. While the Obama administration did not find the war rhetoric Netanyahu employed to be helpful, it certainly did not want Iran to be-lieve that the military option was off the table. In late 2009, the Obama administration transferred to Israel fifty-five bunker-buster bombs, which had the capacity to take out Iran's underground facilities. These were bombs for which even the George W. Bush administration had rejected an Israeli request in 2005. Meanwhile, the British government signaled its readiness to deploy Royal Navy ships to the Persian Gulf to assist the United States.[3]

If Obama saw utility in military pressure in order to elicit diplomatic movement, Israel's intentions were more complex. Israel certainly welcomed that its military threats helped harden the West's position and accelerate the drive for sanctions. The Israeli Foreign Ministry even directly credited Israel's threats for the international sanctions. "Had Israel not spoken out about its intention to attack, none of this [sanctions] would be happening," an Israeli official told *Haaretz*. And the sanctions were essential to keeping Iran isolated and weakened and to preventing a rise in Iranian power that could constrain Israel's strategic maneuverability in the region.[4]

Moreover, Israel's threats to take military action and the West's consequential escalation of its own pressure on Iran could eventually lead to U.S. military action against Iran. "Should sanctions fail to stop Iran's nuclear program, there will be a need to consider taking [military] action," Israeli Defense Minister Ehud Barak argued on many occasions. The Israeli desire for the United States to attack Iran was made crystal clear to me and a group of American experts and former U.S. officials while visiting Israel in 2012. A recently retired Israeli general told our group that the United States' use of nuclear weapons against Japan at the end of World War II had secured five decades of "American glory." "We want," the general told us, "America to enjoy another five decades of glory," insinuating that Israel wanted Washington to take drastic action—perhaps even use nuclear weapons—to take out Iran's nuclear facilities. Needless to say, the Americans were stunned—not necessarily by the idea of Israel wanting the United States to attack Iran, but by the general's callous way of making his case.[5]

During the Bush administration, the United States began to suspect that if the Israelis weren't bluffing, the purpose of an attack would primarily be to force the United States into a war. General Michael Hayden, the former head of both the CIA and the NSA, explained that Washington's fear was that "the real goal of an Israeli attack [against the nuclear facilities in Iran], would be to drag us into war," because Israel's own attack capabilities were limited. Israel might not have been able to destroy the Iranian nuclear program, but few doubted its ability to pull the United States into the war. Classified war games conducted by the Pentagon made that abundantly clear.[6]

The Iranians often brushed off Israeli threats and accused Netanyahu of bluffing. At the same time, Iran did not attempt to hide the fact that it would strike back if Israel—or the United States—attacked it. According to a commander of the Revolutionary Guards, Iran intended to launch missiles at U.S. bases throughout the Persian Gulf within minutes if an attack on Iran took place. "These [U.S.] bases are all in range of our missiles, and the occupied lands [a reference to Israel] are also good targets for us," the commander told Iranian media. The U.S. military estimated that a single such missile attack would kill two hundred American soldiers. The Iranian army's chief of staff, General Hassan Firouzabadi, was even more direct, stating that an attack by Israel would lead to Iranian retaliation against the United States on American soil. "In case of an attack by the Zionist regime, the United States would also be hit," Firouzabadi said. And Iran would not be alone in this fight. Hassan Nasrallah, the leader of Hezbollah in Lebanon, a close ally of Iran, said that an attack on Iran would lead to a "regional war," indicating that Hezbollah would join the fight. Just as the P5 + 1 was united on how to deal with Iran, they were also united in their analysis that an Israeli attack would lead to a "catastrophic" regional war.[7]

At the White House, a large number of meetings focusing on the immediate and longer-term consequences of an Israeli strike were held at the deputy principals' level. It would be the worst of all options, they concluded, since it would produce all the negative reactions of a unilateral military strike without being as effective as a U.S. military operation. "You'd be rattling a hornet's nest without destroying it," a former White House official explained. To make matters worse, a strike would give Iran the legal pretext to withdraw from the Non-Proliferation Treaty and kick out all IAEA inspectors. Iran would be able to continue its nuclear activities, but without the international community having any insights into its progress. And once Iran retaliated against the Israelis, it would be very difficult politically for the United States not to come to Israel's aid. At that point, the United States would be at war at a time of Israel's, not the United States', choosing. "Even if we didn't [start the war] and the Israelis did, we evidently would be in that war within a matter of hours. Because the moment the Iranians or Hezbollah hit Israel, then we are in," Obama's Deputy National Security Advisor Ben Rhodes told me.[8]

Given the disaster unilateral Israeli action would cause, the Obama administration went overboard seeking to convince the Netanyahu government to give sanctions and diplomacy more time. In early 2012, the frequency of those meetings increased significantly. Senior officials from National Security Advisor Thomas Donilon, to Director of National Intelligence James Clapper, to Central Intelligence Agency Director David Petraeus, to Secretary of Defense Leon Panetta all visited with their counterparts in Israel to push back against Israeli military action. Tensions were high between the two allies as public comments revealed the depth of their disagreement. General Martin Dempsey, chairman of the U.S. Joint Chiefs of Staff, had told CNN in February 2012 that an Israeli strike "would be destabilizing" and "not prudent." The general added: "I don't think a wise thing at this moment is for Israel to launch a military attack on Iran." The comments infuriated the Israelis, who took the unusual step of publicly accusing Dempsey of making statements that "served Iran's interests."[9]

Israel refused to commit to not attack Iran, or even to provide the United States with notice prior to launching a war with Iran. "We are not committing to anything," Israeli Defense Minister Ehud Barak told Israel's Army Radio in April 2012. "The dialogue with the Americans is both direct and open," he added while declaring diplomacy with Iran a waste of "precious time."[10]

The public war of words reached a new height during the annual conference of the American Israel Public Affairs Committee (AIPAC), the hawkish pro-Israel lobby based in Washington. In his address to AIPAC, Netanyahu argued that Israel had waited for the world to stop Iran for fifteen years, but its patience was now running out:

> For 15 years, I've been warning that a nuclear-armed Iran is
> a grave danger to my country and to the peace and security

of the entire world. For the last decade, the international community has tried diplomacy. It hasn't worked. For six years, the international community has applied sanctions. That hasn't worked either. I appreciate President Obama's recent efforts to impose even tougher sanctions against Iran. These sanctions are hurting Iran's economy, but unfortunately, Iran's nuclear program continues to march forward. Israel has waited patiently for the international community to resolve this issue. We've waited for diplomacy to work. We've waited for sanctions to work. None of us can afford to wait much longer.[11]

While Netanyahu did not explicitly call for military action, the message was clear. And his supporters in the Republican Party left nothing to the imagination. Mitch McConnell, the Senate Republican leader, called for Congress to authorize the use of force against Iran in his address at the same conference. Obama quickly hit back, calling out his critics for favoring war without owning the argument. "When I see the casualness with which some of these folks talk about war, I'm reminded of the costs involved in war," he said. "This is not a game. There's nothing casual about it. . . . If some of these folks think that it's time to launch a war, they should say so. And they should explain to the American people exactly why they would do that and what the consequences would be. Everything else is just talk."[12]

A central disagreement between Obama and Netanyahu in the spring of 2012 was not only what the consequences of war would be, but also how much time remained before the Iranian nuclear program would be a fait accompli. The Israelis had introduced the concept of a point of no return in mid-2010. That supposed point—March 2011—had passed with no drama: Iran's nuclear advancement had not become irreversible, and Israel had not launched a war. Now, the Israelis introduced a new concept—the zone of immunity. Ehud Barak explained the concept as "the point at which Iran's nuclear facilities would be immune from any potential Israeli military strike because all the necessary components for developing a nuclear weapon would have been moved further underground, rendering Israeli weapons ineffective."[13]

According to Barak, Iran's nuclear program would be immune to Israeli military action by September 2012, while the United States, with its superior military capabilities, had until March 2013 before the Iranians would have achieved the ability to absorb American military strikes without losing their nuclear capabilities. Just as with the "point of no return" concept, the Obama administration was not convinced by Barak's "zone of immunity theory," dismissing it as "ill-defined" and "too narrow."[14]

Obama's Secret Allies

Unbeknownst to the larger public, the Obama administration had a surprising source of strong allies against Netanyahu: the Israeli security establishment. Netanyahu's assessment of Iran sharply contradicted that of the professionals within Israel's apolitical security institutions. Of these, no institution clashed with him more than Israel's intelligence agency, the Mossad.

On almost every key issue, they differed. Tamir Pardo, the head of the Mossad, flatly dismissed the notion that Iran was an existential threat to Israel—a mantra that Netanyahu had come to personify and that most in Washington accepted uncritically. At a meeting with Israeli ambassadors, he explained his rejection of Netanyahu's claim. "Does Iran pose a threat to Israel?" Pardo asked. "Absolutely. But if one said a nuclear bomb in Iranian hands was an existential threat, that would mean that we would have to close up shop and go home. That's not the situation. The term 'existential threat' is used too freely." Pardo was the third consecutive head of the Mossad to reject the idea that Iran constituted an existential threat. His two predecessors, Meir Dagan and Efraim Halevy, had also dismissed Netanyahu's claim. Iran's capabilities were "far from posing an existential threat to Israel," Halevy stated. "The growing Haredi radicalization poses a bigger risk than Ahmadinejad," he added.[15]

There was more. Netanyahu and much of the political establishment had argued for years that Iran was irrational, messianic, and suicidal. These claims formed the bedrock of the Israeli approach to Iran. As long as it was accepted that Iran did not follow logic, diplomacy and deterrence would be futile. And as long as it was accepted that Iran was suicidal, the West would have no choice but to take preventive military action. If these claims about Iran were not adopted, preventive military action would not become the sole logical policy option concerning Iran. Not only did the heads of the Mossad reject the notion that the Iranian threat was existential, they also rejected that Iran was irrational and suicidal. "The regime in Iran is a very rational one," Dagan told CBS's *60 Minutes*. "No doubt, they are considering all the implications of their actions." Dagan's comments were echoed by Israel's military chief, General Benny Gantz, who infuriated Netanyahu by describing Iran's leaders as "very rational people."[16]

Gantz and others in the security establishment even argued that Iran ultimately would not choose to build a nuclear weapon, precisely because of the deterrence power of the West. Gantz's statement echoed the assessment of the U.S. government, which saw Iran seeking the capacity for the weapon rather than the weapon itself. The political decision to actually build a weapon had not been made by Tehran yet—and might not be made at all. "Are they trying to develop a nuclear weapon? No," Secretary Panetta told *CBS News*. "But they are trying to develop a nuclear capability, and that is what concerns us."[17]

Even still, Netanyahu's alarmist assessment of how close Tehran was to a nuclear weapons option was also rejected by the Israeli intelligence. "Bibi has a tendency to exaggerate security threats," a former senior security chief told Israeli journalist Amir Tibon. "He uses it to invoke fear in the Israeli public. As long as it's just a political tactic, we can live with it. But when it starts affecting fateful security discussions— it becomes a problem." Dagan was less diplomatic, calling Netanyahu's claim that Iran could sprint to a nuclear device in less than a year "bullshit."[18]

The biggest disagreement, however, was over Netanyahu's and Barak's push for war, which they presented as the only remaining option. Dagan did not mince his words: war with Iran was "the stupidest thing I have ever heard," he said publicly. Israel didn't "have the capability to stop the Iranian nuclear program, only to delay it," he added. Not only would a military campaign fail to take out the Iranian program, but it would also bring about three disastrous scenarios for

Israel: it would unify the country and prompt Tehran to speed up its nuclear program; it would spark a regional war that would engulf Israel; and it would prompt Iran to retaliate by firing ballistic missiles at Israel that would have a "devastating impact" on the country. "If anyone seriously considers [a strike] he needs to understand that he's dragging Israel into a regional war that it would not know how to get out of. The security challenge would become unbearable," Dagan said.[19]

Netanyahu Was and Wasn't Bluffing

The Israeli security chiefs didn't go public against Netanyahu for no reason. They knew that his government was not bluffing. In particular, they were worried that Netanyahu and Barak would egg each other on until they got their war. Only by going public did they believe that the "madness" Netanyahu was about to unleash could be prevented. According to Barak's memoirs, Israel came very close to attacking Iran three times between 2010 and 2012. The attack plans had been drawn up by Netanyahu and Barak themselves. "We planned to do it," Barak said. But all three attempts were foiled by the security establishment.[20]

In 2010, Netanyahu and Barak issued an order to prepare for an imminent attack on the Iranian nuclear program. At a small meeting of top ministers, Netanyahu instructed the military to "set the systems for P-plus," a term meaning that an operation would start within thirty days. Four of the security officers present were shocked—chief of staff, General Gabi Ashkenazi, Mossad chief, Meir Dagan, chief of military intelligence, Amos Yadlin, and Shin Bet director, Yuval Diskin. "Not one of them could believe what they just heard," an Israeli report on the meeting stated. The security officials refused to obey the order, questioning both its wisdom and legality. Such an order, they insisted, required a decision of the full cabinet, not a segment of the cabinet. Moreover, issuing the order would be tantamount to starting a war, as it would set off a series of irreversible events, the security officers argued. "This is not something you do unless you are certain you want to execute at the end. This accordion will make music if you keep playing it," Ashkenazi said. Barak and Netanyahu disagreed on both counts.[21]

Netanyahu and Barak had not intended to declare war on Iran, however. Their plan was to "to trigger a chain of events which would create tension and provoke Iran, and eventually could have led to a war that might drag in the United States," according to veteran Israeli intelligence reporter Yossi Melman. The Iranians would be provoked and goaded into retaliating, after which the United States would be forced into the war. Eventually however, Netanyahu and Barak found themselves outnumbered, and the plan was shelved—for the moment. After all, never before had an Israeli prime minister managed to start a war in the face of the direct opposition of the head of the Mossad. The relationship between Netanyahu and his security officers, already tense, took a nosedive and prompted these officials to publicly contradict and criticize the Israeli prime minister. Their criticism was often scathing. Gantz blamed Netanyahu and Barak for creating "hysteria" around the Iran issue. Diskin, the chief of the domestic security service, Shin Bet, accused the two of being "motivated" by a "messianic" drive. The statement was explosive since those charged terms were otherwise reserved for Iranian—not Israeli—officials. (Later, right-wing commentators in Israel castigated Dagan and his allies for having, in their view, squandered a golden opportunity to attack Iran.)[22]

Netanyahu was furious. He couldn't get his way as long as both his own security establishment and the president of the United States stood against him. Netanyahu's relationship with Obama was now so bad—the mood in the White House was "f*** Bibi"—that Netanyahu made little secret of his desire for Obama to lose in the 2012 elections. As the United States entered its election season, and the Republican nominee, Governor Mitt Romney, visited Israel in July 2012, Netanyahu gave him two political gifts. The two of them held a joint press conference in which Romney addressed the Iran issue and echoed Netanyahu's arguments. "I couldn't agree with you more, Mitt," Netanyahu said, providing the Republican contender for the presidency with a much valued soundbite. Immediately thereafter, Netanyahu's close ally, the right-wing American casino magnate Sheldon Adelson, hosted a $1 million fundraiser for Romney at the King David Hotel. According to Israeli journalists Amir Tibon and Tal Shalev, such a high-profile fundraiser in Israel for an American presidential candidate—in the middle of an election—was unprecedented. The fact that Netanyahu agreed to host him was enough to break the unwritten rules of noninterference in American politics, in the view of the Obama camp. Furthermore, when Netanyahu publicly complained that Iran had gotten "closer and closer to nuclear bombs" under Obama, Romney quickly used that in an anti-Obama ad campaign in Florida. For all practical purposes, Netanyahu had allowed himself to become a Republican instrument in the campaign against Obama.[23]

But soundbites in attack ads were the least of Obama's worries when it came to Netanyahu. The real fear was that the Israeli prime minister would launch a surprise attack on Iran in the middle of the U.S. presidential elections—the most sensitive political period, when Obama's maneuverability vis-à-vis the Israeli prime minister would be at its lowest point. U.S. officials feared that "Netanyahu may have believed that if he struck during election season, the White House would be more restrained in its response to the Israelis because of its electoral implications," a former White House official told me. "In some ways the 2012 election gave him—Netanyahu—more leverage, more of a free hand in pursuing military action if he so chose."[24]

Sanctions were biting but not stopping Iran's nuclear program, while diplomacy was proceeding but not succeeding without direct talks. With the risk of an Israeli attack steadily increasing, the Obama administration needed an exit from the pressure track. It was time to try real diplomacy. In secret.

The Arabs Who Brought Iran and the United States Together

On July 31, 2009, three Americans studying and working in Syria decided to travel to Iraq to hike in the Kurdish Mountains. They had heard of the popular Ahmed Awa waterfalls and the great hiking paths of Iraqi Kurdistan. The plan was to spend a weekend away from their day jobs in Damascus. But it would be two long years before they would return. As they were hiking up the mountain, they were waved over by a group of armed guards. Unbeknownst to the three Americans—Joshua Fattal, Sarah Shourd, and Shane Bauer—the soldiers were Iranian border guards. As they walked toward the Iranian soldiers, the three American friends unknowingly crossed the unmarked Iraqi-Iranian border. By answering the call of the Iranian soldiers, they had trespassed into Iranian territory and were consequently taken into custody and charged with espionage. But because of that nightmare, a dialogue between the United States and Iran was born—a dialogue that eventually paved the way for the resolution to the nuclear stand-off.

With no embassy in Tehran and no diplomatic relations with the Iranians, the United States was forced to turn to allies that could intervene with the Iranians. The Omanis answered the call. They were very worried that tensions over the nuclear issue would lead to a regional war and wanted to use their good relations with both Washington and

Tehran to end the conflict. The arrest of the hikers gave the Omanis the opportunity to prove to Washington their ability to deliver what Obama craved—an authoritative channel to Iran's supreme leader, Ayatollah Ali Khamenei.[1]

Over the course of several months, Sultan Qaboos bin Said al Said's personal envoy, Salem Ben Nasser Al Ismaily, shuttled between Washington and Tehran, and brokered a prisoner swap that saw the hikers released in return for three Iranians held by the United States. The government of Oman paid the Americans' $1.5 million bail and flew them on Ismaily's private jet to Muscat, where they were reunited with their families. The day after, President Barack Obama called the sultan to thank him. Oman had proven its sway with the Iranians. "The prisoner swap" was the test case that demonstrated that they could deliver, President Obama's nonproliferation tsar, Gary Samore, explained. The question now was whether it could go beyond that to help broker a direct U.S.-Iran dialogue on the nuclear matter and create a channel that the Iranians had refused since the imposition of sanctions in 2010.[2]

As a close and trusted U.S. ally neighboring Iran that—unlike the other Arab countries in the region—had historically enjoyed strong relations with Tehran, Oman was in many ways perfectly situated to mediate between the United States and Iran. Not only are Oman and Iran linked by trade and cultural ties that go back centuries; the Omani sultan also remains indebted to Iran for its support in quelling the Dhofar province revolt in the 1970s, which helped secure the sultan's reign. At that time, the shah of Iran had sent four thousand troops to assist the Omani army, and more than seven hundred Iranian soldiers lost their lives protecting the sultan. That the sultan remembers this aid has been obvious from his policies concerning Iran since the rebellion. When Saddam Hussein invaded Iran in 1980 and most of the Arab world supported Iraq, Oman refrained from taking sides and retained a strong dialogue with Iran. This, in turn, helped the sultan gain the respect and trust of Ayatollah Khamenei. Since then Oman has extended an offer to the United States to help improve U.S.-Iran relations. That offer was renewed in 2009 when Oman's foreign minister "offered Oman as both an organizer and a venue for any meeting the U.S. would want with Iran—if kept quiet."[3]

Obama believed that true progress on diplomacy with Iran could not occur in the absence of a direct channel to Iran's supreme leader. The United States was not willing to give any meaningful concessions, nor did it expect that Iran could offer any meaningful concessions, unless the channel was directly authorized by Ayatollah Khamenei. While the official negotiation track with the P5 + 1 was authorized by Khamenei, the Iranians refused to engage with the United States directly. Despite several attempts, the Iranian negotiators' communication with the Americans did not go beyond simple greeting phrases. Iran's commitment to diplomacy was deemed insufficient unless it agreed to bilateral discussions authorized by Ayatollah Khamenei. The Iranian strategy was, first, to refuse direct negotiations as long as it seemed that the United States was planning to coerce Iran with military threats while at the negotiating table. "Does it make sense to offer negotiations while issuing threats and putting pressure?" Khamenei asked in one of his speeches. "You are holding a gun against Iran saying you want to talk. The Iranian nation will not be frightened by the threats." Second, Tehran refused a direct dialogue as long as the United States refused to clarify that it would accept enrichment on Iranian soil. Iran, as a weaker party, was loath to engage Washington directly if what it considered to be its rights were not honored in the negotiations, since Iran's walking away from the negotiating table could bring about even greater pressure on Tehran.[4]

According to people involved in the various negotiations, the Obama administration was "obsessed" with securing an authoritative channel to Tehran. Washington even provided the Omanis with names of Iranian officials it believed would have Khamenei's blessing to talk to the United States. Over the years, Obama sent several letters and messages to Ayatollah Khamenei, expressing his desire to resolve their differences in direct talks. And many different channels were used, not just the Omani one. In 2012, Obama sent a message through Turkish Prime Minister Tayyip Erdogan urging Iran to take advantage of the opportunity for diplomacy. While he indicated that Iran could use nuclear technology for peaceful purposes, he still did not touch the central issue for Tehran: whether the United States would accept enrichment on Iranian soil. The letters and messages prompted the Iranian foreign minister,

Ali Akbar Salehi, to comment publicly: "Out in the open [the Americans] show their muscles, but behind the curtains they plead to us to sit down and talk."[5]

The Man in the Shadows

To set up a channel of diplomacy, a desire for negotiations is far from enough. There needs to be an unshakable *belief* that diplomacy can work and perhaps more important, a willingness to accept the political risks involved in such sensitive endeavors. Which is precisely why it was difficult for such an initiative to be driven by Obama himself. Luckily for him, he had a friend in the U.S. Senate who was convinced that U.S.-Iran relations could and needed to improve: Senate Foreign Relations Committee Chair John Kerry.

In many ways, John Kerry operated as a shadow secretary of state during his tenure as chairman of the Senate Foreign Relations Committee. He was close to and trusted by Obama—who later made him actual secretary of state—and thrived on sinking his teeth into the hardest diplomatic challenges. He was more than happy to take on matters that were too sensitive politically for Obama—or, for that matter, for Secretary of State Hillary Clinton, who seemed disinclined to engage in any politically risky diplomacy that could jeopardize her future run for president. (Indeed, as Mark Landler writes, compared to Kerry, "Clinton's record looked meager; her approach, cautious; her achievements, evanescent.") The arrangement was quite unusual because "Kerry had an operational role" in Obama's foreign policy despite not being a member of his cabinet, a Kerry staffer explained. Whether it was facilitating the release of the hikers or negotiating with Bashar al-Assad over the Golan Heights, "He gave Obama space by taking on these issues," a White House official told me.[6]

Kerry's involvement began during the negotiations to release the Americans held in Iran as prisoners. He and Sultan Qaboos's envoy, Salem Al Ismaily—usually referred to simply as "Salem" by all officials involved—began discussing prospects for a broader channel to Iran in order to address the nuclear issue. The Omanis had from the outset viewed their efforts to win the release of the Americans as a stepping stone toward setting up a more robust, direct channel that could resolve the nuclear issue before it led to war. In December 2011, Kerry paid his first visit to Oman and met with the sultan to "test possibilities," a former Senate staffer said. The meeting, which was coordinated with the White House, was shrouded in complete secrecy: to have any chance of success, the discussions had to be completely shielded from the many enemies of U.S.-Iran diplomacy. On the Omani side, only three individuals were in the know: the sultan, Salem, and one person in the sultan's inner circle. Kerry's conversations with Salem continued into early 2012. Over dinner at Morton's Steakhouse in Washington, DC, they drafted the blueprint for what would become a secret U.S.-Iran channel.[7]

The Omanis were very impressed with Kerry and felt that he would be the right person to engage with the Iranians: he was humble, he listened, and perhaps most importantly, he spoke with respect—a matter that the Iranians are quite sensitive about. Kerry also had a detailed knowledge of the tortured history between the United States and Iran and understood the roots of Iran's grievances. This was particularly valuable, the Omanis believed, given the relative lack of Iran expertise in Washington think tanks. Having systematically studied previous attempts at U.S.-Iran mediation by other actors, the Omanis recognized the critical role of personal diplomacy, particularly in a situation where trust between the two parties was so low.[8]

But the qualities that Kerry possessed, which the Omanis believed would help bring the Iranians to agree to a direct dialogue with Washington, were the very same qualities that others in Washington worried would give Tehran a false impression of what the United States' actual negotiating position was. Secretary Clinton worried that Kerry was promising too much in order to lure the Iranians to the table. Others at the White House agreed. Kerry "wasn't necessarily always on point with official U.S. policy," a former White House official told me. The key concern was that Kerry might have told the Iranians that enrichment was in fact on the table—despite the fact that the Obama administration was not quite ready to play this bargaining card. In 2009, Kerry had given an interview to the *Financial Times* in which he had declared the Bush administration's zero-enrichment objective to be "ridiculous" and a "nonstarter." Moreover, he agreed with Iran's view that it had a right to enrich. "They have a right to peaceful nuclear power and to enrichment in that purpose," Kerry said.[9]

Some U.S. officials claim that in his conversations with Salem, Kerry did float the idea of the United States being willing to accept Iranian enrichment in order to get the Iranians to the table. This had created tensions between Kerry and National Security Advisor Tom Donilon, who worried about the domestic political fallout. Kerry, however, flat-out denied having played the enrichment card. "I was very careful from day one," he told Mark Landler of *New York Times*. "There is no, was no, and never is, within the confines of the NPT, a right to enrich. And we made it crystal clear to them: 'You don't have a right to enrich.' " However, considering Kerry's previous comments to the *Financial Times,* the hesitation of Clinton and others in the White House may not have been without basis. A month after Kerry had visited with the sultan, a doubtful Clinton stopped by Muscat to have her own discussion with the Omani leader. "Even under the best of circumstances, this was a long shot," she wrote in her biography.[10]

"Hillary and company were skeptical," Kerry said of Clinton's disposition. But Obama was closer to Kerry's assessment of the Omanis than to Clinton's, and by extension he was closer to Kerry's assessment of the Iranians. There was a risk in trying the channel, but there was also a risk in rejecting it, Kerry warned Obama and Clinton during a briefing in the Situation Room. If the United States did not give diplomacy a chance, the sultan would conclude that Washington was not serious about pursuing a diplomatic solution with Iran. News of the United States' dismissal of diplomacy would eventually leak, undermining the sanctions coalition against Iran and risking that world opinion toward Tehran could turn sympathetic. With Obama, Kerry was pushing an open door. "Kerry and Salman were both encouraging us to pursue this course," Ben Rhodes told me. "So then we essentially agreed to test it. But we wanted it. I'm not suggesting that we didn't want it; I'm trying to give Kerry and Salman credit." Obama agreed to proceed, calling Qaboos twice to probe him on the first litmus test of the channel: Could the sultan deliver Iranians who spoke with the authority of Khamenei? A few weeks later, Obama gave the channel his green light. The White House now took ownership of the new backdoor diplomacy.[11]

Convincing Khamenei

The Iranian side of the story further confirms the pivotal role played by the sultan and his envoy, Salem. Just like the Americans, the Iranians were at first suspicious of the Omani mediation effort, unsure as to whether they were acting on behalf of the United States. "I didn't really take it seriously at first," Iran's then foreign minister Ali Akbar Salehi told me of Salem's first attempts to convey the American desire for a bilateral channel in the fall of 2011. Salem's initial outreach was not to Iranian officials, but to Iranian businessmen with strong government connections. These businessmen, in turn, conveyed the message to Salehi, who at first did not know what to make of them, since it was unclear who Kerry spoke for. Why was the chairman of the Senate Foreign Relations Committee so involved in this while Secretary of State Clinton was not?, the Iranians asked themselves. "We did not know whether the message really came from the U.S. government or whether it was an effort by the Omanis or whether the Omani individual [Salem] had come up with the message himself," Salehi commented.[12]

After weeks of silence, Salem contacted another Iranian businessman, Mohammad Souri, the managing director of the National Iranian Tanker Company, who was in Oman negotiating a trade deal. Salem complained to Souri that the Americans were interested, but that Iran was not responsive. And Oman was ready to be a facilitator, he added. Souri conveyed the message to Salehi, who realized that not testing the channel could be a big mistake. Salehi gave Souri a piece of paper with four demands on it to take back to the Omanis and Americans. The demands ranged from the recognition of Iran's right to enrichment to the lifting of sanctions. The *Wall Street Journal* reported that the demands also included adding Jundollah, an al-Qaeda offshoot active in the Balochistan region of Iran, to the U.S. State Department's terror list, though Salehi would not confirm this to me. "I said that if they [the Americans] first express readiness to address our demands, we are also ready," Salehi said.[13]

But the Iranian foreign minister had an additional demand. For Iran to be convinced that the United States was serious, it wanted Washington to officially express its readiness. Washington could do no such thing, but Oman could. So instead, the sultan wrote a letter to Ayatollah Khamenei, assuring the Iranian leader that the United States was serious about entering into negotiation with Iran on a bilateral basis. The letter was delivered to Salehi, who submitted it to Khamenei through Khamenei's close confidant Ali Akbar Velayati—without informing Iran's firebrand President Mahmoud Ahmadinejad.[14]

At the time, a fierce debate was raging within the Iranian foreign policy elite on the form of the relationship Tehran should have with the great powers. The question was no longer *whether* there should be a relationship, but rather the *nature* of that relationship. But the debate had not reached a conclusion and no green light had yet been given for bilateral talks with the United States. Khamenei was at first skeptical, rejecting the offer on the grounds that the Americans were not trustworthy and would not fulfill their obligations. But Salehi countered that Iran would not end up in a worse situation if it tried diplomacy and the United States betrayed its word. On the contrary, the clerical regime could demonstrate to the Iranian public that it had "taken all measures to solve things peacefully, and people will also know that the establishment was ready for negotiations and that it was the Americans who refused." Eventually, despite strong resistance from Saeed Jalili and Iran's Supreme National Security Council, Khamenei came around. "He said ok, but you have to be very vigilant because we do not trust the Americans," Salehi explained to me.[15]

But Salehi was not given a carte blanche. Rather, Khamenei insisted on several conditions to guide and limit the talks: they had to be held at a level below that of foreign ministers, they could not proceed unless progress was made, and the agenda would cover only the nuclear issue and not broader U.S.-Iran relations. There was also a fourth condition, but to this day the Iranians have refused to reveal it. For the United States, these conditions were both a blessing and a curse. By making the Iranian Foreign Ministry responsible for the talks, instead of Iran's Supreme National Security Council (which was headed by the hardline Jalili, who had spearheaded the official P5+1 talks), Khamenei created a degree of distance between himself and the bilateral channel. "We tried to pin down the supreme leader, because we wanted [Khamenei] to have ownership of this process," Gary Samore explained to me. "But of course he refused to do that. He insisted on doing it through the Foreign Ministry." On the other hand, Obama also needed a degree of separation between himself and the talks. After all, that is why he let Kerry handle it at the outset. Still, this was the closest the Obama administration had gotten to an authorized channel to Khamenei. And there was only one way to find out whether it could bring results or not. Khamenei and Obama both green-lighted the channel around March 2012. But it would take another three months—and a lot of wrangling by the Omanis—before the Iranians and Americans would find themselves in the same room.[16]

Finally in Muscat

On July 7, 2012, a small team of American and Iranian diplomats met in the city of Muscat, Oman. The meeting took place in the midst of Israeli threats of war, escalating Western sanctions, and expanding Iranian nuclear facilities. Only a few days earlier, tensions had flared up again over Iranian threats to close the Strait of Hormuz—the world's most important oil transit chokepoint—and a U.S. military buildup in the Persian Gulf aimed at signaling to Iran, "Don't even think about it." Both the Iranians and the Americans were skeptical and distrustful. Only the Omanis, who hosted and facilitated the meeting, remained optimistic. In the end, both sides walked away from the meeting disappointed. The long-awaited direct channel to Iran had gotten off to a bad start.[17]

The American delegation was small and low-profile—secrecy and discretion was the name of the game. It was essentially a two-man team: senior National Security Council staffer Puneet Talwar and Clinton's deputy chief of staff, Jake Sullivan, accompanied by Emmett Beliveau, who handled communications and logistics, and a translator. To avoid being spotted, Talwar and Sullivan stayed in an empty house owned by the U.S. embassy, instead of checking into a luxurious Omani hotel where they risked being recognized by journalists and intelligence agents. Still, a key benefit of having Sullivan and Talwar lead the U.S. team was that they were both relatively unknown at the time.[18]

Talwar was a former staffer to Senator Joe Biden, who had followed his old boss to the White House. Unlike most U.S. government officials working on the Iran issue, Puneet did not have a nonproliferation or a sanctions background. He held regional expertise and was very knowledgeable about Iran—the country, and not just Iran as a nuclear dilemma. And he was the only White House staffer who had actually visited the country. In 2001, in between serving on the State Department's Policy Planning staff and returning to serve on Senator Biden's staff, Talwar paid a brief visit to Iran. Later, he published an article in *Foreign Affairs* arguing for engagement. "By slowly helping Tehran reintegrate into the world community through various multilateral arrangements, Washington can encourage and strengthen positive forces within Iran. This tactic could eventually lead to a rapprochement between the two long-time enemies," he wrote. Later on, Talwar participated in several informal (Track-II) conferences with U.S. and Iranian officials, deepening his knowledge of Iranian politics while earning the respect of the Iranians. I attended a few of those Track-II meetings, and the respect the Iranians showed Puneet was noticeable; others involved in the mediation efforts attributed this to his being knowledgeable and firm while never seeking to bully the Iranians.[19]

Jake Sullivan, a rising star within Washington's foreign policy elite, was the youngest person inside the negotiations. At only thirty-one years of age, he had advised Hillary Clinton on foreign policy during the 2008 primaries. Once Obama clinched the nomination, he was quickly recruited by the Illinois senator, who used his expertise and debating skills to prep for the presidential debates with Senator John McCain. A Rhodes Scholar and Yale Law alumnus, Sullivan was inseparable from Secretary Clinton, accompanying her on all of her 112 foreign trips as secretary of state. And like Clinton, his disposition was to err on the side of suspicion and hawkishness. He felt very comfortable playing the bad cop within the U.S. team negotiating with Iran. "He didn't have the high profile and years of experience that others had who could have been sent," Clinton told Mark Landler of the *New York Times*. "But he had my full confidence, and he was still low-enough profile that he could travel back and forth without inciting undue interest."[20]

The Iranians brought a four-man team headed by Deputy Foreign Minister Ali Asghar Khaji, head of the North America office in Iran's

Ministry of Foreign Affairs, Reza Zabib, Reza Najafi, who later became Iran's ambassador to the International Atomic Energy Agency in Vienna, and Mohsen Baharvand, who was responsible for Latin America at the Foreign Ministry.[21]

The talks took place in a beautiful room at one of the sultan's palaces. The Iranians, ever so wary, given how previous secret negotiations with the United States had hurt the careers of those conducting them, arrived through a different entrance and avoided shaking the hands of their American counterparts. The head of the Iranian delegation, Ambassador Khaji, stayed in a different room and did not interact with the Americans at all. The Iranians even insisted that Salem, who had preferred to let the two sides discuss matters on their own, stay in the room so they would not have to be in the room alone with the Americans.

Nevertheless, the atmosphere of the talks was far better than the strained and often tense ambience in the P5 + 1 rounds. There were some heated moments, but the tone was cordial and businesslike, devoid of high rhetoric and posturing. Most important, because they were far away from the eyes of the media, the Iranians no longer felt the need to speechify and present a litany of their grievances against the United States. "That basically never happened," Sullivan recalled. There were even a few lighthearted moments with the two sides developing a certain degree of sympathy for each other's domestic political dilemmas.[22]

But the improved atmosphere did not change the fact that the two sides were still far apart in their objectives and ambitions. While the Iranians wanted to discuss substance—particularly getting the United States to accept Iranian enrichment—the American delegation was there only to discuss process. For the U.S. side, it was "meant to be a kind of reconnaissance just to see if the Iranians would engage," Deputy Secretary Bill Burns explained. For a second meeting to occur, the Obama administration wanted to authenticate that the channel was real and that the Iranians had the authority of the supreme leader to negotiate, as well as to find out whether they could agree on an agenda. "The first meeting was an exploratory meeting to see whether the channel could be formally set up," Jake Sullivan explained. "It was really intended to confirm face to face that the Iranians were serious," Richard Nephew, who worked at the White House at the time, added. The

Iranians, on the other hand, had only one objective: to pin the United States down on the enrichment issue. If the United States wanted real negotiations, it had to first accept that the parameters for the talks would not include forbidding Iran from enriching uranium, Tehran insisted.[23]

The talks lasted only one day, most of which was spent with the U.S. side rejecting never-ending attempts by the Iranians to win the United States' acceptance of Iranian enrichment. While the United States wanted to see what restrictions to its program Iran was willing to consider, Iran wanted a firm commitment that at the end of the talks, Iran would not lose what it considered to be its sovereign right. "We recognize that you have some concerns, although we do not buy your justification for those concerns," the Iranians told Sullivan and Talwar, according to Iran's Foreign Minister Salehi. "But you should also recognize our right, why otherwise should we enter into negotiations?" The U.S. side was frustrated by Iran's relentlessness on the enrichment issue. They suspected that the Omanis might have overpromised in order to get the Iranians in the room. "The Iranians came to the meeting with the misimpression that we were prepared to sign a document that recognized their right to enrichment," Samore said. "I think the Iranians were terribly disappointed when they showed up and found out that they had been given false assurances." The Iranians left empty-handed on the enrichment issue, and the Americans left convinced that while the channel was authoritative and that the Omanis could deliver, the Iranians were not fully serious, since they were not willing to discuss restrictions to their program. "It didn't go very well," Sullivan recalled. "It didn't seem the Iranians were all that serious."[24]

Salem was concerned that a second meeting would not be scheduled. The United States was entering its presidential elections, which further increased the damage any leak about the channel would cause, while also reducing the Obama administration's willingness to show flexibility. Any concession to the Iranians in a secret negotiation months before the presidential elections was a nonstarter. However, while the U.S. side was not in a position to offer any concessions, it did not want the channel to collapse. After all, the channel had the backing of Khamenei, and the diplomats Iran had sent to Oman were "serious." "That was enough to indicate to us that the supreme leader could be invested in diplomacy," Rhodes explained. Sullivan told Salem the United States would be open to a second meeting, but that the Iranians "need to go back and think hard about whether they're going to keep insisting on refusing to talk in any serious way about the restraints that they need to accept." Whether Salem conveyed the message to the Iranians in those precise words remains unclear, given the Omanis' apprehension that Tehran would only dig in its heels if it felt the Americans were talking down to them and ordering them around.[25]

The United States had hoped the mere fact that the Iranians had approved a secret channel was an indication that they were ready to show flexibility and give concessions. There was not optimism, but there was a hope that perhaps the sanctions were working and forcing the Iranians to get "serious." "That the Iranians were prepared to send a delegation to Oman for secret talks, I saw that as an indication that they might be looking for a way out," Samore said. But save for the speechifying, the Iranian position in the secret talks was no different from its immovable stance in the P5 + 1 negotiations. Despite sanctions, assassinations, and threats of war, the Iranians were not going to budge unless the United States yielded on enrichment.[26]

The "Concession"

By early 2013, while Iran's firebrand President Mahmoud Ahmadinejad was still in power, the most consequential American decision on Iran since 2009 was reached: the United States was now ready to signal acceptance of Iranian enrichment. It was a card Obama had always planned to play, because he did not believe that it was possible to completely roll back the Iranian nuclear program. The question for the Obama administration was not whether to play the card, but when. The plan had all along been to relinquish zero enrichment at the *end* of a fruitful negotiation—once Iran had accepted restrictions to its program. "When we talked about it internally, obviously, we envisioned enrichment," Deputy National Security Advisor Ben Rhodes explained. "The president, in his mind, . . . had made this decision long ago." Offering it too soon, however, would be giving away the United States' best negotiation card. But now, as sanctions had failed to halt Iran's nuclear progress and no meaningful progress had been made in the P5+1 process, Obama was ready to do what previously had been unthinkable: play the enrichment card upfront. It was a momentous decision, and one the Obama administration preferred to bring as little attention to as possible, even after the secret channel was revealed in November 2013. Whether the gambit would work or not, its consequences would no doubt be immense. After all, the biggest leverage the

United States had over Iran was not the damage its sanctions could inflict, but the nuclear flexibility its acceptance of Iranian enrichment could elicit.[1]

While the world's eyes were locked on the ongoing P5 + 1 talks that had moved to the freezing cold of the Kazakh steppes, the real show was taking place in secret in the heat of the Omani mountains overlooking the Arabian Sea. While the Americans in Kazakhstan provided Iran with a new proposal that offered no major sanctions relief and no movement on enrichment, in Oman obstinacy had given way to realism.[2]

Since the inception of the nuclear crisis, the main sticking point had been the enrichment issue. The United States wanted to prevent the spread of that technology, since the risk of nuclear proliferation would grow as more countries developed indigenous enrichment capabilities. This was particularly worrisome in the case of Iran, a country that challenged the United States' regional and global leadership and was embroiled in a lethal rivalry with Israel. As a result, the Bush administration had adopted the zero-enrichment objective, meaning that any nuclear program in Iran could not include any enrichment capacity whatsoever. Key nonproliferation advisors in the Obama administration, such as Gary Samore, did not disagree with that objective. But increasingly, discussion was less about whether such an outcome was desirable and more whether it was actually achievable. By insisting on zero, the Bush administration had squandered earlier opportunities to limit Iran's enrichment capacity. All measures to stop and roll back the program through coercive measures, sanctions, and assassinations had failed. Iran's centrifuges had instead steadily grown in numbers and efficiency.

This also held true for the Obama years, when the Iranians repeatedly insisted that there could be no meaningful movement unless the issue of enrichment was clarified upfront—at every meeting from Geneva to Istanbul to Baghdad to Moscow. The Obama administration was careful not to publicly adopt a clear position rejecting enrichment. Obama didn't "want to stake out an adamant position that zero was the only solution, because that would have made negotiations futile," Robert Einhorn explained. Signaling openness to enrichment down the road, however, was trickier. For instance, Obama officials were careful to always articulate that their objective was to prevent an Iranian nuclear weapon, not an Iranian nuclear *capability*—which was a euphemism for enrichment. "We always said nuclear weapon," the president's Deputy National Security Advisor Ben Rhodes told me. "The Israelis and others would always urge us to say 'nuclear capability.' So we had already signaled [that enrichment could be accepted] by deliberately refusing to say 'nuclear capability.' I actually thought that the enrichment question was resolved on that debate."[3]

But Iran's mistrust of the United States made such rhetorical distinctions hopelessly impotent. The Iranians required a crystal clear commitment from the United States—*in writing*. According to Jake Sullivan, "That was the overriding message [the Iranians] were sending: We are not going to talk seriously about any kind of nuclear deal that is a zero-enrichment nuclear deal. Period. Period. Period. Period. Exclamation point." On this point, there was universal agreement within the P5+1. "The main purpose of the Iranian engagement in this negotiation was exactly a desire to achieve universal recognition of their right to enrich," the head of the Russian negotiation team, Ambassador Sergey Ryabkov, told me.[4]

The United States' position was largely supported by the West, but it was a clear minority position in a global context. In August 2012, the Non-Aligned Movement, a group of 120 states, endorsed Iran's claim to enrichment rights, undercutting the American argument that Iran was an isolated outlier nation. Both Russia and China also recognized enrichment as a sovereign right. In early 2012, Russian Prime Minister Vladimir Putin penned an op-ed arguing that the international community should recognize Iran's right to enrich in exchange for putting the Iranian program under IAEA supervision. "We propose recognizing Iran's right to develop a civilian nuclear program, including the right to enrich uranium," Putin wrote. "But this must be done in exchange for putting all Iranian nuclear activity under reliable and comprehensive IAEA safeguards." In the view of the Russians, the insistence on zero enrichment was an obstacle to an agreement. "I couldn't believe and I still don't believe that any agreement would ever be possible if the U.S. all along would stick to the position that zero enrichment is the only option," Ryabkov argued.[5]

While the European Union had started off supporting the American position, there were divisions within the European Union on the matter as well as a gradual shift on this issue. Back in 2004, "the Europeans were pretty firm on enrichment too," the British ambassador to Washington, Peter Westmacott, told me. (Fluent in Persian and having served in Iran, Westmacott later played a critical role in making the case for the nuclear deal with Iran on Capitol Hill.) "Up to 2005, we did not consider enrichment, even limited enrichment like we have now on the Iranian side," one of the leading EU negotiators, Helga Schmid, explained. The Germans had always held a softer position on enrichment and had early on pushed the United States to shift its position. The French, on the other hand, had earned a reputation for being more hawkish on this issue than the Obama administration. The matter was discussed regularly between the European Union and the United States, but during Obama's first term, Washington simply wasn't ready to shift its position. Diplomatic proposals developed by the European Union had to be stripped of any language on enrichment, for instance. "We obviously favored that at some stage we'd have to play the enrichment card, but the U.S. was the problem," a key member of the EU negotiating team told me. Privately, however, senior U.S. officials conceded to the Europeans that enrichment had to be accepted. And within the U.S. intelligence agencies, this question had been settled long ago.[6]

But for Washington, the issue had repercussions beyond Iran. If enrichment as a "right" was conceded, the United States would find it difficult to convince other states to refrain from acquiring the technology—or limiting enrichment, for that matter. "The Iranians said, 'Once you recognize my right, I will be able to limit it. . . . But you can't impose on me to limit my rights,'" Javier Solana told me; he had headed the EU negotiations with Iran up until 2010. Given Washington's distrust of Iran, confidence that Iran would stick to its promise to limit its enrichment activities once the right had been recognized was next to zero. So the trick was to accept limited enrichment in Iran without conceding that it was a right.[7]

After the U.S. elections in November 2012, months after the failed July meeting in Oman, the years'-long debate within the White House reignited. President Obama felt that the time had come to play the enrichment card. Within the White House, Ben Rhodes, Puneet Talwar, Richard Nephew, and the president's chief of staff, Denis McDonough, agreed. Secretary Clinton, Gary Samore, and National Security Advisor Tom Donilon were skeptical. "They were worried about the strategic implications, they were worried about the political implications, they were worried about legacy. There were a lot of problems associated with this," Nephew recalled.[8]

Beyond the fact that in its second term political considerations began to play a less decisive role, the Obama administration's pivotal decision to shift its policy at this point was born out of several critical factors that all were coming to a head, from the failure of sanctions to elicit Iranian flexibility, to the risk of war increasing precisely as a result of negotiations getting stuck on the enrichment issue, to the fear that the pain from sanctions had reached its peak and would be dwindling as time passed on.[9]

Meanwhile, the Omanis had continued to press upon the Americans the need for a more realistic position on the enrichment issue throughout 2012, as their mediation efforts continued. They deliberately played the role of making Iran's case to the United States, partly to ensure that the Americans "fully understood and appreciated the depth of Iranian mistrust toward the U.S.," but also because of a conviction that Washington didn't fully understand Iran and made several false assumptions about the motives of the Iranians. For instance, the Omanis questioned the assumption that remained unchallenged within the United States: that the true motive behind the Iranian nuclear program was to obtain a weapon or weapons capability. This had earned the Omanis a reputation within the Obama administration of being "sympathetic to the Iranian point of view."[10]

Oman was not alone in questioning Washington's analysis of Iran. Even strong U.S. allies like Germany felt that the United States' understanding of Iran was limited, and that this lack of comprehension impacted its policies. "Germany has normal diplomatic relations, which makes a huge difference in our understanding of Iran," a senior German diplomat told me. "Just relying on intelligence, as the U.S. is forced to do, can distort things. It becomes all about drama, doom and gloom, and never about the normal things. Till this day, the U.S. still has an unnatural relationship with Iran."[11]

With the dual-track policy failing to produce results and the risk of war increasing, the patience of some P5+1 states with the sanctions policy was growing thin. Even in Washington, where the political constituency favoring diplomacy often found itself hopelessly outgunned, that group began feeling some wind in its sails. In an open letter to President Obama in December 2012, twenty-four prominent former diplomats, military officers, and Iran and arms control experts urged the president to pursue more robust and creative diplomacy to try to reach a negotiated settlement with Iran. "We strongly encourage you to take immediate action to reengage in the direct multilateral and bilateral diplomacy with Iran," the letter stated. In the prestigious magazine *Foreign Affairs,* renowned international relations scholar Robert Jervis urged the Obama administration to "up its game and take an unusually smart and bold approach to negotiations." Even Iranian critics of the clerical regime in Tehran voiced their disapproval of the state of diplomacy. Seven former Iranian reformist members of the Majlis penned an open letter urging for a new, more generous P5+1 package that included acceptance of enrichment, in order to avoid war.[12]

In addition to these calls, there were signs that the Iranian economy had started to adjust to the sanctions at the same time that concern in the White House was growing that the sanctions discipline was fracturing among several countries, since the policy had failed to produce results. The White House was getting reports from the Treasury Department indicating that with every passing month, the United States' ability to sustain the sanctions coalition was weakening. "Oil exports were circling back up, there's going to be more leakage, there's going to be more cheating, there's going to be more fraying at the seams of this whole thing, as countries begin to get unhappy with us for making them hang in there for so long," Sullivan explained.[13]

To a large extent, the problem was that the United States and its partners had already hit Iran's main industries with sanctions. Any additional sanctions would only marginally increase the pressure. A point had been reached where the sanctions policy was starting to have diminishing returns. "It was certainly becoming clear in 2012, when I started at the NSC, that we were starting to get close to peak pressure," White House staffer Chris Backemeyer explained to me. "The sanctions pressure wasn't going to last forever." Iran's strategy of nuclear escalation did not suffer from similar limitations. It was becoming "increasingly evident Iran could dramatically increase its uranium enrichment capacity far more quickly than the United States and the international community could botch it up with sanctions pressure," according to Kelsey Davenport of the Arms Control Association, a leading nonproliferation organization in Washington. "If Iran chose to move toward a nuclear weapon, it could have the fuel to move more quickly than the international community could bring Iran to its knees via the sanctions route."[14]

Moreover, since the goal was to roll back Iran's program to whatever extent possible, the more time passed, the taller that order would be, considering Iran's incessant expansion of its nuclear activities. This was an important factor in the decision to play the enrichment card in Oman: "If you were going to not only freeze but also roll back their program in an interim step, and then embark on a comprehensive agreement, the sooner you got going on that the better," in the words of Deputy Secretary Bill Burns. This, combined with the fact that there was an "expiration date for both oil sanctions and for keeping the allies on board," meant that there was "little doubt that time worked against us," according to several Obama administration and State Department officials involved.[15]

This meant that Iran's nuclear clock was ticking faster than Washington's sanctions clock. The Iranians would achieve an unstoppable breakout capability before the United States could cripple their economy (or have economic mayhem bring about regime change in Iran). This was the third factor that led to the change in the Obama administration's approach. And not only was the Iranian nuclear program growing; it was reaching alarming levels. "Sanctions never stopped their program," recalled Wendy Sherman, one of Obama's lead negotiators. "Every year that went by, they had more centrifuges, more capacity, and more capability."[16]

In January 2012, Secretary of Defense Leon Panetta had estimated that Iran's breakout time stood at twelve months. By January 2013, Iran had reduced its breakout time to only eight to twelve weeks. If Iran decided to dash for a bomb, the United States might not have enough time to stop Tehran militarily. "We recognized that there was some urgency to get a freeze on the progress of their program by the beginning of 2013, because their breakout time was falling to the point where it could go under two months in just a matter of weeks," Sullivan pointed out. In addition, the heavy-water reactor at Arak was almost within twelve to eighteen months of being turned on, providing Iran with a plutonium path as well as uranium path to a nuclear device. At a public event in Washington, former senior National Security Council Director Phil Gordon explained that "Iran was essentially on the threshold of a nuclear weapons capability when the United States initiated the secret nuclear talks with Iran in early 2013."[17]

The growth of Iran's nuclear program and the failure of sanctions to stop it gave the Netanyahu government an additional opportunity to push the United States to take military action. The Israelis argued that the sanctions track—the very same pressure policy they had been the main driver for—was failing and that the United States must be prepared to take out Iran's facilities militarily. "We've seen the consequences of a rogue regime having atomic weapons," Netanyahu told reporters, making reference to North Korea. "Tough sanctions and talk don't always do the job." His defense minister, Moshe Yaalon, was even more explicit: "The Western states must understand that only assertive action will curb the threat. Only forcing the Iranian regime to choose between a bomb or survival will bring Iran to halt the project." Similar pressures were also emanating from Saudi Arabia and some Arab countries in the Persian Gulf, though they primarily pressed the U.S. government privately. Leaked U.S. government cables in 2011 revealed that King Abdullah of Saudi Arabia had repeatedly urged Obama to attack Iran, or more precisely, exhorted the United States "to cut off the head of the snake."[18]

The shrinking of Iran's breakout time—which was not just a manifestation of the failure of sanctions to halt Iran's program but also a direct result of Iran's reaction to the sanctions policy—caused the threat of war to peak by late 2012. In fact, it was higher at this point than at any moment during the G. W. Bush administration, despite Obama's extensive efforts to avoid war. "Before the negotiations for the nuclear deal began," according to former CIA deputy director Michael Morell, "we were closer to war with the Islamic Republic than at any time since 1979." If a diplomatic exit was not found, the sanctions and nuclear escalation would eventually make war next to inevitable. "I expected that if we continued to intensify the sanctions, at some point they would have said, 'Now we need to start producing [enrichment at] 60 percent. Now we need to produce [it at] 90 percent,'" Samore said. "At some point that would have ended in a war. . . . That was certainly Obama's view."[19]

This dire assessment was shared by the other P5 + 1 states. "The actual threat of military action was almost felt as electricity in the air before a thunderstorm," Russian Deputy Foreign Minister Sergey Ryabkov pointed out. For Russia, another war on its southern border would be a greater disaster than an Iran with a nuclear capability. For the European Union, which also felt that the pressure gambit had brought the situation dangerously close to war, this "was a nightmare scenario."[20]

Washington had miscalculated. The expectation and calculation had been that the sanctions policy would change Iran's cost-benefit analysis: Iran would resist, but eventually its breaking point would be reached. The key was to sustain the pressure, keep the Israelis at bay, and provide Iran with a face-saving exit. It was important that the off-ramp for Iran was not humiliation. This analysis was premised on the theory that when push came to shove, Iran's leaders would fear war and economic collapse more than nuclear retreat. But this was a false premise.[21]

This brings us to the fourth factor that led to the shift regarding zero enrichment: not only did the Iranians insist that they still had escalation options, while the West had ran out of things to sanction— "Iran can vastly expand the nuclear program, build more plants, add centrifuges, grow the stockpile, enrich beyond 50 percent, etc. What additional sanctions can the U.S. impose?" an Iranian analyst close to the Iranian Supreme National Security Council said—but Iran's internal political dynamics were drastically different from what Washington and its allies had expected.[22]

The heart of the matter was Ayatollah Khamenei's incentive structure—and the domestic constraints the Iranian leaders faced. The

Iranians had tied themselves into a narrative that contended that the nuclear issue ultimately was a pretext the West used to pressure Iran, to deprive it of access to science, and to deny it the ability to live up to its full potential. An Iran that would actualize its full potential would be the most powerful state in the Middle East, the Iranians contended, due to its population size, human capital, natural resources, and scientific progress. Such an Iran would be a potent challenger to U.S. domination of the region—a prospect the West desperately sought to prevent. This was a historic reality, the Iranian narrative maintained, and not just a recent phenomenon. For the past two centuries, Western colonialist designs for the region had necessitated balancing Iran by undercutting it while building up Iran's Arab neighbors. The nuclear issue was just the latest chapter in a long list of Western efforts to subjugate Iran.

The Iranians pointed to British interference in Iranian domestic politics in the nineteenth and twentieth centuries, including the 1953 coup against Iran's democratically elected prime minister, Mohammad Mossadeq, in order to prevent Iran from nationalizing its oil industry (Mossadeq demanded that 50 percent of Iran's oil income belong to the Iranian state, a demand the British—who had control of the industry and offered Iran only 19 percent—found unacceptable). Even the shah, whom the United States and Britain put into power after the 1953 coup, was subject to the same treatment from the West. When the Iranian monarch sought to make Iran a steel producer and exporter, the United States and the United Kingdom denied Iran access to the necessary technology to establish a steel industry. Washington and London argued that Iran should meet its steel needs by buying on the international steel market. Instead—in an eerie parallel to the nuclear issue—the shah had to turn to the Communist leaders in Moscow (whom he loathed) to acquire the required steel technology. (Today, Russia is the biggest outside actor in the Iranian nuclear program.)[23]

According to the Iranian narrative, history proved that collaboration with the United States would not end the West's efforts to subjugate Iran. From the Conoco deal in 1994, to Iran's crucial assistance in Afghanistan in 2001, to its negotiation offer in 2003, to the Tehran Declaration in 2010, history was ripe with examples of instances when Iranian conciliatory gestures had only invited even harsher Western policies. In a speech in February 2013, Khamenei specifically pointed to this in arguing in favor of a strategy of resistance:

> Sanctions are painful and they are a nuisance, but there are two ways to react to such pain: one group are those who start begging for forgiveness, but a brave nation like Iran will try to mobilize its inner resources and to pass through the "danger zone" with determination and courage. . . . The Americans should show that they don't want to bully us, that they won't engage in evil acts, show us that their words and deeds are not illogical and that they respect the rights of the Iranian people, show that they won't push the region into further confrontations and that they won't interfere in the internal affairs of the Iranian people—they will see that the Islamic Republic has good will and the people are logical. This is the only way to interact with the Islamic Republic.[24]

Khamenei thus insisted that as long as Iran stood firm and refused to back down, global sanctions fatigue would ultimately cause the collapse of this policy and force the West to come to terms with Iran once and for all. No competing narrative had emerged in Iran precisely because of Iran's past experiences with the West. "Even though regime members outside the core can have a voice and influence, it is sad to say that none of them actually has a strategy on how to amend the national security policy," a regime insider explained. "Therefore, the core around Ayatollah Khamenei is not only the most powerful, but also the only group that has a strategy."[25]

The failure of critics within the regime to formulate an alternative strategy and narrative rested partly on the failure of Western countries to paint and convincingly communicate an alternative path for Iran. Mindful of the United States' refusal to offer any meaningful sanctions relief in the P5 + 1 negotiations, these critics could not make the case that a softer Iranian nuclear stance would provide an honorable exit from the nuclear standoff. No convincing indications had been provided by the P5 + 1 on how the dynamics of nuclear negotiations would change if Iran changed its behavior. Consequently, the hardline narrative was not only unchallenged during internal debates, but it was further cemented by the escalatory dynamic of the pressure policies both sides pursued. In addition, precisely because the pressure was focused on Iran's nuclear program, which the Iranians viewed as their sovereign right, it helped fuel nationalist sentiments inside Iran, which further unified the country. In the words of Iran's Foreign Minister Javad Zarif:

> [The outside pressure] provided a means for ensuring domestic national consensus [in favor of the enrichment program]. So interestingly enough, you had this dichotomy where internationally, the nuclear issue provided consensus [against Iran within the P5+1] and domestically it provided consensus [against the United States]. . . . This was the single most effective way of uniting the Iranian people.[26]

In the absence of the emergence of an alternative Iranian narrative to pave the way for a shift in policy, the sanctions strategy simply could not succeed in changing Iran's nuclear calculus. Even the stark divisions among the Iranian elite failed to affect regime cohesion when it came to the nuclear issue or the response to sanctions. Instead, sanctions seemed to have been a uniting rather than a dividing factor for the Iranian elite. Moreover, although the Iranian private sector was devastated by the sanctions, its players did not lobby the Iranian regime to shift its nuclear policy—as the sanctions strategy had predicted—precisely because of the absence of an alternative narrative. Instead, it lobbied to maximize concessions from the government *within* the existing strategy of resisting the pressure from the West.[27]

Proponents of the sanctions strategy within the White House, however, contended that the sanctions policy would not yield results in a linear manner. In this narrative, Tehran would be able to resist sanctions for an extended period of time, only to yield to the pressure after an inflection point had been reached. Before such an inflection point was reached, the success or failure of sanctions could not be determined. Nevertheless, inflection points do not emerge randomly; the factors causing them to emerge can be predicted. These include the development of a narrative within the elite that challenged the status quo policy and signs that important constituencies in Iran, like the business community, had begun pressing the government to change its nuclear policy. But as of late 2012, it was clear that an inflection was not likely to be reached before the sanctions pressure started to wane down and the risk of war became unavoidable. In the words of Roberto Toscano, Italy's former ambassador to Iran:

> Pragmatic voices within the regime . . . should be capable of convincingly stressing that both national interest and regime survival would be better pursued by abandoning not only [Iran's] provocative rhetoric but also its ideological intransigence. The problem is that this is made more difficult by sanctions, a godsend for those who are trying to rally Iranians around the regime and against external pressure.[28]

The pressure strategy was working in the sense of hurting Iran's economy, but overall it was not succeeding. This was due to its failure to shift Iran's nuclear calculus, precisely because it lacked the sophistication to help unravel the dominant Iranian narrative and entice elements within the Iranian elite to push for policy changes. Moreover, as the game of chicken initiated by the sanctions policy was leading the United States and Iran to accelerate toward the cliff, the belief that the Iranians would eventually yield in order to avoid war was also failing to pan out. Once again, the West had miscalculated Ayatollah Khamenei's incentive structure.

Iran's supreme leader was well aware that the fraudulent elections of 2009 had cost him several constituencies, making him all the more dependent on the few remaining constituents who supported the regime and believed it to be legitimate. These supporters also tended to be the ones who were most fervently committed to the narrative that resistance against the West was necessary to uphold Iran's independence. Any shift in that policy would be perceived by these constituencies as a capitulation to Western demands—that is, a violation of the regime's narrative of resistance—and could put Khamenei's—and the regime's—survival at risk by causing the last constituencies supporting the clerical system to turn against it.

"We felt we had to resist despite the cost because we were presented with a choice: either resist despite the cost or capitulate and show a green light for the West to pressure us on other issues as well," said President Hassan Rouhani's chief of staff, Mohammad Nahavandian, who at the time served as the head of Iran's Chamber of Commerce. Perhaps more importantly, from Khamenei's vantage point such a scenario was a greater threat to the regime's survival than even a military confrontation with the United States. While Khamenei likely did not believe Iran could win a war against the United States, he certainly believed he could survive a war—and even come out of it stronger at home.[29]

This was the most consequential factor of them all, and by early 2013, this reality had dawned upon decision-makers in the White House: war with Iran was more likely than Iran capitulating to the sanctions strategy. "I think we were coming to the realization that unless something changed, we were headed in a bad path," a former White House official said. "We were headed toward some sort of military conflict with Iran." Washington's Omani interlocutors had on numerous occasions conveyed that Iranian officials such as Salehi had insisted both that Iran would risk war and that it would not give up enrichment, and Oman's own analysts had also reached this conclusion. Oman believed that Iran knew it would lose the war but believed war would also be the end of American influence in region.[30]

Iranian officials told me throughout 2010–2012 that the Iraq war had already transformed the United States from a superpower to a "limping giant." Another war in the region, and the United States would be finished as a superpower, and its domination in the Middle East would be brought to an end. Iran would also be devastated by the war, but it would bounce back after a decade or two, and benefit from the opportunity to shape the new order in the region that the United States' exit from the Middle East would help bring to pass. While this was at first dismissed as nothing but Iranian bravado, by 2013 it had become more difficult to reject the idea that this might be a serious Iranian calculation.[31]

When my colleagues Bijan Khajehpour and Reza Marashi and I presented a report to the U.S. government with these very conclusions in early 2013, one of the architects of the sanctions regime challenged us

by arguing that it was not the business community that they had envisioned lobbying for a shift in Iran's nuclear strategy. Rather, a point
would be reached, he argued, in which a senior Iranian Revolutionary
Guard Corps official would have no choice but to confront Khamenei
and implore him to succumb to Western demands lest Iran's economy
collapse. I acknowledged that sanctions could produce such a point of
crisis but asked him in turn: With what confidence do you believe that
the IRGC official would recommend Khamenei to capitulate instead of
urging him to prepare for war? He provided no answer, but his facial
expression was revealing.[32]

At a different meeting at the White House two years later, a senior
White House official shared Obama's conclusion that Iranian capitulation
simply was not in the cards. The manner in which he explained it, however, hinted that the Obama administration had acquired a deeper understanding of Iran's calculations. "The Iranians simply won't capitulate
[even if faced with war]," the official said. "Because they're *Iranians*," he
added after a brief pause.[33] Obama himself publicly acknowledged when
the negotiations were starting to make progress that Iranian capitulation was not a viable outcome:

> Iran is not going to simply dismantle its program because we
> demand it to do so. That's not how the world works, and
> that's not what history shows us. Iran has shown no willing-
> ness to eliminate those aspects of their program that they
> maintain are for peaceful purposes, even in the face of unpre-
> cedented sanctions.[34]

And even if playing the enrichment card would not help prevent war, it
would still fulfill a crucial function. If the United States did end up taking military action against Iran's nuclear facilities, it would have to justify to the American public and to the international community that all
efforts had been made to resolve the conflict peacefully. Given the near
consensus among key U.S. allies—including other P5+1 nations—that
the zero-enrichment objective was hopelessly unrealistic, not testing it
would open up the United States to significant vulnerabilities. After all,
because multilateralism was a cornerstone of Obama's foreign policy

philosophy, going it alone or with a "coalition of the willing" would be a betrayal of the very ethos of his presidency. "We would have to justify it [the war decision] to history," a former White House official soberly explained.[35]

By all accounts, all of these factors created a strong sense of urgency in the Obama administration by spring 2013. According to some of the EU decision-makers involved, the United States was getting desperate. After all, it was the United States and not Iran that was making the first concession. While acknowledging that enrichment was the United States' most significant card, senior U.S. officials flatly reject that it was played out of desperation and argue that if anything, the United States was in a position of strength. The crucial decision to play that card was made "against the backdrop of strong leverage with the impact that sanctions had had, [prompting] the president to decide that we were going to take a run at serious negotiations," Deputy Secretary of State Burns explained. The United States' leverage was at its peak, and with the sanctions pressure declining, the United States had to "strike while the iron was hot," according to Sullivan. Waiting any longer was inadvisable, because the United States did not know how much longer it could sustain the leverage it had over Iran. Moreover, as Iran's nuclear program was growing, the likelihood of reversing their progress was diminishing, causing the enrichment card to lose value. "You get to a certain point where you've built up a certain amount of leverage, and you either use it, or you lose it," Burns concluded. "Much of that leverage depended on the international cooperation we had built up painstakingly, and it could erode if we were not seen to be engaging seriously in negotiations."[36]

But there was also another factor: the enrichment card may have been virtually played already. According to some White House officials, Kerry had "essentially played that card before he was secretary of state," during his personal diplomacy with the Omanis. That had been done without coordination with or endorsement by the White House, but "when Kerry became secretary of state, in a way the card played itself," according to Rhodes. "Because Kerry had taken that position in his own conversations with the Omanis, it became the U.S. position in a way when Kerry became secretary of state." Kerry denies having enticed the

Iranians by signaling acceptance of enrichment, but in the larger scheme of things, it didn't matter. The bottom line was that by spring 2013, the United States had decided to officially shift its position on the issue that mattered the most to the Iranians and had caused previous diplomatic attempts to fall short. This decision indicated neither strength nor weakness, but rather unprecedented commitment to give diplomacy a real chance.[37]

Iran, like the United States, was acting from neither a position of strength nor one of weakness. If enrichment was the United States' main concession to Iran, agreeing to a bilateral negotiation with the United States was Iran's main concession (albeit procedural rather than substantive) to the United States. And just as Obama had been careful not to categorically rule out acceptance of enrichment in Iran, Ayatollah Khamenei had always kept the door open to giving his blessing to such a dialogue with "the Great Satan," once it was in Iran's interest to do so. In January 2008, for instance, Khamenei rejected relations with the United States, but argued that "on the day this relationship becomes beneficial for Iran, I will be the first to start [it]."[38]

So why did Iran offer the United States this concession? Just as the United States' pressure strategy alone could not elicit Iranian flexibility, neither could an Iranian strategy be centered solely on escalation. While Iran appeared willing to risk war, since capitulation was deemed a greater threat to the regime's survival, war would nevertheless have been a manifestation of the failure—not success—of the Iranian strategy. Yes, Iran might have had more escalatory options left in its arsenal than the United States did, but if escalation did ultimately lead to war, this would still have been a negative outcome from Tehran's perspective. "While everyone knows that Iran will resist pressure, it was clear that nobody wanted, or at least nobody in their right mind on either side, should want a confrontation," Zarif explained to me. "And certainly we didn't." The reality was that both sides were running out of de-escalatory opportunities while their escalatory options were becoming increasingly dangerous. If one of the objectives of Iran's escalation was to clarify to Washington that its pressure strategy would lead to war, it was incumbent on Iran to test exits from the escalatory cycle once the Obama administration had accepted that reality. American capitulation was no more in the cards than Iranian capitulation.[39]

Furthermore, if the dangers of war and the impact of sanctions were Iran's weak points, the advancement of its nuclear program was its strength. With Iran's breakout capability measured in weeks, Iran had essentially reached its nuclear objectives, some within the Iranian system argued, so continuing to endure sanctions made little sense if temporary and reversible limitations to the program could bring about relief from the economic pressure. "At that point, it made no sense to continue to pay the price of sanctions," explained Professor Nasser Hadian, an advisor to Iran's foreign minister. "It could negotiate from a position of strength. Even if sanctions hadn't been so costly, Iran would have moved to talks because the nuclear circumstances were in its favor."[40]

The question was whether Ayatollah Khamenei could be convinced that the time had come to test the United States' willingness to accept Iranian enrichment in a direct negotiation. This is where the enrichment card played a critical role: the sultan of Oman—whom Khamenei held in the highest regard—insisted that the Obama administration was planning to accept enrichment during the secret negotiations. The prospect of the United States conceding this important issue played a pivotal role in convincing Khamenei to give a green light to direct negotiations and the second Oman meeting. Then foreign minister Ali Akbar Salehi made the case to Khamenei as to why Washington was ready to take this crucial step. "The argument that I raised with the supreme leader was the fact that the P5+1 had realized it wasn't really making progress in its [pressure] approach," Salehi explained to me.[41]

Many of Salehi's arguments were mirror images of arguments used on the American side to justify playing the enrichment card. In fact, the similarities between Washington and Tehran's reasoning behind their decisions to offer a painful concession to the other side reflected the symmetrical situation in which they both found themselves: neither could force the other to capitulate, neither could rely solely on pressure, neither would benefit from war, and neither had a more attractive option than to finally—when all else had failed—give diplomacy a real chance.[42]

Back to Muscat

Nine months after what was universally considered a failed meeting in Muscat in July 2012, the United States returned to the Omani capital with a larger and more senior delegation armed with the authority to test if the enrichment card could break the nuclear deadlock and steer the United States and Iran away from war. To signal the United States' sincerity, the delegation was now headed by none other than Deputy Secretary William "Bill" Burns, one of the United States' most well-regarded and most efficient diplomats. Much like Secretary John Kerry, Burns was soft-spoken and had courteous manners, both of which made him able to win the respect of the Iranians. With the United States having elevated the rank of their delegation, Iran's Deputy Foreign Minister Ali Khaji—who shared Burns's rank in the Iranian foreign ministry—no longer participated in the talks from afar, but instead joined them directly (the Iranians tend to be adamant about protocol). Another addition to the U.S. delegation was Robert Einhorn, a senior nonproliferation hand with extensive experience dealing with the Iranians, both from earlier negotiations during the Obama years and from informal (Track-II) meetings dating back as early as the early 2000s.

While the discretion and secrecy of the first Oman meeting continued to characterize the channel—the State Department public schedules mysteriously showed Burns's calendar as blank for the first four days in March 2013—both the atmosphere and venue were more relaxing: a beachside Omani officers' club overlooking the warm waters of the Arabian Sea. The Omanis had also changed the modalities. The diplomats were divided into different teams, working in parallel and occasionally taking walks in the garden of the club to build a stronger personal rapport. Salem, the Omani interlocutor, usually opened the meetings but then left the room to let the Iranians and Americans continue the conversations on their own.[43]

The talks were businesslike, with none of the pontificating over past slights that had characterized the P5+1 talks, though the Iranians continued to insist on getting their right to enrich recognized. "They had their own grievances to get off their chests, but that didn't dominate the discussion," Burns recalled. "So it was practical, it was professional." While both sides suffered from significant constraints, they were constantly searching for possible openings and flexibility on the other side. "They were doing what professional diplomats do. They were probing us, asking intelligent questions, and so forth," Einhorn said.[44]

But as it had in their previous encounters, the conversation quickly got bogged down on enrichment. The moment of truth had arrived: the United States was for the first time going to indicate its conditional acceptance of enrichment. The consensus within the Obama administration was that Burns was the right person to play the card. "If there was a true opening, Bill Burns would know it. And if there wasn't, people in Washington including the president of United States would trust his judgment," Sherman explained.[45]

The U.S. side had carefully crafted the language Burns was authorized to use. The language had gone through numerous iterations to ensure it was properly hedged—it was critical that the Iranians not be able to pocket the concession; it had to be made conditional upon Iran agreeing to significant limitations to their program. The key verb in the formulation was "explore," which was sufficiently ambiguous for the Iranians not to be able to pocket it and sufficiently concrete to signal a real opening. Moreover, Burns was authorized to test but not to agree to the proposition—it was a hint of what the United States could potentially agree to rather than a commitment. Instead of directly offering acceptance of enrichment, the intent was to dangle the offer and examine the Iranian reaction. Burns presented the idea as a theoretical possibility in which the United States was willing to contemplate and explore a future in which Iran possessed a nuclear enrichment program subject to a lot of restraints and constraints. "The way it was couched was quite carefully done," Burns recalled. "It was basically [that] whether we would be prepared to explore a very limited domestic enrichment program would depend on whether Iran was prepared to explore the kind of sharp constraints and sharp limitations on the program that the international community would need to see."[46]

The Iranians showed little reaction at first. This was likely part of their negotiating strategy of downplaying the value of the American concession. But it was also because they had been told by the Omanis that the United States would play the enrichment card, and their focus was on reducing any ambiguity or limitations in the American offer, and perhaps most importantly, on ensuring that they get the offer in writing. That was a nonstarter for the U.S. side, however. If they had the U.S. offer in writing, what would stop them from publicizing it and going to the P5+1, thereby fracturing the consensus and unity the Obama administration had carefully built up? "We did not want the Iranians to be able to publicize it," Rhodes said.[47]

After two days of talks, the two sides were stuck. Political constraints in Iran, including vehement opposition to the secret channel from Saeed Jalili, who headed Iran's formal negotiations with the P5+1 at the time, made it difficult for the Iranians to return to Tehran with only an oral offer on enrichment—particularly one as cautiously couched as the one Bill Burns had presented. Once again, the Omanis intervened to find a way to finesse the situation. They arranged it so that both delegations would brief the sultan on the state of the negotiations. The Americans went first, represented by Burns. The sultan had planned to press Burns on the enrichment issue, but Burns beat him to it. The U.S. deputy secretary of state repeated the formulation he had presented to the Iranians but further clarified the signal by pointing out that the Obama administration was willing to do what no other administration had done before. To the Omanis, the American message was clear enough.[48]

The sultan then called in Iranian Deputy Foreign Minister Khaji for a debriefing. Khaji praised the progress that had been made but complained that the enrichment issue remained unresolved—the American formulation was too vague, and unless it was put in writing, Tehran would likely not schedule a third meeting. "We thought that if we don't get anywhere in the sense that the Americans will not show the willingness to recognize our enrichment, then it will be of no use to continue the negotiations," Salehi argued. The sultan reassured the Iranians that based on his debriefing with the Americans just minutes earlier, the issue was settled: the Americans would accept enrichment in Iran, granted that Iran agreed to international inspections and limitations on their nuclear activities. According to Burns, his message to the sultan had not gone beyond what he had told the Iranians, though the sultan might have added his own interpretation when conveying it to Khaji. "I carefully repeated what I had said to the Iranians when I talked to the sultan," Burns explained. "What the Omanis did with that in their own voice is a different issue," he added, indicating that the sultan might have overstated the American position in order to break the deadlock.[49]

The sultan also offered a solution to the Iranian request to receive the American offer in writing. Instead of the United States providing Iran with a written offer—which the Obama administration categorically refused—the United States could convey the written offer to the sultan. The Omani leader would then write a letter to the Iranian president conveying the American message. Once again, the Omanis saved the day. Though both sides wanted further guarantees—the Iranians wanted clearer assurances that the United States would accept enrichment in Iran; the Americans wanted solid affirmation from the supreme leader that he was committed to the bilateral track—the sultan's proposal was enough to get the talks going again.[50]

According to an official involved in the Omani channel, the sultan received a letter from John Kerry reiterating Burns's verbal offer from the Muscat meeting. The Omani leader then sent a letter to Iranian president Mahmoud Ahmadinejad providing his own personal guarantees that the Americans were serious. At that point, the distrust the Iranians had for the United States was overcome by their trust in Sultan Qaboos. The sultan's letter gave the Iranian negotiators the confidence to schedule a third meeting, Salehi said, because "we have this paper in front of us and this is tacitly understood that the right to enrichment is recognized." That meeting was first scheduled for May 2013 but had to be postponed because of the Iranian presidential elections in June of that year. "Once they were in the thick of their presidential campaign, it just wasn't plausible that they would stick their neck out again to do a meeting, so everything basically went on pause," Sullivan recalled.[51]

Obama had cautiously tested the enrichment card, but because of the debilitating distrust between the United States and Iran, it did not generate the immediate breakthrough the White House had hoped for,

even after Sultan Qaboos's priceless finessing. Such a breakthrough required more daring Iranian leadership that would have the courage to
exit the comfort zone of enmity—a leadership that saw strength in diplomacy and compromise, and not just in resistance. Three months after
the meeting in Muscat, the Iranian people shocked the world by electing a new president who prided himself in conducting diplomacy and
striking deals: "the Sheikh of Diplomacy," Hassan Rouhani.

The Sheikh of Diplomacy

The Iranian political system was in dire need of a dose of legitimacy in 2013. Eight years of Mahmoud Ahmadinejad and the fraudulent 2009 election had left Iranians with few reasons to pay attention to the presidential elections. The elections in Iran have never been fair and free. Rather, they've always been a "cat-and-mouse game between a regime that needs to sustain an image of legitimacy, and a civil society that uses every opportunity, however small, to push for change." But after the 2009 debacle, the question was whether there really was much of an opportunity to begin with. If the regime was bound to cheat once more, why bother to vote? On the other hand, boycotting the elections would only have ensured a victory for the hardliners.[1]

Iranian elections are also known for being notoriously late in generating public enthusiasm. The Green movement in 2009, for instance, didn't gain momentum until a few weeks before election day. In 2013, however, indifference toward the political spectacle was pervasive and persistent, leading many to believe that voter participation would be at an all-time low. Even the minimum amount of hope needed to prompt people to cast a vote within a system they lacked confidence in seemed to be lacking.[2]

With only three weeks left before the election, things were getting worse. At the last minute, Iran's former president, the centrist Hashemi

Rafsanjani, decided to throw his hat in the ring. A vocal critic of Ahmadinejad and his confrontational policies, Rafsanjani—who had lost to Ahmadinejad in 2005—had rehabilitated himself with much of Iranian society during the 2009 election debacle by defending the Green movement and opposing the harsh crackdowns. Although being the ultimate regime insider would have counted against Rafsanjani in the elections under normal circumstances, in 2013 it worked in his favor, because he was seen as one of the few politicians that could change the system from within. But on May 21, 2013, Iran's Guardian Council—which is tasked to vet the candidates—shocked the country by rejecting Rafsanjani's candidacy. Apparently, a former president and one of Ayatollah Khomeini's closest confidents no longer passed the regime's arbitrary ideological test. Iran's political spectrum had never been more contracted, and now it left almost no space for dissent.[3]

But with this decision, which in retrospect was likely made in order to balance out the rejection of Ahmadinejad's preferred candidate, Esfandiar Rahim Mashaei, for whom Ayatollah Khamenei had no tolerance, an unlikely boost was given to moderate and reformist politicians in Iran. Faced with the prospect of being permanently sidelined in Iranian politics, they were now forced to set aside their past grievances and present a united front. Ultimately, this proved to be a decisive factor for the unlikely comeback of Iran's moderate forces. "Rafsanjani's disqualification was critical," a member of Rouhani's inner circle told me. "Here's a man who could say 'I am the revolution,' and he was disqualified. This caused people to pause. This created an anger and a momentum for change."[4]

The Guardian Council approved only eight candidates out of 686 registered hopefuls. Six of the approved candidates were conservatives: Iran's chief nuclear negotiator, Saeed Jalili; the mayor of Tehran, Mohammad-Bagher Qalibaf; former foreign minister and Khamenei confidant Ali Akbar Velayati; former parliamentarian Gholam Ali Haddad-Adel; former Iranian Revolutionary Guard Corps commander, Mohsen Reza'I; and former oil minister Mohammad Gharazi. The other two candidates were reformist Mohammad Reza Aref, who had served as vice president in the Khatami government, and the centrist former secretary of the Supreme National Security Council,

Hassan Rouhani. But both Aref and Rouhani were seen as political nonstarters. Aref was uncharismatic and lacked the following that had brought Khatami to power in 1997, and Rouhani's political career was declared dead in 2005, when he became the scapegoat for the failed nuclear negotiations with the European Union, in which Tehran agreed to voluntarily suspend enrichment without the West dropping its zero-enrichment objective. In the eyes of the hardliners who came to dominate Iran's political scene after 2005, Rouhani was a "sellout" who had committed near treason by showing weakness in those negotiations. The Guardian Council seemed to have designed the election slate to ensure a conservative victory, with only symbolic participation by long-shot reformist and moderate contenders.[5]

That was the conservative forces' second crucial mistake. With the conservative vote divided among six candidates, the moderates and reformists would have a fighting chance if they could overcome two obstacles. One was the population's apprehension about partaking in the elections. Hardliners in Iran tend to win elections in two scenarios: when they cheat, and when they convince the population that they will cheat. In the latter scenario, they win by suppressing the non-conservative vote by convincing them that their votes simply won't count. At no point since 1979 had this obstacle been as enormous as it became in 2013. Second, if the two sides could unite around one candidate, they could conceivably finish second in the first round of the elections and face off with the top conservative contender in the second and final round.

The hardliners, however, seemed to have been completely oblivious to this reality, arrogantly believing that the elections were an internal conservative matter. And they were not alone in this belief. Most Western governments expected a conservative victory and had their eyes locked on the presumptive frontrunner, Saeed Jalili. A Jalili victory would have signified a continuation of a policy of "resistance." At his campaign rallies, his supporters chanted the slogan "No compromise, no submission, only Jalili!" while waving placards saying, "Negotiating with Satan is against the Koran." Although Khamenei claimed he did not favor any of the candidates, it was assumed that he backed Jalili because of Jalili's inflexible stance. (While Jalili took the most uncompromising position among the eight candidates, none of them argued in favor of giving up enrichment as a right.) The only positive aspect of his winning, the joke went inside the White House, was that at least he would no longer be the head nuclear negotiator.[6]

But once the televised presidential debates were aired, it started to become clear that the elections might be more dynamic than initially assumed. Rouhani distinguished himself by addressing the nuclear issue and how the Iranian people were suffering from sanctions. "It is good for centrifuges to operate," he said, "but it is also important that the country operates as well, and that the wheels of industry are turning." The country's deteriorating economy had presented Rouhani with an opportunity to aggressively defend his record as nuclear negotiator, mindful of his success in preventing the nuclear file from being referred to the UN Security Council in 2003–2005 (Iran was taken to the Security Council in 2006 under Ahmadinejad's watch). "All our problems [under Ahmadinejad] are because all efforts were not made to prevent the [nuclear] dossier from being sent to the Security Council," he argued, accusing Ahmadinejad and Jalili of mishandling the situation. Among the eight candidates, Rouhani was the only one promising to improve the economy by resolving the nuclear issue through negotiations, and he did so by pointing to his track record of successfully preventing a crisis.[7]

Rouhani's line contradicted the hardline narrative held by the political elite. Within the halls of power, his arguments had failed to make headway. But now, Rouhani took his critique directly to the Iranian people. And he found an unlikely ally in doing so. In a shocking turn of events, Khamenei's personal advisor, Velayati—who was often assumed to speak for Khamenei due to their close relationship—turned on Jalili and criticized his handling of the negotiations. Making unrealistic demands that the West lift all sanctions right away signaled only that Jalili was not seeking to make any progress at all, Velayati charged in one of the debates. An unmistakable signal had been sent: three months after the United States had played the enrichment card, a member of Khamenei's inner circle had for the first time hinted that a shift in Iran's negotiations posture was needed. The conventional wisdom in the West that Khamenei preferred a Jalili victory had to be reassessed.[8] But perhaps more important, the assumption that Khamenei's ideological fervor would not allow him to show flexibility—even if the United States accepted enrichment—had been called into question.

The Reformists and Centrists Unite

Rouhani was fighting a two-front war. On the one hand, he was challenging the hardline candidates. On the other hand, he was courting the Reformist supporters of Aref while delicately trying to convince the former vice president to drop out of the race and throw his support behind him. At first, Aref resisted. He had served as vice president once before and had no interest in being the number two person yet again. Furthermore, the biggest voting bloc was the supporters of the Green movement— that is, reformists who naturally gravitated toward him and not Rouhani. Time was short, and Rouhani knew that unless he could form a united front with the reformists, the elections were lost.

It wasn't until a week before election day that Rafsanjani, who at the time was privately backing Rouhani, managed to convince Aref's former boss, reformist president Mohammad Khatami, that Aref had to call it quits and back Rouhani. Not only was Rouhani a stronger candidate, Rafsanjani argued, but even if Aref were to win the elections, he would be incapable of implementing his agenda, since the hardliners would refuse to work with a reformist. Rouhani, on the other hand, had a history of working with both conservatives and reformists, and would be a more effective president. Moreover, only Rouhani had the experience and expertise to resolve the nuclear issue diplomatically, and besides, Aref wasn't strong enough to stand up to Khamenei.[9]

Khatami was convinced. The next day, Khatami sent Aref a handwritten note, urging him to drop out. Aref, who was in the southern city of Shiraz campaigning, didn't get a chance to get back to Khatami until later that evening. The two reformist leaders held a lengthy phone call but despite Khatami's best efforts, Aref refused to concede. At the end of the call, Khatami could only get a commitment that Aref would mull it over. The next day, Aref bitterly decided that it would be for the greater good if he withdrew his candidacy. As so many Iranian politicians have begun to do, he took to Facebook to announce his resignation and his endorsement of Rouhani. Although the endorsement was lukewarm, it served its purpose: for the first time in the Islamic Republic's history, a unified coalition of centrists and reformists had been formed to defeat Iran's hardliners.[10]

As soon as Aref had dropped out, the Rouhani campaign's focus turned toward convincing the public—particularly the supporters of the Green movement—that despite the 2009 debacle, their votes would count this time around. Their main argument was that although the hardliners had emerged victorious in 2009, the political infighting had severely fractured the regime. Another such episode and the entire regime could collapse. Simply put, the hardliners could afford to cheat once, but they could not afford to cheat twice in a row, lest they risk the lethal delegitimizing effects of another election scandal. At rally after rally, Rouhani pressed upon his supporters that "2013 will not be like 2009."[11]

Within a day after Aref's exit, Khatami and Rafsanjani publicly endorsed Rouhani through prerecorded YouTube videos that quickly went viral. The main message of the videos was to convince the public not to sit out the election. All along, their plan had been to make a big push for a unified candidate but they had needed clarity first: Would Aref drop out, or would Rouhani? The strategy was to deliberately avoid creating momentum for the unified candidate too early in the campaign in order to avoid giving the hardliners enough time to organize any foul play—however foolish that might be. A surprise spike in the last few days before election day would be much preferable to early winds in the coalition candidate's sails, which would give the hardliners time to overcome their divisions and unify around one candidate. "It was very deliberate and clever to wait and not have Rafsanjani and Khatami endorse Rouhani until a few days before the election," said Iranian American journalist Hooman Majd, who is related by marriage to Khatami.[12]

With only four days left to the elections, Rouhani was still trailing far behind his conservative competitors. Rouhani was polling in fourth place, with both Jalili and Rezai ahead of him, while Tehran's popular mayor, Qalibaf, had what appeared to be an insurmountable lead ahead of the rest the pack. But once Khatami and Rafsanjani's YouTube videos came out, everything changed. Within a day, Rouhani's numbers went from 14.4 percent to 26.6 percent, while Qalibaf dropped from

27.1 percent to 24.8 percent. Overnight, Qalibaf's lead had vanished. Over the next two days, Rouhani's support skyrocketed, reaching 38 percent the day before the elections. This, however, was not enough to win. It would secure Rouhani a spot in the runoff elections, but if all the conservative voters united behind the top conservative candidate, the conservatives would still clinch the presidency. (This is likely why the conservatives never bothered to create a unified front—since no candidate could win the elections in the first round, it was better to let the voters decide which conservative candidate should be on top rather than hash that out through backdoor negotiations.) This was a remarkable turn of events—only five days before the elections, Rouhani was uncertain he could get more than 10 percent of the votes, according to one of his advisors. The day before the elections, he had become the front runner.[13]

Election 2013: Correcting for Election 2009

Tehran was calm on June 12, 2013. But underneath the surface, there was an unmistakable buzz. There had never been any doubt about the collective desire for change. The last four years under Ahmadinejad had been worse than the first four, with repression intensifying, the security atmosphere in Iran strengthening, and corruption and economic mismanagement skyrocketing. The hardliners had criminalized everything from academia to tourism. The population was suffocating. What was unclear, however, was whether change could be ushered in through the ballot box. Thanks to Khatami and Rafsanjani, the population had in the last days before the election become convinced that a real opportunity for peaceful change lay in front of them. On election day, Iranians spontaneously went through their entire address books, calling everyone they knew to urge them to vote. In just a week, apathy had given way to almost unhinged enthusiasm. Things moved so fast that election-day polling differed dramatically based on the hour of the day it had been conducted. Early in the morning, polls showed that Rouhani's support stood at around 38 percent. By the end of that day, it was clear that something unprecedented had happened. In the last twenty-four hours, not only had Rouhani's support exploded, but voter turnout was reaching record levels.

Around 2:00 a.m. on election night, Rouhani's house was surrounded by approximately two hundred Revolutionary Guards. They
provided no explanation for their presence; they only ordered Rouhani
to remain in his house. It was unclear to Rouhani and his wife whether
the soldiers were there to imprison or protect him. As the situation became more tense, Rouhani's wife started feeling ill, and the former national security advisor managed to convince the soldiers that she had
to be taken to hospital. Once beyond the purview of the soldiers, Rouhani changed course and went to the Interior Ministry, where he was
given the stunning results: he'd beaten all of his rivals by securing
50.88 percent of the vote. There would be no second round. Once again,
the Iranian people had shocked their government—and the world. It
was a striking repudiation of Iran's conservative establishment. Young
Iranians quickly took to the streets to celebrate their victory. Playing on
their slogan from 2009, when they chanted "Give me my vote back,"
Rouhani supporters now shouted "Didn't I tell you I would get my vote
back!" To many of them, this victory corrected the wrong they had been
subjected to in 2009.[14]

Never before had social media had such an impact on Iranian
presidential politics. And by all accounts, it was Khatami's endorsement
that had had the greatest impact. In an irony of epic proportions, the
former reformist president—whose name and picture Iranian media
was not allowed to mention or show as a result of his role in the Green
movement—had become the kingmaker of the 2013 elections, using social media to circumvent the Iranian government's censorship. It was a
reminder of the strength and resilience of the reformist movement inside Iranian society.[15]

Rouhani's campaign strategy had worked. By convincing Aref
to drop out, courting the Green vote, and getting Khatami and Rafsanjani's help with voter turnout, what started off as a lost cause had
been turned into a historic victory. But Rouhani's win cannot be fully
attributed to strategy. There was also a tremendous amount of luck
involved. Since Rouhani's surge in the polls happened so late, most voters
expected that the elections would go to a runoff. A poll conducted by
Tehran University and the University of Maryland later revealed that
many Qalibaf supporters believed that the Tehran mayor was a shoe-in

for the second round and as a result decided to cast their first-round ballots for their second choice—Rouhani—in order to secure a Rouhani-Qalibaf runoff. The problem was that they overdid it. According to the poll, almost one fourth of voters who preferred Qalibaf cast their votes for Rouhani, pushing him over the 50 percent mark. Had they not engaged in this strategic voting, Rouhani wouldn't have won in the first run—in fact, he might have lost the elections altogether.[16]

Washington Is Taken by Surprise

No one in the U.S. government had foreseen this scenario. Even some of the more experienced Iran hands at the State Department had predicted a Jalili victory. Rouhani was given "a snowball's chance in hell to win" by the U.S. intelligence community. "Everyone was surprised," a White House staffer told me. "We had a bet—an office pool, and nobody got it right." And at first, Western governments concluded that the elections could still be stolen from Rouhani, since they believed Khamenei did not view his victory as desirable. "He was elected in our analysis over the objection of the supreme leader," Deputy National Security Advisor Ben Rhodes explained. In fact, Khamenei did not favor Rouhani's candidacy and had subtly tried to discourage it. But while some U.S. think tanks argued that Rouhani could have won only with the support of Khamenei—an almost conspiratorial view of Iranian politics in which whatever happened did so because Khamenei willed it—the U.S. government quickly concluded that Khamenei and other hardliners simply lacked the capacity to change the election outcome. Advisors to the Rouhani government also point out that Khamenei realized that his acceptance of Rouhani's victory could also "help heal the country" and reduce the distance between the ruling elite and the population. After all, they say, while Khamenei might not have wanted Rouhani to win, his very narrow margin of victory rendered a conservative challenge to the election results and demand for recount very likely. The most probable reason such a challenge never was mounted, they argue, "must have been because of direct orders from Khamenei."[17]

In a rather peculiar turn of events, Western governments went from surprise over the elections to taking credit for them. Rouhani had been elected, the argument went, as a result of the sanctions pressure. He was, after all, the only candidate to run on a platform of securing sanctions relief. This was a strongly held view at the Treasury Department, in some quarters in Congress, among the primary backers of sanctions, and in Europe. "The people of Iran wanted change and sanctions helped bring about the change," said the German ambassador to the United States, Peter Wittig. At a minimum, Rouhani was elected in a context that sanctions had helped to create, Western officials and some analysts maintained. The bad economic situation clearly intensified people's desire for change, but the Western narrative assumes that in the absence of sanctions and the economic distress they caused, Iranians would have been content with a conservative victory. The 2009 election counters that notion, since Iranians voted in even greater numbers for moderation *prior* to the imposition of sanctions.[18]

Moreover, the Tehran University–University of Maryland poll provides data countering the idea that sanctions played a key role in the election of Rouhani. Only 2 percent of Rouhani's supporters listed the lifting of sanctions as a reason for supporting him, while 7 percent cited his ability to fix the economy. A poll by Zogby International showed that Iranians were primarily concerned with civil liberty issues—a main focus of the Green movement—and that 96 percent of Iranians believed that sanctions were worth the price to pay in order to retain the country's enrichment right. The focus on sanctions, which was the only policy instrument the West employed at the time, comes at the expense of focus on the internal dynamics in Iran and the sheer unpredictability of the elections. In the words of one of Rouhani's advisors, How could sanctions be credited when five days before the election, most Iranians hadn't even planned to vote—and only changed their minds as a result of the YouTube videos of Khatami and Rafsanjani, whose message did not focus on sanctions?[19]

Indeed, what if the conservatives had united around a single candidate? What if Khatami had failed to convince Aref to drop out? What if fewer Qalibaf supporters had decided to vote strategically in the first round? And perhaps most important, What if a greater segment of reform-minded Iranian voters had stuck to their earlier decision to boycott the vote? To credit Rouhani's victory to sanctions at best showcased how little the West understood Iran's internal dynamics and at worst reflected a near desperate desire to credit the sanctions policy with some success, however flimsy the evidence.

The Sheikh of Diplomacy

Rouhani's election was on balance a *positive* surprise, but it also carried a risk for Washington. On the one hand, there "was real excitement that this may be the break that we needed to have a serious and constructive" diplomatic engagement. The Rouhani government was also putting additional pressure on itself by raising the Iranian people's expectations. Rouhani had, for instance, promised a breakthrough on the nuclear program within his first one hundred days in office. On the other hand, there was the realization that Rouhani was a "true believer" in the revolution and the nuclear program. He would be no pushover. On top of that, Rouhani would benefit from the momentum of his favorable public relations. "Many countries would give Rouhani the benefit of the doubt and say, 'as long as Ahmadinejad is gone,'" a White House official said, pointing out that Obama had benefited from the same thinking when he replaced George W. Bush. "The world cut Obama a lot of slack simply for not being Bush." And just as much as Obama turned the table on Iran in 2009 by being the reasonable party in the equation, it would be difficult for the United States to sustain the sanctions pressure on Iran if the United States once again came across as the inflexible and unreasonable side. The stakes were simply higher now. "It was easy to blame the Iranians for the lack of progress in the first four years because it was so obvious," Rhodes said. "They didn't make an effort to conceal it. These guys, Rouhani and [his team], were not going to make that mistake."[20]

Born in 1948 into a family of businessmen and clerics in the Kerman province in central Iran, Rouhani began his education to become a Muslim cleric at age thirteen, a choice he described in his memoirs as fulfilling his destiny. At the religious seminars, he became acquainted with anti-shah students and clerics. Later, on a train ride to Mashad to perform his compulsory military service, he befriended another young cleric who went on to become Iran's supreme leader, Ayatollah Ali

Khamenei. But unlike Khamenei, who never set foot outside of Iran until the late 1980s, when as president of Iran he gave an address to the UN General Assembly in New York, Rouhani's exposure to the West was far more extensive. In 1978, he moved to Britain to teach Islamic jurisprudence at Lancaster University. He was about to relocate to Massachusetts to attend a graduate program at Harvard University when the revolution broke out. Instead of going to Boston, he flew to Paris to join Ayatollah Khomeini, whom he had befriended while the aging cleric was based in Iraq. He soon became a close confidant of Khomeini and the quintessential regime insider: he served in Iran's parliament for twenty years, rising to the rank of vice speaker; for sixteen years he was the secretary of the Supreme National Security Council, where he headed Iran's earlier nuclear negotiations. He has been a member of the Assembly of Experts since 1999 and the Expediency Council since 1991. And even when his political star dimmed, he continued to serve as the chairman of the Center for Strategic Research, an organization that advises Iran's supreme leader.[21]

Throughout his career, Rouhani has stood out for his tilt toward pragmatism and expediency and against ideological rigidity. He was part of the 1986 delegation that met with Bud McFarlane in Tehran in what later became the Iran-Contra affair—a sign of his openness to dealing with the United States. He played a key role in preventing a push by hardliners to ally with Saddam Hussein when he invaded Kuwait in 1990. Instead, Iran officially adopted a neutral line but helped the United States behind the scenes. He was at the center of Iran's efforts to assist the United States against the Taliban in 2001. When a massive earthquake hit the ancient city of Bam in 2003, Iran accepted aid from the United States, including the building of an emergency hospital. Rouhani traveled the region within days of the catastrophe and took the unusual step of visiting the hospital and taking photographs with the American doctors and aid workers. Perhaps most importantly, when nuclear talks with the European Union had reached a dead-end in 2013, he personally called Khamenei on his cellphone and convinced the hardline supreme leader to agree to a voluntary suspension of enrichment (a move Rouhani later came to pay a high price for). "He was the only one able to sell something deeply unpopular to the other leaders," said Stanislas de Laboulaye, who was a member of the European delegation at the talks. Somewhat fittingly, Rouhani's thesis at Glasgow Caledonian University in Scotland, where he received his doctorate in Constitutional Law, was on "the flexibility of Shariah, Islamic law."[22]

When Rouhani picked Javad Zarif, Iran's brilliant former UN ambassador and lead negotiator in almost all of Iran's major negotiations, from the diplomacy to end the Iran-Iraq war in 1988 to secret negotiations with the United States in 2001 to defeat the Taliban, as his foreign minister, confidence grew in Washington that with the enrichment issue settled in principle, Iran was getting ready to take the negotiations to the next level. Like Rouhani, Zarif had earned the respect of his Western counterparts not only because of his skills and acumen, but also because of his ability to engage constructively and make tough decisions. Zarif "is a smooth operator, a very clever and successful diplomat," Gary Samore told the *Al Monitor*. And like Rouhani, he had become a political outcast after the 2009 elections. Zarif had retreated to the university world, where with some luck he had managed to secure a small cubicle at Tehran University.[23]

Like that of many at the core of the revolution, his career within the regime started when he was in his teens. Zarif had moved to the United States at age seventeen to attend school, though he spent much of his time organizing against the regime of the shah. When the revolution began, the nineteen-year-old Zarif was tasked with taking over Iran's embassy in Washington and acting as its spokesperson. From then on, he became a critical player inside the regime's inner circle of foreign policy hands, often arguing for a more reconciliatory approach toward the West. In his autobiography, he defended his position in favor of establishing relations with the United States on the basis that doing so would advance Iran's interest. In my own interactions with Zarif since 2002, I found him to be a fierce advocate of Iran's national interest and a true believer in the principles of the revolution, though privately he does not mince his words when complaining about the extremism of his conservative rivals. He is unique within the Iranian foreign policy elite precisely because of his linguistic and cultural fluency in both the ways of the West and the political traditions of Iran. Effectively utilizing his wit and charm, he has a likability that's off the charts. And although his Western counterparts are rarely exposed to his religiosity, many of my conversations with him have been interrupted as he made his way into the corner of the room to pray.[24]

Netanyahu Sees Rouhani as a Threat

While those favoring diplomacy saw cause for optimism with Rouhani's election, those fearing diplomacy viewed it as a threat. Neoconservatives like Daniel Pipes did not hide their desire for a Jalili victory (Pipes had also expressed his hopes for an Ahmadinejad victory in 2009). It "is better to have a bellicose, apocalyptic, in-your-face Ahmadinejad who scares the world than a sweet-talking Mousavi who again lulls it to sleep, even as thousands of centrifuges whir away," he wrote in 2009. In an article named "Rooting for Jalili," Pipes stated that the same argument now applied to Jalili. Likewise, Israeli officials dismissed the elections beforehand, stating that elections in Iran do not matter. "It makes no difference who wins," Israeli Minister for Strategic Affairs Yuval Steinitz said. "If there are those who want to delay their decision about what to do with Iran for the election, they can, but we think this is high time to give Iran a credible military threat. That is the only way to get them to change their ways."[25]

Once Rouhani won, Israeli analysts argued that his election was a threat to Israel's national interest, since his promises to improve relations with the West would ease international pressure over Tehran's nuclear program. To minimize this potential effect, the main Israeli talking point was that as president, Rouhani had little influence over policy, since most of the power was in the hands of the supreme leader. It was the opposite of Israel's public posture on Ahmadinejad, whom Israel had cast as a powerful leader in control of Iran's nuclear policy precisely because he was president. After all, Ahmadinejad's confrontational style and venomous rhetoric played right into Israel's hands. As Israeli columnist Amos Harel pointed out, "Today Israel bids a sad farewell to Mahmoud Ahmadinejad, that unexpected asset to Israeli public diplomacy, who served it so well during his eight years as president of Iran."[26]

Within a month of Rouhani's election, Netanyahu intensified the campaign for more sanctions and military threats. Rouhani, the Likud leader warned, was a "wolf in sheep's clothing. Smile and build the bomb." To add urgency, the Israeli prime minister warned that Iran was developing intercontinental ballistic missiles capable of reaching "the American mainland." "It's to reach you, not us," he ominously told *CBS News* in July 2013. The United States should not let down its guard, he warned. Now was the time to intensify, not reduce pressure on Iran. "They have to know that you are prepared to take military action. It's the only thing that will get their attention," Netanyahu said, while reiterating Israel's demand for zero enrichment. "We cannot accept anything less than the total cessation of all enrichment of nuclear materials at all levels, removal from Iran of all enriched nuclear material, closure of Iran's illicit nuclear facilities," Netanyahu said during a meeting with Canadian Foreign Minister John Baird. "Until Iran meets these demands, pressure must be stepped up and the Iranian nuclear program must be stopped. Period." Undoubtedly, Rouhani's election had made "Israel's diplomatic path much more difficult, because it was much easier to warn against Ahmadinejad than to warn against Rouhani," Israeli journalist Tal Shalev pointed out. While the U.S. and Israeli approach toward Iran had diverged for some time, Rouhani's election "was a milestone in that respect," as Washington began to see light at the end of the diplomatic tunnel, while the Netanyahu government feared that its opportunity to sabotage the negotiations and put the United States and Iran on a path to war was slipping out of its hands.[27]

Netanyahu found a trusted ally in the Republican-controlled Congress for his push for new sanctions. Before the elections, the Senate had unanimously passed a new sanctions bill on Iran, which not only called for a de facto commercial embargo on Iran, but also preemptively committed the United States to support Israel militarily if it decided to bomb Iran, as well as taking away the president's ability to waive sanctions. The American Israel Public Affairs Committee (AIPAC), the hawkish pro-Israel lobby, hailed the passage of the bill. Furthermore, rather than taking a cautionary approach after Rouhani's surprise election, U.S. lawmakers—under pressure from AIPAC and the Netanyahu government—moved swiftly to pass new sanctions just days before Rouhani was inaugurated. Sending a provocative signal to Tehran that reinforced the hardline narrative in Iran that whatever Iran did, the

United States would always pursue a confrontational approach, the House of Representatives moved to tighten sanctions on the oil, automotive, and mining sectors with a measure that passed 400 to 20. "Iran may have a new president, but its march toward a nuclear program continues," California Republican Ed Royce said. "The economic and political pressure on Tehran must be ratcheted up."[28]

The provocative measure, which seemed aimed at sabotaging the opening for diplomacy Rouhani's election had brought about, did not go down well with the other P5 + 1 powers. Russian Deputy Foreign Minister Gennady Gatilov complained that "any extra sanctions effectively aim at economic suffocation of Iran, not at non-proliferation objectives." But the congressional measure was backed by former secretary of state Clinton, who often landed on the hawkish end of internal Obama administration debates, particularly on Middle East issues. According to a person close to her, she was swayed by Netanyahu's line that Iran was hurting so badly, that it was desperate for a deal. As a result, the United States could afford to tighten the pressure to extract greater concessions from Tehran. "She would have squeezed them again," a person close to her said, "and the only debate is what they would have done." It was not only a profound misreading of the situation—while the economy was suffering, there was no evidence that the pressure had softened Iran's position on the nuclear issue—but also a measure that could have directly jeopardized the opening that Obama and Kerry had finessed through the help of the Omanis. (Later, as the diplomacy progressed, the Obama administration managed to delay the measure in the Senate and eventually threatened to veto it and other sanctions measures.)[29]

Rouhani Shakes Up Washington

But while the Republican-controlled Congress could be counted on to pursue a confrontational approach regardless of developments in Iran, Rouhani's election had elicited a more profound phenomenon underneath the surface—both in Congress and in Washington's larger foreign policy scene. Just as moderate forces in Iran had little to hang their hat on prior to the enrichment concession when arguing in favor of a softer approach, proponents of diplomacy in Washington had suffered from the same challenge. With Iran escalating its program, Khamenei insisting on resistance, and Ahmadinejad endlessly engaging in provocative rhetoric, diplomacy was a hard sell in Washington, which few politicians and organizations dared to push, with the noticeable exception of progressive lawmakers like Keith Ellison (D-MN) and Earl Blumenauer (D-OR), as well as organizations such as the Arms Control Association (ACA), Americans for Peace Now, the Friends Committee on National Legislation, the National Iranian American Council (NIAC), Peace Action and Peace Action West, Win Without War, the Ploughshares Fund, and the Rockefeller Brothers Fund.

But Rouhani's election dramatically changed the political cost of advocating for diplomacy, particularly given his immediate outreach to the United States. While he insisted that Iran would never give up its rights and dignity, and that the time for suspending enrichment had passed, he indicated that the nuclear issue could be resolved through constructive engagement. "We have to enhance mutual trust between Iran and other countries," Rouhani said at his first press conference after the election. Iran's first step toward building trust would be to show "greater transparency." Perhaps more importantly, Rouhani deplored the nonexistent relations between Iran and the United States. It is "an old wound, which must be healed," he explained in what became headline-grabbing comments. A few weeks later, he went even further and called for direct U.S.-Iran talks. Rouhani even published an op-ed in the *Washington Post*, calling for a win-win approach to international disputes in general and the nuclear standoff in particular. "In a world where global politics is no longer a zero-sum game, it is—or should be— counterintuitive to pursue one's interests without considering the interests of others," he wrote. Unlike Ahmadinejad, who dismissed the risk of war and whose bravado at times made it seem almost as if he welcomed a military confrontation, Rouhani put his opposition to war front and center. "I don't believe in war," he said a week after the elections. "War is not to our benefit. It's not to America's benefit. I don't think that the Americans are after war at this point."[30]

The most daring and savvy move Rouhani and Zarif pulled off, however, was neither the op-ed in the *Washington Post* nor the win-win sound bites. In a PR maneuver that brilliantly showed their understanding of U.S. domestic politics, the role of the special U.S.-Israel relationship, the need to differentiate themselves from Ahmadinejad, and the power of social media—all while making Netanyahu come across as a radical and an obstacle to peace—Rouhani tweeted well wishes for the Jewish New Year, Rosh Hashanah. "As the sun is about to set here in #Tehran I wish all Jews, especially Iranian Jews, a blessed Rosh Hashanah," he tweeted. Within hours, the tweet went viral. The contrast with Ahmadinejad could not have been starker. Through this tweet, Rouhani positioned himself as the anti-Ahmadinejad. By denying the Holocaust, the most painful chapter in Jewish history, which had precipitated the establishment of the Jewish State, Ahmadinejad had denied both Jewish suffering and by extension, the right of Israel to exist. By sending Rosh Hashanah greetings and indirectly pointing out that Iran has its own Jewish community, Rouhani recognized and celebrated the Jewish people. (He later also condemned the Holocaust.) And just as Ahmadinejad's anti-Israel rhetoric had made it more politically costly for Washington to engage with Iran, Rouhani's openness and outreach to the Jewish people lowered the political resistance to engagement.[31]

Within the organized Jewish American community—the DC-centric Jewish organizations and their leadership—Rouhani's Twitter outreach was largely dismissed as irrelevant at best or nefarious at worst. But progressive leaning organizations, which have a minority voice but whose positions tend to be more representative of the views of the Jewish community at large, recognized that this could be an opening. "In our portion of the community it was noted that this is not just a change in tone; he's actually recognizing the peoplehood, traditions, and history of the Jews," said Dylan Williams, vice president of government affairs of the progressive Jewish American lobby group J Street. "It wasn't that [Rouhani] was being nice, or that we genuinely believed that he liked Jews. It was that he was signaling that he had the political space to do something that his predecessor hadn't."[32]

While some pro-diplomacy groups had continued to argue for the merits of negotiations even in the darkest hours of U.S.-Iran relations, for others the election of Rouhani was "a big turning point," as it provided a positive opening they could point to, rather than just arguing that "war was not the answer." This was particularly true on Capitol Hill, where receptiveness to the argument that "sanctions are needed to prevent war" was strong. Now, lawmakers favoring diplomacy could point to Rouhani's election and argue that an opportunity existed that additional sanctions would ruin; that is, sanctions undermined diplomacy rather than enhancing it. Rouhani's election prompted two lawmakers, David Price (D-NC) and Charles Dent (R-PA), to organize a letter backing diplomacy and, in what was an unprecedented move, call for sanctions to be lifted in return for Iranian nuclear concessions. To the surprise of the White House as well as the lawmakers themselves, the letter gained signatures from 131 members of the House. Astonishingly, seventeen of the lawmakers were Republicans. Never before had the U.S. Congress sent such a strong bipartisan message of support for diplomacy. The letter signaled to a surprised White House that there was more political support for diplomacy in Washington than many had thought.[33]

"We've just had an unusual election there," Congressman Price told me of his decision to write the letter. "It's foolish not to probe this, not to at least explore what it might mean. That's all we were saying." At a moment when the Iranian people had, against all odds, managed to steer the country in a potentially more moderate and conciliatory direction, not taking note and reciprocating with a positive signal would be a significant mistake, pro-diplomacy lawmakers reasoned. "Here the Iranian people take a chance [by electing Rouhani] because they think we're serious, and then we go offend them by looking at new sanctions," Congressman Ellison explained. "I just thought that was very much in poor taste." A winning argument for Price, Dent, Ellison, and the key lawmakers behind the letter was that Congress had already abdicated its responsibility once by not pushing for all peaceful options to be explored before giving the green light to war in Iraq. Most members of Congress have come to regret that mistake deeply—and many have paid the political price for it. If the Rouhani opening was not explored, Congress would risk repeating that mistake, the pro-diplomacy lawmakers argued. "If it comes to war, if it comes to a real crisis, you want to be on the record as never advocating any effort at diplomacy?" Dent asked his colleagues.[34]

The congressional letter followed another unusual signal from Washington's foreign policy elite. A group of twenty-nine former senior U.S. government officials, diplomats, military officers, and national security experts sent a letter organized by my organization (NIAC) to President Obama urging him to take advantage of the opening Rouhani's election presented, while avoiding "any provocative action that could narrow the window of opportunity for a more moderate policy out of Tehran." All in all, these measures showed that momentum had dramatically shifted in favor of diplomacy, even within parts of the U.S. government that otherwise fed off of enmity with Iran.[35]

A similar momentum emerged on the Iranian side, though their calls for diplomacy were directed at Obama rather than at Rouhani. In an article published in the British daily the *Guardian,* Khatami urged the West to work with Rouhani so as to not risk losing an unprecedented opportunity for peace. Failure to do so, he warned, would strengthen extremists on both sides. Khatami's words echoed a letter signed by five hundred prominent Iranian intellectuals, artists, and activists— including Oscar-winning film director Asghar Farhadi and imprisoned reformist Mostafa Tajzadeh. "The people of Iran seized the opportunity to elect Hassan Rouhani," the letter said. "It is now your turn, and that of the international community, to reciprocate Iran's measures of goodwill and pursue a win-win strategy."[36]

What the Iranian and American pro-democracy groups and lawmakers didn't know, however, was that behind the scenes, Obama was racing way ahead of them.

From Muscat to Geneva

B
arack Obama didn't miss a beat. Soon after Hassan Rouhani was elected, he took the unusual step of sending the Iranian president a letter of congratulations. One and a half pages long, the letter reiterated Obama's hope that the nuclear issue could be resolved diplomatically. But according to the Iranians, it went further than previous communications, in both tone and substance: Obama offered to lift sanctions if Tehran would "cooperate with the international community, keep [its] commitments and remove ambiguities." The Iranians, including hardliners in the supreme leader's office, viewed the letter very positively, which may indicate that it also addressed the enrichment issue. Moreover, the Iranians were likely further impressed by the letter as its message was reinforced by someone they trusted: the sultan of Oman, Qaboos bin Said.[1]

The sultan officially visited Iran to attend Rouhani's inauguration, but his real purpose was to confirm for Washington that Iran's supreme leader was fully committed to the Oman channel and the diplomacy Obama was proposing in the letter. Just as the Americans could not put their acceptance of Iranian enrichment in writing in a letter to Iran but could do so in a letter to the sultan, so Ayatollah Khamenei could not convey his commitment to bilateral negotiations directly to the United States, but could do so to the Omani leader. Ayatollah

Khamenei's personal pledge, conveyed to the sultan in a face-to-face meeting, was the best Obama could hope for. Washington didn't trust Khamenei, but they trusted that he would be loath to break his word to the sultan. Rouhani, in turn, promptly responded to Obama with a letter of equal length that also had a more positive tone than previous letters—and was void of the litany of grievances that had defined earlier Iranian communication with the United States.[2]

Khamenei's commitment to the Oman channel, Rouhani's reply, and the crucial decision in Tehran to move the nuclear file from the Supreme National Security Council to the Foreign Ministry—that is, under Javad Zarif's control—boosted Washington's confidence that a deal could be reached. The Rouhani team was of the same view—particularly when they were briefed on the Oman channel. The Muscat meetings had been a well-kept secret within the Iranian system. Neither Rouhani nor Zarif was aware that secret negotiations had been conducted and that Washington had finally played the enrichment card. The Rouhani team's original diplomatic strategy entailed renewed negotiations only with the P5 + 1, not direct negotiations with the United States. "As one of Rouhani's advisors, I had worked out a rough plan on how to engage with the P5 + 1, but absent the U.S. element," Zarif explained.[3]

Once it became clear that the United States had expressed openness to accepting enrichment in Iran, Zarif recognized the opportunity, and the pace of diplomacy picked up dramatically. The Iranians and Americans reconvened in Muscat only days after Rouhani's inauguration—but with a new cast of characters on the Iranian side and a new Iranian posture. The Iranian delegation was now led by Iran's new deputy foreign minister, Majid Takht-Ravanchi, a soft-spoken career diplomat with Master's degrees from the University of Kansas and Fordham University and a doctorate in Political Science from the University of Bern. Like Zarif, he was as comfortable negotiating in English as he was in Persian.[4]

With the new team, the tenor of the discussion changed dramatically. The Iranians shifted to English, which sped up the discussions, since translations were no longer needed. "We determined that we could communicate our positions more effectively in English," Ravanchi told me. At the first meeting with his counterpart Deputy Secretary of

State Bill Burns, Ravanchi read his opening statement in English. From there on, it was natural to continue the conversations in English, Ravanchi said. But something more profound happened as a result of the change in atmosphere: with the greater political space the two sides enjoyed, they could finally begin humanizing each other. During coffee breaks, the Iranians mingled with the Americans, exchanging stories about their children, families, hobbies, and, in the case of the more senior negotiators, their ailments and illnesses.[5]

Zarif, for instance, suffered from intense back pain during some later sessions and had to be wheelchaired into the negotiating room. Part of that session was spent sharing stories about back ailments and the best tips on how to overcome them. "Everybody had a piece of a back story for him—books they thought he should read, thing he might try—because we all have suffered," a senior U.S. official said. Being able to discuss their day-to-day issues went a long way in humanizing the delegations to each other, which in turn was critical for any attempt to build trust and confidence. "There's a shift in perspective when you can humanize," a White House official told me. And by being very sensitive about showing the other side dignity and respect, significant headway could be made in the talks without the United States necessarily having compromised on substantive issues. (The United States had, for instance, in official statements referred to Rouhani using his clerical title, Hojjatoleslam, as a sign of respect.) "To me it was just normal. This is the way you normally engage in diplomatic engagement," a White House official involved in the talks said.[6]

Between August and November, the United States and Iran held an additional seven secret bilateral meetings. The venues shifted, starting off in Muscat in August, then moving to New York during the annual meeting of the UN General Assembly, and then returning to Oman in October and November. The talks still got tense at times, but they were no longer hostile. Instead, they were businesslike, sober, and professional. "It was clear that the Iranians were serious and wanted a deal," a U.S. official said. For the United States, the objective was to change the dynamics so that time no longer would be on Iran's side. Its nuclear advances had reduced its breakout time from years to weeks. At a minimum, something needed to be done to stop the growth of the program. The Obama officials' strategy was essentially to offer sanctions relief in return for nuclear restraint. The more restrictions and limitations Iran was willing to accept, the more sanctions relief the United States would put on the table. The Iranians could opt for a big deal or a smaller one, depending on their preferences and political limitations— as long as the growth of the program was arrested.[7]

For the Iranians, it wasn't just about sanctions relief; it was about codifying the acceptance of Iranian enrichment while guarding against restrictions that would permanently make the Iranian nuclear program treated differently from all other countries' nuclear programs. And, perhaps most important, it was about using the diplomatic process to "desecuritize Iran." Over the past decade, the Rouhani government believed, the West had been viewing the country solely from a security perspective. Iran was seen as having a menacing nuclear program, before it was seen as a country or a nation. Anything pertaining to Iran— whether it was regular trade or even Iran's participation in sporting events—had to be seen through the lens of the nuclear program. Bringing Iran's case to the UN Security Council under Chapter VII in 2006, which meant that Iran's nuclear activities had become defined as a threat to international peace and stability, had been a critical step in this process. The sanctions imposed on Iran, in turn, were a small but important part of the securitization of Iran. "Sanctions were both an outcome of this securitization environment and also perpetuated by it," Zarif argued. "It showed that this country [Iran] is a security threat because of the sanctions." Sanctions and securitization were mutually reinforcing. Consequently, one couldn't eliminate one without eliminating the other. And if neither could be done, the ultimate consequence of securitization would be a military confrontation, the Rouhani government believed.[8]

But while desecuritization was the ultimate objective, the immediate goal was to finalize the enrichment acceptance and negotiate restrictions that the Rouhani government could sell at home. For instance, the Iranians put forward significant resistance to restrictions on Iran's nuclear research and development precisely because of the dominant narrative in Iran that the nuclear issue was a Western pretext to subjugate Iran by, among other things, depriving it of modern technology. The U.S. concern was that as Iran continued its R&D, it would develop faster new centrifuges, which would further reduce its breakout time. But it was clear that the Iranians had very little negotiation room on this issue, because of Iranian sensitivity to putting limits on research. The diplomats finessed the matter so that the text of the agreement would say that Iran agreed to continue its planned R&D activities. With that formulation, the Iranians implicitly accepted that they wouldn't go beyond the existing research, but since the limitation wasn't stated explicitly, rattling Iranian political sensitivities could be avoided.[9]

Moreover, while the United States made further clarifications on its position on enrichment—a more straightforward formulation with less caveats—accepting enrichment and negotiating the details of the issue on paper were entirely different matters. The shape and dimension of Iran's future enrichment program was continuously negotiated and not fully settled until the very end of the talks. But thanks to the new pace—the number of interactions between the United States and the Iranians between September and October 2013 was twenty-fold the number of interactions the international community had had with Iran over the preceding four years, a former White House official said—the two sides were very close to finalizing a deal by mid-September.[10]

Around that time, Ayatollah Khamenei did something few in Washington had expected. On September 17, Khamenei gave his strongest endorsement of diplomacy and used Shia theology and history to justify flexibility in the negotiations—a sharp departure from his emphasis on resistance. "We are not against proper and reasonable moves, whether in the world of diplomacy or in the world of domestic policies," he said in the speech, which was addressed to Iranian Revolutionary Guard Corps commanders.

> I believe in the idea which was referred to as "heroic flexibility." Flexibility is necessary in many areas. It is very good and there is nothing wrong with it. But the wrestler who is wrestling against his opponent and who shows flexibility for technical reasons should not forget who his opponent is and

what he is doing. This is the main condition. Our politicians too should know what they are doing, who they are faced with, who their opponent is and which area the opposing side wants to attack.[11]

The phrase "heroic flexibility" originates in a key event in Shia history. Hassan Ibn Ali, the second holy imam in Twelver Shia Islam, sought to negotiate peace with Muawiyah I, the founder of the Umayyid Dynasty, rather than opting for resistance (which would have led to confrontation). In 1970, Ayatollah Khamenei translated into Persian a book that attempted to show why Imam Hassan's decision was in line with Shia doctrine. Khamenei titled the book "Imam Hassan's Peace: The Most Glorious Heroic Flexibility of History." Most Shia Muslims see Hassan's peace treaty as a heroic act to avoid senseless bloodshed rather than as a sign of surrender. Khamenei had mentioned heroic flexibility in earlier speeches as well, but few in Washington had considered how he could use this specific episode in Shia history to justify a shift in Iran's posture on the nuclear front. And since the direct U.S.-Iran talks were a remarkably well-kept secret, even fewer understood that Khamenei's shift toward flexibility came in tandem with American flexibility on the central issue of enrichment.[12]

Rouhani was scheduled to arrive in New York to address the UN General Assembly only days after Khamenei's speech on heroic flexibility. Obama would be there as well, addressing the UN body just hours before Rouhani's speech. A direct conversation between the two leaders could go a long way both to advance the talks and to instill confidence that both presidents were investing sufficient political will into diplomacy. Whether Iran's heroic flexibility would extend to a face-to-face conversation with the American president remained to be seen. But while Obama's team was laying the groundwork for an unprecedented encounter between the American and Iranian presidents, another world leader was heading to New York with a different plan in mind. Israeli Prime Minister Benjamin Netanyahu was making his way to the United Nations to pour cold water on Rouhani's charm offensive and Obama's dreams of a diplomatic win.

Netanyahu Versus Rouhani and Obama

As diplomacy advanced, Obama's relationship with Netanyahu deteriorated further. Not only had Netanyahu exhausted Obama as well as the Israeli public by repeatedly stirring tensions and threatening to bomb Iran, but his appearances with Republican presidential nominee Mitt Romney during the 2012 U.S. presidential elections was perceived in most quarters as clear interference in U.S. election politics. Netanyahu had simply gone too far, according to some Israeli commentators. "Instead of Washington and Jerusalem slinging arrows together at Iran, they're slinging arrows at each other," Israeli journalist Ari Shavit wrote.[13]

With Rouhani aiming to put a new face to Iran and escape the sanctions corner Iran had found itself in, Netanyahu decided to go on the offensive to prevent diplomacy from kick-starting and Rouhani from convincing the international community to ease the pressure on Iran. Prior to leaving for New York, Netanyahu announced four conditions that the international community would have to set before lifting the sanctions on Iran: zero enrichment, removal of Iran's stockpile of low-enriched uranium (LEU) from Iran, a shutdown of the facility at Fordo, and an end to the plutonium program in Arak. "Israel would welcome a genuine diplomatic solution that truly dismantles Iran's capacity to develop nuclear weapons," Netanyahu said. But these goals were delusional, many experts, including former Israeli military commanders, complained. "The Israelis were always suggesting they had the same goal—a diplomatic resolution to the nuclear deal, but the requirements on the Israeli side were always unrealistic," commented Israel expert Dalia Dassa Kaye of the RAND Corporation.[14]

While Netanyahu sought to undermine Obama by issuing unrealistic demands for diplomacy, Obama decided to respond in kind by playing the Palestinian card. In his address to the United Nations, the American president declared that his two goals for the coming year were to solve the Iranian nuclear crisis and to reach an Israeli-Palestinian peace agreement. "While these issues are not the cause of all the region's problems, they have been a major source of instability for far too long, and resolving them can help serve as a foundation for a broader peace," he said. This echoed a package deal Obama had tried to sell Netanyahu in 2009: the United States would take care of the Iranian nuclear threat, and in return Israel would reach a settlement with the Palestinians. The United States would get Iran to dismantle its centrifuges, and Israel in turn would take down Jewish settlements in occupied Palestinian territory and pave the way for a lasting peace. For the right-wing in Israel, this was a nightmare scenario. Essentially, the United States was now using the same linkage between Iran and the Palestinian issue that the Rabin-Peres government had used in the 1990s. Rabin and Peres's argument had been that for Israel to risk negotiating peace with the Palestinians, Washington had to take on and isolate Iran. Now the Obama administration was telling Israel that since Washington was neutralizing the threat of Iran's nuclear program, Israel had to get serious about finding a solution to the conflict with the Palestinians.[15]

In the 1990s, the Iranians calculated that they had to undercut the Israeli-Palestinian peace process in order to undermine the United States' efforts to isolate Tehran. Now the Netanyahu government had an added reason to oppose U.S.-Iran diplomacy, as it would help stymie any efforts to drag Israel back to negotiations with the Palestinians. If diplomacy succeeded, pressure would mount on the Netanyahu government to compromise with the Palestinians, Israel feared. But whether the Obama administration was serious about finding a solution to the Palestinian-Israeli conflict remains unclear. At a minimum, as a tactical maneuver, pushing Israel on the Palestinian issue helped put Netanyahu on the defensive and reduced his ability to create problems for diplomacy with Iran. Prior to the 2012 presidential elections, a White House official suggested to me that once Iran diplomacy got serious, it would be valuable to also make a push on the Palestinian issue, as it would keep Israel busy.

In the short run, however, the strategy seems to have only fueled Netanyahu's motivation to undermine Obama's Iran diplomacy. The Israeli prime minister's thirty-three-minute address to the United Nations focused mainly on Iran and Rouhani, with only a brief passage on the Palestinian issue (Netanyahu mentioned Iran and Rouhani ninety-five times, and Palestine only seven). "Ahmadinejad was a wolf in wolf's clothing. Rouhani is a wolf in sheep's clothing," Netanyahu said. "I wish

I could believe Rouhani, but I don't," the Israeli prime minister continued. "Because facts are stubborn things and the facts are that Iran's savage record flatly contradicts Rouhani's soothing rhetoric." While Rouhani smiled during his speech and spoke of the need to oppose extremism, Netanyahu could not avoid coming across as angry and bitter. While many world leaders were curious but slightly skeptical of Rouhani, Netanyahu's condemnation of the Iranian leader only months after his inauguration was unconvincing and seemed to betray political motives.[16]

Netanyahu had not only overestimated his own ability to sway world public opinion against Iran; he had also grossly underestimated the degree to which the international community welcomed Rouhani's election and the idea of the United States and Iran resolving their tensions diplomatically. His determination to stop diplomacy in its tracks was matched by Obama's commitment to resolve the nuclear dispute peacefully.[17]

The Historic Phone Call

"Just now, I spoke with President Rouhani of the Islamic Republic of Iran," Obama told a stunned White House press corps on September 27, 2013. Although the phone call was historic—Iranian and American presidents had not spoken to each other since 1979—Obama showed hardly any emotions as he delivered the news to the unsuspecting reporters. Without delving into too many details about the call, Obama reconfirmed what he had said all along: "I believe we can reach a comprehensive solution [to the nuclear dispute]," he said. "I do believe that there is a basis for a resolution."[18]

The phone call was the result of an extensive back and forth between the White House and Rouhani's office in the lead-up to the UN General Assembly meeting. American and Iranian leaders rarely show much respect for each other. But the UN meeting in September 2013 was an exception to this decades' long rule. Rouhani attended Obama's address to the United Nations in a show of respect. Obama, in turn, mentioned Ayatollah Khamenei's fatwa against developing and using nuclear weapons in his address, which the Iranians deeply appreciated. But

Obama wanted to take it a step further—he wanted to meet with Rouhani at the United Nations. He tasked Jake Sullivan, an original member of the U.S. negotiation team in Oman, to reach out to the Iranians. At first the Iranians were receptive to the idea. They agreed to a chance encounter with Rouhani in one of the corridors at the United Nations. There would be no cameras allowed, and the two sides would have come to an agreement on exactly how they would describe their meeting to the press. The accidental run-in was scheduled for September 24, 2013.[19]

But at the last minute the Iranians got cold feet. The idea of a handshake was too politically risky for Rouhani. "It was clear that it was too complicated for them," a senior U.S. official said. Obama was disappointed, but hardly surprised. The White House decided to leak the story to the media to point out that Obama had been open to the idea, but that Rouhani didn't seem ready for this crucial step. Three days later Rouhani's office contacted Sullivan and proposed that the two leaders speak on the phone instead. Obama accepted. Rouhani received the call from the White House as he was making his way to Kennedy Airport outside of New York City. The two leaders spoke to each other through a translator for about fifteen minutes. Although the White House did not share many details about the call to the U.S. media, a miscommunication between Rouhani's press people and his social media team caused the Iranians to tweet a detailed summary of the conversation—in violation of the agreement between Sullivan and his Iranian counterpart. The Iranians promptly deleted the tweets, but the media had already taken note.[20]

Obama congratulated Rouhani on his election, expressed his "respect for [Rouhani] and the people of Iran," and thanked the Iranian leader for encouraging diplomacy. A historic opportunity to resolve the nuclear issue existed, Obama said, and both Iran and the United States should seize it. The United States respected Iran's right to civilian nuclear energy, granted that it would accept limitations and inspections that would prevent it from building a bomb, Obama continued. While both leaders agreed that the talks had to focus solely on the nuclear issue, Obama left the door open for a broader opening between the two countries. A "breakthrough on the nuclear issue could open the door to a [more constructive] relationship between the U.S. and Iran," Obama hinted, while pointing out that U.S.-Iran diplomacy could also have a positive effect on the situation in Syria. As the conversation came to a close, Rouhani switched to broken English to bid Obama farewell: "Have a nice day." Obama leaned over to one of his senior staffers who had some limited knowledge of Persian and asked him how to say goodbye. Seconds later, Obama responded in equally broken Persian: "Khoda hafez"—May God protect you.[21]

With the phone call, the dialogue could begin in earnest. The call signified that both presidents had publicly blessed the talks and accepted ownership of the process. The cost of failure was now higher for both. The same went for their two foreign ministers, John Kerry and Javad Zarif. Kerry, who had played an instrumental role in setting up the Oman channel while he was chairman of the Senate Foreign Relations Committee, was now Obama's secretary of state and could enjoy the fruits of his earlier labors by engaging directly with the Iranians in his new capacity. His first meeting with Zarif took place a day before the Obama-Rouhani phone call.

The foreign ministers from the P5 + 1 states and Iran were meeting at the UN headquarters. Topping the agenda was a presentation by Zarif on the parameters for a possible resolution to the nuclear standoff. After Zarif's twenty-minute presentation and brief comments from the other foreign ministers, Kerry leaned over to Zarif and asked him: "Shall we chat?" One by one, the foreign ministers left the room—except Zarif and Kerry. Reporters waiting in the halls of the UN building quickly realized that something historic was happening. With the exception of a brief encounter between Secretary of State Colin Powell and Iranian Foreign Minister Kamal Kharrazi in 2001, when Kharrazi had approached Powell in that very same building to express his condolences over the September 11 terrorist attacks, there had been no direct face-to-face meeting between Iranian and American foreign ministers for more than three decades. While he was UN ambassador, however, Zarif had gotten to know several senators who later became key members of the Obama administration. He had on numerous occasions spoken with Joe Biden and Chuck Hagel, for instance, and he had gotten to know Senator Dianne Feinstein over the course of his years in New York. She had at one point in 2004 invited him to her Senate office, where he ended up having an intense conversation with several high-ranking senators, including Harry Reid. But this was Zarif's first encounter with Kerry. Their historic chat lasted a full half-hour. They exchanged emails and cell numbers and instructed their staffs to do the same. It was almost as if they wanted to make up for the past decades of noncommunication.[22]

Both Kerry and Zarif praised their encounter in comments to the press afterward. "We had a constructive meeting, and I think all of us were pleased that Foreign Minister Zarif came and made a presentation to us, which was very different in tone and very different in the vision that he held out with respect to possibilities of the future," Kerry told the media. "I sense that Secretary Kerry and President Obama want to resolve this," Zarif said, explaining that the two sides had agreed to reach a final settlement on Iran's nuclear program within a year. The first step, he explained, was to agree on the parameters of the end game. This was a critical hint that some form of agreement on enrichment already had been struck, as the United States had long sought to avoid addressing the end game since any such conversation would inevitably have to deal with the question of enrichment. Indeed, Zarif's and Kerry's upbeat comments to the press were motivated by something that not even the other P5+1 states knew: Iran and the United States were already at the finishing line of an interim agreement, thanks to the Oman channel.[23]

Back to Geneva

The P5+1 and the Iranians reconvened in Geneva, Switzerland, on October 15, 2013. The media interest had swelled dramatically, with hundreds of reporters congregating at the Intercontinental Hotel as the expectation of a breakthrough steadily rose. The rest of the P5+1 were still unaware of the existence of the Oman channel and the extensive progress the United States and Iran had made toward an interim agreement. None of the drafts developed in that channel was discussed in Geneva—though the discussions covered exactly the same topics.

Despite massive back pains caused by his stress and anger over attacks on him by the hardline media in Iran, Zarif decided to attend the talks, bringing with him his Iranian physiotherapist (who had advised against his attendance). Zarif had to spend most of the day lying down, including on the plane to Geneva, where a special couch was installed for him. Pictures emerged of him lying on the couch while briefing the Iranian press corps traveling with him to Geneva, his facial expression fraught with pain. Sitting in his temporary wheelchair, Zarif kicked off the talks by giving a one-hour PowerPoint presentation in English, titled "Closing an Unnecessary Crisis: Opening New Horizons." The presentation laid out a six- to twelve-month roadmap toward a final deal. The ensuing talks focused on four key issues: suspension of enrichment at the 19.75 percent level, suspension of enrichment at the underground Fordo bunker, limits on Iran's production and stockpile of enriched uranium, and sanctions relief if Iran agreed to restrict its program.[24]

The talks lasted for two days and were praised by all sides. "I have never had such intense, detailed, straightforward, candid conversations with the Iranian delegation," a senior U.S. administration official said. Zarif, in turn, spoke of the United States and the P5+1 as "Iran's partners"—language that was striking, considering the rhetoric that characterized the Ahmadinejad government. Although no agreement was reached on the core issues, one very important breakthrough did take place. The two sides decided that the venue for the talks would continue to be Geneva until a deal was reached and that the two sides would meet about every two to three weeks. A matter that usually took an entire afternoon to decide during the Jalili years was settled in less than ten minutes.[25]

While the diplomats were enjoying their limited breakthrough, Netanyahu and his Senate allies were dismayed. Rather than returning home to Washington after the talks, Wendy Sherman hopped on a plane to Israel to brief Israeli National Security Advisor Yaakov Amidror on the progress made in Geneva. The Obama administration had made a point of keeping the Israelis fully up to date on the developments in the P5+1 talks—though the Omani channel remained a secret. The U.S. side held out on the small chance that they could bring Netanyahu on board—or at least temper his opposition. But the regular briefings the Obama administration provided the Israelis with tended to be "a one-way street," according to Robert Einhorn, a senior nonproliferation hand in the U.S. negotiating team. "We told them what we intend to do, our assessment of the situation. Instead of [engaging], they would simply repeat their position." In some aspects, attempting to engage with the Netanyahu team wasn't too dissimilar from attempting to do so with Iran's former negotiator, Saeed Jalili. "They wouldn't say, 'It would be helpful to modify your position this way or that way,' or 'We could really be much more supportive, if you did x, y, and z,'" Einhorn continued. This was a major mistake made by the Israelis, because when they came across as being unable or unwilling to be satisfied, there was no longer any incentive for the U.S. side to try to take their view into account. "Because their views were extreme, and there was no way we were going to satisfy them, it allowed us to make our policy without reference to specific Israeli proposals," Einhorn concluded.[26]

Annoyed by how the Israelis were shooting down all variations of the deal, the Omanis at one point went to the Israelis directly to get their buy-in, but were asked by the U.S. government to disengage. Still, the U.S. side had left little reason for the Israelis not to understand that Washington would at the end of the day settle for continued enrichment on Iranian soil. This infuriated the Israelis, as it violated their redline and significantly increased the prospects of a deal. Calculating that this concession would be the weakest point in Obama's strategy to sell the deal to Congress and the American public, Netanyahu and his Senate allies zeroed in on the enrichment issue. Ten U.S. senators wrote a letter to Obama on the day of the talks, insisting that Iran end all enrichment activity while pushing for more sanctions.[27]

But Netanyahu went a step further. Kerry organized a meeting with Netanyahu on November 8 to assure him that a deal with Iran would not come at the expense of Israel's security. Instead of engaging with Kerry, the Israeli prime minister took the opportunity to lecture him in front of the cameras—as he had done with Obama in the past. Disinclined to clash with Netanyahu publicly, Kerry tried to convince him not to do a public press conference. But Netanyahu refused to back down. "Wait right here," he bluntly told Kerry before facing the cameras alone to slam Obama for offering Iran "the deal of the century." "Iran must not have a nuclear weapons capability, which means that they shouldn't have centrifuges or enrichment," Netanyahu said, his face red with anger. "They shouldn't have a plutonium heavy-water plant, which is used only for nuclear weapons. They should get rid of the advanced fissile material, and they shouldn't have underground nuclear facilities, underground for one reason—for military purposes," he said while warning Kerry that he was about to strike a "bad deal." Behind the cameras, matters got even worse. As the two leaders headed off to their private meeting, Kerry asked Netanyahu if senior aides should be included or not. "I don't care," the prime minister muttered. "Do whatever you want." An Israeli official later told journalists Amir Tibon and Tal Shalev that their discussion "was the worst meeting between an Israeli leader and an American secretary of state I've seen in decades."[28]

Netanyahu's public lashing put Kerry on the defensive, and he repeatedly had to reassure American journalists that the Obama administration was not about to strike a bad deal. Instead of putting the diplomacy in a positive light and bringing attention to its historic quality, the Obama administration's communications strategy was reduced to insisting that they were not about to do something disastrous. Ironically, however, within the Jewish community, Netanyahu's attacks on Obama and diplomacy were failing to resonate. A poll by the American Jewish Committee showed that support for military strikes against Iran had dropped from 64 to 52 percent since October 2012, while 45 percent said they would oppose a strike, up from 34 percent in 2012. The change was primarily attributed to the "Rouhani effect"—whom Netanyahu had cast as a wolf in sheep's clothing.[29]

Dealing with Netanyahu, however, was not the only difficulty for the Obama administration. Its other challenge was to inform its allies in the P5 + 1 that the United States and Iran had been conducting secret negotiations since July 2012—and that they had reached a draft agreement they wanted the others to sign off on.

Unveiling Oman

By early November 2013, the United States and Iran had secretly reached a nearly complete deal with only a few loose ends left. The plan was to present the proposed draft at the next P5 + 1 meeting in Geneva on

November 7. That meant that the time had come for the rest of the P5 + 1 to know about the secret negotiations. But first, the rest of the U.S. government needed to be informed.[30]

The Oman channel was such a closely held secret within the U.S. government that only those directly involved in it were in the know. No one in the U.S. Treasury was brought in—even though Treasury handled much of the sanctions implementation. The same was true for most of those working on the State Department's Iran team. Bureaucrats and political appointees rarely take news of major decisions being made without their involvement particularly well. The Oman revelation was no exception to that rule. Treasury officials at the Office of Foreign Assets Control (OFAC) were livid. Because their communication with the Israelis on sanctions implementation was so intimate, the White House had not wanted to risk any leaks to the Israelis by briefing them on the Oman meetings too early. Moreover, many Treasury officials had a reputation of being more sympathetic to Netanyahu's arguments that more sanctions and less compromise would yield a better deal. "Treasury believed we had our foot on the neck of Iran and that we just needed to keep on squeezing them," a White House official told me in December 2013.[31]

The White House saw no evidence of an Iranian capitulation lurking around the corner. "They were not anywhere close, from an economic perspective, to completely giving up the ghost on their nuclear program," Sullivan told me. "[The Iranians] were moving to the point on their own [nuclear] development that we and the Israelis were going to be forced to make some really tough decisions with respect to military action."[32]

Treasury Secretary Jack Lew had to personally sit down with David Cohen, the assistant secretary for terrorist financing in the Treasury Department, to inform him of the Oman channel and the shift in the U.S. policy toward lifting sanctions rather than tightening them. As a consolation, Adam Szubin, who headed OFAC, would become a part of the U.S. negotiating team for the upcoming Geneva session. Officially, this was because of Szubin's sanctions expertise, but in reality it was to soothe the anger of the Treasury Department.[33]

The next step was to inform the P5 + 1. In between the two Geneva meetings, the political directors had a coordination meeting in Brussels. Wendy Sherman led the U.S. delegation and was tasked with informing the United States' partners of the Oman negotiations. "[The meeting] was terrible," she recounted. Sherman gave an oral presentation—no documents—where she walked the others through how far the two sides had come. Though she emphasized that there were "plenty of brackets left," it was clear to the Europeans that the draft agreement was "almost a fait accompli." They weren't happy. Their irritation—even anger—was rooted in several factors. First, there was a sense of betrayal. It was one thing for the United States to pursue a dialogue with Iran—in fact, the European Union had consistently pushed Iran to agree to direct talks with Washington—but it was another thing to do it behind the back of the EU countries.[34]

Second, the EU states were frustrated by the United States' crediting its banking sanctions with providing the main leverage against Iran. In the EU view, it was Europe's oil sanctions that really made the sanctions regime different from previous attempts at coercing Iran economically. And unlike the United States, which had no trade with Iran, the European Union paid a high price for sanctioning Iran. "It is both a point of amusement and frustration that the United States believed that it paid the economic price for the sanctions," a senior German diplomat told me. "It was the EU that paid the price, not the U.S." In eastern France for instance, an entire town was devastated by the sanctions, since its economy was dependent on a Peugeot plant that served the Iranian market. The sanctions forced Peugeot to close the plant, depriving the town of its main source of income and employment. "It was a painful decision," France's ambassador to the United States, Gerard Araud, said. Indeed, a study my colleagues and I conducted in 2014 showed that Germany lost between $23.1 and $73.0 billion between 2010 and 2012 in lost exports to Iran. France lost between $10.9 and $34.2 billion during that same period. For the United States to use the EU oil sanctions as the United States' own bargaining card in a secret negotiation with Iran behind the back of the European Union was inappropriate at best, and a violation of EU sovereignty at worst. "For us it was very unexpected and not considered appropriate—they had already sold our sanctions in the oil sector," a senior member of the EU negotiating team told me. "This was something that diplomatically did not go down well."[35]

But perhaps most important was that the European Union feared that it would be deprived of its fair share of credit for having helped resolve the conflict. For Europe, the P5 + 1 talks were about more than just Iranian proliferation. The European Union had initiated the talks in 2003 in an effort to prevent a U.S.-Iran war and to prove that multilateral engagement was a superior policy option to unilateral militancy. Both the United States and the European Union were better served by the two working in tandem than working at cross purposes. Although the European Union wasn't softer on Iran than Washington was, it had consistently pushed the United States in the direction of diplomacy—a task that began to become redundant with the election of Barack Obama in 2008. And throughout the entire P5 + 1 process, the diplomacy was directed by the European Union's foreign policy chiefs—from Javier Solana (2003–2009), to Lady Cathy Ashton (2009–2014), to Federica Mogherini (2014–present). The European Union understandably sought—and deserved—a tremendous amount of credit for its role in the diplomacy with Iran—something it feared it would be deprived of if the United States and Iran struck their own deal behind the scenes. (To the Russians and Chinese, the United States' secret talks with Iran were far less problematic.)[36]

Sherman's revelations didn't come as a complete surprise to the European Union, however. There had been suspicions that something was going on. For instance, EU diplomats suggested once again to the United States in September 2013 that it would be wise to put some degree of enrichment on the table to get the talks going. While the United States usually would argue against that point, this time around the behavior of the U.S. diplomats was different. They remained silent, while their body language signaled agreement with the EU suggestion. "This was very surprising to me, so this was the point where I thought there was something fishy going on," a member of the EU team told me. What surprised the Europeans more, however, was how advanced the U.S.-Iran draft was. "I was surprised about the detail that they had discussed, because it went quite into a lot of detail," said Helga Schmid, who headed the technical talks on the EU side.[37]

The U.S. side was well aware of the emotions that the revelation of the Oman talks likely would elicit. But it felt it had little choice but to pursue the talks in secret, mindful of the political sensitivities in Washington and Tehran, as well as the risk of sabotage by opponents of diplomacy in Congress, Israel, and Saudi Arabia, as well as in some quarters of the Iranian government itself. "This was just a difficult choice that we had to make, because obviously not telling people could create some backlash, but telling people would risk blowing the whole thing up," Sullivan explained. There was also anger on the U.S. side over the European anger. "I think that it was unfair of them to be so mad at us for doing what they'd been asking us to do for years," Richard Nephew said. "I still find that really offensive."[38]

While most of the Europeans ultimately came to terms with the U.S. decision—and indeed understood the American dilemma—the French were the most unforgiving. And they were the ones who decided to exact revenge on the Americans.

France's Temper Tantrum

It was a tense atmosphere on November 8, when the P5+1 and Iran reconvened in Geneva. The United States put all of its cards on the table during the plenary session and fully revealed how far the secret negotiations had advanced. The U.S. side presented the draft deal, and the Iranians quickly affirmed they were in agreement. With the two principals of the conflict in agreement, the only remaining step—getting the rest of the P5+1's approval—seemed merely ceremonial. But Washington had underestimated France's injured pride. Publicly, French Foreign Minister Laurent Fabius complained that the American-Iranian text was weak on the Arak plutonium plant. But at the negotiations, his objections were procedural—that is, rooted in French anger over the United States negotiating with Iran behind France's back. "They were faced with what was already a highly developed text and felt that the Americans simply wanted them to endorse it," Ravanchi said.[39]

The French knew exactly what to strike from the agreement to make the Iranians walk. While the Iranians had already secured acceptance of enrichment on Iranian soil (with restrictions), their objective was to ensure that Iran's file would eventually be "normalized"; in other words, once Iran had satisfied the concerns of the international community, Iran would enjoy the same freedoms and restrictions as all other members of the Non-Proliferation Treaty (NPT). Otherwise, Iran would risk being put permanently in a separate category. This would be unacceptable to Tehran—just as Iran had to accept limitations for a period of time as a result of its past violations, the West had to come to terms with the fact that once Iran had restored trust, it could no longer be treated differently from other NPT states, Iran maintained. Otherwise, Iran would be the only party to the NPT in good standing that nevertheless enjoyed less rights than all other NPT *and* all non-NPT states. Such a scenario would strengthen the voices of those in Iran favoring exiting the NPT altogether. The original draft presented to the P5+1 by the United States included language specifying that Iran's future enrichment would be within the confines of the NPT—that is, Iran's case would be normalized. The French insisted that the reference to the NPT be struck, which predictably caused a deadlock with the Iranians.[40]

All efforts to compromise with Fabius failed as it became clear that the French intent was to block a deal, not improve the text. When U.S. officials "spoke with him bilaterally and asked what positions he was not comfortable with—he had almost no answer to that question," a senior administration official said. After a late evening ministerial meeting on November 9, where the sides once again failed to satisfy Fabius, the French foreign minister quickly exited the room and rushed over to the hotel lobby where the media had congregated. There, against protocol, he announced that the talks had failed. "There is an initial text that we do not accept," Fabius said, adding that France would not fall for a "fool's game." The comments, and Fabius's airing of internal disputes within the P5+1, infuriated the American side and frustrated the other P5+1 states.[41]

Negotiations with the Iranian side had to be postponed because of the internal divisions caused by France, leaving Western and Iranian diplomats alike confused and irritated. Some publicly blamed the French, describing the situation as "outrageous." At the end of that evening, a furious Sergey Lavrov (the Russian foreign minister), was spotted entering the hotel bar ordering a full bottle of vodka. At that point, it was clear that the deal had slipped out of the hands of Kerry and Zarif.[42]

This wasn't the first time the French had created obstacles to diplomacy, but never before had they managed to ruin an opportunity to actually strike a deal. "At every major juncture they threw a wrench in the wheel," a White House staffer working on Iran told me. Yet, the U.S. side was surprised that the French would go so far as to sabotage the deal. While it was well known that a few individuals in the French president's office held very negative views of Iran, this particular incident was believed by U.S. and EU diplomats to have been motivated by France's sharing economic interests with Israel and some Arab states in the Persian Gulf. "We know who the French were pampering to," an EU diplomat quipped.[43]

A few days after the debacle in Geneva, French president François Hollande landed in Israel, where he received a hero's welcome. Netanyahu had praised France's role in the Geneva talks, telling the French daily *Le Figaro* that Israel "salutes Hollande's firm stance on the Iranian issue." The Iran talks dominated the welcoming ceremony at Ben Gurion Airport. Hollande reassured his Israeli host that France wouldn't allow the pressure on Iran to wind down. This was music to the ears of Netanyahu, who in turn told the French president that "Israel sees in France a true friend," a not-so-veiled jab at the Obama administration.[44]

Netanyahu had been on the phone with Obama the night before Fabius caused the talks to collapse. He was still furious about the Oman negotiations, which Obama had revealed to him in person only weeks earlier. The U.S. side suspected that the Israelis already knew that something was taking place in Oman—they kept close tabs on Bill Burns's travels, for instance—but decided to inform Netanyahu in person nevertheless. Still, Netanyahu had been shocked to find out just how close the United States and Iran were to a deal. Veteran U.S. diplomat Dennis Ross saw the Israeli prime minister immediately after the phone call with Obama and described him as being "as disturbed as I had ever seen him." Netanyahu had drunk his own Kool-Aid: after decades of declaring that diplomacy with Iran was futile, he had lulled himself into a false belief that the deal couldn't happen. But his read of Iran was as erroneous as his read of Obama, and he began to panic. He issued four desperate public statements within twenty-four hours condemning the impending deal, calling it "the deal of the century" for Iran and "a historic mistake" and a "very dangerous and bad deal" for the international community. Obama had called to calm him down, but to no avail; in his moment of need, the French came to his aid instead.[45]

Kerry tried to put on a brave face. The Geneva meeting was not a failure, he insisted, because the two sides were now closer to an agreement. "I can tell you without any exaggeration we not only narrowed differences and clarified those that remain, but we made significant progress," he told skeptical reporters who had followed the drama in Geneva. But though it was clear to all that the obstacle in Geneva was France, Kerry later chose to put the blame on the Iranians. "The French signed off on it, we signed off on it," Kerry said during a visit to the United Arab Emirates, where he sought to reassure Arab allies about the nuclear talks. "Iran couldn't take it."[46]

Kerry was motivated by the need to re-create P5 + 1 unity after Fabius had shattered it. Blaming Iran carried little cost, compared to failing to bring France back in line and allowing them to continue to sabotage the talks. "It would have made no sense for us tactically to call out the French for this sort of disingenuousness in their position," a senior administration official told me. "It would have been much better to present to the world and to the Iranians that the P5 + 1 were unified and that there were no weak links in the chain." (President Obama himself had to call his French counterpart to ensure that France would get back in line.)[47]

The Iranians, however, did not appreciate being scapegoated for the sake of P5 + 1 unity. Zarif took to Twitter to lambast Kerry for exonerating France at the expense of Iran. "No amount of spinning can change what happened," Zarif wrote in one of a series of tweets. "Mr. Secretary, was it Iran that gutted over half of U.S. draft Thursday night?" he asked.[48]

Third Time's the Charm

After Obama calmed down the French, the P5+1 reconvened in Geneva on November 20—the third round of talks would begin in less than six weeks. With the French on board, the prospect of working through the draft and tying the few final loose ends was good. Unless any of the parties, particularly Iran's supreme leader, got cold feet at the last moment, a deal should have been in the offing. Added to the growing optimism was a revelation by Zarif: Iran no longer demanded a formal recognition of enrichment as a right—granted that the West accepted that Iran would continue to enrich. "Not only do we see Iran's right to uranium enrichment as non-negotiable, but we do not see any need for it to be recognized by others, since it is an integral part of Iran's rights under the Non-Proliferation Treaty," Zarif told the Iranian media three days before the talks resumed. This was critical for the West as accepting enrichment in Iran was doable, but recognizing a "right to enrich" was far more complex. While this shift already had taken place in earlier talks, Zarif's going public with it increased expectations that a deal could be reached—and put pressure on the West to be flexible on other issues.[49]

Zarif and the Iranian delegation arrived in Geneva on November 20. The other delegations landed that same day, but without their foreign ministers. Secretary Kerry and his peers would arrive only when the parties were close to striking a deal—or if the talks were close to collapse and needed saving. But the Americans also had a secret delegation in Geneva that arrived before Kerry—Bill Burns, Puneet Talwar, and Jake Sullivan. The trio who had led the Oman talks had also been in Geneva during the previous round, but had managed to escape detection by the media. They stayed at a different hotel across town, and though some journalists had seen Talwar arriving and leaving the Intercontinental via the city's public bus system, few realized that he was shuttling messages to and from the secret negotiations conducted on the other side of town.[50]

I met with Zarif on the first day of the talks. He looked supremely confident and was in a good mood—his back pain was gone, and the French debacle of the previous meeting had in many ways worked in his favor. All along, his strategy was to play the role of the reasonable party.

He represented not a "Holocaust denying, wipe Israel off the map" country, but a peaceful nation that simply sought to stand up for its sovereign rights, he insisted. It was a win-win for Iran: it would either elicit American flexibility or, if the talks failed, it would put Iran in a good position to win the blame game and peel off countries from Washington's sanctions coalition.[51]

The day before the talks began, Zarif had released a YouTube video message addressing a global audience. It was the pinnacle of his "reasonableness" strategy. "What is dignity? What is respect? Are they negotiable? Is there a price tag?" he asked in the opening line of the video, which also contained plenty of B-roll footage of Zarif awkwardly walking the halls of the Iranian Foreign Ministry. He continued:

> Imagine being told that you cannot do what everyone else is doing, what everyone else is allowed to do. Would you back down, would you relent? Or would you stand your ground? . . .
>
> The choice is not submission or confrontation. This past summer our people chose constructive engagement through the ballot box. And through this they gave the world a historic opportunity to change course. To seize this unique opportunity we need to accept equal footing and choose a path based on mutual respect and recognition of the dignity of all peoples. And more so, on the recognition that no power, however strong, can determine the fate of others. . . .
>
> We all need a sober appreciation of our common destiny, our common challenges, and our common opportunities. We also need the conviction that imposition is not sustainable. A conviction that we cannot gain at the expense of others. A conviction that we either win together or lose together; that balance is key to success. . . .
>
> The Iranian people are determined to explore this path. Join us in ending an unnecessary crisis and opening new horizons. My name is Javad Zarif and this is Iran's message.[52]

Zarif had taken Iran's narrative of resistance and packaged it in a language appealing to audiences in the West. Iran was simply standing up for its rights, and through the election of Rouhani, it had created a path where both sides could realize their interests while upholding their rights and dignity. Iran had showed reasonableness. The ball was now in the United States' court, Zarif conveyed in the video.

It remains unclear, however, if Zarif's video had any impact on the three main remaining issues the negotiators had to settle in Geneva: putting the conceptual compromise on enrichment in writing, finalizing a compromise on the Arak plutonium plant, and settling the timing and size of the sanctions relief with which Iran would be provided. Although they were very close to finalizing a deal, both sides negotiated ferociously until the last moment. The worst thing that could happen would be for them to finish early and be accused by their domestic critics of not having negotiated hard enough. Letting the talks drag over time, however, was a time-honed negotiation tactic that both sides had mastered. Twice they extended the talks, as neither side was willing to let go of the chance to push the envelope a bit further.

The enrichment part was the trickiest. While the U.S. side had accepted enrichment on Iranian soil, it was still seeking ways to make it conditional on other factors. The Iranians vehemently resisted such conditionality: they could accept a Western refusal to recognize a formal right, but they were not going to compromise on what such a right—recognized or not—would entail. That was Iran's redline. It could not sign on to an agreement in which Iran was subject to enrichment restrictions that other NPT states were not. "We wanted to be sure that nothing was connected to the provisions related to enrichment," Ravanchi explained to me. "This was our primary concern: we had a clear mandate that the right to enrich not be rendered in any way conditional." Relentless efforts by the United States to insert phrases such as "if agreed" in order to connect the enrichment issue to other factors were consistently rejected by Zarif and his team.[53]

The Arak reactor was another sticking point. The Western side wanted the plutonium plant closed, but the Iranians were not authorized to make that concession. Negotiations on this issue continued till the very last day, when a compromise was finally struck that ended work at Arak while allowing some processes there to continue. As a result, the Iranians could say that they had not agreed to a closing of Arak, while the West achieved its objective of ending the proliferation-sensitive activities there. Strikingly, however, the French objections to the Arak provisions during the earlier session in Geneva did not have a significant impact on the final compromise on this issue.[54]

By all accounts, the last night of the negotiations was tense and terrible. The negotiators were exhausted; even the ministers could no longer refrain from snapping at each other and showing their irritation. The text of the final brackets was shifting back and forth as all sides tried to optimize the language, although at some point the text was merely changing, not improving. Richard Nephew was in charge of typing the never-ending amendments into the computer. As emotions flared, Nephew took the brunt of the heat. "I have the distinction of being yelled at by two foreign ministers, two deputy foreign ministers, and an undersecretary in like an hour and a half," he proudly told me.[55]

It was not until around three o'clock in the morning on November 24—two days past the original deadline—that the ministers finally signed off on the agreement. Frustration between Zarif and Kerry was so palpable that the final bracket had been delegated to Burns and Ravanchi to resolve. At that point, it was less about substance and more about who got the last word. But even after the ministers had signed off on a text, attempts to restart the negotiations continued. Around half an hour before the ministers were scheduled to face the press, Burns was contacted by one of the Iranian negotiators, Abbas Araghchi. "Predictably, I got a call from Araghchi saying, 'Well, there's just three more things we need to change,'" Burns said. "I started laughing, and I said, 'We're done.'" Burns's conversation with Araghchi didn't last long, but demonstrated how hard all sides had negotiated. "I think the Iranians, being the good negotiators that they are, weren't satisfied until they tested it to the last."[56]

Confusion reigned among the journalists who had staked out at the Intercontinental. Most reporters were convinced that the two sides would fail once again—just as they had when Fabius had thrown a tantrum two weeks earlier. Journalists who adhered to the narrative that Tehran was desperate for a deal since sanctions had brought the Iranians to their knees had a hard time explaining why the diplomats were crashing through deadline after deadline. After all, if the Iranians were so desperate for a deal, why was it taking so long for them to capitulate?

For hours, almost no news was leaking out from the negotiations. The American delegation strictly avoided the media (outside of their invitation-only briefings), the French loved the spotlight but had little of substance to offer, and the Russians seemed oblivious to the existence of the non-Russian-speaking media. The Iranians, however, were not as disciplined. Iranian diplomats occasionally passed by the lobby where the press had congregated and chatted with the large delegation of Iranian journalists who had traveled to Geneva on Zarif's airplane. Over the course of the preceding weeks, they had also developed a relationship with some of the Western journalists, who took advantage of the Zarif team's friendlier attitude toward the media.

Around 2:40 a.m., an Iranian journalist ran down the stairs from the second floor into the lobby and began typing ferociously on her laptop. The other journalists rushed to her side to quiz her on her scoop. "They got a deal," she said without taking her eyes off of her screen and without offering any other details. But without an official confirming her story, none of the other journalists could file a story—and no Western official was responding to emails or phone calls. All the reporters could do was to tweet yet another unconfirmed rumor. The confusion deepened. It would take another twenty minutes before an official confirmation came.

At 3:03 a.m., Zarif announced on social media: "We have reached an agreement." History had been made, and in a sign of the times, it was tweeted.

The Pressure Paradox

The skeptics had been proven wrong. A deal with Iran limiting its nuclear activities could be struck. Although a final deal was not yet made, the fact that the Iranians had agreed to negotiate directly with the United States and to discuss limits to their nuclear program was in and of itself a vindication of Obama's investment in diplomacy. But negotiating with Iran might prove easier than dealing with Congress. The ink on the agreement hadn't even dried before congressional hawks and Israeli Prime Minister Benjamin Netanyahu tried to kill it.

The interim agreement—or the Joint Plan of Action (JPOA) as it came to be known—was a genuine compromise that gave both sides a critical gain while ensuring that neither side's redlines were crossed. Iran agreed to stop installing new centrifuges, halt production of 20 percent enriched uranium, and stop most of the work at its heavy-water reactor near the town of Arak. The International Atomic Energy Agency (IAEA) would be given unprecedented access to its nuclear facilities and unparalleled ability to monitor and inspect. In turn, Iran would be given access to about $4.2 billion of its foreign currency holdings, which had been frozen in banks overseas as a result of American financial sanctions. Meanwhile, sanctions on Iran's trade in petrochemical products, precious metals, and airplane and automobile parts would be eased. Finally, the P5 + 1 states committed to not imposing any new nuclear sanctions on Iran during the term of the agreement.[1]

Overall, Iran gained formal acceptance of its enrichment program; secured both sanctions relief and a halt to new sanctions; and developed a path to break free from its international isolation. The final deal "would enable Iran to fully enjoy its right to nuclear energy for peaceful purposes under the relevant articles of the NPT in conformity with its obligations therein," the preamble of the JPOA states. "For the first time six countries of the P5 + 1 . . . [have] recognized that enrichment is part of any solution, and another part of this solution is to remove all sanctions," Iran's Foreign Minister Javad Zarif told Iranian TV. In short, Iran had taken a big leap toward desecuritization.[2]

The win for the United States and its P5 + 1 partners was that the JPOA halted Iran's nuclear advances and reversed a dynamic in which time was on Iran's side. With the Iranians halting their nuclear growth, Iran's breakout time would now remain stable, which meant that Iran's leverage over the West would no longer be growing. "The JPOA was very advantageous to us, because it took away their main source of leverage, which was to expand their [nuclear] capability," said Robert Einhorn, a senior nonproliferation expert who took part in the negotiations up until spring of 2013. And with a stable breakout time, the pressure to take military action against Iran began to weaken. The urgency that had compelled the United States to finally play the enrichment card was gone. In fact, viewed strictly from the prism of leverage, the JPOA was arguably more advantageous to the United States than to Iran, since it neutralized much of Iran's advantage while keeping most of Washington's bargaining chips intact.[3]

In Washington, President Barack Obama was quick to praise the deal. "Today, . . . diplomacy opened up a new path toward a world that is more secure—a future in which we can verify that Iran's nuclear program is peaceful and that it cannot build a nuclear weapon," he said. "For the first time in nearly a decade, we have halted the progress of the Iranian nuclear program, and key parts of the program will be rolled back," he added, while pointing out that Iran's sanctions relief would be reversed should Tehran fail to comply with the deal. Kerry tweeted that the JPOA was a first step that "makes the world safer," echoing statements by European leaders.[4]

Nowhere was the interim deal as warmly received as in Iran. Zarif received a hero's welcome upon arriving in Tehran. A large crowd had gathered at the airport, chanting slogans reflecting both Iran's demand for mutual respect and the Iranian people's happiness that Iran had not submitted itself to Western demands: "Na jang, na tahrim, na toheen, na taslim" (neither war, nor sanctions, nor insult, nor submission). Most Iranians first found out that a deal had been struck via social media. "When I checked my Instagram when I woke up, someone had posted a picture of an Iranian and American flag," a young Iranian woman said. "After I read the comments saying a deal was made, tears started rolling down my cheeks of happiness. I couldn't believe it." Rouhani praised the deal and said it would "open new horizons." More important, Khamenei threw in his support for the deal, tweeting that "the nuclear negotiating team deserves to be appreciated and thanked for its achievement." Still, the supreme leader's support did not prevent Iranian hardliners from blasting the agreement, accusing Rouhani of selling the people of Iran a "chalice of poison." But no one opposed the deal more furiously than Benjamin Netanyahu.[5]

Obama's Two-Front War

If Iran was jubilant, Israel was overcome by shock and anger. Netanyahu did not mince his words in condemning the JPOA. Visibly angry, the Israeli prime minister took to the podium and called the deal a blunder of "historic" proportions. "Today the world became a much more dangerous place," he said, refuting the Obama administration's argument that the deal reduced the risk of war. "Israel cannot participate in the international celebration, which is based on Iranian deception and [international] self-delusion," Israeli Minister of Intelligence Yuval Steinitz added. The Netanyahu government blamed the deal on Obama's "inner circle" of advisors which "wants to avoid a military conflict with Iran and are seeking an agreement with it at any price." The Israelis were particularly skeptical of Ben Rhodes, Obama's chief of staff, Denis McDonough, and his long-time advisor Valerie Jarrett.[6]

The thirty-minute phone call between Obama and Netanyahu that took place within hours after the deal was announced did little to tone down Netanyahu's public criticism. Trust between Netanyahu and Obama had gradually been depleted due to their many disputes and confrontations—both public and private. But from the Israeli perspective, the revelation of the Oman channel killed what little trust was left. Obama's negotiating with the Ahmadinejad government behind Israel's back—and giving away the enrichment card on top of that—was simply the last straw for Netanyahu.[7]

With trust depleted, the Israeli prime minister faced a strategic choice. On the one hand, he could have expressed his disappointment with Washington's accepting enrichment in Iran and focused on retaining pressure on the clerical regime in Tehran. Instead, he chose to take on the American president and try to kill the deal—despite its clear nonproliferation benefits (which prompted key members of the Israeli security establishment to consistently express satisfaction with the deal). "That's when we knew there was never going to be a deal that was satisfactory to [the Israelis]," Deputy National Security Advisor Ben Rhodes told me. There was no deal that would satisfy Netanyahu. He was simply opposed to the idea of striking a deal with Iran, because any realistic deal would do two things: it would accept some degree of enrichment in Iran, and it would end Iran's global isolation. Although it deprived Iran of nuclear weapons, the deal would still unleash Iran and help it challenge Israel's geopolitical maneuverability in the region. While Obama kept the channels of communication with Netanyahu open, he could no longer afford to share much information about the state of play in the P5 + 1 talks, lest the Israelis undermine the talks. In the earlier rounds of talks, the United States had made a point of briefing the Israelis both before and after the negotiations. After her talks with the Iranians, Wendy Sherman often traveled to Israel before returning to DC. But after Netanyahu's categorical denunciation of the deal, Obama believed he had no choice but to cut out the Israelis. The briefings stopped.[8]

With Netanyahu on a warpath against the deal, Obama had to shift his focus from Geneva to Congress, where the prime minister's allies were sharpening their knives. In preparation for this showdown,

the White House had begun reaching out to likely opponents and supporters of the nuclear deal a week before the JPOA was struck. The purpose was to minimize the risk of any domestic political backlash or
outright rebellion against the deal in Congress, while strengthening
support for the president's diplomacy. Jewish and pro-Israeli organizations were on top of the administration's list, due to their receptivity
to Netanyahu's arguments against the deal—and because of his specific
targeting of these groups.[9]

The four main Jewish groups skeptical of the deal were the American Jewish Committee, the American Israel Public Affairs Committee (AIPAC), the Anti-Defamation League, and the Conference of
Presidents of Major American Jewish Organizations. On the other side
were J Street and Americans for Peace Now, which had long supported
the president's line. The White House had no expectation that the Jewish groups sympathetic to Netanyahu would come out in support of the
pending nuclear deal with Iran. Rather, the aim was to temper their
opposition. "We didn't ask them to come out and support the [deal],"
an administration official said. "We just wanted them to be quiet."[10]

The first meeting with the skeptics didn't go as planned. The White
House laid out where the negotiations were and the contours of the
likely deal, including the sanctions relief the United States was considering, while signaling that the president would oppose any new sanctions that would derail the talks. The ask was for groups to continue
their dialogue with the White House. The meeting was off the record,
but one by one, the groups began leaking information from the briefing
and declaring their support for new sanctions and opposition to the
pending deal. The White House strongly suspected that the hawkish
groups wouldn't have taken these strong measures without some signal
from the Netanyahu government. A month later, Netanyahu removed
any lingering doubt: at a conference with thousands of Jewish Americans in Jerusalem on November 10, he blasted Obama and his envoys
and accused them of imperiling Israel's survival. He warned that the
United States itself would soon be threatened by Iran's power and urged
the Jewish community to stop the nuclear deal. "Coming to a theatre
near you. Do you want that?" he growled. "Well, do something about
it." Seldom had an Israeli prime minister so openly urged the American

Jewish community to take his side against the president of the United States.[11]

But Obama knew more about Netanyahu's activities than he was letting on. After embarrassing revelations of the United States spying on leaders of some of its closest allies, Obama announced that he would curtail eavesdropping on friendly heads of state. That decision, however, did not apply to Netanyahu. The Obama administration decided to continue spying on his activities precisely because of his unrelenting efforts to undermine diplomacy. Through the National Security Administration's eavesdropping, Obama learned that Netanyahu had leaked details of the nuclear negotiations in order to undermine the talks and coordinated talking points with Jewish American groups against the deal.[12]

With the pro-Netanyahu Jewish groups revealing their hand, and Netanyahu proving that he would reject any plausible deal, the White House had no choice but to take off its gloves. Israeli terms for a deal would "close the door on diplomacy," the administration shot back, and would "essentially lead to war." The idea that sanctions should not be exchanged for nuclear concessions was nonsensical, the administration maintained, because sanctions were imposed not for the sake of driving matters toward a confrontation with Iran, but for the sake of stopping Iranian proliferation. From Obama's perspective, sanctions were imposed to provide the United States with leverage in a negotiation with Iran. And the time had now arrived to use that leverage to clinch a deal. "We got our leverage and we want to use it," a senior administration official told the press. Iranian capitulation due to escalating sanctions pressure, the administration official explained, simply wasn't in the cards—a conclusion Obama had drawn in early 2013, fueling the search for a diplomatic exit from the sanctions strategy. "Unlike Bibi, we are skeptical that there will ever be a time when the Iranian government totally capitulates," the administration official continued. "Due to the nature of this regime, the thought that they will surrender to the West is a long shot. If, as Netanyahu says, this regime is an apocalyptic and messianic cult, why would they surrender because of more sanctions?"[13]

Netanyahu had lost control over the narrative of Iran and diplomacy. He had failed to prevent a deal. He had failed to convince the world (and much of the Jewish American community) that there was no difference between Rouhani and Ahmadinejad. His relationship with the American president was in pieces. But he was far from giving up. He had a secret weapon that he had not yet fully employed—Israel's new ambassador to Washington, Ron Dermer.[14]

The American-born Dermer started off his political career in Florida as a Republican strategist, working for the Republican pollster Frank Luntz. He moved to Israel when he was in his twenties and became an Israeli citizen in 1997. During his years there, he became very close to Netanyahu, who saw much of himself in the young Dermer. His jack-of-all-trades role in Netanyahu's inner circle—he is the prime minister's strategist, pollster, and speechwriter—earned him the title "Bibi's brain." According to *Tablet Magazine*, "Bibi doesn't move an inch without talking to him." Like Netanyahu, Dermer errs on the side of hawkishness and has a brash style, always threading the line "between being a foreign diplomat and being an active player in American politics."[15]

Dermer took up his post in December 2013, only weeks after the interim deal was signed. The Obama administration was dismayed by the appointment, as they viewed Dermer as a GOP hack who would only intensify Netanyahu's interference in American politics by encouraging the Republicans to attack Obama's Iran diplomacy. Which was exactly what the Israeli prime minister planned for him to do. Netanyahu and his Republican allies in Congress could not force Obama to abandon diplomacy, but they *could* pass new sanctions on Iran in an attempt to kill the deal. The United States had, through agreeing to the JPOA, committed itself against imposing any new nuclear-related sanctions on Iran, and any passage of such sanctions would violate the agreement. The Iranians stated in no unclear terms that the negotiations would be dead if the United States were to betray the JPOA so quickly after signing it. Asked by *Time Magazine* what would happen if Congress imposed new sanctions—even if they would not go into effect for six months—Zarif curtly replied: "The entire deal is dead." While the Washington narrative on Iran maintained that the critical obstacles to improved U.S.-Iran relations were Iran's domestic politics and the ideological impulses of the regime, an unexpected picture was now emerging: the most immediate threat to the nuclear deal and continued negotiations lay in Washington—not Tehran.[16]

"I know the domestic complications and various issues inside the United States, but for me that is no justification," Zarif said. "I have a parliament. My parliament can also adopt various legislation that can go into effect if negotiations fail. But if we start doing that, I don't think that we will be getting anywhere." The White House recognized that a violation of the deal would betray not just Iran's confidence in the Obama administration, but also that of the other P5+1 partners. That would cause the international coalition against Iran and the remaining sanctions regime to crumble, giving the Iranians de facto sanctions relief while allowing them to walk away from their responsibilities under the deal. "I don't want to give the Iranians a public excuse to flout the agreement," Kerry told the House Foreign Relations Committee. "It could lead our international partners to think that we're not an honest broker, and that we didn't mean it when we said that sanctions were not an end in and of themselves but a tool to pressure the Iranians into a diplomatic solution."[17]

An Issue of War and Peace

Despite Kerry's protests, Senators Bob Menendez (D-NJ) and Mark Kirk (R-IL) introduced new sanctions legislation—the Nuclear Weapon Free Iran Act of 2013—on December 20, 2013, with twenty-four additional cosponsors. The bill would further cut Iran's oil sales, provide military and other support to Israel if it "is compelled to take military action in legitimate self-defense against Iran's nuclear weapon program," and impose on Obama the zero-enrichment objective, which would ensure that the talks would fail.

The bill, fully backed by AIPAC, was a gutsy move. Since it was a clear violation of the deal, it would force the Senate to choose between the JPOA and the powerful, hawkish pro-Israel lobby. However, it was also a test for AIPAC: the organization doesn't like to directly clash with sitting presidents; it picks its fights carefully. Now it was following Netanyahu's lead and was convinced that it could halt Obama's Iran policy in the Senate. Moreover, there may also have been practical considerations. According to former senior AIPAC executive Douglas Bloomfield, pushing for Iran sanctions was a potent fundraising tool for the organization. "It's good for business," he told Inter Press Services. "AIPAC has spent the last 20 years very, very effectively making a strong case against Iran, and Iran has been a great asset to them."[18]

The president quickly threatened to veto the bill, and during his State of the Union address in January 2014 he reissued the threat directly to the House and the Senate. He also added that it was in the national interest of the United States to continue diplomacy. "If John F. Kennedy and Ronald Reagan could negotiate with the Soviet Union," Obama argued, "then surely a strong and confident America can negotiate with less powerful adversaries today." But the sanctions legislation did put Obama in a bind with Congress, precisely because the administration had so aggressively pushed the narrative that sanctions had forced Iran to soften its position and "come back to the negotiating table." Since most of the sanctions had been pushed for by Congress and resisted by Obama, many senators felt that they, rather than the White House, deserved credit for the diplomatic opening. In addition, they didn't trust Obama's judgment when he took credit for the previous sanctions policy and argued that more sanctions would be harmful to diplomacy.[19]

This might have been why, for the first time, Obama credited diplomacy ahead of pressure when explaining the opening with Iran in his State of the Union address in January 2014. "And it is American diplomacy, backed by pressure, that has halted the progress of Iran's nuclear program," he said. This was a little-noticed but very important deviation from the standard narrative of the White House that put sanctions at the center and portrayed diplomacy as having played a peripheral role in the nuclear opening.

The White House was alarmed by the Kirk-Menendez bill for good reason. By mid-January, it had secured cosponsorship of almost sixty senators, which meant that it could become filibuster-proof. If it reached sixty-seven cosponsors, it would also be veto-proof. It was at this point that the White House decided to put front and center an argument they knew would further raise the temperature between Obama, Netanyahu, and Congress, but could effectively sway the undecided senators against the bill. On January 9, when Menendez was only two cosponsors away from making the bill filibuster-proof, National Security Council spokesperson Bernadette Meehan issued a statement declaring a vote for the Kirk-Menendez bill tantamount to a vote for war:

> The American people have been clear that they prefer a peaceful resolution to this issue. If certain members of Congress want the United States to take military action, they should be up front with the American public and say so. Otherwise, it's not clear why any member of Congress would support a bill that possibly closes the door on diplomacy and makes it more likely that the United States will have to choose between military options or allowing Iran's nuclear program to proceed.[20]

Republican lawmakers and some of their Democratic allies were absolutely livid. The White House had essentially accused them of seeking war through the backdoor. Some high-level Democratic senators called the White House and complained about the statement, but were told in no uncertain terms that their objections carried little weight, since they were essentially complaining that the war accusation created problems for their efforts to undermine the president. In an op-ed published in the *Washington Post* the next day, Senator Menendez categorically rejected the accusation and argued that his bill actually would boost diplomacy—a claim the White House and pro-diplomacy groups found laughable. "It just stands to reason if you close the diplomatic option, you're left with a difficult choice of waiting to see if sanctions cause Iran to capitulate, which we don't think will happen, or considering military action," Ben Rhodes told the *New York Times*.[21]

Supporters of the president, on the other hand, strongly favored the statement and believed it was long overdue. At a meeting at the White House, several Democratic lawmakers banged their hands on the table demanding more "Meehan statements," which could provide them with political fodder against pressure by AIPAC and pro-Netanyahu organizations. From Obama's perspective, not only was the statement

true—the collapse of diplomacy would lead to war; it was also important, as it forced the opponents of diplomacy to "own the consequences
of their recommendation." The short-term goal of the Meehan statement and the war-or-peace framing was to kill the Menendez bill. The
longer term goal was to force the sanctions proponents to articulate an
alternative to diplomacy that they then would have to defend. Up until
that point, the sanctions proponents had "gotten away with pretending
that their efforts would help advance diplomacy." They positioned themselves as supporting the same policy and objectives as the president. In
Obama's mind, there was no doubt that their push was actually aimed
at undermining diplomacy, but until the war-or-peace frame was put
forward, the sanctions proponents had never had to "answer for the
consequence of their policy option." (U.S. intelligence had also briefed
lawmakers on their conclusion that new punitive measures would "undermine the prospects for a comprehensive nuclear agreement with
Iran.")[22]

The White House knew of the American public's war fatigue and
had drafted the statement weeks earlier. They were just waiting for the
right moment to launch their offensive. With the Menendez bill picking up steam, that moment had arrived. And it did the trick. The statement dramatically changed the debate over the JPOA as it became less
about striking a deal with a much-disliked theocratic government and
more about a choice between war and peace. The Menendez bill never
made it beyond fifty-nine cosponsors, and as a result, it was never put up
for a vote, since it would have been filibustered. "Our statement killed
his bill," a former National Security Council staffer proudly told me. "It
was a turning point as it changed the entire debate."[23]

For AIPAC, this was a humiliating defeat. In an unusual move, the
organization issued a press release on February 6 in which it expressed
continued support for the bill but said "there should not be a vote at this
time on the measure." AIPAC's retreat angered the Republicans, as well
as some of the Democratic supporters of the bill. Senator Chuck Schumer
(D-NY) reluctantly joined AIPAC in backing down, but only after "consultations on both sides of the ocean," an apparent reference to the Israeli prime minister. Although the defeat in the Senate did not provide
the Obama administration with much reprieve from AIPAC or Netan-

yahu, it was an important victory for the Obama administration and supporters of diplomacy, as it showed that the balance of power in Washington had shifted. With the war-or-peace framing, Obama had managed to give the backers of diplomacy the upper hand.[24]

Geopolitical Flux

The implementation of the interim deal began on January 20, 2014, with Iran halting its production of uranium enriched to 19.75 percent (MEU) and diluting half of its MEU stockpile. The IAEA quickly confirmed that "all their [Iran's] requirements have been fulfilled." Within a month, the IAEA noted that Iran's MEU was shrinking for the first time in four years and that Iran now had far less MEU than was needed to build a bomb. The negotiations quickly resumed, and the parties agreed on a July 20 deadline to complete the final deal. But despite their best efforts, progress was negligible, hampered by the fact that the Oman channel had been closed at the request of the Europeans. Most of the progress in the talks had been done in the bilateral U.S.-Iran discussions, and with that channel closed, progress in the nuclear talks became painfully slow.[25]

But there were also other complicating factors. Geopolitical and global instability rendered it increasingly difficult to insulate the nuclear talks. Instability in Ukraine led to Russian military intervention in its Western neighbor in March 2014 and a subsequent crisis in the West's relations with Russia. Although the P5 + 1 ultimately managed to prevent the Ukraine tensions from spilling over into the nuclear talks, the Russians at one point did threaten "retaliatory measures" against the West that could hurt the nuclear talks. "We wouldn't like to use these talks as an element of the game of raising the stakes taking into account the sentiments in some European capitals, Brussels and Washington," Deputy Foreign Minister Sergey Ryabkov said. "But if they force us into that, we will take retaliatory measures here as well."[26]

Two regional developments had a more direct impact on the talks—or at least Tehran's view of Washington. The first was diplomacy over Syria. While the P5 + 1 talks were supposed to be exclusively on the nuclear issue, the United States and Iran had used their bilateral channel to discuss regional developments, particularly in Syria. With the JPOA concluded, an opening existed to bring Iran into the diplomatic efforts to end the Syrian civil war. The United States had long recognized that without the participation of the Assad regime's closest ally, diplomacy was unlikely to get far. Tehran had also indicated that it would participate if invited without preconditions. For the United States' Arab allies—particularly Saudi Arabia—this was very alarming, as it would further enable Washington to extract itself from the region while paving the way for Tehran's political rehabilitation. While France and Saudi Arabia insisted that Tehran could partake in the Geneva talks on Syria only if it first accepted that Assad would have to hand over power to a transitional body—a step Iran had consistently refused—Kerry began to signal some flexibility. In January 2014, Kerry indicated that the United States might accept a compromise on the terms of Iran's role so that the conference could proceed. Kerry later altered his position and suggested that Iran could only be "present on the sidelines"—a proposal the Iranians found profoundly insulting. Kerry's conflicting signals were followed by UN Secretary General Ban Ki-Moon's inviting Iran to the talks—only to have the invitation rescinded within twenty-four hours.[27]

It was Kerry who personally lobbied Ban Ki-Moon to rescind the invitation, since the main Syrian opposition group and Saudi Arabia had threatened to boycott the talks if Iran attended. This in turn made the Iranians blame the United States for the debacle. While the entire affair was embarrassing to Tehran, Iran's main worry was that the episode proved Washington remained under the influence of Saudi Arabia, and as a result, its regional policies and attitude toward Iran were unlikely to shift even after the nuclear issue was resolved. This doubt about the United States' independence from the Saudi bloc was further strengthened when the Iraqi city of Mosul fell in June 2014 to the terrorist organization Daesh (also known as ISIS or ISIL), which had emerged out of the ashes of al-Qaeda in Iraq and Saddam Hussein's inner guard. The surprise advance of ISIS took both Washington and Tehran off guard. ISIS's anti-Shia and anti-Iranian tilt was no secret to Tehran: after taking Mosul an ISIS spokesperson threatened to continue onward to Baghdad and the holy Shia cities of Najaf and Karbala. Similarly, Washington knew that an ISIS takeover of Baghdad would be a major victory for the jihadists and a disaster for the United States. The United States and Iran had a clear common interest in halting the advance of ISIS and boosting the defenses of the Baghdad government. Whether they would be able to collaborate against ISIS was a different matter, however.[28]

The Iranians swiftly came to Baghdad's aid. According to a senior Iraqi defense official, Iran immediately responded to Baghdad's request for more ammunition—particularly Russian ammunition. Tehran was the first to respond and put no conditions on the Iraqis for the delivery. No Arab state came to Iraq's aid, while American support came at a slower pace and with several political conditions. As a result, Iraqi officials publicly credited Tehran for saving Baghdad from falling into ISIS hands, much to Washington's annoyance.[29]

Both Washington and Tehran were divided on whether they welcomed collaboration with the other to defeat ISIS. While Kerry and Rouhani publicly welcomed the opportunity to collaborate, hardliners in Tehran and the Pentagon officially rejected the proposition. "There is absolutely no intention and no plan to coordinate military activities between the United States and Iran," Pentagon Press Secretary Rear Admiral John Kirby said. Washington's concerns with such a collaboration were plentiful. For one thing, open collaboration could suggest that a linkage had been created between the nuclear issue and the campaign against ISIS, which critics in Washington would argue put Iran in a more advantageous position. For another, the conflict in Iraq already had a strong sectarian dimension. Further involvement by Iran and Iraqi Shia militias to drive out ISIS from predominantly Sunni areas would likely only further fuel sectarian tensions—a point Iranian officials privately conceded. Then, too, given how Iraqi Shia militias (supported by Iran) were responsible for many American deaths in Iraq, opposition to open collaboration with them was intense among Pentagon officials. "I will not—and I hope we will never—coordinate or cooperate with Shiite militias," General Lloyd J. Austin III, commander of the U.S. Central Command, told Congress in March 2015. But most importantly, open U.S.-Iran coordination in Iraq would cause further panic in Riyadh about the trajectory of U.S.-Iran relations and the new regional order that could emerge out of a nuclear deal. This, in turn, could prompt Saudi Arabia to devote more resources toward derailing the nuclear talks.[30]

The emergence of ISIS radically changed the geopolitical landscape and reinforced the White House's view that the main threat to stability in the region was not Iran, but the jihadi Sunni extremist movements financed and inspired by the strictly orthodox Wahhabi school of thought in Saudi Arabia, combined with weak, failing states. "Obama knew that Iran was a 75-million-strong viable state," German Ambassador Peter Wittig told me. "There are not a lot of viable states left in the Middle East, and this is critical for the long-term power configuration in the region." In an interview just weeks before ISIS's takeover of Mosul, Obama was asked if he viewed Sunni or Shia extremism as more dangerous. His answer was revealing. He chose to clarify the negatives of Sunni extremism by devoting his answer to pointing out that the Shia government in Iran was rational, calculating, self-interested, and susceptible to logic. "If you look at Iranian behavior," he said, "they are strategic, and they're not impulsive. They have a worldview, and they see their interests, and they respond to costs and benefits. And that isn't to say that they aren't a theocracy that embraces all kinds of ideas that I find abhorrent, but they're not North Korea. They are a large, powerful country that sees itself as an important player on the world stage, and I do not think has a suicide wish, and can respond to incentives." Implicitly, Obama indicated that the Sunni radical movements were none of these things, which made them inherently more dangerous and destabilizing.[31]

And it was no secret to the Obama administration that Saudi money and ideology fueled these jihadi terror organizations. "A lot of the money, the seed money if you will, for what became al-Qaeda, came out of Saudi Arabia," Ben Rhodes said in a radio interview in 2016. The White House was clear-eyed about the challenge Iran posed in the region, from the proxies it supported and enabled to the threat it posed to some of Washington's allies in the region. But it was also cognizant of the fact that the region had changed and that the proxies and ideological movements supported by U.S. allies in the region had emerged as the main threat to stability in the area. "Are [the Iranians] way worse than any other powers in the region?" a White House staffer told me. "Personally I don't think so. . . . I think there are other actors in the region who are super unhelpful who we have much better relationships with."[32]

The rise of ISIS also sparked a debate in Iran over its regional posture, which transcended political factions. One side of the debate argued that ISIS was a Sunni creation—a Sunni problem that required a Sunni solution. Iran was already overextended in the region, and besides, ISIS would never be able to threaten the Iranian mainland. It wasn't Iran's fight. Tehran should just protect the Shia population and shrines in Iraq and Syria, while letting the United States and its Sunni Arab allies deal with what ultimately was a problem of their own making. The other side argued that the entire region was becoming more unstable and that Iran would not be able to maintain its own stability in this new context unless it devoted resources to actively stabilize the region. Iran had no choice but to export security—and if that required collaborating with the United States and even Saudi Arabia, that would be a bitter pill Iran had to swallow.[33]

Ever so paranoid about American intentions, Ayatollah Khamenei was skeptical about collaborating with the United States to export security, since he didn't believe the United States sought stability in the first place. The slow American reaction to ISIS and its lukewarm support for the Baghdad government had fueled suspicions in Tehran that Washington wanted to overthrow the Maliki government and use ISIS as a pretext to increase Washington's military presence in the region. "What is happening in Iraq is not a war between Shiites and Sunnis. Arrogant powers want to use the remnants of Saddam's regime and *takfiri* (ISIS) extremists to deprive Iraq of stability and tranquility," the supreme leader said. "The real fight is between those who want to bring back a U.S. presence and those who want Iraqi independence."[34]

In return, the United States held that due to its harsh policies against Iraqi Sunnis, Iraq's Shia-dominated government was partially responsible for the rise of ISIS. Although the United States and Iran ended up coordinating some activities against ISIS indirectly through the Iraqi government, the rise of the terrorist organization undermined Iranian trust in the United States and further confused Tehran about its intentions, Zarif told me. From Tehran's perspective, the United

States' deference to Saudi Arabia "caused it not to take action against ISIS in the manner it said it would," which in turn increased fear in Tehran that after the nuclear deal, the United States would once again pursue aggressive policies toward Iran.[35]

Unrealistic Deadlines or Unrealistic Opening Positions?

U.S. and Iranian negotiators were pessimistic as the last round of negotiations began in early July. Both sides took maximalist positions, driven by a fear that the other side would pocket any flexibility they showed and buy the view that they would end up short if they didn't match the other side's position. Though they retained the discipline to avoid negotiating in public, both sides did take their case public to put pressure on their counterparts.

Zarif penned an op-ed in the *Washington Post* arguing that the United States' unrealistic demands and singular focus on pressure and sanctions had cost it a golden opportunity to limit Iran's nuclear activities in early 2005, before Mahmoud Ahmadinejad was elected president. In Zarif's narrative, Iran's response to those unrealistic demands was to harden its position and posture, causing its centrifuge program to grow from "200 to 20,000 centrifuges." The United States was now once again faced with such an opportunity. It could either seize it, by matching Iran's constructive approach, or squander it, by clinging onto maximalist fantasies, Zarif argued. Kerry had said the same of Iran, arguing it had to choose between taking "the steps necessary to assure the world that their country's nuclear program will be exclusively peaceful" and squandering "a historic opportunity."[36]

At the heart of the matter was the two sides' inability to come to agreement on criteria that would give confidence that Iran's nuclear program was solely peaceful. The Israelis had pressed for the breakout concept (a state's capability to produce one or more weapons quickly and with little warning), which the United States adopted and sought Iran's agreement to. However, the Iranians rejected it on two grounds. First, the concept assumed that Iran was pursuing nuclear weapons—an assumption that Iran had consistently rejected. If the intent to break out was lacking, the breakout time would essentially be infinite, the Iranians argued. Second, Tehran questioned the methodology behind the breakout and presented its own way to calculate breakout—which was rejected by the West. "They insisted on calculating breakout timeline on their own, and we said that we don't care how you calculate it," a senior administration official explained. "It's not relevant how long you think it'll take. It's how long we think—that's our whole interest in this." Meeting after meeting was held throughout the spring (and later in the fall) debating both the validity of the breakout concept and how best to calculate it. The Iranians presented a version in which, according to their calculations, breakout would occur in four years—which the U.S. side found to be "crazy."[37]

The Iranians preferred a different solution: to reconfigure the centrifuges in a manner that would make it impossible to produce nuclear weapons. Under this concept, Zarif had strict instructions not to agree to any reduction of centrifuges below 9,000. The United States' opening bid under that formula was hard to swallow for the Iranians: Iran should keep only 500 centrifuges, the United States insisted. In the midst of the negotiations, Iran's supreme leader made a statement declaring that Iranian experts said Iran would need 190,000 SWU (separative work units) in the long run, which was widely interpreted as him demanding 190,000 centrifuges. Both demands—500 versus 190,000—were bizarre positions, but they were the outcome of Washington's and Tehran's falling for the maximalist trap. The 500 centrifuge opening position "was absurd," according to one of the U.S. negotiators, Rob Malley. "We knew it was absurd, they knew we knew it was absurd, and we knew that they knew that we thought it was absurd."[38]

With both sides having adopted a strategy of leading with maximalist positions, blowing through deadlines was almost inevitable. As the two sides gradually shifted their positions, they revealed that their original positions were nothing but bargaining positions. This created uncertainty about what the other side's true bottom line was—and an almost endless desire to keep pushing in order to reach that bottom line. Whatever position one ended up taking, the other side would still not be convinced that it was the true bottom line, and hence would seek to push further. This, combined with the fact that the most important shifts in each side's position would take place close to the deadline, dramatically increased the likelihood that the lion's share of bargaining would take place right before the deadline—and that the target date would be missed.

When I met with Zarif in mid-July, he was downtrodden and pessimistic. It was clear that the two sides were stuck, and he feared he would suffer the same fate as he did in 2005, when he presented the European Union with the last Iranian negotiation offer before Ahmadinejad was elected. The European Union never responded to that proposal, and Zarif and Rouhani were blamed in Iran for having naively agreed to suspending enrichment. Zarif and Iran lost the blame game back then, but he was determined not to lose it again. If the talks collapsed, he told me, he would resign and send a letter to the UN secretary general explaining Iran's position, attach both Iran and the P5+1's positions, and let the world decide who was at fault. I was unsure whether Zarif was bluffing or not, but a few days later, the parties announced that the talks would be extended until November 24. Few were surprised by the extension, but while there was a sense that the negotiations could survive one extension, most were convinced that domestic political pressures in Tehran and Washington would not permit a second delay. For every day that passed, opponents of diplomacy were closing in on Kerry, Zarif, and their teams.

The Pressure Paradox

After the predictable failure in July 2014, the very same Europeans who had been irked by the secret negotiations in Oman were now telling Washington that the direct U.S.-Iran channel needed to be resurrected. Negotiating the deal among seven different parties was a recipe for failure. A direct channel between the principals of the conflict was needed to come to an agreement on the contours of a deal before it was put in front of the other parties. The difference this time, of course, was that the rest of the P5+1 would be fully briefed on the U.S.-Iran deliberations.[39]

But a change of methodology was not sufficient to get the talks back on track. The parties needed a more profound shift in how they understood each other and how their positions could be altered. Each side was fully convinced that the other side had agreed to negotiate seriously only as a result of the pressure that it had been subjected to, while strongly rejecting the idea that the pressure it was itself subjected to prompted its own shift in behavior. While the gospel in Washington held that sanctions brought the Iranians to the negotiating table, Iranian hardliners maintained that the expansion of Iran's nuclear program compelled Washington to drop its zero-enrichment position. The centrifuges brought the United States to its senses, the Iranian argument read.

This excessive focus on pressure as the sole instrument to compel changes in behavior contributed to the deadlock in negotiations. Since the two sides believed that pressure had generated flexibility on the other side, they were both loath to ease said pressure, fearing that it would cause their counterpart to revert back to its previous policy. Following this logic, Washington insisted on significant concessions from the Iranian side, but in return offered only to suspend some sanctions upfront, postponing the actual lifting of sanctions to a much later date. The U.S. side feared that if the sanctions—its main leverage—were lifted earlier, Iran would no longer have any incentive to comply with the agreement. Once sanctions were lifted reimposing them would be a monumental task, leaving Iran with the freedom to expand its nuclear program with impunity. Absent pressure, the belief went, Iran would not move in the right direction.[40]

Similarly, Tehran agreed to freeze some of its nuclear activities, but insisted on maintaining its functioning centrifuges—the core of its leverage. Just as the United States and the European Union wanted to reduce the centrifuge count to lengthen Iran's breakout capability, Tehran calculated that a shorter breakout period would give it leverage over the international community to ensure that it followed through on the sanctions relief it had promised.

Operating in this pressure paradigm, neither side could imagine alternative drivers of behavior. The notion that a deal could change Iran's incentive structure and make it not *desire* actions that would violate the deal simply did not fit within this paradigm. Similarly, the Iranians did not trust that the West would see adhering to the deal as being in its interest, absent Iran's being on the verge of breakout.

But the premise of this paradigm was incorrect. In reality, the negotiations took off because the pressure path was leading to a dead end: a war neither side wanted. And just as the pressure paradigm did not bring about diplomacy, it was also incapable of delivering a durable deal. For an enduring solution to be reached, both sides had to feel that they won something. Pressure cannot bring about that sentiment. No one can be pressured into feeling like a winner. Durable solutions are found when both sides feel that they have gained something that they do not want to lose and that they cannot obtain through other means. Their incentives are transformed. They no longer want to cheat, because they are more satisfied within the agreement than outside of it—not necessarily because of the punishment they would suffer, but because of the gains they would lose.[41]

Clearly pressure is also needed as one of many components in a broader strategy. But a strategy that is centered solely on pressure suffers from an inescapable paradox. To compel the other side to negotiate, you need pressure and leverage, it is assumed. For the other side to agree to change its behavior, however, you need to offer giving up that leverage as an incentive. But once the pressure is relieved, so is the incentive of the other side to comply with the agreement, according to the paradigm, causing the deal to fall apart. The paradox is caused by a flaw in the paradigm's foundational assumption: the behavior of the other side can be changed only through pressure. There is no solution to this paradox; the paradigm needs to be discarded altogether. Any deal then needs to be embedded in a web of other arrangements, which changes the incentive structure of both sides. The leap of faith both sides must take to strike a deal must be balanced by measures following the deal that tie the two together and raise the cost for reverting back to the previous posture and policies.[42]

Washington and Tehran were clearly stuck in this paradox. As soon as they got to negotiating the final deal, in which they had to give up much of their leverage—sanctions and centrifuges, respectively—the entrapment of the paradox revealed itself. The U.S. side moved its position to agreeing to 1,500 centrifuges remaining in Iran, still far off from the Iranian redline of 9,000 under the reconfiguration scheme. The Iranians in turn insisted that the UN sanctions be lifted at the front of a final deal rather than toward its end. For Tehran, this was important, because most of the unilateral sanctions imposed on Iran by other nations used the UN sanctions as their legal basis. If the UN sanctions were lifted, these other bilateral sanctions would lose their legal foundation and begin to crumble, Tehran calculated. Since neither the United States nor Europe was open to lifting its own sanctions at the initial stage of the final deal (rather, the U.S. position was to lift those sanctions gradually as Iran complied with its obligations), the P5 + 1 would have to put the UN sanctions on the table, Tehran argued. But precisely because of the value of the UN sanctions, the United States was disinclined to give up that leverage. With the two sides so far apart, a final accord remained unlikely.[43]

On November 9 and 10, Kerry and Zarif met again in Oman without representatives from the other P5 + 1 countries. Kerry presented the Iranian foreign minister with a confidential eight-page paper outlining ideas for enrichment capacity and sanctions relief, as well as the issue of Iran's stockpile of enriched uranium. The Iranians were given the paper to read but not to keep. The encounter grew heated, and for the first time, the two foreign ministers found themselves yelling at each other. It wouldn't be the last time. It was a terrible outcome for what was supposed to be a coming together of minds between the two prior to the final round of talks before the November 24 deadline.[44]

Only days earlier, President Obama and the Democratic Party had suffered a defeat in the midterm elections, with the Republicans gaining control of the Senate while increasing their majority in the House. With Congress firmly in Republican hands, Obama was even more vulnerable to diplomacy-killing sanctions being passed. Moreover, it was now even harder for Obama to credibly offer Tehran sanctions relief, since it was very unlikely that Congress would approve such measures. Instead, Obama had to rely on his waiver authority through which he could suspend congressional sanctions for 90 or 180 days at a time. This presented a problem in itself though, since waivers had to constantly be renewed—including by the next president of the United States—in order for the sanctions relief to remain in place. As such, relief through waivers was fundamentally reversible, rendering them a weak bargaining chip for the United States, since a principle both sides

had agreed to was that reversible measures by one side would be pro-
portionally reciprocated with reversible measures by the other. Obama's
ability to deliver was a growing question mark for the Iranians. To
boost the prospects of a deal, Obama sent another letter to Ayatollah
Khamenei, emphasizing the two countries' shared interest in defeating
ISIS, though prospects for such cooperation depended upon them first
resolving the nuclear question. Khamenei responded that Iran could
not accept having a mere "decorative, caricaturistic nuclear industry."
Prospects for a breakthrough in Vienna, where the final round of talks
were to be held, looked increasingly grim.[45]

Saudi Intervention?

The negotiators were back at the Palais Coburg in central Vienna, where
they had failed to reach a deal only four months earlier. The talks had
the same rhythm as had previous rounds: a slow start, with the technical deliberations preceding those led by the political directors, then
halfway through, the foreign ministers arriving and the talks approaching their climax, then some drama arising, with one or more delegations threatening to walk or giving comments to the media that more
time was needed and that the other side had a historic choice to make,
followed by great uncertainty in the last hours before the deadline, with
the media not knowing whether the talks were heading toward collapse,
extension, or success.

By Saturday the 22nd, the Iranians were signaling that important
progress was being made and that a deal could be forthcoming. Zarif
had presented the P5+1 with a new reconfiguration proposal that the
Western powers at first found very satisfactory, according to the Iranians. At this point, the American and Iranian accounts of what tran-
spired in the final hours of the talks came to differ dramatically. The
Iranians maintain that substantial progress was made and that if the
talks had been extended for only two days, they could have reached a
deal. But on the last day, Secretary Kerry took a break from the nuclear
talks to meet with the Saudi foreign minister at the airport in Vienna.
The two met on the Saudi minister's private airplane for roughly one
hour. Upon his return from that meeting, everything changed.[46]

"We were almost ready to call it a success, that we have a frame-work," Zarif told me of the moment right before Kerry left for the meeting with Foreign Minister Saud bin Faisal. While Kerry was with him, Zarif was talking to Dr. Frank-Walter Steinmeier, the German foreign minister, about how to announce the breakthrough. "Do we need a piece of paper or do we just say that we have reached a framework?" Zarif recalled. "Because we were concerned if we put it on a piece of paper, it would leak." The Iranians and the European Union leaned toward a two-page statement listing principles that had been agreed upon. "The document would express our complete agreement on a list of three or four principles we had agreed to on [the nuclear facilities at] Arak as well as three or four principles related to Natanz [one of Iran's enrichment plants]," Deputy Foreign Minister Majid Ravanchi explained. It would not have been a full agreement; rather it would be an agreement on the framework of the final deal. Kerry was supposed to come back at 5:30 p.m. for a meeting with Zarif, but was a half-hour late, after having spoken to both the Saudi minister and to the White House. Almost apologetically, he looked at Zarif and said: "I'm sorry, but we need to extend." The Iranians were shocked. All of the critical progress that had been made in the past two days was undone, and success was turned into failure, the Iranians maintain. "I was very frustrated," Zarif said of the episode. In retrospect, the Iranians became increasingly convinced that Kerry's about-face was due to Saudi Arabia. "I'm almost sure that it was the Saudis who intervened because of what happened afterward with the drop in oil prices," Zarif said.[47]

The American narrative paints a dramatically different picture. Though some progress was made in the final hours, it was too little, too late. Neither the United States nor the Europeans were impressed by Zarif's new proposal and as a result, the parties were never close to reaching an agreement. "None of us [in the P5 + 1] thought we were on the brink of a deal," Malley said, who took part in the negotiations. The Iranians had reached their conclusion by misreading Kerry and by overinterpreting his conversations with Saudis and with the White House. "[The Iranians] looked at two data points: that Kerry had met with foreign minister Saud and that there had been a phone call with the White House," Malley explained. "And they put two and two together and they came up with five." Moreover, Kerry's conversation with Saud bin Faisal centered on Syria, not Iran. "The Saudis were trying to pressure the Russians, essentially using oil prices as a tool to extract some concessions on Syria," a senior administration official told me. "I can see how circumstantially the Iranians could argue and believe that [Saud impacted the United States' negotiation position], but I can tell you it was simply not true."[48]

That evening, the parties announced that instead of a breakthrough, another extension had been agreed upon. I ended up having dinner with Zarif and the Iranian negotiators later that night and was struck by how relieved rather than disappointed they looked. It was as if a major weight had been lifted off of their shoulders. When I asked Zarif about it months later, he told me he was relieved he wouldn't have to sell the deal at home and face his domestic critics. "At that time, I would have had a hard time trying to sell it at home," he said. Instead, Zarif, Kerry, and their colleagues had to deal with selling another extension. Once again, they had to put up a brave face to the media and focus on the distance that had been traveled, not the distance that remained. A series of "new ideas surfaced" in the last several days of that talk, Kerry told reporters as he tried to fend off criticism that it was time to abandon diplomacy. In a move that raised a lot of eyebrows, Kerry went out of his way to heap praise on Zarif. "The Iranian foreign minister has worked hard and he has worked diligently," Kerry said. "He has approached these negotiations in good faith and with seriousness of purpose."[49]

Even more surprising was the length of the extension. The first extension in July 2014 had given the negotiators four added months to reach a deal. Now, they extended the talks until June 2015—a full seven months, with a deadline of March 31 for a framework agreement and a June 30 deadline for a final deal. The lengthy extension strengthened the impression that the talks were on life support. In reality, it was motivated by the realization that the political climate would not tolerate a third extension and that the month of May would be consumed by the NPT review conference. Since many of the negotiators on the technical side would be involved in those talks, limited time and resources could be allocated to the nuclear talks during that month.

While proponents of diplomacy were disappointed that the talks had once again failed to lead to a breakthrough, the extension decision found an unlikely supporter: Israeli Prime Minister Benjamin Netanyahu. The biggest opponent of the interim deal was now cheering the decision to extend that very agreement. "No deal is better than a bad deal. The deal that Iran was pushing for was terrible," he said. "This result is better, a lot better." Netanyahu even took credit for the failure in Vienna and highlighted the extensive efforts of his government to convince the P5 + 1 not to strike a deal with Iran. "I can testify that Israel has made an enormous effort, in all areas and on every level, to prevent the signing of that agreement," Netanyahu told his cabinet. "That is why we have reason to be pleased, at least for now."[50]

"Our Eyes Were Bleeding"

Today, the United States of America is changing its relationship with the people of Cuba," President Obama said on December 17, 2014, stunning the world. For eighteen months, two of his aides had been conducting negotiations with the Castro regime in complete secrecy. What had started off as talks over prisoners had morphed into discussions on U.S.-Cuba rapprochement. Obama had achieved the politically impossible—he had created an opening to Havana and put an end to a five decades' long failed sanctions policy.

As he explained the remarkable turn of events, he didn't hold back in blasting the policy of isolating and sanctioning Cuba, calling it "an outdated approach that, for decades, has failed to advance our interests." He decried how U.S. sanctions had "denied Cubans access to technology that has empowered individuals around the globe" and insisted that the United States could not "keep doing the same thing for over five decades and expect a different result." Perhaps most importantly, he argued that the policy of sanctioning Cuba stood in direct contradiction to the desire to see democracy flourish there:

> Moreover, it does not serve America's interests, or the Cuban people, to try to push Cuba toward collapse. Even if that

worked—and it hasn't for 50 years—we know from hard-earned experience that countries are more likely to enjoy lasting transformation if their people are not subjected to chaos. We are calling on Cuba to unleash the potential of 11 million Cubans by ending unnecessary restrictions on their political, social, and economic activities. In that spirit, we should not allow U.S. sanctions to add to the burden of Cuban citizens that we seek to help.[1]

Obama recognized that changes in U.S. policy wouldn't lead to immediate change in Cuba, but that change would eventually come as the Cuban people became empowered by the positive outcomes of engagement.

Everything Obama said on Cuba he could have said on Iran as well, from the inefficacy of sanctions in bringing about change, to lack of engagement reducing the United States' influence in Iran, to sanctions increasing the burden on the Iranian people rather than empowering them, to destroying Iran's economy ultimately making a transition to democracy only more difficult. Indeed, the parallels to Iran were obvious. No one in Washington expected any change in U.S.-Cuba relations precisely because of the domestic political minefield surrounding them. Only a very small minority in Washington believed the decades' long embargo had been a success, or that its continuation served U.S. interest. Yet, very few believed the United States' Cuba policy could be altered due to the stranglehold imposed by this small but dedicated constituency, who insisted that the embargo be kept on Cuba until Castro fell—come what may. Similarly, proponents of a confrontational policy on Iran had prevented exploration of several openings with Iran, such as the Tehran Declaration of 2010, since doing so was associated with devastating political costs.

This had prompted the White House to pursue direct negotiations with both Iran and Cuba in secrecy. The fewer cameras, the fewer opportunities for spoilers to derail the talks or exact a price on Obama. Once a deal had been struck, it would be easier to fend off the attacks from supporters of the status quo. As in Iran, contact with the Cubans centered on a prisoner swap—in the case of Cuba the United States was seeking the release of detained USAID contractor Alan

Gross and CIA operative Rolando Sarraff Trujillo. In addition, both negotiations had a mutually trusted interlocutor who helped overcome the deep mistrust between the United States and the other country. With Iran it was the sultan of Oman; with Cuba, it was His Holiness Pope Francis.[2]

However, while Obama was reaching the end game with Cuba, the negotiations with Iran were in crisis. The two sides could not come to an agreement on the formula to use for ensuring that Iran's path to a bomb would be closed, and without a breakthrough on this issue, nothing else could be agreed upon. More than a year had passed since the interim agreement had been signed, and domestic critics of the nuclear deal were closing in on Obama and Rouhani as they had little to show for their efforts during that time. As tensions inside Iran increased, Rouhani began to fight back with increasing ferocity. Recognizing that those opposing a deal were a small, albeit fervent, group, he threatened to take the matter directly to the Iranian people and have them vote in a referendum. Rather than opposing the deal on the grounds that Iran was giving up too much, these critics were opposed to an agreement because they benefited financially from the sanctions, an angry Rouhani charged. In a particularly colorful speech, he told the critics of diplomacy to simply "Go to hell!"[3]

Obama's situation was arguably even worse, with some in Congress constantly pushing to kill the talks by allying with Israeli Prime Minister Benjamin Netanyahu and imposing new sanctions. Frustrated, Obama issued a threat echoing Rouhani's strategy: if Congress wouldn't play ball, Obama would bypass it and let the American public decide. "We'll see how persuasive I am. But if I'm not persuading Congress, I promise you, I'm going to be taking my case to the American people on this," he told reporters in mid-January 2015. Obama repeated his veto threat and declared that Congress would have to own the war that was likely to break out if diplomacy was scuttled by new sanctions.[4]

Things were getting increasingly tense between Obama and supporters of sanctions in the Senate. At one point, the president suggested—in a closed meeting—that the lion's share of their opposition to the talks was political, due to pressure from political donors, and not rooted in the substance of the issue. Senator Menendez said he took "personal offense" to that suggestion and later publicly accused the White House of getting its talking points "straight out of Iran."[5]

With momentum in Congress building up against Obama, the Europeans decided to make an intervention of their own. British Prime Minister David Cameron took the rare step of personally calling key senators to lobby them against imposing new sanctions, while the ambassadors of the United Kingdom, France, and Germany published an op-ed in the *Washington Post* echoing that message. "Rather than strengthening our negotiating position," they wrote, "new sanctions legislation at this point would set us back."[6]

Netanyahu's Magnificent Own Goal

A few phone calls from Cameron and an op-ed in the *Washington Post* was nothing compared to what Netanyahu, former GOP-operator turned Israeli ambassador to Washington Ron Dermer, and Republican leaders in Congress had planned. Going against protocol and tradition, House Speaker John Boehner extended an invitation to Netanyahu to give an address to Congress without consulting the Democrats or the White House. This was an unprecedented move. Invitations to foreign leaders to address Congress are usually a bipartisan decision and made in conjunction with the White House. To have one party invite a foreign leader for the explicit purpose of criticizing the president of the United States was unparalleled, and even opponents of Obama said "it didn't show a lot of class." However, Speaker Boehner insisted he was not going to "stand idly by and do nothing while [Obama] cuts a bad deal with Iran." "Two words," Boehner told reporters, " 'Hell no!' . . . We're going to do no such thing." The invitation strengthened the partisan characteristic of the Iran debate, a development that may have served Boehner and the GOP's interests, but would prove disastrous for Netanyahu.[7]

The plan to invite Netanyahu was devised between Boehner, Senate Majority Leader Mitch McConnell, and Dermer. Boehner probably knew the invitation would infuriate the Democrats, but from his perspective this was arguably a bonus: it made Israel a wedge issue that the GOP could use to present itself as a better friend of Israel and thereby persuade Jewish voters and campaign donors to shift to the Republican Party. Dismissing warnings from his aides that the address would cause irreparable damage to his relationship with Obama, Netanyahu argued that he could outmaneuver Obama by relying on U.S. public opinion. "It is my obligation as prime minister to do everything that I can do to prevent this agreement," he said before arriving in Washington. Due to his own extensive network in the United States, Netanyahu has always had a strong conviction that he can play the domestic political card in the United States and "move America."[8]

But Netanyahu never realized how the United States had changed since the disastrous Iraq war—how antiwar sentiments have grown, how disinclined the American public has become to agree to military involvement abroad, and how distrustful they have grown of politicians who advocate hawkish policies. "He is enslaved by his old knowledge of the American political system," retired Israeli Brigadier General Shlomo Brom told me. "Whenever he comes to the United States, he meets the same Jewish leaders that are closest to the Republicans, and he gets the impression that it's the same U.S. he always knew."[9]

But the United States had changed. In a major embarrassment to Netanyahu, fifty-eight Democratic lawmakers boycotted the speech. This was a first: while many lawmakers may have missed the address of an Israeli prime minister, they had never actively boycotted one before. Now, nearly sixty of them, including several Jewish members of Congress, made a point of not attending the speech in protest. "I can't think of any other example in the thirty-four years I've served in the House or Senate of anything even close to that," Senator Dick Durbin (D-IL) told me. "That's never happened before. Never." Representative Jan Schakowsky (D-IL) was one of the prominent Jewish lawmakers who decided to boycott Netanyahu's address. "This was inappropriate in every possible way," she explained. On all other issues, the U.S.-Israel relationship had strengthened significantly during Obama's term, she maintained, despite the tense personal relationship between Obama and Netanyahu. A case in point was the Iron Dome air-defense system, which had saved numerous Israeli lives during its war with Hamas in Gaza in July 2014. Just seven months before Netanyahu came to Congress, both chambers of Congress had passed a bill—that Obama signed—awarding Israel another $225 million to operate the Iron Dome. Given all the help Obama had provided Israel, for Netanyahu to come and take on Obama on U.S. ground "felt like, as my mother would say, biting the hand that feeds you," the Illinois lawmaker said.[10]

While the commotion surrounding Netanyahu's stunning move was immense, the speech itself was predictable and uneventful. Iran's ambition is to destroy the Jewish people, Netanyahu said, drawing parallels to the story of Esther in the Bible, in which a viceroy to the Persian King Xerxes conspires to kill the Jews in the Persian capital of Susa. But Queen Esther—the Persian king's Jewish spouse—exposes the plot and saves the Jews. "Today the Jewish people face another attempt by yet another Persian potentate to destroy us," Netanyahu said, pointing to Iran's supreme leader, Ayatollah Khamenei. Under Khamenei, Iran seeks to dominate the Middle East, Netanyahu charged, and if its power is left unchecked, it will become a threat to all. The United States should not fall for the lure of collaborating with Iran against ISIS, since Iran is no different from ISIS. On the contrary, Iran is more dangerous than ISIS because it is on the verge of getting nuclear weapons, whereas ISIS is "armed with butcher knives, captured weapons and YouTube."[11]

In the harshest line of the speech, Netanyahu charged that President Obama's nuclear deal "would all but guarantee that Iran gets those weapons, lots of them. . . . That's why this deal is so bad. It doesn't block Iran's path to the bomb; it paves Iran's path to the bomb." Netanyahu essentially accused Obama—on U.S. soil—of being so misguided and naive that he was aiding Iran's nuclear ambitions. Nor would rejecting Obama's deal lead to war, Netanyahu explained. Rather, the alternative to this deal was a much better deal—one that didn't "leave Iran with a vast nuclear infrastructure and such a short breakout time" and that kept "the restrictions on Iran's nuclear program in place until Iran's aggression ends." Sanctions should not be lifted until Iran ended "its aggression against its neighbors in the Middle East," stopped "supporting terrorism," and "stopped threatening to annihilate" Israel. Netanyahu had blatantly moved the goal post. Having insisted that any diplomacy with Iran should focus solely on the nuclear issue, he now demanded that sanctions could not be lifted until a whole set of other, non-nuclear policies had changed.[12]

From Obama's vantage point, Netanyahu was deliberately putting forward unachievable goals in order to render diplomatic success an impossibility. The track record on Iran showed that pressure alone could not elicit changes in Iran's policies. Besides, the sanctions pressure the United States had managed to assemble now was because of the buy-in of the European Union, Russia, and China on the nuclear issue—which was the one issue they could all largely agree on. If the United States suddenly changed the goal post per Netanyahu's demands, the sanctions coalition would fall apart, leaving the United States with no other option but to take military action—which the Israelis had privately demanded for more than a decade. "The logic is that they wanted the conflict," Ben Rhodes told me. "I don't know how else to explain it. Because I truly think it's analytically impossible to believe that you could keep sanctions around until they just abandon their nuclear program."[13]

Netanyahu's demands made good soundbites, but were so unrealistic that he didn't move the needle in Congress. If anything, he undermined his own cause. Siding with Netanyahu was becoming tantamount to siding with the Republicans, and vice versa, and the more partisan the issue became, the more Democrats in Congress felt compelled to side with their president and their party. But beyond partisan calculations, Netanyahu had managed to insult lawmakers from both sides who perceived his action as a slight to the office of the presidency and American sensibilities. At a press conference immediately following Netanyahu's address, Democratic lawmakers took turns condemning the Israeli prime minister's unprecedented move. A visibly livid Nancy Pelosi called the speech an "insult to the intelligence of the United States." When I spoke with her months later, her anger was still evident. "I think it was really totally unacceptable," she told me, her facial expression revealing her frustration with the episode. "The nature of his speech was so—how dare you criticize—it was as if he came here to say, 'Your president doesn't even know what he's doing.'"[14]

At the White House, Obama's inner circle drew a sigh of relief. There was nothing new in the speech, nothing that would complicate their already tricky task of selling the negotiations to Congress. Obama dismissed the speech as mere theatrics. "I am not focused on the politics of this. I am not focused on the theater," Obama said. "As far as I can tell, there was nothing new." Rather than challenging Obama with new arguments and claims, Netanyahu's speech provided proponents of diplomacy with new fodder to take on Netanyahu and his allies. For groups supportive of Obama's efforts, Netanyahu had turned himself into their new Dick Cheney—a resented pro-war figure whose ability to mobilize antiwar constituencies was unparalleled. A video of Bibi testifying in Congress in 2002 in favor of the invasion of Iraq—"If you take out Saddam's regime, I guarantee you, that it will have enormous positive reverberations on the region, he said"—resurfaced, adding credence to Obama's argument that the opponents of the Iran deal were "the same people who got us into Iraq."[15]

The Scientists Step In

Roughly a month before the Netanyahu address to Congress, Zarif and Kerry met on the sidelines of the Munich security conference in Germany. They were still far apart on how to limit the Iranian enrichment program, but they agreed on one thing: it would be "impossible" to extend the talks any further. A deal had to be struck before July, or the talks would collapse. At that point, Tehran had itself turned against the reconfiguration proposal, opening the door for Zarif to give the nod to the breakout formula presented by the United States. This was an important development that gave the White House a lot of hope—it was the first critical breakthrough since the Joint Plan of Action itself.[16]

Inside the White House, however, the real concern was not breakout—since that would happen in the open with IAEA inspectors quickly detecting the deviation toward military use. The real concern was "sneak-out"—a secret effort to weaponize that would be more difficult for the inspectors to discover. Breakout was deemed "extremely unlikely," whereas the track record of countries seeking nuclear weapons was that they would quietly weaponize at undisclosed facilities. The Israelis pushed for the breakout approach, however. Moreover, the breakout formula was more practical to calculate. "You can't quantify sneak-out," Obama's former nonproliferation tsar Gary Samore told me. "Breakout you can quantify. You can do a mathematical formulation that allows you to define within some level of specificity what breakout time is."[17]

The U.S. redline was that the combination of measures—the size of Iran's stockpile, the intrusiveness of inspections, the degree, quantity, and quality of centrifuges, and so on—would not enable Iran to have a breakout time of less than one year. That number was partly artificial. It needed to be long enough to ensure that if the Iranians broke out, there would be ample time to react so that Washington's only option would not be military intervention. However, a nine-month breakout would be sufficient to provide the United States with other options. There was no meaningful difference between a nine-month and a one-year breakout in that regard. But for Obama's ability to sell it to Congress and the American people, the psychological difference was significant. "The difference was that nine months sounded as months, twelve months sounded as a year," Colin Kahl, a senior advisor to Vice President Joe Biden, explained.[18]

The shift toward the breakout formula complicated the technical aspects of the negotiations. Zarif faced some heat upon his return to Tehran, as Iran's previous redline of 9,000 centrifuges had become meaningless. This ultimately compelled the Iranian foreign minister to bring the head of Iran's atomic energy program, the MIT-educated Dr. Ali Akbar Salehi, into the talks. Salehi was no stranger to the nuclear negotiations, having served as foreign minister under Ahmadinejad and having helped set up the Oman channel. At first, Salehi was reluctant to join the talks, fearing that he would become the scapegoat if the negotiations failed. Eventually, he was convinced to join, but only after putting forward a condition: he would join if the U.S. side brought his counterpart—Energy Secretary Ernest Moniz—to the talks. Iranian negotiator Abbas Araghchi called Wendy Sherman—just as she and Rob Malley were about to meet the president in the Oval Office—and explained that the Iranians would be bringing Salehi to the next round of talks and requested the presence of Moniz.[19]

At first, the president was hesitant. "We each felt that it was a bit crazy," Malley told me. "That's a big step, including the secretary of energy." Past experience with Salehi had not always been positive, fueling fears that his inclusion would lead to a hardening on the Iranian side. Others pointed out that it would make little sense for the Iranians to bring Salehi to scuttle the deal, as Iran would be more likely to bear the blame for the collapse. In the end, the president went with his instinct: Salehi could hardly make matters worse, and if there was a small chance that he could help break the deadlock, then it was worth exploring. Within hours, the U.S. side let the Iranians know that Secretary Moniz would be present at the next round of talks. As it would turn out, Obama's instinct was spot on: Salehi's and Moniz's inclusion was a game-changer.[20]

Moniz and Salehi immediately struck up a respectful relationship. They were both MIT-educated; in fact, their time at MIT overlapped. Salehi was doing his PhD at MIT when Moniz began teaching there as assistant professor of physics. Although they never got to know each other there, they had many mutual friends and colleagues. "The first time we met face to face, I felt as if we had known each other for so long," Salehi recalled. They discussed common acquaintances and exchanged gifts. Moniz gave Salehi baby gifts from MIT for his grandchildren, like onesies with the periodic table symbols of copper and tellurium ("CuTe"). Salehi brought Moniz Iranian fruits and pistachios. While they were both tough negotiators, they developed a strong and solutions-oriented relationship. "We understood each other," Salehi said. "I understood his constraints. He understood mine. That's how we could move forward." In fact, they got along so well that one aide quipped, "If they were on an online dating site, they probably would have been matched together."[21]

Although their meeting in the picturesque Swiss city of Lausanne made progress, it was troubled by two unforeseen events. On March 7, only four days after Netanyahu's address to Congress, freshman Republican Senator Tom Cotton (R-AR) pulled off another first: he organized a letter to the "Leaders of the Islamic Republic of Iran" signed by forty-six of his Republican colleagues in the Senate, declaring that Congress would "consider any agreement regarding your nuclear-weapons program that is not approved by the Congress as nothing more than an executive agreement between President Obama and Ayatollah Khamenei." Such an agreement, the letter declared, would essentially expire in January 2017 when Obama left office. "The next president could revoke such an executive agreement with the stroke of a pen and future Congresses could modify the terms of the agreement at any time."

The message of the letter was unprecedented: in the midst of extremely sensitive national security negotiations, members of the Senate
openly told leaders of a declared enemy state that they should not trust
the agreement the American president would sign because the Senate
would not respect it. Never before had senators defied the authority
of the presidency in such a manner. This was not the conduct of a disciplined superpower. It was a new extreme in the politicization of foreign
policy and a debasement of the institutions that make up the government of the United States. Criticisms of the letter—from both opponents
and supporters of diplomacy—were scathing. "It appears that for most
of my Republican colleagues in the Senate, a war in Afghanistan and a
war in Iraq were not enough," Senator Bernie Sanders of Vermont said.
"They now apparently want a war in Iran as well," he continued, adding
that the letter was "an outrage." The *New York Daily News,* a paper that
has otherwise been critical of Obama's diplomacy, put the picture of
some of the Republicans signing the letter on its front page under the
title "Traitors." On Twitter, the hashtag #47Traitors began trending only
hours after the publication of the letter.[22]

The letter was an insult not just to Obama, but also to the rest of
the P5 + 1, since the agreement with Iran was not a bilateral U.S.-Iran
deal. The idea that the United States would not uphold the deal was just
as disconcerting for the P5 + 1 states as it was for the Iranians. "We just
shook our heads," a senior German diplomat told me. "This upset us
because we had skin in the game as well. It's not just an American issue." But while the Europeans kept their frustrations private, Zarif took
the fight with the freshman senator public, calling it "a propaganda
ploy" that revealed that "some are opposed to any agreement, regardless of its content."[23]

Inside the U.S. government, the letter caused significant concern.
Any suggestion that Obama did not have the ability to deliver on his end
of the bargain weakened the U.S. negotiating position. The cost for the
Iranians to put their faith in Obama would go up, prompting them to
raise the demands they made on the United States. The U.S. team saw the
letter as nothing short of an attempt to sabotage the talks. "It was unprecedented for a member of Congress to try to undermine American
negotiating efforts while they were ongoing, which I found irresponsi-

ble and reckless," Kerry said to me. During their first session in Lausanne, Kerry immediately sought to assure all the players that Cotton did
not have the power to derail the talks. The Iranians were skeptical, but
not unreasonable. After all, Obama's ability to deliver had been a major
question mark of theirs from the outset, and the U.S. negotiators themselves had pushed back on the Iranian demand that the United States
lift congressional sanctions on the grounds that Obama didn't have the
votes. "We did have a little bit of an uphill battle, just as the Iranians
did, of convincing the other side that we would stick to whatever deal
was negotiated in the room," a senior administration official said.[24]

Although the Cotton letter did lead to the Iranians demanding
that everything they agreed upon be written down, particularly on the
issue of sanctions relief, it ended up having a less negative impact than
many originally had feared. There were two reasons for this. First, the
breakthrough in Munich had given both sides newborn confidence that
a deal that both could live with was possible. And as the talks progressed
toward a positive conclusion, desperate attacks by spoilers would intensify. The only way to insulate and protect the diplomatic process from
such attacks was for the two sides to unite against the detractors. "We
had both understood that we have to help each other and handle each
other's hardliners," a senior White House official explained.[25]

But the Iranians had other reasons as well. For Tehran, this was
yet another opportunity to demonstrate Iran's sincerity. "If we want
to walk away from the talks, this is a perfect opportunity," Zarif told
the other foreign ministers. Staying at the table strengthened Iran's negotiating position as well as its ability to win the blame game in case
the talks failed. And the more sincere and reasonable Iran was, the
more it would further its efforts at desecuritization. A harsher reaction to the Cotton letter also carried dangerous risks. Zarif had learned
that the hard way as a young diplomat at the Iranian Permanent Mission to the United Nations in New York in the early 1980s. Saddam
Hussein had invaded Iran, but the UN Security Council had refrained
from condemning Iraq and treating the matter as a threat to international security and stability. To show Iran's dissatisfaction with the UN
Security Council's negligence, Zarif recommended to his ambassador
that Iran boycott the next Security Council meeting in protest. But

Zarif got more than he had bargained for. Not only did Tehran approve his request; it also decreed that Iran would boycott all further UN Security Council meetings. Zarif spent the next years at the UN mission trying to convince the leadership in Tehran to reverse the very same decision he himself had recommended. "What I took away from that experience was that it is easy to close diplomatic doors, but it can take years to reopen them," he told me two weeks after his meeting with Kerry about the Cotton letter.[26]

The second unforeseen event was the passing away of President Rouhani's mother on March 20, 2015. The talks had begun on March 16, and the Iranians had indicated that they would be willing to continue negotiating through the Iranian New Year on March 21 in order to meet the March 31 deadline. But with the passing away of Rouhani's mother, and with his brother Hossein Fereydoun being a member of the negotiating team, the Iranians had to cut the talks short and return to Tehran. But before they made their way back to Tehran, the U.S. delegation took an unprecedented step: they visited the Iranian delegation in their quarters of the Beau Rivage Hotel to express their condolences and show their respect. A picture of Kerry embracing a sobbing Hossein Fereydoun showed that something extraordinary had happened. After thirty-five years of mutual demonization and distrust, the two sides had not quite managed to reach a final deal, but they had managed to humanize each other. Beyond just reaching a deal, no enmity can be ended without recognizing the humanity of the other side.[27]

Seven Days in Lausanne

As the negotiators reconvened in Lausanne on March 25, the mood had once again turned sour over a regional development. At midnight that day, Saudi Arabia launched a bombing campaign against Houthi rebels in Yemen. The Houthis, who belong to the Zaidi branch of Shia Islam, had descended on the capital, Sanaa, ousting the Saudi-backed president of Yemen, Abdrabbuh Mansour Hadi. The Saudis, accusing the Houthis of being proxies of Tehran, assembled a small coalition of Arab states to put Hadi back in power and expel the Houthis. What was in fact an internal power struggle between various Yemeni factions was depicted by

Saudi Arabia as an effort by Iran to expand its influence in the Arab world—even though U.S. intelligence revealed that the Iranians had urged the Houthis not to attack Sanaa. Apparently, the supposed Iranian proxies decided not to follow Tehran's advice.[28]

It was no longer a secret that the true Saudi worry about the nuclear talks was not that it would leave Iran with a nuclear weapons capability, but that "the talks could lead to a broader détente or even alliance between Washington and Tehran." Some speculated that the rather unusual Saudi step of involving itself directly in Yemen was aimed at undermining this prospective U.S.-Iran rapprochement by forcing Washington to side with Riyadh against Tehran in Yemen. Much like Israel, which charged that Iran was seeking to dominate the Middle East—Netanyahu's comment on the Houthi takeover of Sanaa was that Iran was seeking to "take over and occupy the entire Middle East" and that the "Iran-Lausanne-Yemen axis is very dangerous to humanity and it must be stopped"—the Saudis were desperately seeking to tie the United States down in the region to uphold an order based on Iran's isolation and containment. To Tehran's great disappointment, Washington was poised to walk straight into the Saudi trap.

Although the U.S. side was skeptical of the wisdom of Saudi Arabia's campaign, and although it viewed the complete defeat of the Houthis as a negative since they constituted the main fighting force against al-Qaeda in Yemen, Washington still ended up supporting Riyadh. Right before Kerry's first session with Zarif in Lausanne, he took part in a conference call with the foreign ministers of the Arab nations partaking in the Saudi-led campaign, praising their offensive. The White House also announced that the United States would provide intelligence and logistical support to the Saudis and their allies. In Iranian eyes, the United States had once again shown itself too close to and too dependent on Saudi Arabia. For Washington, however, it was better to provide the Saudis with some limited support than to risk antagonizing them further at a time when the nuclear talks were reaching a do-or-die moment.[29]

With the Iranians having agreed in principle to the breakout formula, the negotiations now focused more on the specific variables, including the number of centrifuges, the size of Iran's stockpile, and the length of the agreement. The American negotiation strategy also shifted accordingly. Having started with a bargaining strategy in which both sides opened with outrageous maximalist positions, the approach increasingly became centered on putting on the table a proposal that was "internally consistent and externally defensible," the idea being to present a "principled position with room to maneuver." While the negotiations remained tough and fierce, they became much more constructive and solution-oriented. What had been a zero-sum competition increasingly turned into "a joint enterprise," according to Rob Malley, a senior member of the U.S. delegation. "You put your proposal on the table and say: 'Tell me where I am wrong,'" Malley explained. "'If you need something to change, how does it affect the overall coherence of the proposal?' And we got there little by little."[30]

Not surprisingly, Moniz and Salehi proved invaluable for this process, both because of the highly technical nature of the breakout concept and their predisposition to seek out solutions. Moniz "managed to sort of wrap the deal in a way that made internal sense even from an Iranian perspective," Malley continued. Similarly, Salehi was very honest about the various aspects of the Iranian program, including its deficiencies, and showed an unusual degree of openness to what needed to be done. Both Salehi and Moniz could make a distinction between mere posturing and positions that made scientific and technical sense, relieving the process from the time-consuming haggling that had characterized previous rounds. Moniz also had the additional benefit of being completely trusted by the president, both because of his scientific credentials and because his advice and judgment were void of political baggage. And few could match his ability to validate ideas and proposals in the eyes of the president, precisely because of his scientific expertise.[31]

Still, the United States drove a hard bargain, pushing Iran on the breakout timeline, transparency measures, the IAEA's access to Iranian facilities, and so on. Many of the U.S. demands were hard for the Iranians to swallow, but the U.S. negotiators had strict redlines and showed little flexibility on Obama's key priorities. The breakout time, for instance, could not go below one year. At the same time, though, there were no redlines on the number of centrifuges. In that regard the United States could be flexible as long as the combination of variables kept Iran at a breakout of twelve or more months. Under the breakout scenario, Iran would end up keeping fewer operating centrifuges than under the reconfiguration proposal. Iran put up fierce resistance, with Kerry and Zarif going at it till early morning on March 31. With the negotiators testy and sleep deprived, the exchanges between Kerry and Zarif became increasingly emotional and loud. They broke around 9 a.m. to get an hour of two of sleep. At that point, the situation looked hopeless, and the American delegation was preparing to return to Washington. But when they reconvened four hours later for a final session, something vital and unexpected happened. Suddenly, the Iranians were ready to give on the centrifuges. "I think everybody got so close to the brink that it became apparent that we needed to do something," Backemeyer recalled.[32]

Ultimately, the Iranians argued, reducing the number of Iran's outdated centrifuges was not a problem, because Iran would be phasing out the older centrifuges anyway—a point recognized by the United States as well. "Even if we didn't have this agreement we would have removed those machines," Salehi said. "We are in other words proceeding on a path that we would have gone through anyway." The aggressive expansion of Iran's enrichment program was, after all, aimed at providing Tehran with leverage in the negotiations—the centrifuges were supposed to be negotiated away. "It was the principle that mattered, not the numbers," President Rouhani's chief of staff, Mohammad Nahavandian, told me. "The numbers were part of the negotiation, what was not up for negotiation was the principle that Iran would keep enrichment. The right to enrichment was sacred, the dimensions of enrichment, however, were negotiable."[33]

With the breakthrough on centrifuges, both sides agreed to set aside the March 31 deadline for the talks and continue negotiating until a full framework deal had been reached. But nothing could be agreed upon until everything was agreed upon. Progress on the breakout timeline was meaningless unless other sticking points also were resolved. Those remaining were Washington's insistence on snapback sanctions (a mechanism to quickly reimpose sanctions if Iran violated the deal), Iran's ballistic missile program, how to handle the sensitive issue of Iran's activities with possible military dimensions in the past (PMD), Iran's insistence on a UN Security Council resolution lifting sanctions and declaring the Iranian nuclear dispute resolved, and the issue of sanctions relief.[34]

Washington wanted the deal to include a mechanism that automatically reimposed sanctions on Iran if it violated the deal. The consequences should be clear—and swift, Washington maintained. This was a necessity because of the difficulty in putting the sanctions regime in place in the first instance. Otherwise, Iran would have an incentive to sign the deal in order to have the sanctions dismantled only to later cheat, since it knew that it would be very difficult for the United States to reimpose sanctions. A snapback mechanism would resolve that problem, the Obama team argued. Though Iran resisted the proposal, the main opposition to the idea did not come from Iran, but from Russia and China.

Russia's disagreement was rooted in the events of December 1998. Saddam Hussein's Iraq was under UN Security Council sanctions and was suspected of having continued its weapons of mass destruction program. On December 15, the executive chairman of the United Nations Special Commission (UNSCOM), Richard Butler, presented a report to the UN Security Council asserting that "Iraq's conduct ensured that no progress was able to be made in either the fields of disarmament or accounting for its prohibited weapons program." The recommendation created a conflict inside the Security Council. On the one hand, the United States and its allies viewed it as legitimizing the use of force against Iraq, since Iraq had violated the UN Security Council's decree. On the other hand, Russia, China, and many of the nonpermanent members of the council did not believe that a violation automatically justified military action, but rather that the council had to decide how to react to Iraq's conduct. To the fury of Russia and China, Butler had also shown the findings of the report to the U.S. and British governments prior to sharing them with the Security Council.[35]

In the backroom of the UN Security Council—where all deliberations take place—Russia's then UN ambassador (and current foreign minister) Sergey Lavrov did not conceal his anger. The council members knew that the United States already had or was about to give the order to bomb Iraq, despite the fact that the council had not yet had a chance to react to the UNSCOM report. (I served at the time with the Permanent Mission of Sweden to the United Nations, a nonpermanent member of the council, and I was partly responsible for the Iraq portfolio.) Lavrov, who tends to speak in a loud voice in all circumstances, thundered at the United States and accused it of undermining the UN Security Council. The U.S. ambassador's defense was less than forceful, and he let the Brits do most of the talking (a strategy the United States often used in the internal council deliberations at sensitive moments). As the debate continued, news broke on CNN that the American bombing campaign against Iraq had begun. The meeting broke as all the diplomats went to the adjacent room to follow CNN's coverage. A half hour later, they reconvened and decided—against U.S. wishes—to hold an open meeting in the formal UN Security Council room later that evening for all member states to make public comments on the matter. Many of the council members, as well as UN Secretary General Kofi Annan, scathingly criticized the U.S. decision to take military action before the council had a chance to react to the report.[36]

Ever since the debacle with the Butler report, the Russians have ensured that all UN Security Council resolutions explicitly reject any automaticity mechanisms. If there is a violation of an agreement or if a redline is crossed, the UN Security Council must adopt a new decision on how to respond—the response cannot be predetermined. For the Russians, this was more about the defense of that principle and of their veto power in the Security Council (what use is a veto if a decision is automatic?) than any concern for Iranian proliferation. The Iranians actually conceded on the snapback sanctions before the Russians, leaving the United States in a situation in which it had Tehran's agreement, but not Moscow and Beijing's. This held up the talks and frustrated the Iranians, who expected the United States to be in control of the P5 + 1 instead of them having to negotiate and renegotiate everything with each country separately and help Washington establish a consensus within the P5 + 1.[37]

But time was running out. Breakout and snapback sanctions were resolved, but question marks still remained about the PMD, ballistic missiles, the UN Security Council resolution, and, most important, the issue of sanctions relief. The negotiators were already a day past the

March 31 deadline while working around twenty hours a day. Zarif was also trying to finesse the deal so it wouldn't be presented as a two-stage agreement, as that had been explicitly forbidden by the supreme leader. "At that point, everybody was brain dead," a senior administration official recalled. At this last moment, Zarif pulled a card that at first looked like a major concession, but in retrospect was likely simply a clever way of putting the United States in a tough spot down the road: the Iranians agreed to defer the sanctions question, including the UN Security Council resolution, to the final deal. With the others in the P5 + 1 ready to defer the PMD and ballistic missiles to the next stage, the matter was settled—they had a deal. Back at the White House, staffers drew a big sigh of relief. Until the last twelve hours, Lausanne was on a fast track toward collapse. And with only a few hours of sleep in the past forty-eight hours, the White House team was at the point of exhaustion. "Our eyes were bleeding," Bernadette Meehan, deputy spokesperson for the NSC, told me.[38]

But now Obama had a deal to show for it.

The Unclenched Fist

Obama finally had a framework agreement on the limitation of Iran's enrichment capacity. During the months following the conclusion of the Joint Plan of Action (JPOA), he had suffered from the disadvantage of not being able to publicly reveal his plan for how to reduce Iran's centrifuges. Any leaks revealing the numbers being discussed could cause the Iranians to back out, while also creating undue expectations. This had left the critics of diplomacy with a significant advantage: they could accuse the president of making all kinds of fabricated concessions without the president's being able to defend himself and set the record straight, lest he reveal sensitive data from the negotiations. The same was true for the extent to which the administration could brief Congress on the talks. Not briefing Congress would cause a major political backlash and would also put the president's congressional allies in a bind, since they wouldn't have enough information to defend the talks. But briefing Congress and revealing sensitive information could also lead to leaks that would cause the talks to collapse. The balancing act Obama had to conduct ultimately gave his opponents a considerable edge in the public debate.[1]

But with the framework agreement in the bag, Obama could finally reveal the fruits of his labor—and they far exceeded expectations. In fact, the accusations of monumental American concessions by the president's detractors ultimately played in Obama's favor: expectations were lowered, and Obama came across as overperforming. The Israeli press had reported that the United States was contemplating accepting 6,500 centrifuges in a deal lasting only eight years. But the framework agreement limited Iran's centrifuges to 5,060 (down from roughly 19,000) for ten years and cut Iran's low-enriched uranium (LEU) stockpile from 10,000 kilograms to 300 for a full fifteen years. Nor would Iran enrich above 3.67 percent for at least fifteen years or build any new enrichment facilities during this period. Iran's underground Fordo facility—the one Israel couldn't bomb—would no longer be used to enrich uranium. For the next ten years, Iran would also refrain from using any of its more modern centrifuges (the IR-2, IR-4, IR-5, IR-6, and IR-8 models) for enrichment, although it could use them for research and development.[2]

On the transparency side, Iran agreed to give the International Atomic Energy Agency (IAEA) full access to all its nuclear facilities (using the IAEA's most advanced instruments) and all the phases of its nuclear activities—from the supply chain that supports Iran's nuclear program, to its uranium mines and mills, to its storage facilities. Iran would begin implementing the Additional Protocol to the Non-Proliferation Treaty, which would also give the IAEA the ability to inspect Iran's nondeclared facilities if credible suspicions were to arise. In essence, the IAEA would be deeply embedded in the Iranian nuclear program, making it virtually impossible for Iran to cheat on its obligations. Iran would also redesign and rebuild its Arak heavy-water research reactor, making it impossible for it to produce weapons-grade plutonium, while the original core of the reactor would be destroyed. All in all, these measures dramatically increased Iran's breakout timeline from two months to one year for the next ten years. On sanctions, little specificity was offered to the media, since the details of the relief had been deferred to the final deal.[3]

The Rise of the Congressional Doves

The immediate reaction in the press and by most observers was one of surprise: Obama had gotten much more than most had expected. For congressional supporters of diplomacy, the framework agreement was a game-changer. While the JPOA gave them the confidence that diplomacy had a chance, the framework agreement—and its significant cuts to Iran's enrichment program—gave them the confidence that diplomacy could succeed. For years, supporters of diplomacy in Congress had been outgunned, outspent, and outmaneuvered. Obama didn't have anything to sell to his allies in Congress when he asked them to hold off on sanctions, and they didn't have any concrete diplomatic achievement to rally around and defend.[4]

Now they did: a tight-knit network of Hill staffers had, through collaboration with the National Iranian American Council (NIAC), established a steadily growing circle of lawmakers who wanted to support diplomacy, as well as to create political space and cover for the negotiations. They had opted not to create a formal caucus, since that would likely make the lawmakers targets of the American Israel Public Affairs Committee (AIPAC) and pro-Likud organizations. Instead, the network of staffers and supportive organizations coordinated their efforts through informal channels. When the first extension decision was made in July 2014, lawmakers in the network coordinated and immediately issued press releases supporting the decision to extend the talks while urging for more investment in diplomacy. Their efforts had helped reduce the backlash in Congress against Obama. With the framework agreement secured, however, they now had the opportunity to go on the offensive.

Congresswoman Jan Schakowsky (D-IL) decided to step up and shoulder the responsibility for securing enough congressional opposition to the efforts to scuttle the deal. As a Jewish lawmaker, her high-profile leadership could be particularly valuable, she reckoned. "I came to the conclusion that a relatively high-profile Jewish voice could be especially effective," she explained to me. "So it was a very self-conscious decision to take this stand." Like many other lawmakers supportive of diplomacy, her motivation had only grown after Netanyahu's congressional address. "I was so offended by Netanyahu, who I remember well, because I was in the room when he came here as a private citizen to advocate for the Iraq war and said it was only our cowardice that we had to overcome in order to do the right thing," she continued. Back in

2003, she had spearheaded a campaign that ensured that a majority of House Democrats voted against the Iraq war—despite pressure from Hillary Clinton and more hawkish Democrats who campaigned in support of President George Bush's war. She had failed to prevent the Iraq war, but she was determined not to lose the battle against what she saw as a push for war with Iran.[5]

Together with her congressional allies, and with support from organizations such as J Street, the Friends Committee on National Legislation, and NIAC, Schakowsky organized a letter in support of the diplomatic process. The letter needed 146 signatories to signal that if Congress rejected Obama's nuclear deal, and he chose to veto their resolution of rejection, there were enough supporters in Congress to sustain Obama's veto. Within a few weeks, Schakowsky had secured 150 signatures. "If the president is forced to use his veto to protect an agreement this summer, there are now sufficient lawmakers on the record in support of the envisioned deal to potentially uphold that veto," NIAC's policy director, Jamal Abdi, commented at the time. Not only did the letter achieve this objective, it also made clear that support for diplomacy on Capitol Hill was far greater than many had thought.[6]

The framework agreement and the Schakowsky letter could not have been more timely. On the other side of the aisle, momentum was also growing for potent, legislative measures that could kill any prospect for a deal with Iran. Senator Bob Corker (R-TN), the chairman of the Foreign Relations Committee, was adamant that Congress must have a say in the negotiations and had prepared a bill that authorized the Senate to approve or reject the nuclear deal, even though the nuclear agreement was not a formal treaty (the Senate must ratify treaties that the president signs with other states). A disapproval of the nuclear deal would mean that the president would not be able to lift sanctions on Iran. Corker even threatened to do away with Obama's waiver rights under existing sanctions laws. Such waivers were crucial to any deal, since a key incentive Obama could offer the Iranians was his use of his waiver authority to suspend sanctions.[7]

But the White House would have none of it. Even though such a bill wouldn't be a formal violation of the JPOA, Obama still opposed it since he saw it as nothing more than an attempt by Congress to sabotage the talks. Early on, Obama made clear that he would veto the bill if it was passed by the Senate. In return, the White House said Congress would get a say on the deal toward the end of the negotiations when it would be asked to formally lift the sanctions imposed on Iran. If Congress rejected the deal and its achievements, it could choose to retain the sanctions. The White House calculated that an early vote would be very difficult to win because of the distrust of Iran and the overwhelmingly negative attitudes toward Iran on Capitol Hill. But years down the road, after Iran had dismantled much of its nuclear program and some trust had been built, prospects of getting congressional support for the deal would be much better. Opponents of the deal subscribed to the same analysis, which was precisely why groups such as AIPAC pushed for an early vote.[8]

The White House faced a significant challenge, however. While Democratic members of Congress opposed any efforts to sabotage the deal directly, many of them strongly believed that the Senate had to have a say. This was particularly true since so much of the sanctions infrastructure was created by congressional statute and not by executive order. They reasoned that the president should not have the authority to negotiate away congressional sanctions without congressional approval. One Democratic ally of Obama receptive to the argument was freshman Senator Tim Kaine (D-VA). While a supporter of Obama's diplomacy, Kaine disagreed with the president's efforts to avoid a Senate vote for two reasons. First, in his assessment, congressional noninvolvement wasn't realistic. The Senate would find a way to involve itself one way or another. "The issue wasn't congressional involvement versus noninvolvement, it was congressional involvement according to rules versus congressional involvement according to just a free for all," he told me. Second, Kaine had an "obsession" with the idea of ensuring that Congress upholds its responsibility with regard to its role in war, peace, and diplomacy.[9]

During a visit to the Middle East in January 2015, Senator Bob Corker (R-TN) tried to recruit Kaine for his bill by offering him an opportunity to make amendments to it. Kaine knew that the White House was dead-set against the bill, and he also understood the political sensitivity of the issue. During this visit, the senators made a stop in Israel to meet with the political leadership there. As in most conversations in

the Middle East at the time, Iran topped the agenda. Corker had scheduled a meeting with the head of the Mossad, Tamir Pardo, but upon arrival at Ben Gurion Airport, the senators found out that Netanyahu
had canceled the meeting in an apparent effort to ensure that the Americans didn't get to discuss Iran with the head of the Israeli intelligence
service, who, like much of the Israeli security establishment, disagreed
with Netanyahu's assessment of Obama's Iran diplomacy. Corker, who
had just become the chairman of the Senate Foreign Relations Committee, was furious. He was not going to start off his chairmanship by allowing the Israeli prime minister to take control of his schedule. Corker
threatened to cancel the rest of the visit to Israel and promptly return to
Washington unless the meeting with Pardo was reinstated.[10]

Netanyahu backed down, and Corker and the rest of the delegation ended up meeting with the head of Israeli intelligence. There, it
became quite clear why Netanyahu had tried to cancel the meeting.
Pardo's message on Iran was on some key points diametrically opposed
to Netanyahu's arguments. "More sanctions during the negotiations is
like throwing a grenade into the room," Pardo told the senators, echoing the logic put forward by Obama and the supporters of diplomacy.
Pardo's message only strengthened Kaine's conviction that the best way
to protect the Iran diplomacy was to have a bill—deprived of diplomacy-
killing poison pills—that structured the process for Congress to have a
say on the final deal. But Corker's bill wasn't the right answer, at least
not as it stood. The Republicans were adding amendments to it, such as
requiring that Iran recognize Israel in order for Congress to approve the
nuclear deal—and these kinds of amendments were guaranteed to sabotage the talks.[11]

Kaine carefully reviewed Corker's bill and demanded four crucial
changes to it in order for him to sign on. First, instead of requiring Congress to vote on the entire deal, congressional approval would be needed
only for the congressionally mandated sanctions. Second, Kaine demanded that the presumption must be that the deal is approved unless
Congress votes to disapprove it; the Senate should not have to or be able
to take affirmative action. "Look, the president has Article II powers to
conduct diplomacy," Kaine told Corker. "The presumption should be reversed." Third, the vote should follow normal order, meaning that the

resolution of disapproval would need sixty rather than fifty votes to pass. Over the years this had become the standard in the Senate, and this bill should be no different, Kaine insisted. And finally, the freshman senator argued, the timeframe for reviewing the prospective nuclear deal should be limited. This would give opponents of the deal one shot to kill it, rather than allowing them to continuously challenge the nuclear accord. By February 10, 2015, Corker and Kaine had come to an agreement on these four changes.[12]

The White House wasn't happy. To have an Obama ally and a supporter of diplomacy join a bill the president had promised to veto did little to help diplomacy, it maintained. Moreover, Kaine's support could open the floodgates for other Democrats to join the bill as well, making it impossible for Obama to uphold his veto. Despite Kaine's personal meetings with Obama to convince him of the benefits of the structured process the revised Corker bill established, the White House wasn't persuaded and instead pleaded with Kaine until the last moment to withdraw his support.[13]

Kaine was on the Senate floor on Friday, February 27, the day the bill was formally introduced. Political bickering had held up funding for the Department of Homeland Security (DHS) and a compromise package had finally been found—with only two days left before the DHS's funding ran out. So the senators were forced to keep the Senate in session on a Friday to vote on the package and avoid the immense embarrassment of having the DHS shut down. As the Corker bill was about to be introduced, Kaine received a message that the president wanted to speak to him. He went back to the cloakroom to take the call. "Tim, do not introduce this bill," Obama told the Virginia senator. "You are my friend, you were my chosen person to be chair of the Democratic National Committee. This is going to be spun as one of the president's closest allies is trying to kill the Iran deal." Kaine went over all the arguments he had for why the process he had designed ultimately would be helpful to the president's diplomacy. "Mr. President, I can guarantee you this will be helpful," he told Obama, "because it will force Congress to confront the deal in a time-limited space under rules that are frankly deferential to your Article II powers to negotiate. We should be deferential to your powers, but we still need to have a say."[14]

Indeed, if the president couldn't even secure the support of one third plus one senators—enough to sustain his veto—perhaps the deal he was negotiating wasn't that good a deal, Kaine argued. Obama laughed, but quickly shot back. "Tim, I will concede that point, but I think you overestimate the rationality of the body where you serve," he said, "because why are you there on a Friday trying to vote on whether DHS should be funded?" Kaine conceded that point, knowing he couldn't defend the conduct of the Senate, but stood firm on the bill, confident that the measure ultimately would benefit the negotiations. On the president's most important issue, the freshman Virginia senator had told him no.[15]

The White House's fears proved valid. With Kaine on the bill, it was becoming increasingly difficult to keep other Democrats off of it, particularly since the argument that the Senate must have a say on the deal had such a strong appeal on both sides of the aisle. The White House's strategy was to continue to push against the deal while quietly negotiating with a few key lawmakers to strip the bill of its most dangerous elements, such as the provision that Iran must recognize Israel or cease all support for groups the United States considered terrorists. By mid-April, it was clear that the bill was unstoppable. The president's chief of staff, Denis McDonough, asked for a meeting of all the Democrats in the Senate Foreign Relations Committee on the same day that the bill was going to get marked up in committee. Kaine thought that it might be a last ditch effort by the president to stop the bill. But instead, McDonough walked in and said that with the changes made to the bill, and the support it was gaining, the White House was dropping its veto threat.[16]

Three weeks later, the Corker bill was adopted by the Senate by a vote of 98 to 1. The White House stated that it was pleased with the compromise. In reality, though, "we hated it," according to a senior administration official. The White House had not been convinced by Kaine's arguments; it had simply lost the votes. And the early review process that the bill mandated would directly affect the negotiations, since it prohibited the White House from lifting any sanctions for thirty days after it had submitted the text of a final accord, along with classified material, to Congress. The legislature would use that thirty-day period to review and vote on the deal. If, however, negotiations with Iran continued beyond July 9, the review process would become sixty days long in order to factor in the August recess, when the Senate wouldn't be in session.[17]

The Corker bill was a compromise that ultimately left very few satisfied. Supporters of diplomacy worried that the early review process significantly increased the prospects of a deal being killed in Congress. Hawks were disappointed that the bill did not include more stringent measures that could directly threaten the nuclear negotiations. That group included Netanyahu, who was opposed to the compromise. The Israeli prime minister had signaled his all-or-nothing approach directly to Obama after the Lausanne agreement. The president called the Israeli prime minister from Air Force One, pleading with him to set aside their disagreement on the nuclear issue and instead focus on collaborating on rolling back Iran's regional influence. "Let's put the nuclear issue in the cabinet," Obama told Netanyahu. But Netanyahu refused. He would not agree to any measure that could give the impression that he was coming to terms with the nuclear deal without first having exhausted every possibility for killing the deal in Congress. The president was disappointed but not surprised. A massive showdown with Netanyahu, AIPAC, and other pro-Likud organizations in Congress was now unavoidable.[18]

Post-Lausanne Backtracking

The sleep deprivation of the diplomats in Lausanne became unmistakable when they reviewed the agreement upon their return to their respective capitals. Privately, administration officials conceded that with its many holes and loose ends, it wasn't the best written document. The lack of sleep had definitely left its mark on the document. Both sides expected that the other would seek to renegotiate aspects of the agreement and potentially backtrack on previous commitments. Tensions had already been brewing over the fact sheets the U.S. side had released explaining the agreement. The sheets contained no signs of being the product of the U.S. government, leaving many to believe that it was the text of the agreement itself rather than the aspects of the deal the Obama administration wanted to explain and highlight—and, at times, perhaps embellish. No other party to the negotiations issued their own fact sheets; all others relied on the joint statement issued after each round of talks. This frustrated the Iranians to no end, as they viewed the fact sheets as more spin than fact, adding to the domestic criticism Zarif and his team were already struggling with.[19]

The fact sheets coming out of Lausanne were more risky for the Iranians than those following the JPOA, since the framework agreement was so light and vague on sanctions relief. Without recognition that the sanctions issue had been deferred to the final deal, the framework agreement could give the impression that Iran had given a lot while receiving very little in return. As a result, the Iranians preferred that neither the full agreement nor any American fact sheets be published, a demand the United States couldn't agree to, since it was standard American practice to provide fact sheets when important international agreements were reached. The Iranians also tried to convince the United States to rename the document to "summary of understanding," but the Americans offered instead to show the fact sheets to Zarif before they were published.[20]

As the negotiations restarted, both sides were frustrated. The first meeting after Lausanne was held in Geneva and was predictably disappointing. Both sides accused the other of backtracking. The Iranians argued that whatever was agreed upon in Lausanne was set and could not be reopened, while the United States and the European Union felt that the nuclear provisions were insufficiently detailed—"What does it mean to 'remove' centrifuges? What parts must stay, what parts are going? What timetable?" Instead, the Iranians wanted to focus almost solely on sanctions relief—the one big item that was hardly addressed at Lausanne. In fact, they didn't even bring their nuclear experts to the Geneva meetings. (To make matters worse, Salehi was undergoing surgery and was hospitalized.) The Iranian message was: the nuclear issue is done; now it's the West's turn to reciprocate Iran's flexibility on the sanctions front.[21]

This had been Zarif's strategy all along—to surprise the United States by not pressing very hard on sanctions relief in Lausanne only to "jam the Americans" in the next round of talks. "Our strategy was the sanctions are not negotiable," Zarif explained to me. "So I didn't want to bring sanctions as a part of negotiations. We thought the negotiations should focus on the nuclear issue, and sanctions were a given." By having given the West a deal on the nuclear side that satisfied Obama and his allies, the Iranians calculated that it would become all the more difficult for the United States and the European Union not to be flexible on the sanctions front, since they now knew what they would give up if they failed to meet Iranian sanctions demands. Zarif calculated that "he could not get the U.S. to engage fully on sanctions until the Americans first saw what was within their reach on centrifuges. By first satisfying U.S. demands on enrichment, Iran would then be in a good position to drive a hard bargain on sanctions relief," Malley said of the Iranian strategy.[22]

It was a clever strategy, because it finally helped Iran create some divisions within the P5 + 1, with many of the United States' partners privately pressuring Obama to reciprocate Iran's flexibility from Lausanne. Obviously, it was a very risky move by Iran, given the lack of trust between Washington and Tehran, but it was a strategy that could work precisely because the United States had to manage a coalition with diverse interests and simultaneously hold together a strong line against Tehran. And if it failed, it would put Iran in a strong position to win the blame game. Since the Obama administration had lauded the agreement in Lausanne, failing to be flexible on sanctions would have shown that the United States was either unwilling to or incapable of lifting sanctions. Either way, the United States would come across as the intransigent party, the Iranians calculated. In Zarif's own words, "We would have said: So we gave them a nuclear program that was completely peaceful, but they were so wedded to their sanctions that they were not prepared to divorce them for a nuclear program that would address their concerns." It was a strategy that ultimately would prove successful.[23]

The Final Stretch in Vienna

As the delegations gathered in Vienna in late June 2015 for the final round of talks, sanctions relief topped the agenda together with the unresolved issues of possible military dimensions in Iran's past activities

(PMD), snapback sanctions, additional details on the nuclear front, the UN Security Council resolution, the arms embargo on Iran, and sanctions on its ballistic missile program. All sides knew that an agreement had to be struck in Vienna or they would have to concede that diplomacy had failed. This was the do-or-die moment for diplomacy—there could be no more extensions. While the negotiations could pass the June 30 deadline for a few days, there was no new lease on life for diplomacy to which the negotiators could retreat. For the first time, Zarif looked genuinely worried. When I joked with him that Vienna was cursed—all final rounds in Vienna had failed and ended in extending the talks—and that they should have opted to hold the final round in Geneva or Lausanne, where the JPOA and the framework agreement were reached, he gave me a nervous look and said, "Khoda nakone"— "God forbid" in Persian.[24]

Both sides increasingly played the public game, declaring their positions to the media and using public comments to impact the atmosphere in the negotiations. The blame game was a far more important factor now precisely because there could be no more extensions. As the talks began, Zarif's advisors were concerned that the media coverage was unfavorable to Iran—the Americans were giving regular press briefings, emphasizing the compromises Iran must agree to. For instance, Vice President Biden had publicly laid out the Obama administration's redlines for a final deal in a speech to the Washington Institute for Near East Affairs, a hawkish, pro-Israeli think tank—from the one-year breakout time to the principle of "phased sanction relief, calibrated against Iran taking meaningful steps to constrain their program," rather than the front-loaded, immediate sanctions relief the Iranians had declared to be their redline. The Iranians had responded in kind, with Ayatollah Khamenei giving a speech just days before the final round of talks, ruling out both freezing Iran's nuclear R&D for ten to twelve years and allowing inspections of military sites, while insisting that the process of lifting sanctions begin once Iran signed the nuclear agreement, with specific sanctions being relieved in a phased manner in tandem with Iran's nuclear steps.[25]

The P5 + 1 position was to phase the sanctions relief, but with no initial steps at the front of the agreement. On June 27, the U.S. side presented a shrewd solution that could reconcile the two approaches: the P5 + 1 and Iran would simultaneously adopt a legally binding decision to lift sanctions and begin dismantling centrifuges, but the sanctions relief would not come into effect until the IAEA verified that Iran had met its obligations. This way, the West achieved its goal of ensuring that sanctions wouldn't be lifted until Iran first had verifiably taken its nuclear steps, and Iran safeguarded its redline of parity and equality while ensuring that the decision to lift sanctions "wouldn't be at the mercy of Obama's signature," but would be made in a legally binding way at the very first phase of the agreement. The initial step—or "adoption day"—would begin as soon as the congressional review of the deal was completed and it was clear that Congress had failed to scuttle the deal. The actual lifting of the sanctions would occur on "implementation day," whose specific date would depend on how fast the Iranians could complete their nuclear dismantlement and have the IAEA verify it. By June 28, an agreement on the sanctions relief schedule had been reached, with the U.S. team spelling out in writing a detailed list of actions they would take to prepare private businesses for the changing legal landscape on sanctions, including commitments by the United States and the European Union to directly brief banks to remove any potential ambiguities.[26]

Despite this important breakthrough, the issue still wasn't fully resolved, since nothing was agreed upon until everything was agreed upon. One critical factor that could affect the schedule of the sanctions relief was Iran's past nuclear activities, which the United States believed contained possible military dimensions. It was a very delicate issue. If it was revealed that the Iranians had indeed engaged in illegal military research, that could jeopardize the entire agreement, as voices would be raised to have it punished for its past violations. Completely disregarding it without allowing the IAEA to complete its investigation—which the Iranians had not been cooperating with—was also not an option. What it came down to, from the perspective of the P5 + 1, was a choice between punishment for Iran's past violations and guarantees that those violations would never be repeated in the future. The obvious choice for Obama was the latter: punishing Iran for its past errors was of little value if punishment came at the expense of a deal that would prevent

Iran from building a bomb. Politically, however, this choice was feasible only if the IAEA could complete its investigation—with the cooperation of the Iranians—to make a final judgment on the issue and close the file. The P5+1 needed neither an admission of guilt nor a guilty verdict; they just needed Iran's cooperation to complete the investigation.[27]

The Iranians, however, did not trust the head of the IAEA, Yukiya Amano, due to his controversial report in 2011 that stated that Iran's weapons-related work might have continued beyond 2007, and feared that giving the IAEA more access would only lead to more demands and investigations. It was critical, from Tehran's perspective, that any investigation would be time-limited, so it couldn't drag on indefinitely, and delinked from the sanctions relief process, so that the decision to lift sanctions couldn't be held hostage to the PMD investigation. (The Iranians also objected to the term "possible military dimensions," and insisted that the IAEA report be titled "Clarification of Past and Present Outstanding Issues.") Eventually, a compromise was reached in which the Iranians would make their documents accessible and their scientists (though not their military officials) available for interviews for the purposes of producing a time-limited report that would contain both the IAEA's assessments and Iran's responses and contributions. The report would essentially include two narratives, which meant that there wouldn't be an authoritative judgment. More importantly, the sanctions relief process would be linked to the completion of the IAEA investigation and not its conclusion. That is, the IAEA would have to report only that Iran had cooperated with the investigation and that the IAEA's questions were answered in order for the green light for sanctions reform to be lit.[28]

As the negotiators were continuing their deliberations in Vienna, Amano flew to Tehran on July 2 to meet with Rouhani and Iran's Supreme National Security Council secretary, Ali Shamkhani, and concluded a final agreement that was announced two days later. The agreement established a timeline for resolving the PMD issues whereby Iran would turn over all information requested by the IAEA by August 15, and Amano would provide his final assessment by December 15.[29]

Between Heated and Heartfelt Moments

Overcoming the PMD hurdle was a major achievement. But the negotiators were already four days past the June 30 deadline, and the talks had already gotten tense on occasion. It didn't help that Vienna was struck by an unusual heatwave, with temperatures reaching as high as 95 degrees Fahrenheit. As in any good negotiation, both sides threatened to leave the talks at least once. And voices were raised on more than one occasion. At one point, Zarif objected so strongly to Kerry's proposal on snapback sanctions that they ended up in a shouting match that ended only when an aide to Kerry entered the room and told the two foreign ministers they had to lower their voices, since everyone in the hotel could hear them. The next morning, German Foreign Minister Frank-Walter Steinmeier teased Zarif about the heated exchange. "Seems like you had a constructive meeting last night; the whole hotel could hear you," he quipped.

Zarif, who is known for his temper, at one point threatened to take the entire P5+1 to the International Criminal Court in The Hague for their support of Saddam Hussein in the 1980s. "If we are talking about regional security, I should take every one of you to international courts for supporting Saddam," Zarif charged. In one meeting with Wendy Sherman, Zarif complained that the $7 billion of Iran's money that had been released to it as part of the JPOA had not made any difference to the Iranian economy, thereby downplaying the value of an earlier Western concession. Sherman responded by saying that if it hasn't been of value, the United States would be happy to take the money back. "Whose $7 billion will you 'take back'?" Zarif shot back angrily, offended by the suggestion that Iran's frozen assets actually belonged to the United States.[30]

Despite his reputation for being unflappable, Kerry lost his temper too. At the end of a six-hour session with the Iranians, he was infuriated by what he considered Iranian backtracking on the fate of the Fordo plant—after he had gotten the green light from Obama on a compromise he had worked out with the Iranians. He got so mad and slammed his fist so hard on the table that his pen flew across it and hit one of the Iranian negotiators.[31]

But even at the height of their tense exchanges, the negotiators could at the same time only be moments away from laughter. In fact, laughter was often what saved them from diplomatic dead ends. Late in the evening on July 6, the P5 + 1 presented to the Iranians a package on snapback, military embargo, and missile sanctions. The package had been developed largely by the EU team under Federica Mogherini, the EU foreign policy chief, but it met Obama's redlines, and the United States signed on to it. To the Iranians, however, it was worse than previous packages they had been sent, causing Zarif to push back hard. "Zarif's reaction that night was as belligerent and hostile as I've seen," Malley recalled. The response was so bad, and the atmosphere so tense, that Malley began thinking that the United States must prepare for an exit. The sides were stuck, the talks weren't going anywhere. "Everybody was accusing everybody," Mogherini told me. At that point, Mogherini felt that if the parties continued, they would risk undoing earlier agreements instead of making progress. "Well, if this is the case, then we just stop the discussion here, we just break, and we'll all go home and come back another time," she told Zarif. He, in turn, read Mogherini's suggestion as a warning and angrily shot back: "Never threaten an Iranian!" The room fell silent. For a moment, the entire deal hung on a thread. Then suddenly, Russia's Lavrov unexpectedly came to the rescue, quipping "Or a Russian!" The silence gave way to laughter. Diplomacy had survived yet another near-death experience.[32]

Humor was often used to break impasses, or simply to lubricate the otherwise tense deliberations. A story Zarif told the Americans soon became an inside joke among the negotiators and often helped lighten the mood. An Iranian American friend of the Iranian foreign minister had taken up a job as a limousine driver in New York. One night, he drove a woman to a wedding north of the city, but got lost. As time passed without the driver being able to find his way, the woman got visibly upset. To console her, the driver repeatedly told her, "Don't worry, don't worry. God has a plan." Eventually, he found the wedding, though much precious time had been lost. As the woman was about to leave, she asked him, "What in your religion makes you believe that God has a plan that is going to help you resolve these kinds of problems?" Incapable of explaining his optimism, he told the woman that he'd forgotten the name of the religious concept. "But let's just say it's Eastern philosophy," he told her. "Well, in my religion, we call it hogwash," the woman responded, slamming the door on her way out. From then on, whenever Zarif thought that Kerry and the Americans were giving him hogwash proposals, he would say "John, is that some more Eastern philosophy you're offering me?"

There were other heartfelt moments as well. After more than a week in Vienna, the Americans had grown tired of the Austrian cuisine and envied the Iranians, who had their lunches and dinners catered by a local Persian restaurant. The two sides ate in different but adjacent dining rooms, but Moniz would occasionally wander over to the Iranian side for dessert. Although Kerry and Zarif had met and negotiated for almost two years, between Geneva, Paris, Davos, Lausanne, Montreux, Munich, and New York City, they had still not sat down for a meal together. So on July 4, Zarif invited Kerry and his team for a Persian meal in the Iranian dining room. "It was ten times better than the food we ate on our side of the house," an aide to Kerry told Robin Wright of the *New Yorker.* Remarking on the wall separating the two dining rooms and the delegations, Zarif joked: "Like President Reagan said, tear down this wall!"[33]

The Corker Deadline

It was clear from the outset that the June 30 deadline had never been realistic. But once they were past that deadline, something surprising occurred: instead of working to meet the congressionally mandated July 9 deadline and avoiding the extension of the review period to sixty days, both sides felt it was to their benefit to miss it.

The intent of the Corker bill was to pressure the Iranians and deprive them of the time factor in the negotiations. But the Iranians saw it differently. In their view, the bill primarily pressured the U.S. negotiators: it was the Obama administration that would have to deal with a sixty- rather than a thirty-day review process, not the Rouhani government. The administration's argument to the Iranians that a sixty-day review period would give the opponents of the deal more time to sabotage it proved ineffective—if not even counterproductive. It wasn't Iran's responsibility to ensure the nuclear deal passed in Congress; it was Obama's, Tehran argued. As a result, the Iranians adopted a very relaxed attitude, calculating that the pressure to meet the deadline would force the U.S. side to be more flexible. "As far as we are concerned, we do not see a new deadline," Iran's Deputy Foreign Minister Majid Ravanchi told reporters on July 2. "We understand that the U.S. administration based on its own domestic considerations has certain points that they need to think about, but from our side I think July 7th, July 8th, July 9th does not have much of a difference."[34]

The Iranians had another factor working in their favor: Zarif's focus for the past two years had been almost exclusively on the nuclear issue. He could afford to stay in Vienna for days if not weeks because his other responsibilities were comparatively limited. Kerry, on the other hand, had to "keep the world running." His responsibilities were global. Spending close to three weeks in Vienna was significantly harder for Kerry than Zarif, the Iranians calculated. Using the Corker bill and the United States' global responsibilities against the United States, the Iranians made it abundantly clear that they were not in a hurry. "They did not give a stressed impression at all before the deadline," a senior European diplomat told me. "On the contrary."[35]

The Iranian strategy presented the United States with a conundrum. If the United States rushed to meet the deadline, they'd be accused by congressional hawks of letting the Iranians win. If they blew through it, they'd be forced to deal with a longer review process, but perhaps more important was that during the August recess, many lawmakers would visit Israel and be lobbied directly by Netanyahu, while AIPAC would have an opportunity to use its extensive grassroots network to press the lawmakers when they were home in their respective districts. The White House chose the latter. "We were not going to let anyone else's deadlines drive what we were willing to accept in the deal," Kerry told me.

To deprive the Iranians of any illusion that the Corker deadline would put the U.S. side in a disadvantageous position, Kerry decided to slow the pace of the talks himself. By July 8, the U.S. side withdrew its own proposal on how to solve the remaining issues, ensuring that a deal could not be reached by July 9. "Our total willingness to blow right by that [July 9] marker to make sure we got what we needed neutralized the leverage the Iranians believed this [Corker] bill would give them," a senior administration official explained. On the other hand, once the United States had called Iran's bluff, the Iranians couldn't change their position lest they be accused by their domestic critics of having allowed Congress to impose a deadline on them. "Both of us would have made ourselves vulnerable to criticism that we both gave in order to meet the deadline, so I think it made us both safer to go past it," Zarif told me. Paradoxically, a bill aimed at pressing the negotiators to conclude the deal by July 9 in reality ensured that the talks would proceed beyond that date. It was a telling example of how imprecise Congress's tools for impacting the talks were—and how poorly Congress understood the dynamics of diplomacy.[36]

Saved by the Russians

Once the July 9 deadline was passed, the only remaining big item issues were the arms embargo on Iran, its ballistic missile program, and the IAEA's access to Iranian military sites, as well as a snapback mechanism in the UN Security Council resolution. None of these military issues was central to the nuclear file. In fact, both the arms embargo and missile issue were a concern for the UN Security Council only if question marks remained about Iran's nuclear program. If the Security Council's concerns about Iran's nuclear activities were resolved, the basis for addressing the missile program would automatically be eliminated, since the fear was that Iran would be using ballistic missiles to deliver nuclear weapons. The missile program was in and of itself not a violation of any international treaties; only when combined with an illicit nuclear program did it make it to the Security Council's agenda.[37]

But with Iran's regional gains and the sense of alarm in Riyadh, Abu Dhabi, and Tel Aviv, Washington was under pressure to push back on variables that affected—or were perceived to affect—Iran's maneuverability in the region. The Obama administration knew its arguments were weak, particularly on the missiles issue, but the prospects of immediately lifting those sanctions would be very problematic. According to a leaked transcript of a briefing that Iranian negotiator Abbas Araghchi gave to the directors of Iran's state TV station, Kerry argued that the arms embargo had to be kept in place because not doing so would enable opponents of the deal to kill it:[38]

> Mr. Kerry said a few times: "You are the victim of your own successes in the region. You have had successes in Yemen, Syria, Iraq and Lebanon and have gained influence. Under these conditions, if we lift the arms embargo against you, we would kill the deal and we would no longer be able to defend it—not with our own allies, not with Arabs, not with Israel and not with Congress. There will be no deal. So we have to keep the arms embargo."[39]

For the Iranians, these were sensitive issues that quickly got entangled with Iranian feelings with regard to their independence and political factionalism, as well as legitimate security concerns. During the Iran-Iraq war, Iran's lack of missile technology gave Saddam Hussein a major advantage. While Saddam could hit Tehran from the most western point in Iraq due to Iraq's long-range missiles, the Iranians had to be deep inside of Iraqi territory in order to reach Baghdad with their missiles. Tehran scrambled to get other countries to sell it missiles, but only Muammar al-Ghaddafi's Libya and a few East European countries responded. The vulnerable situation in which Iran found itself and the humiliation of having to beg for defensive weapons while under attack left deep scars both within Iran's society and among its leaders.[40]

While the Iranians rejected leaving the arms embargo and sanctions on its missile program in place for a few more years, opening its missile facilities for inspection became even more sensitive, since Obama administration officials had referred to inspections as "anywhere, anytime." This was a mischaracterization of the actual process. In reality, the IAEA would have to receive credible evidence of suspicious activities at an undisclosed site in Iran, after which the agency would request access to that site from the government in Iran. This process was more accurately described as "managed access," rather than "anytime, anywhere," which the Iranians read as complete denial of their independence. The conversation in Iran quickly turned into a categorical rejection of giving international bodies access to its military sites. In reality, Iran had a long history of allowing international monitors to visit its military sites—for instance, both under the Chemical Weapons Convention as well as during the 2003–2005 period when Iran voluntarily implemented the Additional Protocol to the NPT. The difference was that Iran was comfortable giving access if a request was made, but not if it was ordered to provide that access. "The barrage of attacks against Iran—that Iran must do this, must do that—that has created problems domestically and this is when the question of dignity comes into play," one of the Iranian negotiators explained.[41]

The issue of snapback sanctions had reopened with the Iranians demanding parity. If the United States could go to the Security Council and demand that sanctions snap back due to an Iranian violation, Iran should also be able to go to the Security Council if the United States failed to lift sanctions on Iran—but without the United States being able to use its veto to squash the Iranian complaint. The U.S. proposal was that a single state could charge that Iran had breached its commitments and initiate snapback sanctions, a process that only a decision of the Security Council could halt. No reciprocal process was suggested in case Iran sought to file a complaint if the P5 + 1 violated its commitments. The U.S. side no longer insisted on automaticity, however, recognizing that it would be to its own detriment if all sanctions were snapped back on Iran in response to a minor violation. Proportionality was needed in order to ensure that any punishment would compel Iran to get back into compliance with the agreement, rather than having the punishment itself blow up the deal. Thus, the United States developed "a menu of proportionate responses to any potential Iranian violation."[42]

At first, the Iranian position on these issues was backed by Russia. But something happened around July 10 that prompted Russia to reverse its position on snapback sanctions and the arms embargo. On the latter issue, the Russians agreed to a compromise that required that states wishing to sell conventional arms to Iran obtain advance approval from the Security Council on a "case-by-case basis" for a period of five years. In essence, that meant that the arms embargo would remain intact for that period. Similarly, the Russians also backed down on new U.S. demands regarding snapback sanctions, much to Tehran's chagrin. Mindful of the importance the Russians ascribed to defending their veto, the Iranians were convinced that Washington had given Moscow a major concession behind the scenes. (The White House believed they simply got "lucky.") The Iranians felt betrayed by the Russians, but considered the nuclear agreement as a whole to be too valuable to reject on account of snapback sanctions or arms embargoes. Moreover, the Iranians had their own snapback—they could always start spinning more centrifuges in response to P5 + 1 violations. And on the issue of missiles, Tehran actually scored a small victory. The Security Council called on Iran "not to undertake any activity related to ballistic missiles designed to be capable of delivering nuclear weapons" for a period of eight years. Since Iran's missiles were not designed to deliver nuclear weapons, and since the operative term in the resolution was "called on," the measure did not carry much legal weight.[43]

At Last, Iran Unclenches Its Fist

With all of the major issues resolved, everything should have been set. But the Iranians still would not sign. They insisted on a few more changes and additional measures from the United States—some of which had no clear connection to the nuclear deal. "The Iranians just assumed that we wouldn't say no to any last minute requests out of fear that we would risk the entire deal," Malley recalled. The sides continued negotiating for another two days, and by July 12 optimism rose as the foreign ministers of the other P5 + 1 states all returned to Vienna.[44]

The U.S. team was exhausted. Most of the American diplomats had by now spent nineteen straight days in Vienna. Others, like Wendy Sherman, had been staked out in the Austrian city even longer—twenty-seven days in her case. Diplomacy was not only a contest of power, but one of persistence and perseverance. Both sides negotiated hard and absent political will and determination, diplomacy would have fallen at the first hurdle in the road. Now, the negotiators had reached the final hurdle, but patience was running short. On July 13, Kerry, Lavrov, Zarif, and Mogherini met to sort out the final differences. Helga Schmid and the technical people had negotiated the final text till five o'clock in the morning and handed it over to the ministers to finalize the few remaining issues. As the meeting began, all aides were kicked out of the room as only the ministers were authorized to make the political calls that could settle the last items on the agenda.[45]

It was a tense meeting. The raised voices of the testy, sleep-deprived ministers could easily be heard in the adjacent hallways where aides held their breath and hoped that last-minute incidents or interference by Israel or Saudi Arabia wouldn't jeopardize almost two years of diplomatic work. Kerry used every argument under the sun to convince Zarif to finally agree to the deal, including appealing to his sense of history. "He told him he had the chance to be known as the person who took the steps to ultimately end the nuclear sanctions against Iran," a senior State Department official said. Zarif, in turn, tried to convince Kerry to agree to a few final changes by dangling the prospects of a different relationship with Iran. The nuclear deal could be more than just a nonproliferation agreement; it could be an investment in an Iran that could be part of the international community and not at odds with it.[46]

Suddenly, a visibly frustrated Kerry exited the room and called on Chris Backemeyer. "I need one more thing," Kerry told Backemeyer. "I need to give them an excuse." The U.S. side had prepared a list of minor "meaningless" measures they could offer the Iranians in case they held up the talks to get the United States to make one final concession. Backemeyer handed him a list of eleven individuals—non-Iranians— designated on the U.S. sanctions list. "That's all we have left," Backemeyer said. Kerry glanced at the list briefly and walked back into the room. It was a last-minute measure, an inconsequential concession. "Sometimes, they argue over the smallest things," a senior administration official complained. The last two days of talks were nothing more than "pointless posturing where Zarif insisted on one more thing," probably for nothing more than its symbolic value.[47]

But that last pointless measure was enough to get them over the goal line. Zarif finally accepted, and years of diplomacy successfully came to an end. It was 11:00 p.m. on July 13. Against all odds, against conventional wisdom in Iran and in the United States, and in spite of extensive efforts by Netanyahu, the Saudi government, hardliners in Iran, and Republicans in Washington, pragmatists in the White House, in Europe, China, Russia, and Iran proved that even the most contentious

international conflict could be resolved peacefully if all sides were willing to negotiate in earnest, accept painful concessions, and muster the
political will to defend their peaceful path against domestic critics.

Immediately after Zarif's acceptance, Mogherini assembled the
other Europeans to go over what had been agreed upon. The agreement
would be announced tomorrow morning on July 14, she told them. As
usual, like clockwork, the French foreign minister, Laurent Fabius, objected. "Ah, mais non, c'est le quatorze juillet, c'est impossible," he complained. July 14 is Bastille Day, the French national holiday. Kerry lost
it. He had spent the last two days negotiating meaningless measures
with Zarif; the last thing he was in the mood for was more obstruction-
ism from the French. Throughout the talks, the French had annoyed the
others in the P5+1 to no end. Publicly, they adopted a hard line and
pretended to be more hawkish than the others. But at the negotiating table,
they adopted a very different posture. During one of the last rounds of
talks, I had a sit-down with Zarif immediately after one of his bilateral
meetings with Fabius, only hours after Fabius had given a very harsh
statement to the media. Mindful of that, I asked Zarif how the meeting had gone. "Very well," Zarif responded without hesitation. "But
publicly, he was saying . . . ," I said before Zarif interrupted me. "Publicly, Fabius says a lot," he said. "He likes the attention. But when I
meet him, he raises those same points only once. After I push back, he
changes the topic to how French companies can reenter the Iranian
market." The Americans were well aware of the French double-game,
calling the idea that the French were hardliners "a mythology" created by the French themselves. "Fabius is a lion in front of the cameras, but a mouse at the negotiating table," Kerry had complained to
Zarif at one point.[48]

Kerry angrily responded to Fabius in perfect French. "Listen, I've
spent two Fourth of Julys negotiating in a row." After all their sweat and
tears, the deal would not be delayed any further, certainly not for Bastille Day. The other Europeans began embracing and celebrating, but
Fabius refused. "No, I'm not going to do that," he said curtly. But the
others were not going to let Fabius's endless desire to complicate matters
ruin their celebrations. It was a fitting reflection of how inconsequen-

tial many—if not most—of Fabius's gambits had been. They caused headlines, even delays in the talks. But their impact on the substance of the deal was often minuscule at best.[49]

Later that day, a final plenary was scheduled with all the principals to celebrate and share their last thoughts. All foreign ministers gave a brief statement, reflecting on what the agreement meant to them and to their respective countries. Both Mogherini and Zarif's comments focused on the importance of multilateral diplomacy and finding win-win solutions. That in the modern world, neither force nor coercion could work. And that through the deal, a new era in Iran's relations with the West and the international community could be made possible. Kerry spoke last. He reflected on his youth as a soldier in Vietnam and later as one of the foremost advocates against the war. How he had learned that war was the ultimate failure of mankind and that his desire to spare the younger generation what he had to endure in Vietnam was a major motivator behind his drive to resolve the nuclear issue peacefully. "It was not a prepared statement, but it [was] a sentiment I had thought a lot about during the negotiations," Kerry told me. "I came back from Vietnam with the deeply held belief that we should never send our men and women in uniform into harm's way unless we've exhausted every other option." At the end of Kerry's comments, half of the other ministers were teary-eyed. No one in the room doubted that they had avoided a war that would have left all of them, and all of their countries, worse off.[50]

The Win-Win

Obama was in the Oval Office when his senior aides broke the news that the deal had been sealed. He drew a sigh of relief, reflecting back on the long road he had journeyed to get to this point. "It was a long time coming," he told his aides and joked about placing a call to Senator John McCain (R-AZ), his 2008 presidential rival who had called him naive for thinking diplomacy with Iran could work. But the celebrations were short-lived. All knew the congressional review process would begin promptly, and that the opponents of the deal would use every possible argument to diminish their diplomatic victory. At the National Security

Council, staffers popped a bottle of champagne. And then they went promptly back to work. "It was a surreal moment," NSC Deputy Spokesperson Bernadette Meehan told me.[51]

The Iranian celebrations were more cheerful. People were dancing in the streets of Tehran till late in the morning, some youth sporting T-shirts saying "I Love USA"—a sight rarely seen in the Islamic Republic of Iran. The supreme leader lauded the agreement as a victory for Iran. "After 12 years of struggling with the Islamic republic, the result is that they have to bear the turning of thousands of centrifuges in the country," the ayatollah said.[52] At an off-the-record briefing with Iranian state TV, Abbas Araghchi of the Iranian negotiating team revealed some of Tehran's calculations and why it considered the deal a victory. The Americans had one key demand: preventing Iran from acquiring a nuclear weapon, Araghchi said. "We had no problem with that, and granted it to the enemy. . . . The other side got what it wanted and can say that they prevented an Iranian atomic bomb." This, however, was not a defeat for Iran, Araghchi insisted, according to the leaked proceedings. "If we had wanted the bomb, then the JCPOA [Joint Comprehensive Plan of Action] is an utter defeat. But if we are after internationally legitimate enrichment and a completely peaceful nuclear program, then this agreement is a great victory." After all, Araghchi explained, Iran's nuclear program never made much sense from an economic standpoint. The program was needed, however, to force the West to come to terms with Iran's independence and standing in the region. "If we calculate the cost of the products, it makes no sense at all," the Iranian negotiator said. "But we paid these costs for our honor, our independence and our progress. We will not be bullied by others."[53]

This defense of Iran's independence and dignity came at a significant price, Araghchi admitted, not only because of the economic pain inflicted by sanctions, but also because the Iranians were convinced at times that war was a real possibility. Tehran, however, saw that risk primarily during the last years of the Bush administration. "Maybe people are not aware of the details, but our Revolutionary Guards and military friends know that there were nights in 85–86 [2006–2007] when we were worried that by the morning Iran would be surrounded," he said. Araghchi also assured the hardline leadership of Iran's state TV that

Iran had little to worry about the congressional review process. If Congress were to reject the agreement, Iran wouldn't lose anything. "We can return to our own program and the world will consider us to be justified," he argued.[54]

The supreme leader's endorsement was crucial. Hardline elements in Iran had been kept in check by Ayatollah Khamenei throughout the negotiations and prevented from undermining the talks. The discipline of the Iranian system had surprised many observers, given its past history of out-of-control political factionalism. The discipline reflected the fact that the Iranian elite as a whole had agreed to settle the nuclear issue. Even the top leaders of the Iranian Revolutionary Guard Corps (IRGC) expressed support for the Iranian negotiators. "Up until today the nuclear negotiation team have defended the Iranian nation's rights well, and the nation and IRGC is grateful for their honest efforts," IRGC commander Mohammad Ali Jafari said. In fact, once diplomacy began in earnest, the debate was never between resolving the issue and reverting back to resistance. Rather, the debate was on the extent of concessions Iran had to accept and, more important, whether the nuclear deal should be allowed to pave the way for a broader rapprochement between Washington and Tehran. The opposition to the deal was often motivated by the fear that a nuclear accord would initiate an irreversible opening to the West rather than by a true disagreement over the details of the deal itself. And the opening to the West was opposed, not primarily on ideological grounds, but because of the understanding that improved relations with the West would increase Western influence in Iran and shift the balance of domestic politics in favor of the more moderate political factions.[55]

To Obama, the deal was an equally valuable achievement for the United States. At a press conference at the White House the day after the deal was brokered, Obama called it "historic" and "a powerful display of American leadership and diplomacy." Obama emphasized that the deal could lead to "conversations with Iran that incentivize them to behave differently in the region," although the United States wasn't counting on such changes. Nor was the success of the deal dependent on any change in Iran's overall foreign policy orientation. "This deal is not contingent on Iran changing its behavior," Obama explained. At his

moment of triumph, the president also took a swipe at his critics, knowing very well that he had to convince the American public on the merits
of the deal in order to count on them to push back against any attempt
to kill the deal in Congress. "What is your preferred alternative?" he
asked rhetorically. The reason the opponents of the deal had not presented an alternative policy, Obama argued, was because the only other
option was war. "There really are only two alternatives here: either the
issue of Iran obtaining a nuclear weapon is resolved diplomatically
through a negotiation, or it's resolved through force, through war. Those
are the options." The option of just increasing sanctions until the Iranians gave up completely simply did not exist, the Obama team maintained. "Sanctioning Iran until it capitulates makes for a powerful
talking point and a pretty good political speech, but it's not achievable
outside a world of fantasy," Kerry said on the eve of the deal.[56]

In an interview with Tom Friedman of the *New York Times* the day
after the deal, Obama expanded on his thinking as to why the deal was
good—and why it was necessary. Containing Iran definitely was not an
option, Obama hinted, because the Iranian demand to be recognized as
a major power in the region had merit. "The truth of the matter is that
Iran will be and should be a regional power," he said. "They are a big
country and a sophisticated country in the region." This recognition by
the United States was one of the main reasons for Israel's and Saudi Arabia's opposition to the deal, as it clearly signaled the United States' acceptance of Iranian inclusion in a new regional order. While recognizing
aggressive Iranian behavior, Obama also pushed back against the near-
hysteria in the region about Iranian ambitions. Iran's involvement in the
conflict in Yemen, for instance, had been "overstated." Instead, the Iranians were opportunistic and sought to exploit crises as they emerged,
rather than being the driver behind them. The United States' regional
allies should stop giving Iran opportunities for mischief, Obama argued. "Strengthen your own societies. Be inclusive. Make sure that your
Shia populations don't feel as if they're being left out. Think about the
economic growth," was his advice to Iran's Arab neighbors; he would
not indulge them in their fear of "Iran's rise" or request for the United
States to confront and contain Tehran. Moreover, Obama argued against
the idea that the Iranians were bound to cheat on the agreement. "That's

not what we saw during the last two years of the interim agreement," Obama argued, pointing out that Iran had lived up to its commitments under the JPOA and that it had strong incentives to stick to the deal. These were remarkable statements coming from an American president. After decades of mutual demonization, entertaining the idea that Iran could honor its word or that it deserved a major role in the region was nothing short of political heresy. But it was also the honest assessment of a president whose views were shaped by his administration's interactions and dealings with Iran, rather than by the emotional entrapment of past wounds.[57]

Opponents of the deal were unfazed, however. After all, for most of them, as for Iran's hardliners, the details of the nuclear deal were irrelevant. Their fear and the motivation for their opposition was the very idea that a deal with Tehran had been struck since it signaled an end to Washington's policy of isolating Iran. The geopolitical fallout of this move could lead to Washington's losing Iran as an enemy—a proposition that was as frightening and unappealing to Washington's hawks as it was to Israel's and Iran's hardliners.

The War Zone in Washington

The nuclear agreement was celebrated throughout the world as a historic triumph of reason and dialogue over militancy and warmongering. For more than a decade, war between the United States and Iran had loomed. Now, as a result of the deal, the talk of war had ended, and the U.S. government asserted that all paths for Iran to build a nuclear bomb had been blocked. Nevertheless, global celebrations failed to reach three critical places: the U.S. Congress, the palace of the Saudi king, and the office of the Israeli prime minister. Everywhere else, the benefits of the deal were self-evident. Yet even from their minority position, Republican hawks and their Israeli and Saudi allies mustered ferocious opposition, leaving President Barack Obama with no option but to organize the greatest mobilization since his fight for health care reform in order to save his signature foreign policy achievement. For opponents of the deal, it wasn't just about the way to deny Iran nuclear capability; it was about the very idea of striking a deal with the clerical regime in Tehran. For decades, the U.S.-Iran enmity had been institutionalized in Washington and Tehran. To come to an agreement with Iran necessitated not just a policy shift but a paradigm shift. The fight to pass the deal in Congress was a fight Obama knew he could not win alone.

The Israeli security establishment found itself in a bind. The U.S. president had just significantly reduced the threat of Iran's nuclear capabilities. However, the Israeli prime minister's vehement opposition to the deal was replacing that threat with a much graver one: a deteriorating U.S.-Israel relationship. Israel had found itself in a "diplomatic war" with the United States and the P5+1 even though the Israeli security establishment's assessment of the nuclear deal tended to be positive. The Israeli military intelligence credited it for turning the nuclear program into a "threat in decline." The Israeli Atomic Energy Commission endorsed the deal, concluding it would "prevent Iran from developing a nuclear bomb." Even the Israeli Defense Forces published a thirty-three-page overview of its strategic doctrine that barely mentioned Iran or its nuclear program. The chief of staff of the Israeli military, Gadi Eizenkot, described it as a "strategic turning point" for Israel. "It is a big change in terms of the direction that Iran was headed, and in the way that we saw things," he said.[1]

Nonetheless, the rift between the security and the political establishments' assessments of the nuclear deal could not have been any greater. It wasn't just Netanyahu—even his political opponents preferred to sound hawkish rather than side with their own security experts and the president of the United States. "It's bad politics to confront an American president, but it's good politics to confront Obama," Israeli journalist Tal Shalev told me. After decades of portraying Iran as an existential threat, for a politician to come across as weak on Tehran was simply political suicide. With no political opposition to Netanyahu's line, and with the security establishment limited in its ability to raise its concerns publicly, Israel simply did not have a debate on the merits of the nuclear deal. "In Israel it became easy to play with our fear," said Ami Ayalon, the former head of the Shin Bet, Israel's secret service.[2]

But Netanyahu was not motivated solely by the technical aspects of the nuclear deal. The geopolitical fallout of the deal—regardless of its technical details—was largely the same: the United States would recognize Iran as a major player in the region, it would cease its many efforts to contain it, and it could create a new order that no longer entirely excluded Iran. So while some in the Israeli security establishment wanted to press the United States to ensure a stronger deal, Netanyahu was not interested in *any* deal. Netanyahu "has no interest in any agreement," Efraim Halevy, the former head of the Mossad, charged.[3]

Two days after concluding the nuclear deal, British Foreign Secretary Philip Hammond flew to Israel to mend fences. What was supposed to be a visit to convince Netanyahu of the deal's merits turned into a testy public confrontation. Only a day earlier, Hammond had blasted Netanyahu in the British Parliament, accusing Israel of wanting "a permanent state of standoff" with Iran. "The question you have to ask yourself is what kind of a deal would have been welcomed in Tel Aviv. The answer of course is that Israel doesn't want any deal with Iran," Hammond said. These were astonishing comments that fundamentally contradicted the Western narrative that Israel was the victim of an ideological assault by Iran's clerical rulers. Absent ideology, Iran and Israel would be natural allies, this narrative claimed, completely disregarding the conflict's geopolitical roots, which prompted Israel to oppose any measures in the region that would allow Iran to escape its international isolation regardless of shifts in Iran's ideology. Hammond's comments indicated that the Western powers had realized the limitations of understanding the Israeli-Iranian conflict solely from an ideological lens.[4]

Netanyahu vehemently rejected the notion that Israel sought permanent conflict with Iran, insisting instead that Israel wanted "a genuine and effective diplomatic solution." He pointed out that only four days before the nuclear deal was concluded, protesters in Tehran called for the destruction of Israel. Rather than continuing their discussion in private, Hammond could not restrain himself and responded to Netanyahu. "We will judge Iran not according to the chants of the crowds on the streets of Tehran but by the actions of its government," he observed, mocking Netanyahu for letting protesters in Iran determine Israel's posture on Iran.[5]

Netanyahu's press conference with Hammond made it clear that he and his political allies determined Israel's position on the nuclear deal, not the Israeli security establishment. "We consider the deal a very bad one," Netanyahu's defense minister, Moshe Yaalon, said even before the agreement had been struck. "The deal is going to allow Iran to actually become a military nuclear threshold state." From the perspective of the opponents of the deal, the American position had gone from demanding "a peaceful nuclear program to just enough to detect breakout. From no right-to-enrichment to getting an alarm system." Although almost no American observers believed that zero enrichment was achievable, Israel blasted the deal since it didn't aspire to eliminate Iran's program.[6]

"We thought the goal should be to get rid of the Iranian nuclear threat, not verify or inspect it," Israeli Minister of Intelligence Yuval Steinitz said. The real risk was not breakout, Steinitz continued, but that Iran would quietly weaponize its program in a few years when the West was preoccupied with other crises. To allow the restrictions on Iran's program to be lifted in fifteen years presumed that Iran would have a democratic government by then—a dangerous assumption according to Steinitz. Both arguments contradicted earlier Israeli positions, however. First, it was Israel that had pushed for the breakout concept at the expense of other considerations. Second, the expectation of eventual democratization in Iran was assumed when Israel itself propagated recurring military action against Iran's nuclear program. Since Iran would be rebuilding its program, the "mowing the lawn" strategy would continue until the Iranian regime fell or was replaced with a pro-Western government.[7] And with the lifting of sanctions, Iran would rehabilitate its economy and be in a greater position to "dominate the region." Consequently, Yaalon contended, Iran posed a greater threat to the region than ISIS, repeating an argument Netanyahu had unsuccessfully made in Washington before. "This is a war of cultures" taking place in the Middle East, Yaalon wrote in December 2015, between a "culture that values death and destruction" and the culture of the "Western world," as represented by Israel. To top it off, he declared, "the driving force behind this opposing, evil culture is Iran," not ISIS. Even to sympathetic voices, Yaalon's claims bordered on the hysterical.[8]

But having already burned all bridges with the Obama administration and with most Democrats in Congress, Netanyahu had little to lose. At one point, National Security Advisor Susan Rice complained to the head of the Anti-Defamation League that Netanyahu had done everything but "use 'the N-word' in describing the president." As far as the White House was concerned, Netanyahu's interference in American affairs had already caused "irreparable scars."[9]

However, to Netanyahu the damage to U.S.-Israel relations would have been worth it if he managed to kill the deal in Congress. After all, he paid no domestic political price for having "gone to war against Obama." In fact, he had calculated that even his controversial speech to Congress had helped him domestically, since the Likud Party ran political ads in Israel with clips of his speech within days of his address. Even if he failed to stop the deal, the mere fact that he had tried could enable him to "go down in history as one of the prophets who warned of doom and were subsequently vindicated," Peter Beinart explained to me. Furthermore, by putting up a fierce fight, Netanyahu could help prevent the deeper danger posed by the deal: a broader U.S.-Iran rapprochement. By fighting the deal, Netanyahu could force "the U.S. to maintain its Cold War posture vis-à-vis Iran" and constrain Obama's ability to make the deal go beyond its nonproliferation core, Beinart argued. Steinitz, however, maintained that "Iran is part of the problem and not part of the solution—unless you think Iran dominating the Middle East is the solution."[10]

It was precisely this fear of Iran's political rehabilitation that pushed Israel and Saudi Arabia closer together. Both of them had been primary benefactors of the American-led order prior to 2003 and believed that they would be the main losers if Iran was let in from the cold. According to European diplomats, the prospect of a deal had prompted Israeli and Saudi officials to secretly meet as early as 2014 to coordinate efforts against it and what they described as Iranian expansionism. While Saudi officials were loath to acknowledge this collaboration with the Israelis—just as the Iranians had hidden their ties to Israel decades earlier—Israel was unapologetic about its new alliance. "Iran is a common enemy," Israel's defense minister said. "If we share common enemies along with other common interests, there is room for cooperation." It was a remarkable turn of events: only a few decades earlier it had been Iran and Israel that conspired behind the scenes in order to balance the Arabs. Perhaps even more noteworthy was the fact that the Israeli-Saudi secret rapprochement occurred as Iran's foreign policy was becoming markedly more moderate. It wasn't Iranian radicalism that pushed them together as much as Washington's willingness to deal with a more moderate Iran.[11]

From the Saudi perspective, the United States had gone behind Riyadh to negotiate with Iran, just as it had in 1986 before the Contra scandal. The Saudis feared that the United States was making a "pivot to Iran" and abandoning them in the process. "We were America's best friends in the Arab world for 50 years," the former head of Saudi intelligence Prince Turki told the *New York Times*, using the past tense. The Saudis didn't even pretend to care about the details of the nuclear negotiations. They neither pushed for nor spoke publicly of any specific nuclear solutions or positions. "We never had a single conversation with [the Saudis] about the number of centrifuges," Colin Kahl, a senior advisor to Vice President Joe Biden told me. "It was rather: How can you make a deal with this regime, legitimize them and empower them?" Once again, the United States' sin was not its allowing enrichment in Iran but the very idea of making a deal with it. If forced to choose, Riyadh preferred an isolated Iran with a nuclear bomb to an internationally accepted Iran without nuclear weapons.[12]

In an attempt to bind the United States to Riyadh through mutual rivalry with Tehran, the Saudis pushed for a formal defense treaty between the United States and Saudi Arabia. Such a treaty, the Saudis calculated, would prevent a full-scale American betrayal of Saudi interests. From the U.S. perspective, however, it could lead to further entanglement in the Middle East at a time when the United States sought to reduce its footprint in the region. Given Washington's immense military sales to the Arab states in the Persian Gulf, a defense pact would be overkill, as well as provoking Iran and increasing tensions in the region, Obama calculated. Furthermore, the Gulf Cooperation Council (GCC) as a whole spent $135 billion on their defense, with the Saudi share constituting more than $80 billion, while Iran spent less than $15 billion on defense and arms purchases. The numbers simply didn't give credence to the Saudi narrative of a rising Iran that necessitated a Saudi-U.S. defense pact. If you're concerned about Iran feeling emboldened by sanctions relief, the White House told the Saudis, how do you think they would feel if they obtained a nuclear weapon?[13]

Back on the Hill, AIPAC found itself torn. The group raised a record $20 to $40 million to take on the president—a position it had historically sought to avoid. However, because it was "tied at the hip to

Netanyahu," its ability to act independently was severely limited. "Once the Israeli government went all in, AIPAC didn't have any choice," Beinart commented. Since 1995, Iran had been AIPAC's top policy priority and its most valuable fundraising cause. Taking on the president of the United States would be tough and could do long-term damage to AIPAC's standing regardless of whether it won or lost. Of all scenarios, the worst one would be if AIPAC were to be deemed irrelevant; it was better to fight and lose than to not matter at all, particularly on the issue that had become AIPAC's raison d'être during the past two decades and that had proven a remarkably lucrative fundraising tool. "They were caught in a bind," Israeli columnist Chevi Shalem told me, pointing out that had it been up to AIPAC, the organization would likely have chosen a different course. AIPAC's lack of maneuverability was a sign of its declining influence. It had been manipulated by both the Israeli government and House Republicans and had lost the ability to shape its own options.[14]

Kaine Sets the Rules

Having considerable confidence that Israel "knows how to sway public opinion" in the United States, the Netanyahu government launched a massive campaign on Capitol Hill to stop the nuclear deal. When U.S. intelligence officials listened in on his conversations with lawmakers, they discovered that he and Ron Dermer directly lobbied Congress regarding the deal and explicitly asked lawmakers: "How can we get your vote? What's it going to take?" Dermer even coached hawkish Jewish American groups on which talking points to use with lawmakers. The intercepts also revealed—much to the White House's surprise—that Netanyahu truly believed he could win this fight. "Netanyahu thought he could outflank Obama by making Israel a partisan issue," a senior administration official told me.[15]

Senator Tim Kaine's earlier changes to the Corker bill had, however, heavily tilted the rules in favor of Obama. The opposition in the Senate would need sixty votes to force a vote on a resolution to reject the deal, and then sixty-seven votes to override Obama's veto of that resolution. If supporters of the nuclear deal in the Senate could secure thirty-four votes, Obama's veto would be protected. If they could secure forty-one votes, the resolution to reject the deal would not even come to the floor for a vote. In the House of Representatives, the resolution could not be prevented from being voted on, but similar rules existed on the president's veto. By securing 146 votes out of 435, proponents of diplomacy would have protected the president's veto. With these rules, the monumental mistake Netanyahu had committed by making the Iran vote a partisan issue became clear. Not only did it turn Democrats away from Netanyahu; now, they also began fundamentally questioning his position. "It really caused many Democrats to step back and question the message he delivered about the threat of Iran," Senator Dick Durbin (D-IL) said. "He created doubt and skepticism about this position."[16]

Although the Republicans controlled both chambers of Congress, they needed to win over several Democrats in order to break Obama's veto, since the Republican majority was not large enough to override the president's veto on its own. The more partisan the issue became, the tougher the task would be. Turning the issue into a choice between Obama and the leader of a foreign nation only made it more likely that the Democrats would choose their own president—even if that foreign nation was Israel. "For a lot of people, [choosing between Obama and Netanyahu] was actually pretty easy," Congresswoman Jan Schakowsky (D-IL) pointed out.[17]

The strategy of Netanyahu and his allies to win over U.S. public opinion and get a veto-proof majority in Congress was surprisingly uncreative. First, frame a vote for the deal as a vote against Israel. Next, activate the grassroots of all allied organizations, from AIPAC to evangelical churches, to pressure lawmakers through constituency lobbying (particularly during the August recess). Last, overwhelm the Obama administration with a deluge of arguments against the deal—hoping that at least a few would stick—and saturate the TV networks with ads against the deal. Since the partisan nature of the deal ensured that very few Republicans would jump ship, almost all of the focus was on getting twelve Democratic senators and forty-three members of the House to shift sides.[18]

No Democratic senator faced more pressure from AIPAC than Chuck Schumer (D-NY), the likely successor to Harry Reid (D-NV) as majority leader in 2017. Schumer's clout within the Democratic caucus was considered so strong that if he shifted, he could potentially bring another five to six senators with him, providing them with political protection against the wrath of the White House. "If Schumer says this [the deal] doesn't do it, it lifts the arms embargo and doesn't have anytime, anywhere inspections, then we have a fight on our hands," Noah Pollak, executive director of the Emergency Committee for Israel (ECI) said. "He's a linchpin or a bellwether," he added. The main players Netanyahu had in his corner were hawkish pro-Israeli groups such as ECI, AIPAC, the Israel Project, and Republican and neoconservative outfits, as well as factions of the evangelical movement.[19]

For Obama, the path to securing 34 votes in the Senate and 146 in the House was more difficult to chart. No president had tried to get an agreement with Iran through Congress before, while AIPAC had extensive experience in doing so with anti-Iran measures. Obama had hoped to avoid a fight in Congress, but now had to beat AIPAC and win support for the deal before Iran had proven that it would honor the agreement. Early on, two key conclusions were drawn. First, the opponents of the deal could not be allowed to frame a vote such that it would be in favor of Iran and against Israel; if this happened, Obama would surely lose. Rather, opposition to the deal must be understood as a vote in favor of war with Iran, the White House strategized. As long as the war-or-peace frame prevailed, Obama's prospects for victory were favorable. Second, the White House needed the broadest possible political coalition of outside groups to counter the pressure from AIPAC and Netanyahu. It would not be enough for the nuclear deal to be good policy—it also had to be good politics. Obama could not afford to have lawmakers turn against the deal because they feared they'd face AIPAC's wrath in the next elections and not have a strong constituency backing them. But beating back AIPAC and Netanyahu on Capitol Hill was not something the White House could do on its own. Support from outside groups would prove "critical" for the survival of the nuclear deal.[20]

The Spider in the Web

Joseph Cirincione was not new to nonproliferation or to fighting against the expansion of war in the Middle East. A renowned nonproliferation expert with a long career in Washington, DC—from staffing the House Committee on Armed Services to directing Washington think tanks— Cirincione was the ultimate DC insider. In 2003, he lost the fight to prevent the Iraq war and was now determined to prevent war with Iran. In his position as president of the Ploughshares Fund, he soon emerged as the spider in the web. All efforts by outside groups to support the Iran deal led one way or another to him and his organization.

Ploughshares is an unusual foundation. Founded in 1981 to reduce nuclear threats, it has distinguished itself by taking an active role in the policy process and working closely with its grantees. Early on, Ploughshares had diagnosed that the entities pushing for diplomacy with Iran were too scattered and uncoordinated. Their prospects for turning U.S. policy on Iran toward diplomacy were minuscule unless an infrastructure for greater collaboration was put into place. Ploughshares was uniquely positioned to create that "central location" for the pro-diplomacy groups, and no one was a better fit for the job than Cirincione himself. Some years before, he had successfully created such a central hub, the Coalition for Nuclear Dangers, to get the Comprehensive Test Ban Treaty ratified, and he reused that strategy to support ratification of the new Strategic Arms Reduction Treaty (START) in 2011. Once START was secured, Ploughshares shifted its focus to preventing a nuclear-armed Iran and a consequential war.

Ploughshares had already been funding key groups in the pro-diplomacy coalition, such as the Arms Control Association (ACA) and the National Iranian American Council (NIAC) for years, but in 2011, it began coordinating and expanding the existing coalition supporting the nuclear talks. The coalition addressed all aspects needed to muster a tectonic policy shift toward diplomacy. It started by creating intellectual space for nonproliferation experts to imagine what a good deal would look like and plan a diplomatic path to it. Ploughshares and Rockefeller Brothers Fund (RBF) funded the Iran Project, a group of highly regarded former senior American officials led by Ambassador Bill Luers, who produced numerous influential reports on the nuclear crisis that paved the way for diplomacy. Then, it created political space by investing in organizations mobilizing grassroots pressure on Congress and the executive branch. Finally, it shaped public debate by providing resources for experts favoring diplomacy to be heard and coordinating groups to ensure that resources were properly allocated and message discipline was maintained. These efforts connected people and created synergies in ways that otherwise probably would never have been possible. "People that normally wouldn't talk to each other, like former generals and MoveOn.org's activists, got to talk and got to share information and experiences," Cirincione explained to me.[21]

At its height, the Ploughshares coalition was composed of eighty-five highly diverse organizations—from Jewish American groups such as Americans for Peace Now and J Street, to peace and security groups such as Council for a Livable World, Win Without War, and the Friends Committee on National Legislation, to nonproliferation organizations such as the ACA, Iranian American groups such as NIAC, and progressive groups with vast grassroots followings such as MoveOn and CREDO. The administration began meeting with the coalition in 2013 after the election of Hassan Rouhani, providing updates on the negotiations and requesting advice on both the talks and the public debate around the negotiations. For the coalition groups that had advocated diplomacy during the sanctions years and criticized Obama for rejecting the Tehran Declaration, this was a welcome development. Throughout the summer of 2015, the coalition generated 150,000 phone calls to Congress, 307,000 emails, 1.1 million signatures on petitions, 199 editorials, 442 op-eds, and over 200 letters to the editors of local newspapers in support of the nuclear deal. These feats would not have been possible had it not been for the central hub Ploughshares had established and the clarity it provided regarding the deal—namely, that it was a choice between war and peace.[22]

The coordination within the coalition was also essential because the pro-diplomacy groups were hopelessly outfunded by AIPAC and its allies by a factor of five. Worse still, Ploughshares could not fund all of the groups in its circle. Moreover, with the Republicans controlling the House and Senate, experts opposing the nuclear negotiations were more than twice as likely to be invited by Congress to testify on the matter. With the scales tipped against it, the Ploughshares circle had no choice but to fight smarter. Once they created the central hub, Cirincione and his colleagues could take their case to other foundations and seek their support for the effort to prevent war and nuclear proliferation.[23]

One foundation that collaborated closely with the Ploughshares Fund was the New York–based Rockefeller Brothers Fund (RBF), headed by Stephen Heintz. RBF's involvement in the Iran issue was deeper and longer than that of any other major U.S. foundation. Until this day, it remains the biggest American funder of projects and activities focused on U.S.-Iran diplomacy. RBF's involvement started in late 2001, when Stephen Heintz talked about Iran with Ambassador William Luers, a member of the RBF board of trustees and then the president of the United Nations Association of the USA (UNA-USA). Luers had also been interested in U.S.-Iran relations and told Heintz about the work of his UNA-USA colleague, Suzanne DiMaggio, who was serving in the secretariat responsible for activities associated with the designation of 2001 as the "United Nations Year of Dialogue among Civilizations," an idea first proposed by President Mohammad Khatami as a counter to Samuel Huntington's "Clash of Civilizations." In that context, DiMaggio had been working with then deputy foreign minister Javad Zarif on the Dialogue among Civilizations beginning in 2000, and the two had determined that a Track-II dialogue between the United States and Iran was both needed and feasible—though it required tremendous political courage from both sides since dialogue between the two remained a taboo in both capitals. Luers greenlighted the idea, he and DiMaggio then contacted Heintz, and the three of them agreed to move forward as a UNA-RBF partnership. Heintz reached out to the Stockholm International Peace Research Institute (SIPRI) to enlist the well-respected think tank as a third partner, as the highly sensitive meetings between Iranians and Americans would need to take place on neutral ground and with utmost confidentiality.[24]

Between 2001 and February 2008, when the Ahmadinejad government in Iran put a stop to the Track-II with the set of interlocutors associated with Zarif, fourteen meetings were held between American and Iranian academics, former and serving officials, and, occasionally, lawmakers. Most of the meetings were hosted by SIPRI and took place in a small inn outside of the Swedish capital of Stockholm. For many of the participants, it was the first time they ever spoke to someone from the other side. Beyond providing the two sides with a deeper understanding of their respective political systems, limitations, and calculations, the meetings also connected key players on both sides who later came to have leading roles in the nuclear negotiations. Zarif was a central supporter of the Track-II meetings. The U.S. side included Puneet Talwar, who years later headed the Oman negotiations with Jake Sullivan, and Robert Einhorn, a nuclear expert who went on to be a senior member of the U.S. negotiating team. Two highly regarded former diplomats, Ambassadors Thomas Pickering and Frank Wisner, were also actively involved throughout.[25]

Thanks to their contact with high-level Iranian officials and their stature in foreign policy circles, Luers, DiMaggio, Heintz, Pickering, and Wisner were also given high-level access on the U.S. side. They regularly briefed top Bush and Obama White House officials on their conversations with the Iranians. The more they came to understand the complexities of Iran's decision-making structure and political culture, the more frustrated they grew with the simplistic view of Tehran's motives and calculations that dominated the thinking inside the U.S. government. For instance, the Bush administration consistently dismissed the potential openings the participants in the Track-II identified by insisting that the regime in Iran was "on the brink of implosion" and needed only a small push to collapse. A similar miscalculation was the insistence on zero enrichment, borne out of an exaggerated view of U.S. power and an overly pessimistic assessment of Iranian capabilities.[26]

There were also several U.S. lawmakers involved in the Track-II. Once the nuclear deal had been concluded, the connections between Iranian negotiators and U.S. lawmakers provided by the RBF-funded Track-II proved instrumental.

The Peace Room in the War Zone

Capitol Hill was a war zone in the summer of 2015. The Republican attacks on President Obama had reached a new height, with former Arkansas governor Mike Huckabee accusing Obama of marching the Israelis "to the door of the oven." Republican senators accused the U.S.

negotiators of having been "fleeced" and "bamboozled" by the talks with Tehran. Senator Corker even accused Kerry of having "turned Iran from being a pariah to Congress being a pariah," due to the administration's accusation that opponents of the nuclear deal were seeking war with Iran. To fend off the onslaught of attacks, the White House had to devote its full attention to the congressional fight.[27]

For two and a half years, an interagency meeting had been held twice a week to coordinate all aspects of diplomacy with Iran. As the talks inched closer to a deal, the White House began holding the meetings on a daily basis, and the agenda came to be increasingly dominated by "how we would sell the deal at home." The meetings were held every morning in a room in the basement of the White House dubbed the "peace room." It was the biggest, most encompassing campaign the White House had ever mustered. "Everyone was involved. Absolutely everyone—it took all of our time," recalled Colin Kahl, senior advisor to Vice President Joe Biden. The White House created fact sheets that directly countered arguments from AIPAC and the Washington Institute for Near East Policy. Briefings were held regularly on Capitol Hill to answer detailed, technical questions about the deal and provide arguments for its supporters. Written responses to lawmakers were often provided within twenty-four hours. After being criticized for not paying due attention to Congress, Obama was now receiving high marks for the speed and quality of his answers to lawmakers. "They don't always pick up on supporting their friends, but in this case I'd have to say the White House was exemplary," Congressman David Price (D-NC) told me.[28]

To win a vote in Congress, Obama knew that one-on-one meetings and written responses wouldn't suffice—he would need a congressional leader to whip the votes. On the Senate side, the RBF/UNA Track-II dialogue paid off handsomely as Senator Dick Durbin stepped up to play that role. In May 2015, the Track-II organizers had set up a meeting in New York between Zarif and five U.S. senators, including Durbin. The meeting had a profound impact on his thinking. Durbin put in place a whipping team of five senators, each of whom was tasked with securing the approval of a set number of Democratic senators. The approach was not to push, but to provide information, answer questions, and gently encourage support of the deal. "I know what works and what doesn't," Durbin explained to me. "Don't beg, don't threaten, don't always believe you're right. You have to work with them, and they have to go through a thought process, and you have to be prepared to answer their questions." Durbin ensured that the lawmakers received all the information they needed from the administration, organized off-the-record briefings with Ben Rhodes and Wendy Sherman, and made certain that his whip team knew the senator's whereabouts during the August recess. The most important meeting he organized, however, was not with the U.S. negotiators but with the ambassadors of Germany, France, the United Kingdom, and Russia.[29]

"It crossed my mind that we weren't thinking about this or looking at it through the eyes of other nations," Durbin recalled. On August 4, he arranged for an off-the-record with the ambassadors. This proved instrumental, since the opponents of the deal had argued that the United States should negotiate a "better deal," without taking into account that it was an agreement among seven different nations. The views of those nations were highly relevant. The ambassadors left little doubt that there would be no renegotiation. If the U.S. Congress rejected the deal, the negotiations would collapse, leaving the United States with no other choice but to go to war or acquiesce to Iran's nuclear advances. Rejecting this deal would not get the United States a better deal. The speech by the Russian ambassador, Sergey Kislyak, was particularly persuasive, as many were surprised that the P5+1 unity had survived the Ukraine crisis. Kislyak made clear this unity would not survive a congressional rejection of the nuclear deal. At the end of the session, Durbin turned to his colleagues and said:

> Before you leave, I want you to look across the table and see who's sitting there, and think back not that far in history, and imagine those countries coming together with the United States to reach a national security agreement including ending the nuclearization of a country. This is historic. Not only the agreement but the fact that they're sitting here today defending it for us.[30]

The EU ambassadors had realized that sitting on the fence and watching Congress derail the deal was not an option. They had worked too hard and for too long, and they were painfully aware of the consequences of a congressional rejection—a drift toward military action. But they also understood that winning over Republicans to their side was not a realistic option. The debate was not driven by the merits of the deal, but by Republican opposition to anything Obama was pursuing, as well as being fueled by Israeli and Saudi pressure. The European Union's involvement did not pass without controversy: Republican lawmakers were infuriated by what they considered to be interference in internal American affairs. Some of the exchanges were testy and unusual, given the otherwise strong relations between the United States and its close EU allies. "There were people who gave me a real hard time saying, 'How dare you interfere in our domestic politics?'" according to the British ambassador to the United States, Peter Westmacott. "They said, 'It's none of your damn business.' I had to say rather firmly, 'Well it is part of my damn business, because my government is a signatory of the Vienna agreement.'" The British were particularly upset that the Republicans welcomed Israeli lobbying against the deal—when Israel wasn't even a party to the agreement—but didn't allow for their closest ally, the United Kingdom, to have a say in the debate.[31]

What Durbin did on the Senate side, Nancy Pelosi handled on the House side: the P5+1 ambassadors provided a similar briefing for the Democratic lawmakers in the House at Pelosi's invitation. The ambassadors repeated their message from the Senate briefing: "If you walk away, it's over. We don't come back." For most lawmakers, this was a turning point. Few—if any—wanted to be responsible for the now-obvious consequences of a vote to reject the deal. "The impact of the briefing was stunning," Pelosi told me. "It was really stunning." Pelosi assembled a whip team to ensure that at least 146 House members would uphold the president's veto. As in the Senate, the focus was entirely on the Democrats—there were no prospects of convincing Republicans to support diplomacy. House Speaker John Boehner (R-OH) had vowed that Republicans would "do anything possible to stop" the nuclear deal, and most Republican lawmakers had declared their opposition to the deal within hours of its being reached—that is, well before they actually had a chance to study the deal. "If these people who announced [their opposition] an hour after the deal was announced were in a jury pool," said Senator Angus King (I-ME), "they'd be disqualified."[32]

Pelosi was particularly perturbed by the near-instantaneous Republican rejection of the deal—"They hadn't even read it!" she told me indignantly—and made a point of urging all Democratic lawmakers to read and study the agreement before they decided their votes. This meant, however, that the Democratic support would trickle in slowly rather than come all at once in the review process. The White House strongly preferred House members coming out early in support of the deal, fearing that momentum would go to AIPAC. But Pelosi stood firm: to deliver the House, she needed to educate her caucus with briefings, one-on-one sessions, validation by outside experts, nuclear scientists, generals, and diplomats, and mobilization of the grassroots groups to ensure that the vote would make sense from a political as well as policy standpoint.[33]

Pelosi's team of whips—David Price (D-NC), Barbara Lee (D-CA), Keith Ellison (D-MN), Jan Schakowsky (D-IL), Lloyd Doggett (D-TX), Dan Kildee (D-MI), Ben O'Rourke (D-TX), Paul Tonko (D-NY), Rosa DeLauro (D-CT), Earl Blumenauer (D-OR), Gary Connolly (D-VA), and Sam Farr (D-CA)—met once a day in Pelosi's office to go over the progress and the challenges ahead. For weeks, the whips devoted almost all of their time to securing votes in favor of the deal. But they weren't making the phone calls all on their own. In early August, the president invited the House whip team to the White House to discuss their strategy. Schakowsky presented the president with a list of undecided lawmakers on the House side whose votes the whip team was hoping to secure. "Mr. President, you personally should call the top three," the Illinois lawmaker said. Without hesitation, the president responded: "Give me that. I'm calling all of them."[34]

Beginning in the fall of 2013, there were well over 1,200 separate administration engagements on Iran with members of Congress, including phone calls, meetings, briefings, and hearings. The president himself met with 125 lawmakers during the review period, and placed an additional 30 phone calls while vacationing at Martha's Vineyard during the August recess. Cabinet and other senior administration officials made the case for the deal directly to over 256 House members and senators during that same period. And that's not counting the White House's almost constant email communication with Hill staffers.[35]

With the president's backing, Pelosi and the whip team started securing the votes. Pelosi made it clear to her caucus that their support was useless unless it was strong and unswaying. She needed it in writing for her drip-by-drip strategy of having more and more lawmakers declare their support. "Do not whisper in my ear that you will be there at the end of the day sustaining the veto," she told them. "I want you to put it in writing." On a daily basis, a handful of lawmakers publicly declared their support for the nuclear deal using their own language and arguments. This created a constant drumbeat of support for the deal, building a strong momentum before the August recess began. Later, the Democratic caucus turned all the letters and press releases into a book dedicated to Pelosi, with each letter signed by the lawmaker who issued it.[36]

The big fear was that AIPAC would turn out its massive grassroots machine during the August recess and shift the momentum to its side. "Terrible things go on in the August recess," Durbin said. The bipartisan effort around president's health care reform died over the August recess in 2009, when the opposition got organized and flooded town meetings. Durbin and his team were determined not to let that happen again. "The feeling was that during 2009, everyone went their separate ways and just crossed their fingers," said Senator Chris Murphy (D-CT), one of Durbin's whips. "The decision was made that the whip operation and the White House were going to keep tabs on undecided members throughout that break."[37]

The outside groups went "all in." The Arms Control Association (ACA) organized a letter in support of the deal signed by seventy-five nonproliferation and arms control experts, including Hans Blix, a former director of the International Atomic Energy Agency (IAEA). The letter was referenced by Energy Secretary Ernest Moniz in his testimony to Congress as well as by several lawmakers as they explained why they had opted to support the deal. There was also a letter to Obama from twenty-nine of the nation's top scientists, including five Nobel laureates, backing the deal. The letters made clear that at least within the scientific and nonproliferation community, the overwhelming opinion was strongly favorable to the deal. It was precisely the kind of expert validation Pelosi had requested.[38]

The largest grassroots organization on the progressive side—MoveOn—made securing the Iran deal its top priority for the summer of 2015, directing its millions of followers not only to pressure their lawmakers, but also to turn up at town hall meetings and do the groundwork the Democrats had failed to do in 2009. Despite their massive efforts, however, the proponents of the deal were still outdone by supporters of AIPAC and Netanyahu, whose grassroots machine was considered the gold standard in the business. Obama's side also suffered from their grassroots being overly optimistic. Too many assumed that the agreement was a done deal since they could not imagine Congress scuttling it. At one point, Obama made an unusually frank appeal in a conference call with a record ten thousand activists, urging them to step up their citizen lobbying:

> As big of a bully pulpit as I have, it's not enough. I can't carry it by myself. . . . In the absence of your voices, you're going to see the same array of forces that got us into the Iraq war, leading into a situation where we forgo this historic opportunity and we are back on the path of potential military conflict. . . . I want everybody [on the phone] to get movin'. You guys have to get more active and loud and involved and informed. . . . I'm meeting these members of Congress. And they don't really buy the arguments of the opponents, but I can tell when they start getting squishy. And they start getting squishy because they're feeling political heat. And you guys have to counteract that with the facts.[39]

One of the biggest strengths of the campaign in support of the deal was its diversity. Whereas the opponents of the deal enlisted only the grassroots of the hawkish pro-Israeli community and evangelical Christians, proponents of the deal managed to enlist support from unexpected quarters. For instance, the Steelworkers Union endorsed it in early August and urged its members to push Congress to support it. Forty Iranian human rights defenders, including Nobel laureate Shirin Ebadi, posted videos on Facebook expressing their support for the deal. One of the human rights defenders recorded an audio message in support of the deal from his prison cell and smuggled it out for his friends to post on Facebook. The National Iranian American Council organized a letter signed by eighty foremost scholars on the Middle East, which argued that the deal would help stabilize the region. Perhaps most stunning, however, was the full-page ad published in the *New York Times* on August 20, 2015, which was signed by two dozen leaders of Jewish organizations and argued that "the deal is the best available option to halt Iran's nuclear weapons program." One of the signatories was Tom Dine, the former head of AIPAC.[40]

The Jewish American Schism

Obama's successful diplomacy with Iran had a profound impact on Iranian Americans. Overwhelmingly opposed to the regime in Tehran, yet often divided on how to engage with it, the community quickly rallied behind the deal. "I don't want war to come to my homeland," Amy Zarafshar of McLean, Virginia, told the *Washington Post*. "I don't want to see it bombarded like Iraq, with innocent people killed. We have to find a way out."[41]

But what united the Iranian American community divided Jewish Americans: AIPAC and other hawkish pro-Israeli groups had been the foremost drivers behind the policy of sanctioning and confronting Iran ever since the mid-1990s. At the same time, however, there had always been a schism between Jewish Americans writ large and the pro-Israeli organizations in Washington. While AIPAC and its allies adopted increasingly hawkish policies on Iran, the Israeli-Palestinian conflict, and diplomacy, Jews as a whole tended to be more progressive. This schism widened substantially during the George W. Bush administration after it was revealed that AIPAC—despite its public denials—lobbied in favor of the Iraq war. The *New York Sun* reported in January 2003 that AIPAC had, according to its Executive Director Howard Kohr, "quietly" lobbied Congress to approve the use of force in Iraq. This did not sit well with many Jewish Americans—while the American public was split on the war in Iraq, Jewish Americans opposed it 77 percent to 21 percent, according to Gallup.[42]

As the rift within the Jewish community grew, so did the need for a new pro-peace Jewish lobby. While Jewish American organizations promoting progressive foreign policy existed—including Americans for Peace Now and Israel Policy Forum—they lacked the political bundling capacity of AIPAC and wielded far less influence as a result. When MJ Rosenberg of the Israel Policy Forum met with then senator Barack Obama and asked him if he would listen to pro-peace Jewish voices or just AIPAC on Israel, Obama responded that he couldn't hear him. Taking him literally, Rosenberg spoke louder. But Obama meant that he couldn't hear the voice of the pro-peace Jewish groups because they weren't as active and organized as AIPAC. "Back home, I hear from my AIPAC friend, [AIPAC Chairman Lee] Rosenberg, every week. Is he your cousin?" Obama asked. "Anyway, your side needs to organize. You need to make your voice heard so I can't ignore you."[43]

J Street was founded to become that voice. Its rise created significant rifts as the more hawkish organizations tried to squash it before it gained traction. While the tensions between J Street and its establishment detractors centered primarily on U.S. policy toward Israel and Palestine, it was with Iran that J Street made its mark. J Street provided crucial political cover to lawmakers who wanted to support the nuclear deal but did not want to come across as anti-Israel and feared AIPAC. "J Street gave members of Congress cover to do what was right, whereas before J Street that would not have happened," said Bob Creamer, the head of the nonprofit Americans United for Change. J Street enlisted supporters of the deal with strong pro-Israeli credentials, from former U.S. diplomats and politicians, to Israeli security officials opposed to Netanyahu's crusade against the deal. According to J Street, a vote for the deal had to be understood for what it was: a fundamentally pro-Israeli position, since it eliminated the threat of an Iranian nuclear attack on Israel. "Israel should have been the first to welcome this agreement," Dan Kurtzer, a former U.S. ambassador to Israel, wrote in a piece for CNN.[44]

During the battle over the Iran deal in Congress, tensions within the Jewish community peaked. While differences among Jewish Americans were nothing new, the vitriol on the nuclear deal became so intense that Jewish leaders began speaking openly of long-term damage to Jewish organizations. It was a "brutal" fight. AIPAC and its supporters were infuriated by the insinuation that their aim was to drive the conflict toward a military confrontation. A harsh *Tablet Magazine* editorial even accused the administration of "sickening anti-Jewish incitement," claiming that Obama was using "dark, nasty stuff we might expect to hear at a white power rally." Obama, J Street, and other pro-deal groups were, in turn, incensed by the accusation by the Right that they were pro-Iran and anti-Israel. Senator Bob Menendez (D-NJ) even accused the Obama administration of speaking on behalf of Iran. "The more I hear from the administration in its quotes, the more it sounds like talking points that come straight out of Iran," he said during a hearing in January 2015.[45]

One incident in late July showcased how tense the relations between the White House and AIPAC had gotten. As the president was making his way back from Africa on Air Force One, he learned that AIPAC was flying seven hundred of its members to DC to lobby Congress against the deal. Under normal circumstances, whenever AIPAC brings its members to the capital, it also requests a meeting with the White House. In this case, they didn't. Obama instructed his staff to reach out to AIPAC and invite them to the White House to hear them out. Since getting all seven hundred members to the White House would be a logistical impossibility, AIPAC made a counteroffer to the White House to send three officials over to a downtown hotel the next morning at 8:00 a.m. for a thirty-minute chat, but not a minute more due to scheduling restrictions. AIPAC advocates would be heading to Capitol Hill immediately thereafter, and they had nixed a Q&A with administration officials.[46]

The next morning, lead negotiator Wendy Sherman, senior Treasury official Adam Szubin, and the president's chief of staff, Denis McDonough arrived at the hotel to brief the AIPAC members. After making their presentations, they requested questions from the audience, even though they knew AIPAC had barred them from doing so. They hoped that AIPAC would relent, but a senior AIPAC official promptly stood up and curtly said, "We gotta go. Thank you." This was unheard of. Never before had a group declined an opportunity to meet with the president and then refused to allow their members to engage with the president's chief of staff. It may not have been intended to be an insult, but that was how it was received by the president. I was at the White House the day after the incident, and it was clear that emotions were running high. Discussing the organizing around town hall meetings during the August recess, one White House staffer urged supporters of the deal to counter the "AIPAC screaming loonies." He quickly corrected himself—"I meant nonproliferation passionate people," he said with a smile.[47]

Afterward, Obama decided to confront the AIPAC leadership in person. He invited twenty-two leaders of the Jewish community to meet with him on August 4—his fifty-fourth birthday—in the Cabinet Room. The White House had already conducted numerous such meetings since January to keep the Jewish groups abreast of developments in the negotiations and to deter them from going all-out against the deal, but this one would be different. Obama called AIPAC out for "spreading inaccuracies" and misinformation about the deal and made clear that he was personally hurt by the accusation that he wasn't supportive of Israel. He wasn't going to stand for this. More important, he made clear that he intended to "hit back hard" at his detractors. "You couldn't miss the message that he was sending," one of the attendees said. "That's not O.K. with me, and it will be answered."[48]

The two AIPAC representatives sat right across the table from Obama. One of them was Lee Rosenberg, the former chairman of AIPAC and a major fundraiser for Obama's 2008 presidential bid. Representatives from J Street and the Anti-Defamation League (ADL), as well as other Jewish leaders were also present. "It's my birthday and I'm going to be blunt," Obama said, sitting next to Vice President Joe Biden. He "meticulously" made the case for the deal, explaining how it would prevent all of Iran's paths to a nuclear weapon and why sanctions had to be lifted in return. To Obama, this was not a tough call. As president, he explained, easy decisions rarely reach his desk. It's only the tough ones that make their way up to him. "But I have to tell you," he said to the Jewish leaders, "this is not a tough call." This was not a 60-40 decision. The preponderance of scientific evidence made it a 90-10 call. It was simply obvious, he maintained, that the deal at hand would be better than not having any deal, revealing his frustration that intelligent people, some of whom he had known for years and whom he respected, couldn't recognize this.[49]

It didn't take long for the two-hour meeting to become contentious. Obama sharply criticized AIPAC not only for spending $20 million to campaign against the agreement and sending its members to Capitol Hill armed with misinformation, but also for putting out TV ads in which he was compared to Neville Chamberlain, the British prime minister who signed the Munich Agreement with Adolf Hitler in 1938. Obama also brought up the example of Congressman Jerrold Nadler (D-NY), a Jewish lawmaker who had been subjected to particularly heinous abuse for his support of the deal. He had been called a kapo—a Jew who collaborated with Nazis—and accused of having "blood on his hands" and of having "facilitated Obama's Holocaust." Obama was the "most passionate I've ever seen him," one attendee recalled.[50]

In turn, Rosenberg accused Obama of characterizing opponents of the deal as warmongers, a step he feared would fuel anti-Semitism in the United States. "Some of us in the community are troubled the messaging will be used and abused by bigots," Abraham Foxman of the ADL later commented. In Obama's view, however, there was no moral equivalence between the rhetoric of the two sides. While the opponents made accusations of anti-Semitism, the proponents tended to argue that the consequence of rejecting the deal would be war, without necessarily stating that war was the desire of its opponents.[51]

The next day, Obama delivered a scathing speech at American University in Washington, DC. He not only denounced the deal's opponents, but connected the Iran debate with the Iraq war more directly than ever before. The problem with the Iraq war was not just the decision to invade, but "the mindset that got us there in the first place," Obama said. Now people with that same mindset—in many cases held by the very same people who pushed for the Iraq war—were leading the charge against the deal with Iran. Obama even asked "Does anyone really doubt that the same voices now raised against this deal will be demanding that whoever is president bomb those nuclear facilities?"

The president recognized that Netanyahu was sincere in his criticism and pursued only what he believed to lay in the interest of Israel. Similarly, it was Obama's responsibility to pursue the interest of the United States, and not that of Israel. "I believe [the deal is] in America's interest and Israel's interest, and as president of the United States it would be an abrogation of my constitutional duty to act against my best judgment simply because it causes temporary friction with a dear friend and ally," he said to applause from the audience. As he had promised, Obama was hitting AIPAC hard.[52]

In the end, despite the vitriol, AIPAC lost the argument within the Jewish community, vindicating J Street's line that the "organized Jewish community" was not accurately representing American Jews. Polls showed that American Jewish support for the Iran deal exceeded that of the general population. Sixty percent of American Jews supported the agreement, compared to 56 percent of American adults overall, according to a Washington Post-ABC News poll. "The overwhelming majority of Jewish Americans identify more with Barack Hussein Obama and what he stands for than they do with the leadership of AIPAC," J Street's Jeremy Ben-Ami remarked.[53]

The Rush to the Finishing Line

The White House's first major setback came a day after Obama's speech at American University. Few in the White House expected that Chuck Schumer (D-NY) would come out in support of the deal. His constituency largely overlapped with AIPAC, and he was under tremendous pressure from opponents of the deal, who calculated that Schumer's defection would open up the floodgates for other Democratic senators to shift sides. Throughout the diplomatic process, Schumer had signaled his skepticism. The White House did expect, however, that Schumer would announce his decision toward the end of August precisely to avoid giving the opponents of the deal momentum, the so-called "Schumer effect." Instead, late in the evening of August 6, Schumer announced that he would be voting against the deal.[54]

Schumer, who had studied the issue very closely—he participated in individual meetings with Obama, Kerry, and Sherman, as well as "three hour-long meetings with members of the negotiating team, who answered 14 pages of questions from him"—did not base his decision on the core nonproliferation merits of the deal. Rather, he believed that the deal would not bring about a greater change in Iran's conduct. "I will vote to disapprove the agreement, not because I believe war is a viable or desirable option, nor to challenge the path of diplomacy," wrote Schumer in a blogpost. "It is because I believe Iran will not change, and under this agreement it will be able to achieve its dual goals of eliminating sanctions while ultimately retaining its nuclear and non-nuclear power."[55]

Although his opposition took few by surprise, the timing did catch the White House and Schumer's Senate colleagues off guard. To prevent launching an all-out war against his own party and president, Schumer did make clear that he would not be whipping against the president. He would vote his conscience, but not push others to come to his side. "I'm not going to get on the phone," he told Senator Durbin. "I'm not going to work this issue. This is where I stand. Each individual senator should make their own decision." Still, many were unhappy with his timing. The White House fired a shot across the bow, warning that his defiance of his party and president could cost him his leadership position. Grassroots organizations were furious, too, and MoveOn announced in direct response to Schumer's vote that 185,000 of its members had pledged to withhold more than $43 million in donations to Democratic candidates who succeeded in sabotaging diplomacy with Iran. "This donor strike sends a loud, clear message to any Democrat who risks American lives and chooses war over diplomacy: You will be held accountable and pay a political price if you undermine this deal," said Ilya Sheyman, executive director of MoveOn Political Action.[56]

In the end, there was no Schumer effect. The pushback from the grassroots, MoveOn's pledge to withhold campaign contributions, J Street's pouring $3.5 million into TV ads in support of the deal, and the White House's securing three senators in favor of the deal the day after Schumer's announcement all helped ensure that other lawmakers didn't follow Schumer's lead. Although AIPAC put up a relentless fight, the August recess did not end up becoming the game changer the opponents of the deal had hoped it would be. Nancy Pelosi's strategy of drip-by-drip had succeeded in securing momentum on the side of the president and diplomacy. The original goal in the Senate and House was solely to get to 34 and 146 members respectively to uphold the president's veto. By September 2, that goal had been achieved, with Senator Barbara Mikulski (D-MD) announcing her support for the deal. But with numerous lawmakers still undecided, an opportunity existed to reach forty-one senators and deny AIPAC and its allies even the opportunity to bring the resolution to reject the deal on the floor.[57]

The White House had originally been skeptical about the possibility of scoring such a crushing defeat of AIPAC, but by early September, that possibility was within reach. No celebrations were held on September 2 at the White House. Instead, the Obama administration doubled down and went for total victory. Within a week, they had breached the forty-one-senator barrier. The Republicans tried to bring the resolution to reject the deal to a vote, but had only fifty-eight senators to support it. President Obama and his main whip, Durbin, had managed to secure the support of forty-two senators—an achievement that from the outset no one thought was possible. "For the first time, I'm not looking at the computer with my hair on fire," a member of the legislative team at the White House said. "I'm just sitting and breathing like I'll be able to sleep well."[58]

It was a stunning victory for Obama. In the words of the *New York Times,* it was "a stinging defeat" for AIPAC, as well as a personal humiliation for Netanyahu. Conventional wisdom had been turned completely upside down. Not only could the United States negotiate with the regime in Iran; it could even strike a deal with Tehran and prevent Netanyahu, AIPAC, and the GOP from blocking it in Congress. While the Israeli prime minister's office privately told journalists that they had never expected to win, it's quite clear that at a minimum Netanyahu's goal was to force the president to use his veto. But Netanyahu could not achieve even that. Moreover, out of the eleven Jewish members of the Senate, only two of them ended up siding with Netanyahu and AIPAC—*on a vote in relation to the clerical regime in Tehran.* The isolation of Iran had come to an end: Iran was no longer the most isolated country in the region. "The limits to Israel's and AIPAC's influence have now been painfully exposed," Israel's former deputy national security advisor Chuck

Freilich wrote in *Newsweek*. "An issue that Israel deemed existential was blithely ignored both by the administration and much of Congress." It is not that the Israeli Right didn't have formidable influence in Washington—it did and still does. It's that its ability to dominate was largely based on the absence of the American public. Once Americans were organized and mobilized, as they were in this case by the president and the outside groups in the Ploughshares circle (which included Jewish groups such as APN and J Street), it then became clear that the hawkish pro-Israel lobby did not have a killer left hook. "You pull back the curtain, and they couldn't deliver," Creamer said. "They huffed, and puffed, and bloviated, and then everybody said 'Thanks anyway, but we're going to go with these other guys.' "[59]

For many Israelis, even those critical of Netanyahu's approach, the defeat of AIPAC was worrisome. The organization plays a major role in advancing Israeli interests in Washington. Now, the deterrence capabilities of AIPAC had been badly damaged. "One leader of a Jewish organization recently told me," Israeli journalist Amir Tibon said, "that we are like that famous boxer who is famous for his killer left, that everybody knows his killer left, and even if taking hits round after round, everybody knows that once he puts on his killer left, nobody can stand. And then this boxer puts out his killer left, and his opponent—not only does he not fall, he barely even feels it. That's what happened to the Israel lobby this summer."[60]

For supporters of diplomacy, however, this was their David-beats-Goliath moment. "This is such great evidence that one does not need to simply follow what is perceived to be the conventional wisdom or the popular thing to do," Congresswoman Schakowsky told me. "You can be a leader, and you can change the conventional wisdom. . . . We can stand up for diplomacy and win." The victory in Congress was particularly noteworthy, given Congress's traditional hostility toward anything to do with Iran. When the White House went to look for supporters on the Hill who could whip in favor of the deal, it started with those members who had opposed Obama's sanctions strategy, such as Congressman Keith Ellison (D-MN), knowing quite well that the bedrock of support for diplomacy on Capitol Hill was with those members, since they had stood up for diplomacy at a time when even the president was hesitant. "It just goes to show that if you stick to fight for something that's the right thing to fight for, you can win," Ellison said. "The problem with this place is it moves slowly so people don't always have patience."[61]

At the White House, the president could finally celebrate. He had passed through all the hurdles—securing an authoritative channel to Iran, clinching an interim deal, getting the Iranians to agree to massive cuts in their nuclear program, and winning the battle on Capitol Hill. A few days after the forty-second senator had been secured, the president invited his staff for a small celebration. The president didn't always join such festivities, but he was there for this one. "He just looked genuinely happy to be a part of this," one of his legislative staffers said. "Those votes were as much his as any of ours."[62]

Why Diplomacy Won on Capitol Hill

The primary reason the president and his allies won the battle on Capitol Hill was the strength of the deal itself. Had the Joint Comprehensive Plan of Action (JCPOA) suffered from technical vulnerabilities—that is, had the scientific community identified paths that could allow Iran to pursue a weapons program—chances are that the deal would have been dead on arrival. The combination of the limitations imposed on the program and the intrusive inspections made it virtually impossible for Iran to embark on a weapons program—a point the critics never managed to refute. "I thought it was quite a remarkable agreement," Pelosi told me. "So the substance of the diplomacy was what gave me the confidence to go to my members and say, 'This is why I'm supporting this agreement.'"[63]

Instead, the opposition strategy was to saturate the debate with a deluge of second-rate arguments, none of which held up to scrutiny or even addressed the central aspects of the deal. It was a strategy that smacked of defeatism: charging that better terms were needed without explaining how such improved terms could be achieved gave the impression that the opposition was simply arguing for the sake of arguing. They lacked strong arguments against the deal so instead they went for quantity over quality. It was particularly difficult for them to come across as sincere when their preferred negotiation strategy was simply to demand more and offer less. After all, those who had never negotiated with Iran and had opposed every opportunity for the United States to sit down with the Iranians carried little credibility when they dictated to the administration how such negotiations should be conducted. Their strategy of insisting on a complete dismantling of the Iranian program while offering Tehran next to no incentives had in the past led only to Tehran expanding its nuclear activities. That was the cost of not negotiating with Iran with reasonable bottom lines. "Iran went from 103 or [104] centrifuges to 19,000 [during this period]," Kerry said. "When I became secretary of state, what did I find? I found 12,000 kilograms of material, enough for 10 to 12 bombs."[64]

Indeed, many of the opponents' arguments were so easily dismissed that they harmed the credibility of AIPAC and its allies. Their charges made headlines and captivated the U.S. media, but didn't carry much weight among Democrats on Capitol Hill precisely because they were demonstrably false, according to the scientific and experts' communities. For instance, opponents criticized the deal for lasting "only" fifteen years when most nonproliferation agreements are of that length and ignored the fact the most important restrictions and inspections instruments are permanent, according to the Additional Protocol to the Non-Proliferation Treaty. "The thing I will never understand is how Iran was within a year from having a weapon, and now they're not," Pelosi complained to me. "And people are saying, 'Oh my gosh, with this agreement Iran could have a weapon in fifteen or twenty years.' Instead of fifteen or twenty months. It's weird."[65]

AIPAC claimed that the deal lifted "sanctions as soon as the agreement commences, rather than gradually as Iran demonstrates sustained adherence to the agreement," whereas in reality the sanctions were not to be lifted until the IAEA had confirmed that Iran had completed dismantling or disconnecting two-thirds of its centrifuges, and shipped out more than 90 percent of its enriched uranium. The critics lambasted the deal for not ensuring "anytime, anywhere" short-notice inspections, whereas in reality the deal did provide the most intrusive inspections regime ever devised, in which Iran would be obligated to give the IAEA access to any site it had grounds to suspect housed nuclear activities within twenty-four days—which is far too short of a time for Iran to dispose of or eliminate any trace of nuclear activities (which can remain for decades if not centuries). Again, AIPAC was setting the bar unrealistically high. The kind of inspections it demanded have only been granted by powers invaded and defeated in war.[66]

Supplying lawmakers with such easily refutable arguments did little to help AIPAC's credibility on the Hill and undercut everything members said about the deal. "They constantly made claims about the deal that were wildly overstated," Deputy National Security Advisor Ben Rhodes said. Such a tactic had little prospect of working when lawmakers studied the issue and its technical aspects as closely as they did with the JCPOA. The frustration with AIPAC was particularly strong among its own supporters in Congress who relied on AIPAC to provide them with solid arguments and verifiable facts. "AIPAC was discredited among its own supporters," a former National Security Council official told me. "They felt betrayed by AIPAC and by Israeli Ambassador Dermer" because of the false information they provided.[67]

The second reason the deal passed was that the president succeeded in framing the issue as a choice between war and peace. Mindful of the American public's war fatigue, lawmakers found the idea that rejecting the deal could lead to war tremendously worrisome; lawmakers who deeply regretted their vote in favor of the Iraq war found it even more so. Moreover, the choice between war and peace also enabled the president and his allies to mass-mobilize the American public in favor of the deal with the degree of intensity needed to neutralize the pressure from Netanyahu, AIPAC, and their allies. "For most of our groups, the real concern was that you'd end up in a war," not nonproliferation, Stephen Miles of the Win Without War coalition explained. And the war-or-peace framing was the most powerful line to counter the opposition's emotional rhetoric when it asked such questions as "How can you strike a deal with a regime as distasteful, untrustworthy, and despicable as that of the Ayatollahs in Iran?" On an emotional level, the idea of reaching an agreement with the regime in Tehran was highly unattractive to most Americans. But if the alternative was gravitating toward war with Iran, the emotional argument tended to fall short. The efficiency of the frame was on full display when senators such as Lindsey Graham

(R-SC) had to "bend over backwards to say he didn't want to have war with Iran," Miles pointed out. The frame put Graham and his allies on the defensive, forcing them to explain their positions rather than being on the offensive and challenging the president.[68]

Overall, both Netanyahu and AIPAC underestimated the way the Iraq war had changed the attitudes of the American public toward war in foreign lands. Americans were now more skeptical about war with countries in the Middle East and far more willing to give space for diplomacy with traditional enemies of the United States. Neither Netanyahu nor AIPAC seems to have understood how deep rooted this shift was. "Prime Minister Netanyahu knows the America that elected Ronald Reagan president," former Democratic congressman Robert Wexler (D-FL) said. "He's completely unfamiliar with the America that elected Barack Obama president. And they are in fact very different Americas."[69]

A third factor leading to victory was that throughout this period, the Democrats succeeded in maintaining a strong discipline that prevented the opponents of the JCPOA from splitting the Democratic lawmakers from their congressional leaders or the president. This was largely thanks to Netanyahu and his controversial speech in Congress, which inadvertently made him the Most Valuable Player among supporters of diplomacy. During what must have been a moment of frustration, AIPAC even blamed Netanyahu for its defeat in Congress. "Netanyahu's speech in Congress made the Iranian issue a partisan one," an AIPAC official told Israel's Walla!News. "As soon as he insisted on going ahead with this move, which was perceived as a Republican maneuver against the President, we lost a significant part of the Democratic Party, without which it was impossible to block the agreement." Still, by going along with and supporting Netanyahu, AIPAC lost its nonpartisan credentials and was increasingly seen as "an arm of the Republican Party." With Democrats shunning AIPAC, the organization could not recruit a Democratic leader who would be willing to whip votes against the deal. The White House could count on Pelosi, Durbin, and their teams of whips. AIPAC could count on no one. The end result was that the $20–$30 million AIPAC spent on defeating the JCPOA got them only four Democratic senators and a handful of Democratic House members.

And considering the fact that at least two of those four Democrats on the Senate side were known opponents of the deal from the outset (Senators Menendez and Schumer), the depth of AIPAC's failure becomes even clearer. "What did all that money buy?" asked Steve Rosen, a former senior lobbyist for AIPAC. "This is a very bad moment for AIPAC."[70]

A fourth element that weighed in favor of the JCPOA was that the opponents of the deal were disoriented. They were put in an unusual situation that they had neither prepared for nor anticipated. They were untrained to deal with the Israeli prime minister being seen as a pariah in many parts of Washington. They were unused to being at war with the president of the United States. They were unused to holding the minority viewpoint in a policy debate with many international players. Thus disoriented, they made bad decisions and adopted ineffective strategies. Spending money, for instance, on billboard trucks driving around Washington, DC, denouncing the deal could not possibly have a strong return on investment. John Bisognano, a member of the White House Office of Public Engagement, was walking back to his DC apartment on the night the White House secured the forty-second senator. As he approached his building, he saw that a large billboard had been set up outside opposing the deal. In many ways, that billboard—and its timing—represented the confused and ineffective strategy of the opponents of diplomacy. "That's exactly what this was," he told me. "This was a late, poorly run, ad hoc campaign where no one knew what was going on."[71]

Both Netanyahu and AIPAC overestimated their own influence, and they underestimated Obama's commitment and willingness to fight for the JCPOA. "They seemed genuinely surprised when we issued the veto threat on the very first Menendez sanctions bill," Rhodes said. "I think they thought we would sit down and negotiate something, some trivial sanctions bill. I think they were really taken back by that. They misjudged the political will of the president to really fight to create the space for this deal." This was similar to their misjudgment of Iran's willingness and ability to reach an agreement with the United States—they had fallen for their own talking points that anti-Americanism was such a strong pillar of the Iranian revolution that the regime simply couldn't strike a deal with Washington. Had their assessment and understanding of Iran been more realistic, it is likely that they would not have been caught off guard by the Oman channel or the interim agreement in 2013.[72]

Moreover, the opposition never managed to surprise. They ran a campaign like a twenty-term member of Congress who never had faced a real challenge in the past eighteen races. They were out of shape. They never had to develop new alliances or constituencies, and so they never attempted to do so in the fight against the deal. All of the voices they brought to the debate were either long-time GOP operatives, staunch supporters of Israel, or evangelical Christian supporters of Netanyahu. They all belonged to the same group of usual suspects. Contrast that to the supporters of diplomacy, who managed to enlist a highly diverse set of supporters ranging from the Steelworkers Union, to pro-Israeli groups, to Iranian human rights defenders, to Nobel laureates and scholars of the Middle East.

In retrospect, Netanyahu and AIPAC's attempt to defeat Obama was "irresponsible and delusional," in the words of Israel's former deputy national security advisor Chuck Freilich. AIPAC, whose mythical influence was largely based on its ability to unseat lawmakers who stood in its way, had no choice but to signal that it wouldn't punish Democratic lawmakers who supported the JCPOA.[73]

There were simply too many of them.

Conclusion

T his was never about enrichment." The academics and officials in the room were taken aback. For a former senior Israeli
official to deny the importance of the nuclear issue was unusual, to say the least. The conversations, attended by American civilian and military officials and other Western representatives, as
well as Iranian diplomats and Tehran's then nuclear negotiators, were
shockingly honest.

"Enrichment is not important," the Israeli official continued. "What
Israel needs to see from Iran is a sweeping attitude change." The veteran
Israeli decision-maker—himself a vocal opponent of Prime Minister
Benjamin Netanyahu—explained that Israel could not accept the United
States coming to terms with Iran without demanding that Iran come
to terms with Israel. "Israel is not party to the deal, so it won't be bound
by the deal," he warned. If Iran is not willing to accept Israel's existence, then Israel will stand in the way of the United States reaching a
deal with Iran, the Israeli message read. The Iranians listened atten-
tively, but showed no reaction. In a breakout session later that afternoon,
the Iranians indicated that they could recognize Israel only if Israel
joined the Non-Proliferation Treaty as a non-weapons country—that is,
once Israel gave up its nuclear weapons and opened its nuclear program
to international inspectors.

It was April 2012. Tensions between Israel and Obama were increasing as the latter was pushing back against Israeli pressure for military attacks against Iran, while at the same time continuing the P5 + 1 diplomacy with Iran. There were also only a few months left before the 2012 presidential election. Many Israelis worried that Netanyahu's aggressive style would further damage his relationship with Obama and undermine Israel's influence over American calculations regarding Iran. This was becoming a growing worry for the Israelis as Obama showcased unprecedented dedication to diplomacy, which they suspected would only grow under a second term.

The closed meeting, organized by a prominent U.S. university and held in a small Western European country, revealed drivers of the conflict rarely discussed in public: the Israeli fear that Iran's rise in the region would be accepted by the United States and that it would regard Tehran as a legitimate player in the new regional order without Tehran's accepting Israel's existence. The most potent instrument for ensuring that Washington wouldn't come to terms with Iran was the nuclear issue, which before the breakthrough in November 2013 was viewed as a hopelessly intractable conflict. "As long as the deadlock held, Iran would remain at least a permanently sanctioned pariah," former Israeli official Daniel Levy wrote. For the years when the United States pursued Iran's all-out containment, Israel "enjoyed a degree of unchallenged regional hegemony, freedom of military action, and diplomatic cover that it is understandably reluctant to concede or even recalibrate." Israel's position was directly linked to the United States' upholding Pax Americana in the Middle East. Its status was "underwritten by U.S. preeminence in the region," Levy argued.[1]

Herein lies the tragedy of Netanyahu's miscalculations: by aggressively defining the Iranian nuclear program as an existential threat to Israel, depicting the Iranians as irrational and suicidal, and threatening to bomb Iran, Netanyahu hoped to force Obama to take military action and recommit Washington to Pax Americana. Instead, Netanyahu's strategy eliminated the status quo option of containing the nuclear program while neither resolving the issue nor acquiescing to Iran's nuclear demands. Then, once that option was rejected, Obama did something Netanyahu had discounted—he opted for diplomacy, a measure that by definition could put an end to the United States' efforts to iso-late Iran.

Not only did Obama doubt the efficiency of military action; it also went against his principles and promises to pursue war only after all other options were exhausted. In never considering acceptance of en-richment on Iranian soil, the United States had not tested all diplomatic solutions. War also contradicted Obama's larger geopolitical objectives to reduce the United States' footprint in the Middle East and shift its focus east toward Asia and China. Although the Obama administration has insisted that the nuclear deal was solely about nonproliferation, its commitment to it in spite of the overwhelming domestic risks can best be understood in the larger geopolitical context of the nuclear talks. The real challenge to the United States is the emergence of a peer-competitor with capacity and ambition to be a global superpower. No state in the Middle East has the capacity or the potential capacity to challenge the United States on a global scale. China, on the other hand, does.

From Obama's perspective, the war in Iraq and the United States' overcommitment in the Middle East had served only to weaken the United States and undermine its ability to meet the challenge of prospective peer-competitors. With the Middle East losing strategic significance as a result of a variety of factors, including reduced U.S. dependence on oil, and with the cost of U.S. hegemony drastically in-creasing, the cost-benefit calculation for the United States had decisively shifted. To Obama, the Middle East was unsalvageable, and the more the United States got involved, the worse things would get and the more the United States would be blamed for the region's woes. If Libya showed Obama that the region was best avoided, the rise of ISIS proved to him that the region could not be fixed. In his mind, the difference from Asia could not be more palpable: "Contrast that with Southeast Asia, which still has huge problems—enormous poverty, corruption—but is filled with striving, ambitious, energetic people who are every single day scratching and clawing to build businesses and get education and find jobs and build infrastructure," he told the *Atlantic*. "If we're not talking to [young, ambitious people in Asia and elsewhere]," he continued, "because the only thing we're doing is figuring out how to destroy or

cordon off or control the malicious, nihilistic, violent parts of humanity, then we're missing the boat."[2]

Obama's critics contended that his lack of involvement was the
cause of much of the problems in the Middle East, which in turn had
weakened the United States. On the contrary, Obama believed that the
United States' overextension in the region had and would continue to
harm the United States' strength and global standing. "Overextension
in the Middle East will ultimately harm our economy, harm our ability
to look for other opportunities and to deal with other challenges, and,
most important, endanger the lives of American service members for
reasons that are not in the direct American national-security interest,"
Deputy National Security Advisor Ben Rhodes explained.[3]

Added to this was his growing conviction that Iran's prolonged
isolation was neither possible nor necessarily helpful. This was particularly true if Iran's reaction to its containment was to further challenge
Western interests in the region. "Iran is too large a player, too important a player in this region, to simply leave in isolation," the United
Kingdom's then foreign secretary Phil Hammond said. This sentiment
was widely held in Europe. "No one believes Iran can perpetually be put
in a straightjacket," Germany's U.S. Ambassador Peter Wittig told me.
This belief was also held within the Obama administration, though it
refrained from publicly stating it, mindful of the backlash it would cause
from Congress. After all, it would be to admit the failure of the United
States' policy of containing Iran in the past three decades.[4]

To the contrary, Obama believed giving Iran a seat at the table
could help stabilize the region, particularly in Syria and Iraq, where the
West and Iran shared an interest in defeating ISIS. "There's no way to
resolve Syria without Iran being involved," Obama said a few weeks after
the Joint Comprehensive Plan of Action (JCPOA) had been reached. The
White House believed an opportunity had emerged to end the bloodshed
in Syria diplomatically partly due to the nuclear deal. "Getting beyond
the nuclear deal is a first step to starting a dialogue" on Syria, a senior
administration official told *Foreign Policy* magazine. Syria had been
discussed on the sidelines of the nuclear talks, but it was only after the
deal had been finalized that real deliberations could take place. Had

the JCPOA been reached earlier, the Syrian negotiations could also have begun earlier, EU foreign policy chief Federica Mogherini told me. Meanwhile, the United States and Iran indirectly coordinated their efforts against ISIS in Iraq, prompting Kerry to tell an American audience that Iran had been "helpful." Neither that collaboration—nor the public acknowledgment of Iran's help—would have occurred had it not been for the nuclear deal.[5]

Obama's interaction with Iran convinced him that the leaders in Tehran were rational, self-interested, and pragmatic. "What we've seen, at least since 1979," Obama said in August 2015, "is Iran making constant, calculated decisions that allow it to preserve the regime, to expand their influence where they can, to be opportunistic, to create what they view as hedges against potential Israeli attack, in the form of Hezbollah and other proxies in the region." Beyond that, there was also an unspoken hope that the nuclear deal would strengthen moderate forces in Iran and help bring about broader changes in Iran's regional policies. "Many of us felt there was potentially a bigger prize if we could get this done and if the Iranian government chose to address its behavior in other areas as well," the British ambassador to the United States, Sir Peter Westmacott said. This was not just a European sentiment—the Obama administration shared it as well. However, articulating it would have created vulnerabilities for the Obama administration, given political realities in Washington.[6]

Reducing tensions with Tehran was particularly attractive in view of both the negative role some of the United States' key Middle East allies played and their insistence that Washington fight their battles. American frustration with Saudi Arabia was particularly noteworthy. The ruling family in Riyadh are reportedly Obama's least favorite family in the world. Obama often found himself aggrieved with the Saudis and with the idea that the United States had to treat Riyadh as an ally at all. His understanding of Saudi Arabia's role in exporting extreme Wahhabist Islam may go well beyond that of any previous and future presidents. During his youth in Indonesia, Obama observed firsthand how Saudi-funded Wahhabists gradually moved a populous country "from a relaxed, syncretistic Islam to a more fundamentalist, unforgiving interpretation." The United States' problems with Iran ran deep, but in the

president's mind it was not in American interests to always unquestionably side with Saudi Arabia.[7]

Ultimately, the United States sought to reduce its tensions with
Iran and pave the way for a pivot to Asia. By contrast, Saudi Arabia
sought a return to the pre-2003 order and an intensification of Iran's
isolation and exclusion from regional affairs. It was fundamentally clear
that Riyadh and Washington were on a "collision course." While Saudi
Arabia wanted the United States to define Iran as the root of all problems in the region, Obama viewed the rivalry between those two countries as a source of instability for the region. Rather than placing the
blame on either side, the United States should help resolve the problem.
According to the president:

> The competition between the Saudis and the Iranians—
> which has helped to feed proxy wars and chaos in Syria and
> Iraq and Yemen—requires us to say to our friends as well as
> to the Iranians that they need to find an effective way to share
> the neighborhood and institute some sort of cold peace. . . .
> An approach that said to our friends "You are right, Iran is
> the source of all problems, and we will support you in deal-
> ing with Iran" would essentially mean that as these sectar-
> ian conflicts continue to rage and our Gulf partners, our
> traditional friends, do not have the ability to put out the
> flames on their own or decisively win on their own, and
> [that then] would mean that we have to start coming in and
> using our military power to settle scores. And that would be
> in the interest neither of the United States nor of the Middle
> East.[8]

Yet from the Saudi point of view, American neutrality was tantamount to betrayal. To Riyadh, Obama was abandoning the entire Arab
world and acting on behalf of Tehran by pursuing a policy that "declared support for a more powerful Iran." The Saudis saw proof of this
view when they refused to attend the Syrian crisis talks since Iran
would partake for the first time, and Obama personally intervened. He
called the Saudi king to convince him to participate in the negotiations

and drop the request for Iran to be shut out. Obama appealed to Saudi Arabia to find a way to "share the region with Iran." His reasoning—that the problem was not Iran's alleged aspiration for hegemony, but rather Riyadh's refusal to accept Iran's inclusion into the region—was "patently absurd" to Saudi ears.[9]

From the American perspective, however, the nuclear deal prevented both war with Iran and a nuclear-armed Iran while holding out a promise of improved relations. At the same time, the United States could exercise tougher love with Israel and a more conditional friendship with Saudi Arabia. "We need to re-examine all of the relationships we enjoy in the region, relationships primarily with Sunni-dominated nations," General Mike Mullen wrote in support of the nuclear deal as Congress debated it. "Detente with Iran might better balance our efforts across the sectarian divide." The United States was frozen in a pattern of relations that were no longer productive and could force it into unnecessary wars. To pivot to Asia, these patterns needed to be broken, starting with a new relationship with Iran. Conversely, to prevent the United States' reorienting itself, the nuclear deal needed to be killed—hence Saudi Arabia's and Israel's staunch opposition to it.[10]

While U.S. and Saudi interests were diverging, Riyadh found itself viewing the region in an increasingly similar light as the Israelis. Once clearly taboo, collaboration with Israel was increasingly discussed in the Saudi kingdom. For both countries, Obama's deal largely resolved the immediate matter of the nuclear question. However, it did so by undermining their mutual core interest in excluding Iran from the regional order. The JCPOA addressed the pretext for Israel and Saudi Arabia's tensions with Iran, but not the roots of their conflict.

As noted earlier, this was a direct result of Netanyahu's government defining Iran's nuclear program as an existential threat to Israel, since that enabled the "sidestepping of broader worries that both Arabs and Israelis have about Iran." After all, an existential threat supersedes all other issues; all else became secondary at best. In fact, the Saudis and their allies asked the United States not to discuss their top regional concerns with the Iranians in the United States' bilateral meetings with Iran. Israel did the same, securing a promise from the United States and the European Union "that a total separation will be enforced" between the nuclear file and other issues such as ISIS. Later, both Saudi Arabia and Israel pointed to this division as a weakness of the JCPOA.[11]

The most important implication of the JCPOA, according to Israel, was that it condoned "Iran's drive to obtain recognition as a legitimate regional power to be reckoned with." Moreover, rather than downgrading Iran, the deal upgraded it to "a de-facto threshold nuclear power." With the nuclear issue resolved, the United States would lose interest in countering Iran's "destabilizing activities" in the region, leaving Israel and the Arabs to manage their rivalry with Iran on their own. Israel's singular focus on keeping Iran isolated and constrained also caused tensions with the United States over the struggle against ISIS. To Israel, ISIS was a distraction. "ISIL is a five-year problem," asserted Yuval Steinitz, Israel's strategic affairs minister, while the struggle against Iran would continue for another generation. Israeli Defense Minister Moshe Yaalon publicly rejected that ISIS constituted a threat to Israel, and stated that he preferred ISIS to Iran. Some Israeli think tanks even suggested that ISIS should not be destroyed since it could "be a useful tool in undermining" Iran. "The continuing existence of IS serves a strategic purpose"; by collaborating with Russia to destroy the group, the United States was committing "strategic folly" that will "enhance the power of the Moscow-Tehran-Damascus axis," the Begin-Sadat Center for Strategic Studies argued. The argument underscored the depth of the divergence of interest and perspective between the United States and Israel.[12]

While some have suggested that the nuclear deal caused a rift in U.S.-Israel relations, in reality the geopolitical interests of Israel and the United States had already been diverging for some time. Rather than causing this rift, the deal reflected a preexisting, growing gap between them. "There's no doubt that there's a divergence of interest between the United States and Israel," a senior administration official told me. Differences over the Israeli-Palestinian peace process, the Arab spring, including Iran in the regional order, and the United States' military footprint in the Middle East were all coming to a head. While Israel wanted the United States to retain a strong military presence in the region, the United States' global responsibilities prevented the Middle East from occupying such a large share of its resources. While the

United States continues to have an interest in keeping Israel safe and democratic, it is concerned that the biggest threats to Israeli democracy are coming from inside the country itself—specifically, its ongoing occupation of Palestinian territory. Even senior members of the Israeli security establishment agree that the real existential threat to Israel comes from the inside, and not from Iran. "There is no outside existential threat to Israel, the only real existential threat is the internal division," former Mossad chief Tamir Pardo said. "Internal division can lead us to civil war—we are already on a path towards that."[13]

These profound rifts cast doubts over the suggestion that the conflict over the Iran deal could have been avoided. Certainly, mistakes on both sides made a bad situation worse. But even the best personal rapport could not have prevented the clear divergence of interests between the United States and Israel. The ultimate responsibility falls upon Netanyahu first for pushing the United States to act against its own interest by taking military action against Iran instead of using diplomacy, and then for challenging President Obama in Congress. "If Israel is really threatened by Iran, then he should be doing things that ensure Israel's security, starting with making sure the U.S.-Israel relationship is on solid ground," former U.S. special envoy for Israeli-Palestinian negotiations Martin Indyk said of Netanyahu. "He should read the map, because if he's not going to succeed it will have screwed up the relationship between the United States and Israel, opened up a gap between Israel and its most important friend and most important strategic ally."[14]

Netanyahu's biggest critics were in the Israeli security establishment, who were horrified over the damage to U.S.-Israel relations his vendetta with Obama and his "illogical" opposition to the JCPOA was causing. "Instead of fighting Iran, he's fighting the U.S. Instead of Israel working with its closest ally, he's turned them into an enemy. Does that seem logical to you?" former Mossad chief Meir Dagan remarked to prominent Israeli journalist Ilana Dayan. Netanyahu had the choice of shifting his position on negotiations with Iran once Obama had made clear that the United States would not look at any other options until it had first exhausted diplomacy. By supporting diplomacy, Israel would arguably have had a greater ability to impact the talks and shape the outcome. Instead, Netanyahu chose to declare war on diplomacy and go after Obama. "Once the negotiations had started, Israel should have put itself in a position that would have enabled it to have a continuous dialogue [with Obama] on the positions of the United States in the negotiations," retired Israeli official Shlomo Brom complained. Officials on both sides agree that beyond the geopolitical divide, the fight over the Iran deal has inflicted "lasting damage to the Israeli-U.S. alliance."[15]

The great irony of course is that there was a much easier way for Netanyahu to kill the nuclear deal than by taking on the president of the United States. Negotiations could have been seriously harmed had he embraced the deal and argued that Iran had been defeated through it. The Iranians had no problems handling Netanyahu's opposition to the nuclear talks—on the contrary, they welcomed it. But it would have been very challenging for them politically, particularly for the nuclear negotiators, if Netanyahu had gone on a victory lap and declared the deal a defeat for Iran. "That would have been enough to kill the deal," Iran's foreign minister, Javad Zarif, admitted to me.[16]

Why Diplomacy Succeeded

So why, despite decades of mistrust and immense opposition from Israel and Saudi Arabia, did the nuclear talks succeed? This is a critical question because the JCPOA showed that not only can intractable global conflicts be resolved through diplomacy, but diplomacy is far cheaper and more effective relative to military action. Secretary Kerry has already suggested that the Iran talks can be used as a "model" for how to deal with North Korea. Moreover, it also showed that the United States and Russia could still compartmentalize their geopolitical differences and collaborate on diplomacy with Iran. "Russia was a help on this," Obama told Thomas Friedman of the New York Times. "I was not sure given the strong differences we are having with Russia right now around Ukraine, whether this would sustain itself.... We would have not achieved this agreement had it not been for Russia's willingness to stick with us and the other P5 + 1 members."[17]

The conventional wisdom in Washington is that diplomacy succeeded because multilateral sanctions crippled the Iranian economy and forced Iran back to the negotiation table. Had it not been for the sanctions, Iran's nuclear program would have expanded and the United States and Iran would have drifted toward war. Conversely, Tehran believes the acceleration of Iran's enrichment program during the sanctions and the Rouhani government's improvement of the economy without sanctions relief convinced the United States that sanctions were a dead end and forced it back to diplomacy. "Once Rouhani got elected and we began improving the economy without any sanctions getting lifted, we sent the U.S. a clear signal that sanctions wouldn't break Iran," President Hassan Rouhani's chief of staff, Mohammad Nahavandian, argued. "The utility of sanctions had come to an end and the Americans chose diplomacy."[18]

Though both narratives contain grains of truth, neither explains the full picture. Privately, former White House officials acknowledge Iran was always at the table, even when the United States refused to attend the P5 + 1 talks. Certainly, the Iranians sent more capable diplomats who engaged constructively and did not stall for time after Rouhani was elected. Nevertheless, this was because the United States accepted that any diplomatic solution would entail enrichment on Iranian soil—Iran's redline—granted that Tehran agreed to the necessary restrictions and transparency measures. "We didn't consider that sanctions played an essential role in bringing the Iranian side into the negotiations and subsequently into the conclusion of this document [the JCPOA]," Russian Deputy Foreign Minister Sergey Ryabkov told me.[19]

In reality, it wasn't so much the pressure the two sides exerted on each other that broke the deadlock as it was the compromises they made. The U.S. side pressured the Iranians either to capitulate or to engage with the United States directly without any conditions regarding enrichment. Rather than halting or slowing down its program, Tehran counter-escalated by enhancing its nuclear activities. Iran went from having 123 centrifuges in 2003 to 22,000 by 2013 and grew its stockpile of low-enriched uranium (LEU) from 1,500 kilograms in 2009 to 12,000 by 2013. "In other words, despite sanctions, despite everything that was offered, Iran continued its program because they believed deeply that they had a right to do this as an NPT country, to have a peaceful nuclear program," Kerry told the Council on Foreign Relations on July 24, 2015. "Well, folks," he added, "sanctions hasn't done anything to stop their program."[20]

By mid-2012, the U.S. side started to realize that the Iranians simply wouldn't capitulate despite the pressure. Conceding the right to enrich would be tantamount to political suicide in Iran, as there was no domestic constituency supporting such a step. Without such a constituency, there would be no internal pressure on Ayatollah Khamenei to give in, leaving escalation and "resistance" his only option. "Neither the Iranian government, or the Iranian opposition, or the Iranian people would agree to what they would view as a total surrender of their sovereignty," President Obama acknowledged in an address at American University three weeks after the JCPOA had been reached. Meanwhile, Iran's breakout capability was rapidly diminishing as a result of its expanded enrichment program, reaching as little as eight to twelve weeks by January 2013.[21]

With Iran not capitulating and its breakout time swiftly shrinking, Obama's options were to stay the course and risk war or to reignite diplomacy with renewed flexibility on the enrichment variable. "The president and I both had a sense that we were on an automatic pilot towards a potential conflict, because no one wanted to talk to anybody or find out what was possible," Kerry told *Wall Street Journal*'s Jay Solomon. "I have no doubt we avoided a war. None."[22]

Not only did Obama have misgivings about military strikes, but he understood the difficulty of preventing Iranian retaliation from escalating matters into a regional war. Iran not only threatened to retaliate against American interests throughout the region, but to target any country that hosted U.S. troops for the attack. The Pentagon shared the White House's skepticism about the broader implications of the military option: the United States was already embroiled in two unending wars in the region, and the appetite for a third engagement was limited to say the least. "A generation of commanders forged by inconclusive wars in the Middle East does not want to start another one," *Politico* wrote in July 2015. "More than anyone else in the government, the Pentagon understood what exercising the other options would mean," added Derek Chollet, a former U.S. assistant secretary of defense. "Clearly the vote was for this to be solved through diplomacy."[23]

The risk of war, heightened by the constant drumbeat of threats from the Israeli prime minister, pushed Obama toward diplomacy with previously unseen dedication. "[Netanyahu] and the then defense minister [Ehud Barak] said the only way to prevent Iran from getting the bomb was an attack . . . [and they] signaled to the whole world that this is what Israel is going to do," Dagan said. "As a result, the Americans went into assessment mode. . . . Their conclusion was that such a war was bad for American interests. And that's why they looked for an alternative, a deal."[24]

But several years of talks conducted by the Obama administration itself had led nowhere. The Iranians had not shown any degree of flexibility and refused substantive negotiations unless the United States first accepted enrichment in Iran. Even the first secret meeting in Oman stalled due to the Iranians' relentless insistence on enrichment. Although the Obama administration had intended all along to accept limited enrichment in Iran, the plan was to offer that incentive at the end of a negotiation. By January 2013, however, Iran's breakout time was reduced to weeks instead of years, while the sanctions pressure was beginning to wane. Now that the Omanis had opened a direct channel to Iran's supreme leader, Obama had little choice but to play the enrichment card—even with Ahmadinejad in power at the time. In fact, it might have been the only thing that could provide an escape from what Kerry described as the "automatic pilot" toward war.[25]

For the Iranians, this was the watershed moment they had sought for more than a decade. "It was the U.S. accepting enrichment that opened the issue and enabled a solution to be found," Nahavandian told me. Had enrichment not been accepted, the Oman channel would have collapsed, and there would never have been a deal. "The Ahmadinejad administration would not have entered into negotiations had we not received those indications on the enrichment question," Iranian Deputy Foreign Minister Majid Ravanchi explained. "Both administrations entered into negotiations due to the enrichment indication." According to a senior European diplomat deeply involved in establishing communication between the United States and Iran, it was this step that convinced the Iranians that the United States was serious. It's what made the Oman channel different from all previous diplomatic efforts.[26]

On this crucial point, there is no disagreement between the United States and Iran: American officials acknowledge that without acceptance of enrichment, there would never have been a breakthrough in the talks. "There would not have been the possibility of a deal without the United States putting the prospect of enrichment on the table," a senior administration official declared to me. "Absent that, I cannot fathom a scenario in which we would have gotten to a deal." When JCPOA critics blasted it precisely for conceding enrichment, the White House became more convinced that many of them simply did not want any deal with Iran at all. The zero-enrichment position would have ensured that serious talks wouldn't even commence, let alone elicit Iranian concessions.[27]

Another critical reason the talks succeeded was something the United States had neither control over nor impact on—namely, the election of Hassan Rouhani. Nicknamed the "Sheikh of Diplomacy," he dramatically changed Iran's posture on diplomacy in general and on the nuclear negotiations in particular. With Iranian enrichment secured, he assembled a team of seasoned diplomats spearheaded by Javad Zarif. Zarif already knew the file and Western negotiators, thanks to the Track-II meetings organized by the Rockefeller Brothers Fund/United Nations Association, Pugwash Conferences on Science and World Affairs, and other groups, and had the courage to accept a deal and defend it in Tehran. The Iranian diplomats were praised for their efficiency by all parties, including Israeli officials like Moshe Yaalon. "The Iranian negotiators were brilliant," the Israeli defense minister said. "They played a weak hand superbly." Zarif in particular earned the respect of his counterparts, with Western diplomats describing him as "exceptionally bright" and even "dangerously" clever. "His skills are far beyond those of Western diplomats," one of the P5 + 1 negotiators told me.[28]

Moreover, Rouhani carried none of the political toxicity that Ahmadinejad had amassed from his bellicose rhetoric against Israel. While Ahmadinejad questioned the Holocaust, Rouhani condemned it and tweeted his well wishes to the Jewish people on Rosh Hashanah. He also took measures to improve relations with Iranian Jews by, for instance, unveiling a monument to Jewish-Iranian soldiers killed in the Iran-Iraq war. "The government has listened to our grievances and requests. That we are being consulted is an important step forward," said Homayoun Samiah, leader of the Tehran Jewish Association. "Under former president Mahmoud Ahmadinejad, nobody was listening to us." Despite relentless efforts by Netanyahu, Rouhani's outreach and moderation made it difficult for deal opponents to demonize him. Even Israeli decision-makers privately acknowledged—contrary to the government line—that something "historic" was happening inside of Iran.[29]

Obama now had an Iranian counterpart willing to expend the political capital needed to secure a deal and take a risk for peace. "The single bellwether event was Rouhani's election," a former White House official told me. "I am absolutely convinced that had Jalili been elected, we'd probably be in the same situation today, if not a much more draconian situation." U.S. officials are convinced that had Rouhani not come to power through "the bravery of the Iranian people," the United States would have been headed in a disastrous direction. "If Rouhani hadn't won, we would have been up shit-creek, despite the sanctions pressure," a former senior National Security Council director told me bluntly.[30]

Accepting enrichment in Iran and Rouhani becoming president were necessary factors for the nuclear deal to come about. Although the role of sanctions is more complicated, in the Washington narrative they take center stage. "I've been struck by how in the American media, the narrative that the Obama administration was persistent in pursuing diplomacy and implementing sanctions finally convinced the Iranians back to the table after they recognized the error of their ways, and voilà, we had a diplomatic crack," a former White House official explained. "People just gloss over the Rouhani election, which in my mind was the landmark sea change that produced all of this."[31]

Clearly, sanctions did provide the United States and the West with leverage in the negotiations. In particular, the leverage the West got through the EU oil embargo and U.S. financial sanctions was considerable. The Iranians don't deny their economic impact and made little secret that their second priority after keeping enrichment was getting them lifted. From that perspective, the value of sanctions becomes almost undeniable.

Time did not stand still in Iran, however: while the West imposed sanctions, Tehran aggressively bolstered its own position by expanding its enrichment program, amassing more low-enriched uranium (LEU) and medium-enriched uranium (MEU), and deepening its knowledge of the fuel cycle. Every additional centrifuge and kilogram of enriched uranium increased Iran's leverage. By the time the two sides met, it was not entirely clear if either side actually had an edge. The Iranians were more eager to negotiate, but was that because of the sanctions or because the United States had yielded on enrichment? Or was it because Iran had already reached its nuclear objectives and felt more comfortable negotiating, as Iranian negotiator Abbas Araghchi indicated in a secretly taped conversation? "The actions of the two sides went forward until we reached a point that our hands were full from a nuclear perspective, meaning we had reached an irreversible point," he argued. "When our hands were full, there was no point in paying the costs. So we went after consolidating our achievements. This is how we went after a new round of talks, with our hands full."[32]

Many officials believe that had enrichment been offered earlier, a deal could have been reached before Iran amassed thousands of kilograms of LEU and built 22,000 centrifuges. Under those circumstances, far stronger limitations could have been imposed by virtue of Iran having less nuclear infrastructure. In fact, back in March 2005, when Rouhani was Iran's lead nuclear negotiator and Zarif served as UN ambassador in New York, the Iranians made one last effort to resolve the nuclear issue before the presidential elections that installed Ahmadinejad. Zarif proposed to the European Union that Iran convert its LEU to fuel rods for power reactors, not reprocess spent fuel rods to preclude plutonium production, allow a continuous IAEA presence at Iran's nuclear facilities, and limit Iran to 3,000 centrifuges.[33]

In comparison, the JCPOA limits Iran's centrifuges to 5,060. Thus, prior to any sanctions and to Iran's amassing LEU, the Iranians offered to limit their nuclear program to a far greater extent than they agreed to in the JCPOA. According to then UK foreign secretary Jack Straw, the 2005 proposal failed because the Bush administration refused to accept anything but zero enrichment in Iran. "I'm absolutely convinced that we can do business with Dr. Rouhani," Straw said after Rouhani's election in 2013, "because we did do business with Dr. Rouhani, and had it not been for major problems within the U.S. administration under

President Bush, we could have actually settled the whole Iran nuclear dossier back in 2005, and we probably wouldn't have had President Ahmadinejad as a consequence of the failure as well."[34]

The lead EU negotiator at that time, Javier Solana, concurs: "If you look back in time, we could have done very few centrifuges. We could have got an agreement [with much fewer centrifuges]. . . . No doubt," he told me. In fact, when I raised the issue with Zarif during the Lausanne negotiations, he pointed out that 3,000 centrifuges was just Iran's opening bid. Tehran didn't expect to keep that many centrifuges if the West had engaged on the Iranian proposal. "We would have settled for 1,000," he recalled with a smile. At a White House briefing in the fall of 2013, the Iranian proposal from 2005 was raised by one of the participants. "We would jump on the opportunity to get that deal if it was offered today," one of the U.S. negotiators said, admitting the lost opportunity and that time had not been on the side of the West. "We were constantly chasing the deal we could have gotten two years earlier," a former State Department official commented.[35]

Indeed, if one looks at the total period of the nuclear dispute, and not just the last two years prior to the commencement of direct U.S.-Iran talks, a picture emerges where acceptance of enrichment and the presence of leaders in Washington and Tehran committed to diplomacy remain necessary variables, whereas sanctions or centrifuge escalation do not. What resolved the nuclear issue was ultimately not the pressure the two sides could bring to bear on each other, but the discarding of unreasonable and unrealistic demands—whether the American insistence on zero enrichment or the Iranian belief that it could present Washington with a nuclear fait accompli. If anything, escalation might have been a necessary precondition to both becoming convinced that their coercive approach could not bear fruit, as states usually opt for a compromise only after having reached the realization that forcing their counterparts to capitulate is a mere pipedream.

After compromising, Obama had to disprove that a "better deal" was achievable if the United States stayed with coercion. "The fact is that it wasn't either sanctions or threats that actually stopped and finally stopped the expansion of Iran's nuclear activities," Kerry explained during the congressional battle over the JCPOA. "It was the start of the negotiating process and the negotiations themselves, recently concluded in Vienna, that actually stopped it. Only with those negotiations did Iran begin to get rid of its stockpile of 20 percent enriched uranium. Only with those negotiations did it stop installing more centrifuges and cease advancing the Arak reactor. Only then did it commit to be more forthcoming about IAEA access and negotiate a special arrangement to break the deadlock."[36]

Weeks earlier, Kerry disabused Congress of the idea that the United States could coerce Iran to agree to a better deal. That is, he had to wean them off of the strategy that had been the bedrock of the United States' Iran policy for nearly three decades. "Some sort of unicorn arrangement involving Iran's complete capitulation . . . that is a fantasy," Kerry said at a congressional hearing on the JCPOA. "The fact is that, whether we like it or not, Iran has developed experience with a nuclear fuel cycle, and we can't bomb that knowledge away, nor can we sanction that knowledge away."[37]

Meanwhile, Rouhani faced a similar challenge in Tehran: he had to defend the centrifuge and LEU cuts he agreed to against the charge that Iran would be better off sticking to its policy of "resistance." Although the Iranian parliament did not have the authority to reject the deal, Ayatollah Khamenei ordered it to hold a vote on it regardless. The Iranian parliamentarians mimicked Congress by holding numerous theatrical hearings, grilling the Iranian negotiators, and subjecting them to harsh and blatantly unfounded accusations. Iranian hardliners made little secret of the fact that their goal was to outdo their American counterparts in the U.S. Congress. "I think the drama in my country will be bigger than that of yours," Iran's speaker of parliament, Ali Larijani, told American journalists during a visit to the United Nations in September 2015.[38]

Political Will, Respect, and Dignity

Overcoming three decades of mistrust, engaging in risky negotiations for years, and defending compromises with an "enemy state" takes leaders who are committed to diplomatic solutions to conflict. Lack of political will was why Obama's 2009 attempt at diplomacy with Iran was abandoned. A solution was in reach (as evidenced by the Brazilian-Turkish-brokered Tehran Declaration), but Obama lacked the political will to take on the critics of diplomacy and pay the political price. That political will depends on several factors.

First, even the most committed peacemakers will not invest in negotiations unless they perceive the other side exhibiting similar commitment. It takes two to tango, but many leaders are risk-averse when it comes to negotiations and are more comfortable taking risks for confrontational policies. In their minds, skepticism of diplomacy is conflated with strength and hawkishness. Even when the other side shows readiness, these leaders prefer dismissing opportunities for exploring them. By Obama's second term, Iran and the United States had presidents who saw the will to compromise as a sign of strength, not weakness. Rouhani even accused the Iranian critics of the talks of being cowards. "Some of them chant slogans but they are political cowards. As soon as we negotiate they start shaking," he said of his opponents.[39]

Closely linked to this will to pursue diplomacy is a conviction that a diplomatic way to a solution is possible. While publicly Obama adopted a cautious—if not skeptical—tone about the prospects of a diplomatic breakthrough, many of his officials were privately optimistic. Those pushing diplomacy were all convinced that with the right political determination a solution would eventually be found. "I always thought there was going to be [a deal]," Ben Rhodes said. A similar determination gripped the nongovernment organizations championing diplomacy. Without their certainty, these groups would never have made the necessary investment in advocating for a negotiated settlement. For instance, had the Rockefeller Brothers Fund (RBF) assessed their Track-II project by regular evaluation metrics, the meetings would have ended long before they yielded fruit. "This project would have been out of business three years in," Stephen Heintz, the president of RBF, explained. Instead, proponents of diplomacy took the long view—and stuck to their plan.[40]

Few embody this tenacity more than Secretary John Kerry. As chairman of the Senate Foreign Relations Committee, he was the driving force behind the secret Oman channel with the Iranians. While others in the administration, including then secretary of state Hillary

Clinton, were skeptical that the Oman channel "could deliver on Iran and represent the power echelon like the supreme leader," Kerry insisted that the opportunity be pursued. Had he not won that battle, it is likely that there would never have been a nuclear deal. (While Kerry and his associates deny it, others in the administration claim Kerry covertly promised enrichment to Iran through the Omanis to get them to agree to the channel.)[41]

A third factor that explains the success of diplomacy is Kerry and Obama's unusual ability to see the world through the eyes of their counterparts. This is a significant strength in negotiations, not just because it helps you to predict your counterparts' next steps, but because the ability to understand their perspective is critical for building trust. "Obama really gets Iran," a White House staffer explained. "He can put himself in their shoes and understand their calculations and how they define their interests." This was particularly important, given the troubled history between the United States and Iran and the many grievances both sides had with each other. Obama explained his reasoning on this matter in detail to the *New York Times*:

> I do think that you have to have the capacity to put yourself occasionally in their shoes, and if you look at Iranian history, the fact is that we had some involvement with overthrowing a democratically elected regime in Iran. We have had in the past supported Saddam Hussein when we know he used chemical weapons in the war between Iran and Iraq, and so, as a consequence, they have their own security concerns, their own narrative. It may not be one we agree with . . . but I think that when we are able to see their country and their culture in specific terms, historical terms, as opposed to just applying a broad brush, that's when you have the possibility at least of some movement.[42]

Furthermore, one cannot underestimate the importance of mutual respect, even though it cannot be measured or quantified. For the Iranians, this was essential beyond its particular cultural sensitivities: respect signaled Western acceptance of Iran as a nation, as a society as well as a political system. The Iranians see themselves as heirs to an ancient empire, grieve its fall from grace, and abhor how the West has treated it over the past two centuries. When Zarif insisted that diplomacy could succeed only if conducted with "mutual respect," it was a code for "You need to treat Iran as a real society and political system," Iran scholar Farideh Farhi explained. Iran prides itself on not making key state decisions solely through an authoritarian ruler or clique. Iran has institutions that have to weigh in and set decision-making processes to ensure a proper cost-benefit analysis. In the Iranian mind, these characteristics make Iran a legitimate regional power, unlike its many neighbors, which Tehran believes lack legitimacy and independence.[43]

Finally, a modicum of respect went a long way psychologically in lowering Iran's guard. The Obama administration learned that lesson early, both in creating a diplomatic atmosphere by drastically changing American rhetoric on Iran and from its secret negotiations with Cuba. When Obama extended his hand to greet Raul Castro at Nelson Mandela's funeral, the Cubans were taken aback by the gesture. The next time Ben Rhodes met with the Cubans, their reaction confirmed the importance of courtesy. "Your President treated us with respect, nobody has done that before," the Cuban negotiator said with surprise. The gesture reignited confidence that the political commitment to resolving their decades' long conflict existed, whereas years of tough talk, sanctions, and coercion had done nothing to create a psychological opening. "Nobody had tried treating them with respect," Rhodes said with a hint of bewilderment.[44]

These factors all contributed to diplomacy succeeding. It was the geopolitical context that rendered the political cost of pursuing diplomacy with Iran palpable. In addition to the fact that the U.S. order in the region had been shattered by the Iraq war and that Washington needed to shift its focus toward China, the nuclear crisis had escalated to the point where the two sides no longer could be in a state of neither war nor peace—the cost of leaving the nuclear issue unresolved was simply getting too high. It was the secret negotiations in Oman and the United States' acceptance of enrichment on Iranian soil that created a diplomatic breakthrough and provided Washington and Tehran an exit ramp from the sanctions and escalation policy that had been leading them toward war. It was lack of political will that led to the abandonment of Obama's first attempt at diplomacy in 2009, and it was an unprecedented demonstration of political commitment in 2013–2015 that insulated the nuclear talks from all external shocks and pressures—be they from Israel, Saudi Arabia, or the rise of ISIS.

Thus, against all odds, after twenty-two months of intense negotiations, the P5+1 and Iran finally reached a nuclear agreement that in one move avoided two disasters: war with Iran and an Iranian path to a nuclear bomb. But after all the negotiations and the meeting of minds between Iranian and American officials, did the United States lose Iran as an enemy? Or in other words, was the nuclear deal transactional or the beginning of a broader transformation of U.S.-Iran relations?

Has the United States Lost an Enemy?

Blocking Iran's path to a nuclear weapon through the nuclear deal required neither a transformation of Iran nor a broader change in U.S.-Iran relations. But for the deal to last, a broader opening between the United States and Iran may prove necessary. Neither the United States nor Iran has the capacity to compartmentalize the nuclear deal so that it can remain unaffected by continued and escalating tensions in other aspects of their relationship. This reality will remain a major threat to the durability of the deal, since the enmity between the United States and Iran runs deeper than just the nuclear issue and involves the geopolitical order in the region and Iran's position therein. Over the course of the past decades, the enmity has taken on a life of its own, with significant domestic political interests on both sides benefiting from its continuation.

Nonetheless, desire for change was evident in the Obama administration and among its allies. "This deal does not count on our fundamental relationship with Iran changing," Obama told NPR, but the United States should "welcome" a shift in Iranian politics and policies. While White House officials did not connect the success of the deal to broader change in Iran, they did not shy away from arguing that prospects of change were greater with it. "We believe that a world in which there is a deal with Iran is much more likely to produce an evolution in

Iranian behavior than a world in which there is no deal," Rhodes told the *New York Times*. The same sentiment existed in parts of Congress, with senior lawmakers meeting Zarif to begin a broader dialogue with Iran's parliament and society.[45]

But old habits die slowly. Inside the U.S. bureaucracy, resistance was and remains stiff. "Iran has been toxic in the American foreign policy establishment for quite some time," explained Reza Marashi, a former State Department official and current research director of the National Iranian American Council. Incentives within the bureaucracy are tilted against creativity on Iran and toward preserving the status quo. "We were told to inject political realism into our recommendations," Marashi commented on his time at the State Department. "That simply meant that the political climate in Washington did not allow for recommendations and considerations that could change the broader trajectory of the U.S.-Iran relationship." The fight in Congress revealed more than anything else the fear in some quarters that the United States would lose an enemy. Rather than fearing the deal's impact on Iranian policy, some feared it would push Iran away from being an enemy. "When people would discuss scenarios of Iran evolving in a more positive direction, that seemed to almost be the thing people were opposed to, as if it had to stay in this clenched up conflict," Rhodes pointed out."[46]

A similar challenge existed on the Iranian side. Rouhani clearly wanted to explore opportunities for collaboration on issues where the United States and Iran had common interests, such as in Afghanistan, Iraq, and the fight against ISIS. In fact, the Iranian negotiators were frustrated that the United States was not focused on the bigger picture and creating a larger diplomatic opening between the United States and Iran. "The opponents in Iran don't care about the nuclear issue, they oppose it because they don't want to see the relationship change," a frustrated Iranian diplomat told me. "And these confused Americans don't get this." The frustration was directed primarily against Wendy Sherman and Ernest Moniz, whom some Iranian diplomats described as technicians who easily got lost in details. "For some of them, for every centrifuge they had to accept, it was as if we were pulling off a piece of skin from their bodies." Obama and Kerry, on the other hand, were appreciated for their "grand vision" for the region and desire to "overhaul" the United States' traditional posture in the Middle East.[47]

Immediately after the deal, both sides sent optimistic signals about the trajectory of the relationship. "[The] Iran deal is not a ceiling but a solid foundation. We must now begin to build on it," Zarif tweeted hours after the JCPOA had been reached. Privately, Zarif told Kerry that once a deal was struck, he would have a mandate to engage on other regional issues as well. He said "If we get this finished, I am now empowered to work with and talk to you about regional issues," according to Kerry. Clearly, the process would take time and would proceed at a modest pace. But the critical matter was that the trajectory of relations would be positive. "Are we heading towards amplifying the enmity or decreasing this enmity?" Rouhani asked. "I believe we have taken the first steps towards decreasing this enmity."[48]

Conservatives in Iran, however, cared little about the nuclear deal or its details. They feared that improved relations with Washington would pave the way for American economic penetration of Iran. This in turn would rock the domestic political balance there in favor of reformist and moderate forces. Moreover, hardliners feared collaboration with Washington would force Tehran to adopt a more pro-American policy in the region, abandon its cherished independence, and lose its dignity. In Khamenei's view, without independence, dignity cannot be upheld. Even successful states such as Japan and South Korea suffer from dignity deficits, in his view, due to their dependence on the United States. With sanctions and other Western pressures, Iran paid a significant price for its independence and dignity, Khamenei maintained. If it now agreed to engage more broadly with Washington, it would risk falling within the United States' sphere of influence and lose its dignity and independence. Since the United States' regional objectives are "180 degrees opposed to Iran's," Iran would be forced to make concessions and "play by the rules" set by the United States. "Our policy toward the arrogant government of America will not change in any way despite these negotiations and the document that has been prepared," Ayatollah Khamenei said after the nuclear deal had been struck. "They can only see Iran's surrender in their dreams."[49]

For years, Iranian hardliners fended off this scenario by refusing any dialogue with Washington and making engagement with the United States taboo. Yet by 2011, the Iranian foreign policy elite had reached a consensus that some relationship with the United States served Iran's national interest. The question was what the nature of that relationship should be. After Ayatollah Khamenei permitted direct nuclear negotiations, the debate became over whether the dialogue with the United States could extend to regional conflicts. Khamenei insisted that JCPOA diplomacy be limited to the nuclear issue, but never completely shut the door on broader engagement. If the nuclear deal yielded positive results, then diplomacy could extend to other issues, despite the likely opposition from his hardline base. "The leader is waiting for the permanent result of the agreement," observed Amir Mohebian, a conservative commentator close to Ayatollah Khamenei.[50]

Moreover, some degree of rivalry with Washington was needed in order to sustain and elevate Iran's bid for regional leadership, senior Iranian officials told me. Discarding Iran's ideology or anti-American posture would turn Iran into a normal state whose power and influence in the region would be measured solely by its military and economic might. According to them, Iran should challenge the United States' vision for the region, instead of competing with Turkey, Saudi Arabia, and Israel to be the United States' number-one regional ally. In the long run, Iran could then position itself as a peer-competitor with the United States in the region. The Iranians point to Russia as an example of a state with global ambitions hampered by a lack of ideology and vision that others can buy into.

The Iranians have insisted, however, that the outright enmity between the United States and Iran does not have to continue. Rather, the United States and Iran could potentially enjoy a relationship that encompasses both competition and collaboration. Their rivalry for the future order of the region does not preclude tactical or even strategic collaboration in areas of mutual interest, such as fighting against ISIS. While few in the United States find this arrangement attractive, moderate elements in both Iran and the United States agree that neither wants the enmity to continue, yet neither is ready to replace the enmity with partnership or alliance. At the end of the day, the JCPOA removed only one dimension of the hostility between the United States and Iran—the one most likely to bring them to war. For other tensions to be resolved, a far greater investment in diplomacy is needed. Yet with the election of Donald Trump as president, the question is no longer if the United States can lose Iran as an enemy, but whether the nuclear deal even can survive.

Will the JCPOA Endure?

Today, the JCPOA is under severe threat. A Clinton victory in the 2016 presidential elections would have brought its challenges, but Trump's victory presents a far graver danger. Renegotiating the deal as he promised to do during the campaign would not be easy. After all, it is not a bilateral deal with Iran that the United States can void on its own, but a multilateral one with Russia, China, France, the United Kingdom, and Germany, codified by a UN Security Council resolution. The United States cannot unilaterally void or amend the agreement without violating international law. Any effort to directly kill the deal—or even renegotiate it—will isolate the United States, and not Iran.[51]

But Trump can kill the deal through indirect measures. His future presidency has already added political risk to any Western companies contemplating entry into Iran. Hesitant businesses fear that the United States will impose new sanctions on Iran and force companies that just entered the Iranian market to exit at a hefty cost. After being instilled with doubt about the durability of the deal, businesses will avoid Iran to prevent the cost and embarrassment of being sabotaged by new sanctions. Disappointment with the agreement is already high in Iran, since many expected economic conditions to improve quickly after it went into effect. Additional uncertainty about sanctions relief could undermine Rouhani's prospects for reelection in 2017 and make Iran's continued adherence to the deal domestically indefensible.[52]

Moreover, Trump may also succumb to pressure from Israel and Saudi Arabia to, if not nix the JCPOA, at least revert to containing and marginalizing Iran. "They will continue that pressure," explained Dalia Dassa Kaye, an expert on Israel at the RAND Corporation. "It's all going to be about containing Iran and making sure that this deal doesn't lead to a broader embrace of Iran beyond this nuclear agreement." Key pro-Israel opponents of the JCPOA told me in the spring of 2016 in no uncertain terms that their opposition to the nuclear deal is unwavering. On the contrary, they are holding their powder dry while awaiting President Obama's exit from the White House. In their analysis, their loss in Congress was largely due to the aberrant Obama presidency. As soon as Obama leaves office, they reason, the United States will revert back to its "normal" posture in the Middle East. Its policy will center on sustaining a pro-Israel and pro-Saudi order in the region, while underwriting the cost of containing and isolating Iran. In short, they anticipate that the new administration will repudiate the pivot to Asia, reprioritize the Middle East, reexamine the United States' relations with the Sunni dictatorships in the region, and reconsider the idea that "detente with Iran might better balance our efforts across the sectarian divide."[53]

Returning to the old status quo was also a likely direction in a Clinton victory, and even enjoys some support in Europe. France, for instance, calculates that Iran has become too strong regionally since the Iraq war and that the West should side with Riyadh to balance Tehran. In the words of the French ambassador to the United States Gerard Araud:

> The problem is not the Islamic Republic. The problem is not the Shah. The problem is simply geopolitics, because our American friends have destroyed Iraq and because of the Egyptian crisis, the power in the region is now Iran. Period. . . . So I think it means that on the European side, to solve the geopolitical quagmire in the Middle East, it's not being anti-Iranian to consider that there is an imbalance in favor of Iran.[54]

In fact, Trump's first national security advisor, Michael Flynn (who was fired after only twenty-four days on the job), and his secretary of defense, General James Mattis, clearly consider Iran an enemy. Flynn stunned his subordinates at the Defense Intelligence Agency when he instructed the agency to find evidence that Iran was the culprit for the 9/11 Benghazi attacks (Iran had no role in the attack). Meanwhile, Mattis was reportedly fired by Obama for pushing a much more confrontational line against Iran, while making dubious claims about a supposed ISIS-Iran connection. In April 2016, Mattis gave a talk in which he suggested a link between ISIS and Iran, completely ignoring Iran's role in defeating ISIS in Iraq and preventing the terror organization from capturing Baghdad. "I consider ISIS nothing more than an excuse for Iran to continue its mischief. Iran is not an enemy of ISIS. . . . What is the one country in the Middle East that has not been attacked by ISIS?" he asked. "One. And it's Iran. That is just more than happenstance, I'm sure." (ISIS and other Salafi jihadist groups have tried attacking Iran on numerous occasions, at times successfully.)[55]

Obama questioned the strategic value of the United States' Middle East presence while encouraging U.S. allies to share a greater burden of the security cost—a shift that necessitated eliminating the risk of war with Iran over the nuclear issue. In contrast, Trump's national security team appears to attach far greater significance to the region and favors reestablishing American hegemony in the Middle East. Such a strategy puts the United States back on a collision course with Iran due to Tehran's rejection of Pax Americana and realigns Washington with Tel Aviv and Riyadh since these powers not only welcome American dominance, but need it for their own security. As a result, Iran will still be considered an enemy despite collaborating with the United States against ISIS, while Saudi Arabia will be considered an ally despite its financing of international jihadism, precisely because its interest aligns with the Trump administration on the more important question of U.S. hegemony.

The JCPOA is at risk even short of a direct confrontation between the United States and Iran. While Trump is unlikely to build a strong coalition against Iran due to his lack of international credibility, U.S.-Iran relations must have an at least slightly positive trajectory for the JCPOA to be sustained. It cannot survive if in addition to those attacks on the deal, the broader U.S.-Iran relationship further deteriorates. An all-out containment policy that closes the new communication channels between Tehran and Washington—already too centered on the personal rapport between Kerry and Zarif—would be a major setback to the United States. "What I know is that, both because we have such stark differences to address, and also to see what may be possible over time, it is in our interest to maintain diplomatic communication—to engage Iran," Kerry made clear to me. "Thirty years without much engagement didn't bring us to a place anyone wanted to be." Simply put, the United States has to choose between the JCPOA and a comprehensive containment policy of Iran. It can have one, but it cannot have both. The objective of the deal may not have been to transform their relationship, but a transformation is likely necessary for the deal to survive.[56]

It is important to note, however, that the deal has proven that U.S.-Iran enmity is not inevitable. It has proven that diplomacy can be triumphant. It has proven that war can be avoided and that the United States' true leadership shines through when it chooses multilateral diplomacy over unilateral coercion. But the achievement of the nuclear deal goes beyond that. The norm in recent history has been that diplomacy settles a new peace after devastating carnage—not before. Instead, a global crisis was resolved peacefully through a genuine compromise in which all sides made politically costly concessions and the outcome doesn't just resolve the immediate nuclear question, but also has the potential to transform the relationship between Iran, the United States, and the European Union. The Iran negotiations stand as a progressive counterpoint to the Iraq war: opponents of militant foreign policy can now not only criticize the errors of preventive military action, but also have a successful model for peacefully reconciling nations approaching the precipice of war.[57]

But the triumph may not endure. Ultimately, the Trump administration may act on its stated desire to roll back the deal, whether through a move to nullify or renegotiate the JCPOA or by causing the deal to collapse under the weight of growing U.S.-Iran tensions following Trump's efforts to reestablish hegemony in the region. If so, the demise of the deal will not come about as a result of the deficiencies of the JCPOA or the shortcomings of diplomacy. Rather, it will be the thirst for hegemony that will stand in the way of the United States losing Iran as an enemy.

Notes

ONE Introduction

1. Dan De Luce, "Inside the U.S. Navy's Iran Fiasco," *Foreign Policy,* March 1, 2016, and "Punished U.S. Navy Officer Believes He Prevented a War with Iran," *Foreign Policy,* September 12, 2016.

2. Interview with Iranian Foreign Minister Javad Zarif, April 20, 2016.

3. Interview with U.S. senior administration official, August 16, 2016. Interview with Javad Zarif.

4. Interview with U.S. senior administration official. Interview with Secretary of State John Kerry, September 8, 2016. Interview with senior White House official, April 11, 2016.

5. Interview with Javad Zarif. Thomas Gibbons-Neff and Missy Ryan, "Iran Holds 10 U.S. Sailors but Pledges to Release Them Soon, Pentagon Says," *Washington Post,* January 12, 2016. Interview with U.S. senior administration official. Defense Secretary Carter later publicly admitted that the American sailors made a navigational error that mistakenly took them into Iranian territorial waters. Michael Schmidt and Helene Cooper, "Defense Secretary Says U.S. Sailors Made Navigational Error into Iranian Waters," *New York Times,* January 14, 2016.

6. Interview with U.S. senior administration official. Interview with Javad Zarif.

7. Interview with Javad Zarif.

8. Statement by the president on Iran, White House, January 17, 2016. Interview with senior White House official, April 11, 2016. Interview with U.S. senior administration official.

9. John Kerry's remarks at the Aspen Ideas Festival and conversation with Walter Isaacson, June 28, 2016. Interview with Javad Zarif.

10. Interview with U.S. senior administration official. Interview with senior White House official, April 11, 2016.

11. Interview with former National Security Council official, September 2015. Interview with senior White House official, January 28, 2016. "What we're trying to foster," Deputy NSC Advisor Ben Rhodes said, "is a dynamic where we can have a diplomatic dialogue with the Iranians on issues related to these regional conflicts. Precisely because Iran has had a role in these areas, we would like to try to move them in a more constructive direction. And that requires some amount of dialogue. It also requires vigilance" (quoted in Laura Rozen, "Can US, Iran Maintain Ties After Obama?" *Al Monitor,* April 21, 2016). See also Statement by the president on Iran.

12. Statement by the President on Iran.

13. De Luce, "Punished U.S. Navy Officer."

TWO Israel's Master Stroke

1. Trita Parsi, *Treacherous Alliance: The Secret Dealings of Israel, Iran, and the United States* (New Haven, CT: Yale University Press, 2007), ch. 13.

2. Interview with former national security advisor Brent Scowcroft, Washington, DC, September 27, 2004.

3. Efraim Halevi, *Man in the Shadows* (New York: St. Martin's Press, 2006), 33–34. Phone interview with Efraim Halevi, former head of the Mossad, June 17, 2006.

4. David Kimche, *The Last Option* (New York: Maxwell Macmillan International, 1991), 236.

5. Ibid.

6. Interview with Shlomo Brom, Jaffee Center for Strategic Studies, Tel Aviv, October 26, 2004.

7. Uri Savir, *The Process: 1,100 Days That Changed the Middle East* (New York: Random House, 1998), 27.

8. David W. Lesch, *The Middle East and the United States* (Boulder, CO: Westview, 2003), 278.

9. Speech by Henry Kissinger, U.S. Naval Academy Forrestal Lecture, Annapolis, Maryland, April 11, 2007.

10. James Baker, *The Politics of Diplomacy* (New York: Putnam, 1995), 415, 428.

11. Halevi, *Man in the Shadows,* 33–34.

12. Baker, *Politics of Diplomacy,* 117, 123, 129.

13. "Former Sec. of State Baker Blasts Netanyahu at J Street Conference," *Jerusalem Post,* March 24, 2015.

14. Baker, *Politics of Diplomacy,* 423, 125, 131.

15. Shireen Hunter, *Iran After Khomeini* (New York: Praeger, 1992), 126.

16. Parsi, *Treacherous Alliance,* 142.

17. Ibid.

18. For a discussion of the significance of Secretary Baker's statement, see R. K. Ramazani, "Move Iran Outside the 'Axis,'" *Christian Science Monitor,* August 19, 2002.

19. Parsi, *Treacherous Alliance,* 143.

20. Shahram Chubin, "Iran's Security Policy in the Post-Revolutionary Era" (Santa Monica, CA: RAND, 2001). Interview with Nasser Hadian, reformist strategist in Iran, New York, February 26, 2004.

21. Shane Harris and Matthew M. Aid, "CIA Files Prove America Helped Saddam as He Gassed Iran," *Foreign Policy*, August 26, 2013.

22. Interview with Javad Zarif, New York, April 1, 2004.

23. Kenneth Pollack, *The Persian Puzzle* (New York: Random House, 2004), 259.

24. Presentation by Shahram Chubin, Woodrow Wilson Center for International Scholars, November 9, 2004.

25. Interview with Mahmoud Vaezi, August 16, 2004.

26. Scott Shane, "Saddam Hussein Told of Fearing Iran More than U.S.," *New York Times*, July 2, 2009.

27. Hooshang Amirahmadi, "The Spiraling Gulf Arms Race," *Middle East Insight* 2 (1994): 49.

28. Paul J. White and William S. Logan, *Remaking the Middle East* (New York: Berg, 1997), 203. Hunter, *Iran After Khomeini*, 133. John L. Esposito and R. K. Ramazani, ed., *Iran at the Crossroads* (New York: Palgrave Macmillan, 2001), 217. Interview with Gary Sick, New York, February 25, 2004.

29. Interview with Brent Scowcroft. White and Logan, *Remaking the Middle East*, 202.

30. Amirahmadi, "Spiraling Gulf Arms Race," 204.

31. Baker, *Politics of Diplomacy*, 444.

32. Washington failed to pick up on Iran's readiness because of the image of Iran as an inherently anti-American nation, formed by a decade of tensions between the two countries. According to Dennis Ross, "Certain images get formed, and when they are formed, even when there are behaviors that seem to contradict the image, if there are other images at the same time that tend to confirm it, you give much more weight to those that tend to confirm it, and you dismiss those that should point you in a different direction. . . . The signals from Rafsanjani tended to be dismissed, but they were there. The behaviors that actually tended to fit with the traditional images [of Iran] were treated as if that was the real Iran" (interview with Ambassador Dennis Ross, Washington, DC, May 29, 2004).

33. Interview with Ambassador Robert Pelletreau, March 1, 2004. Interview with Dennis Ross. Interview with Brent Scowcroft.

34. Anoushiravan Ehteshami and Raymond Hinnebusch, *The Foreign Policies of Middle East States* (London: Lynne Rienner, 2002), 85.

35. Interview with Deputy Foreign Minister Hadi Nejad-Hosseinian, Tehran, August 12, 2004.

36. Interview with Mohammad Reza Tajik, counselor to President Khatami and director of the Strategic Studies Center of the President's Office, Tehran, August 25, 2004.

37. Interview with Iranian political strategist, August 2004.

38. Interview with Ali Reza Alavi Tabar, Tehran, August 21, 2004. Interview with Amir Mohebian, August 19, 2004.

39. Interview with Mohammad Reza Tajik.

40. Interview with Amir Mohebian.

41. Interview with Ali Reza Alavi Tabar. Interview with Amir Mohebian.

42. Interview with Dennis Ross.

43. David Makovsky, *Making Peace with the PLO* (Boulder, CO: Westview, 1996), 108.

44. Interview with Itamar Rabinovich, former advisor to Rabin and Israeli ambassador to the United States, Tel Aviv, October 17, 2004.

45. Makovsky, *Making Peace with the PLO*, 83.

46. Shimon Peres, *The New Middle East* (New York: Henry Holt, 1993), 3. Interview with Shai Feldman, Jaffee Center for Strategic Studies, Tel Aviv, October 27, 2004.

47. Interview with General David Ivry, head of Israel's Iran committee, Tel Aviv, October 19, 2004.

48. Israel Shahak, *Open Secrets—Israeli Nuclear and Foreign Policies* (London: Pluto, 1997), 82–83.

49. Interviews with Eynat Shlein, First Secretary, Embassy of Israel, Washington, DC, June 1, 2004; Shai Feldman; and Michael Eisenstadt, Washington Institute for Near East Policy, Washington, DC, June 2, 2004.

50. Charles Smith, *Palestine and the Arab-Israeli Conflict* (Boston: Bedford St. Martin's, 2001), 440. Savir, *The Process*, 5. Makovsky, *Making Peace with the PLO*, 108. Kimche, *The Last Option*, 314.

51. Interview with Efraim Halevi.

52. Interview with David Kimche, Tel Aviv, October 22, 2004.

53. Emma Murphy, "The Impact of the Arab-Israeli Peace Process on the International Security and Economic Relations of the Persian Gulf," *Iranian Journal of International Affairs* 2 (Summer 1996): 437.

54. Makovsky, *Making Peace with the PLO*, 112.

55. "Iran Looms as a Growing Strategic Threat for Israel," *Jerusalem Post*, November 21, 1991.

56. Peres, *New Middle East*, 43.

57. Parsi, *Treacherous Alliance*, 162.

58. "Israel Seeking to Convince U.S. That West Is Threatened by Iran," *Washington Post*, March 13, 1993.

59. Interview with Gary Sick.

60. "Israel Focuses on the Threat Beyond the Periphery," *New York Times*, November 8, 1992.

61. Israel Shahak, "How Israel's Strategy Favors Iraq over Iran," *Middle East International* no. 446, March 19, 1993, 91.

62. Reuters, October 25, 1992. "Iran Greatest Threat, Will Have Nukes by '99," Associated Press, February 12, 1993.

63. Shai Feldman, "Confidence Building and Verification: Prospects in the Middle East," JCSS Study no. 25 (Tel Aviv: Jaffee Center for Strategic Studies, 1994), 25. Peres, *New Middle East*, 41.

64. Interview with David Makovsky, Washington Institute for Near East Policy, Washington, DC, June 3, 2004.

65. Peres, *New Middle East,* 83.

66. "Israel Seeking to Convince U.S. That West Is Threatened by Iran," *Washington Post,* March 13, 1993.

67. "Israel Focuses on the Threat Beyond the Periphery."

68. Interview with former assistant secretary of state Martin Indyk, Washington, DC, March 4, 2004.

69. Interview with Kenneth Pollack, Washington, DC, November 29, 2004.

70. Interview with Keith Weissman, March 25, 2004.

71. Ibid.

72. Interview with Shlomo Brom.

73. Interview with Ranaan Gissin, Jerusalem, October 31, 2004.

74. Interview with Efraim Halevi.

75. Interview with Itamar Rabinovich.

76. Interview with Efraim Inbar, Begin-Sadat Center, Jerusalem, October 19, 2004.

77. Interview with Martin Indyk. Interview with Shai Feldman.

78. "Israel Seeking to Convince U.S. That West Is Threatened by Iran."

79. Interview with Efraim Inbar.

80. Murphy, "Impact of the Arab-Israeli Peace Process," 426.

81. Pollack, *Persian Puzzle,* 263.

82. Chubin, "Iran's Security Policy," 10. Interview with Ali Reza Alavi Tabar.

83. Interview with Hadi Nejad-Hosseinian.

84. Interview with Mahmoud Sariolghalam, Tehran, August 18, 2004.

85. David Menashri, "Revolution at a Crossroads," Policy Paper 43 (Washington Institute for Near East Policy, 1997), 81. Shaul Bakhash, "Iran: Slouching Toward the Twenty-First Century," in *The Middle East Enters the Twenty-First Century,* ed. Robert O. Freedman (Gainesville: University Press of Florida, 2002), 57–58.

86. Interview with Mohammad Reza Tajik.

87. Clark Staten, "Israeli-PLO Peace Agreement—Cause of Further Terrorism?," *Emergency-Net NEWS,* October 12, 1993.

88. Interview with Masoud Eslami of the Iranian Foreign Ministry, Tehran, August 23, 2004.

89. Reuters, March 5, 1994.

90. Interviews with Mohammad Reza Tajik; A. A. Kazemi, former Iranian diplomat during the early years of the Khomeini regime, Tehran, August 16, 2004.

91. Interview with Mustafa Zahrani of the Iranian Foreign Ministry, New York, February 26, 2004.

92. Interview with Masloud Eslami, August 23, 2004.

93. Houchang Chehabi, *Distant Relations: Iran and Lebanon in the Last 500 Years* (New York: I. B. Tauris, 2006), 230.

94. Robert O. Freedman, ed., *The Middle East Enters the Twenty-First Century* (Gainesville: University Press of Florida, 2002), 58. Interview with Shlomo Brom.

95. Interview with Iranian political strategist, March 2004.

96. Makovsky, *Making Peace with the PLO,* 112.

97. Interview with Itamar Rabinovich.

98. Interview with Israeli diplomat, Tel Aviv, October 18, 2004.

99. Interview with Ephraim Kam, Jaffee Center for Strategic Studies, Tel Aviv, October 26, 2004.

100. Feldman, "Confidence Building and Verification," 199.

101. Shahak, *Open Secrets,* 64.

102. Eric Margolis, "Israel and Iran: The Best of Enemies," *Toronto Sun,* July 5, 1998.

103. Interview with David Ivry.

104. Interview with General Amos Gilad, Tel Aviv, October 31, 2004.

105. Interview with Yitzak Segev, former Israeli military attaché to Iran, Tel Aviv, October 17, 2004.

106. Interview with Shai Feldman.

107. Interview with former Israeli minister of finance Dan Meridor, Tel Aviv, October 27, 2004.

108. Interview with Yossi Alpher, October 27, 2004. "There was a fear that if America talks to Iran, Israel will be left out in the cold," explained Gerald Steinberg, professor at Bar Ilan University in Israel. "The Great Satan will make up with Iran and forget about Israel" (interview with Gerald Steinberg, Jerusalem, October 28, 2004).

109. Interview with Israeli diplomat.

110. Farideh Farhi, "Economic Statecraft or Interest Group Politics: Understanding U.S. Sanctions on Iran," *Iranian Journal of International Affairs* 1 (Spring 1997): 67.

111. Reuters, September 12, 1994.

112. Murphy, "Impact of the Arab-Israeli Peace Process," 426. Interview with Keith Weissman of the American Israel Public Affairs Committee (AIPAC), Washington, DC, March 25, 2004.

113. Interview with Kenneth Pollack.

114. Text of Warren Christopher speech, "Maintaining the Momentum for Peace in the Middle East," Georgetown University, October 25, 1994.

115. *Mideast Mirror,* March 10, 1995. White and Logan, *Remaking the Middle East,* 199.

116. Interview with Kenneth Pollack.

117. Lamis Andoni, "When Iran Hedges Closer, U.S. Pushes Away," *Christian Science Monitor,* April 7, 1995.

118. Colin Barraclough, "Iran Seeks Oil Partners, U.S. Firms Can't Join the Dance," *Christian Science Monitor,* December 12, 1995.

119. Pollack, *Persian Puzzle,* 271.

120. John Greenwald, "Down Goes the Deal," *Time,* March 27, 1995.

121. "Clinton's Anti-Iran Move," *Christian Science Monitor,* May 2, 1995.

122. Pollack, *Persian Puzzle,* 273.

123. "Clinton's Anti-Iran Move."

124. Interview with Dennis Ross.

125. Interview with Keith Weissman. G. Moffett, "Push to Widen Libya Sanctions Riles U.S. Allies," *Christian Science Monitor,* January 24, 1996. Pollack, *Persian Puzzle,* 270.

126. Gary Sick, "The Future of U.S.-Iran Relations," *Middle East Economic Survey,* June 21, 1999.

127. Interview with Ephraim Sneh, October 31, 2004.

THREE The Epic Mistake

1. Interview with former assistant secretary of state Martin Indyk, Washington, DC, March 4, 2004.

2. Ibid.

3. Interview with General David Ivry, head of Israel's Iran committee, Tel Aviv, October 19, 2004.

4. Interview with Marshal Breger, professor at Catholic University, Washington, DC, October 11, 2004.

5. Interview with Phil Gordon, senior director for the Middle East at the National Security Council under President Obama, September 8, 2015.

6. Kayhan Barzegar, "Détente in Khatami's Foreign Policy and Its Impact on Improvement of Iran-Saudi Relations," *Discourse: An Iranian Quarterly* 2 (2002): 160–167.

7. Gareth Porter, "How Neocons Sabotaged Iran's Help on al-Qaeda," Inter Press Service, February 23, 2006. Flynt Leverett, "Illusion and Reality," *American Prospect,* September 12, 2006.

8. Interview with Yossi (Joseph) Alpher, former Mossad official and senior advisor to Ehud Barak, Tel Aviv, October 27, 2004. Patrick Bishop, "Worried Israel Feels Spurned as the West Courts Iran," *Daily Telegraph,* September 26, 2001.

9. Letter by the Project for the New American Century to President George Bush, September 20, 2001. Other prominent neoconservatives who courted the Bush administration with the idea of invading Iraq include Bernard Lewis and Fouad Ajami; see Porter, "How Neocons Sabotaged Iran's Help on al-Qaeda." Kenneth Pollack, *The Persian Puzzle* (New York: Random House, 2004), 346–347.

10. Speech by Ambassador James Dobbins to the New America Foundation, Washington, DC, August 24, 2006. Interview with Javad Zarif, New York, October 12, 2006. Pollack, *Persian Puzzle,* 347. Michael Hirsh and Maziar Bahari, "Blowup? America's Hidden War with Iran," *Newsweek,* February 19, 2007.

11. Speech by James Dobbins.

12. James Bennet, "Sharon Invokes Munich in Warning U.S. on 'Appeasement,'" *New York Times,* October 5, 2001. Jack Donnelly, "Nation Set to Push Sharon on Agreement," *Boston Globe,* October 10, 2001. Interview with Ambassador James Dobbins, October 24, 2006. Porter, "How Neocons Sabotaged Iran's Help on al-Qaeda."

13. Ali Ansari, *Confronting Iran* (New York: Basic Books, 2006), 186. Pollack, *Persian Puzzle,* 186–187. Scott Peterson, "Pragmatism May Trump Zeal as Iran's Power Grows," *Christian Science Monitor,* July 6, 2006. Michael Gordon, "U.S. Conferred with

Iran Before Iraq Invasion, Book Says," *New York Times*, March 6, 2016. Interview with Javad Zarif, New York, April 1, 2004.

14. Interview with James Dobbins.

15. Gareth Porter, "Burnt Offering," *American Prospect*, June 6, 2006.

16. Neil Mackay, "Bush Planned Iraq 'Regime Change' Before Becoming President," *Sunday Herald*, September 15, 2002.

17. "Rebuilding America's Defenses: Strategy, Forces and Resources for a New Century," Project for the New American Century, Washington, DC, September 2000.

18. Ken Adelman, "Cakewalk in Iraq," *Washington Post*, February 13, 2002.

19. Pollack, *Persian Puzzle*, 354–355.

20. Gregory Beals, "A Missed Opportunity with Iran," *Newsday*, February 19, 2006. Bernard Gwertzman, "Leverett: Bush Administration 'Not Serious' About Dealing with Iran," Council on Foreign Relations, March 31, 2006. Gordon Corera, "Iran's Gulf of Misunderstanding with U.S.," BBC, September 25, 2006.

21. Gareth Porter, "Cheney-Led 'Cabal' Blocked 2003 Nuclear Talks with Iran," Inter Press Service, May 28, 2006.

22. Trita Parsi, *Treacherous Alliance: The Secret Dealings of Israel, Iran, and the United States* (New Haven, CT: Yale University Press, 2007), 247.

23. Guy Dinmore, "Washington Hardliners Wary of Engaging with Iran," *Financial Times*, March 16, 2004. Corera, "Iran's Gulf of Misunderstanding with U.S." Interview with Larry Wilkerson, October 16, 2006. Porter, "Burnt Offering" and "Cheney-Led 'Cabal.'"

24. Jim Lobe, "Neo-Cons Move Quickly on Iran," Inter Press Service, May 26, 2003. Interview with Larry Wilkerson.

25. Dinmore, "Washington Hardliners Wary of Engaging with Iran." Interview with Larry Wilkerson.

26. Glenn Kessler, "In 2003, U.S. Spurned Iran's Offer of Dialogue," *Washington Post*, June 18, 2006. Gwertzman, "Leverett." Corera, "Iran's Gulf of Misunderstanding with U.S."

27. Corera, "Iran's Gulf of Misunderstanding with U.S."

28. Interview with Hadi Nejad-Hosseinian, Tehran, August 12, 2004.

FOUR American Disorder

1. Ryan Cooper, "Face It: America Is Terrible at Nation-Building," *Week*, October 29, 2015. Gian Gentile, "America's Nation-Building at Gunpoint," *Los Angeles Times*, August 13, 2013.

2. "Public Attitudes Toward the War in Iraq: 2003–2008," Pew Research Center, March 19, 2008. Lydia Saad, "Republicans and Democrats Disagree on Iraq War," Gallup News Service, September 28, 2006. "Army Chief Ray Odierno Warns Military Suicides 'Not Going to End' After War Is Over," *Huffington Post*, September 25, 2013.

3. "More Troops Lost to Suicide than Combat in Iraq, Afghanistan for Second Year in a Row," *CQ Weekly*, May 25, 2011. Ed Pilkington, "U.S. Military Struggling

to Stop Suicide Epidemic Among War Veterans," *Guardian,* February 1, 2013. Paul Rieckhoff, "15-Month Tours in Iraq? The War Is Breaking Our Military," *Huffington Post,* May 25, 2011. Gregg Zoroya, "Repeated Deployments Weigh Heavily on U.S. Troops," *USA Today,* January 13, 2010.

4. Mark Landler, *Alter Egos: Hillary Clinton, Barack Obama, and the Twilight Struggle over American Power* (New York: Penguin Random House, 2016), Kindle Android version.

5. "Iran's Nuclear Program Resolved: When Will That Time Come for Israel's Nuclear Warheads?," Khamenei.ir, May 28, 2016, http://english.khamenei.ir/news/3854 /Iran-s-nuclear-program-resolved-When-will-that-time-come-for.

6. Michael Gordon, "U.S. Conferred with Iran Before Iraq Invasion, Book Says," *New York Times,* March 6, 2016.

7. Dennis Ross, "How Obama Got to 'Yes' on Iran: The Inside Story," *Politico,* October 08, 2015.

8. "Public Attitudes Toward the War in Iraq." James A. Baker III and Lee H. Hamilton, "The Iraq Study Group Report," United States Institute for Peace, December 2006. "Five Ex-Secretaries of State Urge Talks with Iran," Associated Press, September 15, 2008.

9. Democratic Debate Transcript, Austin, Texas, Council on Foreign Relations, February 21, 2008. Michael Cooper, "In AIPAC Speech, McCain Hits Obama on Iran, Iraq," *New York Times,* June 2, 2008. Rick Klein, "Clinton: Obama 'Irresponsible and Naïve,'" *ABC News,* July 24, 2007.

10. Tom Donilon, "The United States and the Asia-Pacific in 2013," Address to the Asia Society in New York, March 11, 2013. Kurt Campbell and Brian Andrews, "Explaining the U.S. 'Pivot' to Asia," Chatham House, August 2013. David Sanger, "ISIS Fight Raises Fears That Efforts to Curb Iran Will Slip," *New York Times,* September 12, 2014.

11. Comments by Ben Rhodes at the Aspen Ideas Festival in Aspen, Colorado, June 29, 2015.

12. Remarks by President Obama to the Australian Parliament, Canberra, Australia, November 17, 2011.

13. Jeffrey Goldberg, "The Obama Doctrine," *Atlantic,* April 2016.

14. Comments by Ben Rhodes. Interview with Phil Gordon, former senior director for the Middle East at the National Security Council, September 8, 2015. Interview with former senior White House official, September 2015.

15. Landler, *Alter Egos.*

16. Angelique Chrisafis, "Sarkozy Admits France Made Mistakes over Tunisia," *Guardian,* January 24, 2011.

17. Mark Mazzetti, "Obama Faults Spy Agencies' Performance in Gauging Mideast Unrest, Officials Say," *New York Times,* February 5, 2011. Helene Cooper, "The United States Supports, Um, Well . . . When It Comes to Diplomacy in Egypt, Words Often Fail," *New York Times,* January 30, 2011. Deborah Amos, "Is the Arab Spring Good or Bad for the U.S.?," NPR, January 9, 2012.

18. Helene Cooper, Mark Landler, and David Sanger, "Crisis Highlights Policy Rifts in Obama's Team," *New York Times*, February 14, 2011. Cooper, "The United States Supports, Um, Well." David Sanger, "Obama Hails Outcome in Egypt, but Sets out Benchmarks for the Military," *New York Times*, February 12, 2011.

19. Cooper, Landler, and Sanger, "Crisis Highlights Policy Rifts in Obama's Team." Mimi Hall, "U.S. Watches and Waits During Egyptian Conflict," *USA Today*, February 1, 2011.

20. "Hosni Mubarak Resigns as President," *Al Jazeera*, February 11, 2011. Sanger, "Obama Hails Outcome in Egypt."

21. "Obama Calls for Peaceful Response in Middle East," *Daily News Egypt*, February 16, 2011.

22. Joel Gulhane, "Obama Re-Election Impact on Egypt," *Daily News Egypt*, November 7, 2012. Sanger, "Obama Hails Outcome in Egypt." Jason Ditz, "Israeli President, Others Slam Obama for 'Betrayal' of Mubarak," Antiwar.com, January 31, 2011.

23. Trita Parsi, *A Single Roll of the Dice: Obama's Diplomacy with Iran* (New Haven, CT: Yale University Press, 2012), 226.

24. Anthony Shadid, "Egypt Shuts Door on Dissent as U.S. Officials Back Away," *Washington Post*, March 19, 2007. Steven Weisman, "U.S. Muffles Sweeping Call to Democracy in Mideast," *New York Times*, March 12, 2004. Martin Indyk, "Back to the Bazaar," *Foreign Affairs* 81, no. 1 (2002): 75–88.

25. Hall, "U.S. Watches and Waits."

FIVE A New Year's Greeting

Sections of this chapter are partially adapted from Trita Parsi, *A Single Roll of the Dice: Obama's Diplomacy with Iran* (New Haven, CT: Yale University Press, 2012), chs. 6–7.

1. Parsi, *Single Roll of the Dice*, 45.

2. Ibid., 9–10.

3. Ibid., 62.

4. Farideh Farhi, "And Happy Nowruz to You Too Mr. Obama!," *Informed Comment: Global Affairs*, March 20, 2009, http://icga.blogspot.com/2009/03/on-khameneis-response-to-obama.html.

5. Farideh Farhi, "On Khamenei's Response to Obama," *Informed Comment: Global Affairs*, March 22, 2009, http://icga.blogspot.com/2009/03/on-khameneis-response-to-obama.html. Interview with Farideh Farhi, June 7, 2010.

6. "Text of Khamenei's Speech to U.S. President," BBC, March 22, 2009.

7. Interview with Peter Beinart, December 10, 2015.

8. Amir Tibon and Tal Shalev, "Scenes from a Marriage," *Huffington Post*, November 12, 2015.

9. Parsi, *Single Roll of the Dice*, 71.

10. Tibon and Shalev, "Scenes from a Marriage."

11. "Peres to Iran: Reclaim Your Rightful Place Among 'Enlightened Nations,'" *Haaretz*, March 21, 2009. "With Obama to Iran," *Haaretz*, March 24, 2009. Interview

with former Israeli negotiator, July 20, 2010. Helene Cooper and David E. Sanger, "Obama's Message to Iran Is Opening Bid in Diplomatic Drive," *New York Times,* March 21, 2009.

12. Asef Bayat, "Iran: A Green Wave for Life and Liberty," OpenDemocracy.org, July 7, 2009.

13. Trita Parsi, "Why Iran's Supreme Leader Wants a Nuclear Deal," *Atlantic,* March 26, 2015.

14. "Codel Kyl's Meeting with Prime Minister Netanyahu: What Will the U.S. Do About Iran?," classified U.S. State Department cable, April 28, 2009.

15. David Sanger, "After Israeli Visit, a Diplomatic Sprint on Iran," *New York Times,* May 20, 2009.

16. Herb Keinon, "Iran Talks Should Last 12 Weeks Max," *Jerusalem Post,* December 18, 2008. "Israel Calls for Time-limit on Iran Talks," United Press International, May 7, 2009. Barak Ravid, "U.S. Puts October Deadline on Iran Talks," *Haaretz,* May 11, 2009. Transcript of State Department press briefing, May 14, 2009.

17. Transcript of remarks by President Obama and Prime Minister Netanyahu, May 18, 2009.

18. "Codels Ackerman and Casey Meetings with Prime Minister Netanyahu," classified U.S. State Department cable, June 2, 2009.

19. Sheryl Gay Stolberg, "Obama Tells Netanyahu He Has an Iran Timetable," *New York Times,* May 19, 2009.

20. Conversation with senior White House official, July 30, 2015.

21. "The Populist's Problem," *Economist,* May 5, 2009. Nader Habibi, "The Ahmadinejad Presidency and the Future of Iran's Economy," *Georgetown Journal of International Affairs,* January 28, 2016. "Iran Says It Can No Longer Afford Ahmadinejad's Cash Handouts," Agence France Presse, May 19, 2015. Interview with Mohammad Nahavandian, chief of staff to President Hassan Rouhani, September 24, 2015.

22. Interview with former U.S. State Department Iran Desk officer, June 14, 2010. "Mousavi: I Stand Firm on Principles, Diplomacy Will Relieve Tensions," Mehr News Agency, April 6, 2009 (Farvardin 17, 1388).

23. Parisa Hafezi, "Iran Candidate Backs Nuclear Talks with the West," Reuters, May 29, 2009. Interview with senior advisor to former president Mohammad Khatami and opposition leader Mir Hossein Mousavi, July 23, 2010. Interview with campaign worker at Mousavi's headquarters, July 28, 2010.

24. Interview with Mir Hossein Mousavi. Interview with campaign worker.

25. Parsi, *Single Roll of the Dice,* 89.

26. "Larijani Criticizes the Guardian Council, IRIB," *Press TV,* June 21, 2009.

27. Scott Wilson, "Muted Response Reflects U.S. Diplomatic Dilemma," *Washington Post,* June 15, 2009. Iason Athanasiadis, "Iran Protest Biggest Since Revolution," *Washington Times,* June 16, 2009. Interview with Michael Ratney, August 10, 2010.

28. David Weigel, "Neocons, House GOPers Demand Obama Take Moussavi's Side," *Washington Independent,* June 16, 2009. Manu Raju, "GOP Tries to Find Its Pitch on Iran," *Politico,* June 17, 2009, http://www.politico.com/news/stories/0609/23827

.html. Anne Flaherty, "House Condemns Tehran Crackdown on Protesters," Associated Press, June 19, 2009. Wilson, "Muted Response."

29. Interview with former Iranian lawmaker and pro-democracy activist, September 17, 2010. Interview with Mir Hossein Mousavi. Interview with Professor Ahmad Sadri, August 10, 2010.

30. Trita Parsi, "What Obama Must Do Now on Iran," *Christian Science Monitor,* June 22, 2009.

31. Borzou Daragahi, "Iran: Report of Second Letter from Obama to Tehran," *Los Angeles Times,* September 2, 2009. Interview with senior Obama administration official, October 27, 2010.

32. Interview with U.S. senior Senate staffer, August 20, 2010.

SIX A Single Roll of the Dice

1. David Sanger, "Obama Order Sped up Wave of Cyberattacks Against Iran," *New York Times,* June 1, 2012.

2. Mark Fitzpatrick, *Iran's Nuclear, Chemical and Biological Capabilities* (London: International Institute for Strategic Studies, 2011).

3. Interview with senior State Department official, July 22, 2010. Interview with State Department official, July 21, 2010.

4. Thomas Erdbrink and William Branigin, "In Iran, Nuclear Issue Is Also a Medical One," *Washington Post,* December 20, 2009. Interview with Ambassador Ali Asghar Soltanieh, June 30, 2010. "IAEA Obligated to Supply Nuclear Fuel," *Tehran Times,* February 10, 2010.

5. Interview with senior State Department official, July 22, 2010. Interview with State Department official, July 21, 2010. Interview with senior EU official, June 14, 2010.

6. Interview with State Department official, July 21, 2010. Interview with senior EU diplomat, May 27, 2010. Interview with senior EU official, June 14, 2010. Interview with senior State Department official, October 27, 2010. Interview with Iranian nuclear negotiator, May 27, 2010.

7. Interview with Iranian nuclear negotiator. Interview with senior State Department official, July 22, 2010. Interview with Ali Asghar Soltanieh, June 30, 2010.

8. Interview with senior State Department official, October 27, 2010. Interview with State Department official, July 21, 2010. "U/S Tauscher's Meetings with FS Miliband and Other HMG Officials," classified U.S. State Department cable, September 22, 2009.

9. Interview with senior State Department official, October 27, 2010. Interview with State Department Iran Desk officer, June 14, 2010. Interview with Iranian nuclear negotiator.

10. Interview with State Department official, October 7, 2010. Interview with State Department Iran Desk officer. Interview with senior State Department official, July 22, 2010. Interview with senior EU official, June 14, 2010. Steven Erlanger and Mark Landler, "Iran Agrees to Send Enriched Uranium to Russia," *New York Times,* Octo-

ber 1, 2009. Interview with Ali Asghar Soltanieh, June 30, 2010. Email and phone exchange with Olli Heinonen, February 21, 2011. Interview with Ambassador Gerard Araud, June 15, 2010.

11. Interview with senior EU official, June 14, 2010. Interview with senior State Department official, October 27, 2010.

12. Interview with French diplomat, July 6, 2010. Interview with Ali Asghar Soltanieh, June 30, 2010. Interview with senior EU diplomat, June 15, 2010. Interview with senior State Department official, October 27, 2010. Interview with senior State Department official, July 22, 2010.

13. Interview with Iranian nuclear negotiator. Interview with Ali Asghar Soltanieh, July 1, 2010.

14. Interview with Ambassador Mohammad Khazaee, June 15, 2010. Interview with senior State Department official, July 22, 2010. Interview with Iranian nuclear negotiator. Interview with Ali Asghar Soltanieh, July 1, 2010.

15. Interview with senior State Department official, July 22, 2010. Interview with Ali Asghar Soltanieh, July 1, 2010. Conversations with Obama administration officials, summer and fall of 2010. Interview with senior Senate staffer, August 20, 2010.

16. International Atomic Energy Agency, "IAEA Receives Initial Iranian Response on Proposal to Supply Nuclear Fuel to Research Reactor," news release, October 29, 2009, http://www.iaea.org/newscenter/pressreleases/2009/prn200914.html. "U.S. Tells Iran Nuclear Deal Offer Won't Be Changed," Reuters, November 5, 2009. Interview with Ali Asghar Soltanieh, June 30, 2010. Interview with senior EU official, June 14, 2010.

17. *Charlie Rose,* PBS, November 6, 2009.

18. Interview with former Iranian diplomat, June 30, 2010. Glenn Kessler, "As Standoff with Iran Continues, U.S. Prepares Targeted Sanctions," *Washington Post,* December 30, 2009.

19. Mir Hossein Moussavi, statement, October 30, 2009, www.kalame.ir.

20. Interview with former Iranian diplomat, June 30, 2010. Interview with Ambassador Peter Wittig, July 7, 2010. Interview with senior State Department official, September 10, 2010. *Charlie Rose.* Interview with senior advisor to former president Mohammad Khatami and opposition leader Mir Hossein Moussavi, July 23, 2010.

21. Interview with Ahmad Sadri, August 10, 2010. Discussion with senior State Department official, November 9, 2010. Interview with former Iranian diplomat, June 30, 2010. Interview with William D. Wunderle, foreign affairs specialist, Joint Staff, September 2, 2010. Interview with Professor Ali Ansari, September 17, 2010. *Charlie Rose.* Interview with Peter Wittig. Interview with Ali Asghar Soltanieh, June 30, 2010. Interview with Robert Einhorn, November 24, 2015. Interview with David Miliband, July 7, 2011. Interview with senior State Department official, July 22, 2010.

22. Interview with senior State Department official, September 12, 2010. Interview with Michael Ratney of the State Department, August 10, 2010. Interview with former Iran Desk officer at the State Department, June 14, 2010. "Staffdel Kessler Discusses Iran with MFA, ENI, PD," classified U.S. State Department cable, January 22, 2010. Interview with Ambassador Pierre Vimont, July 26, 2010.

23. Samuel Charap and Brian Katulis, "Talking to Iran Has Helped the U.S.," *Guardian,* March 4, 2010. Trita Parsi, "How Obama Became Vulnerable on Iran," Salon.com, January 31, 2012.

24. Seymour Hersh, "Iran and the Bomb: How Real Is the Nuclear Threat?" *New Yorker,* June 6, 2011. Interview with former Obama White House official, July 31, 2015.

25. Interview with senior Pentagon official, September 18, 2015. Interview with Deputy Secretary of State Bill Burns, December 21, 2015. Interview with senior White House official, January 12, 2016.

26. David Sanger, "Obama Set to Offer Stricter Nuclear Deal to Iran, Officials Say," *New York Times,* October 28, 2010. John Vinocur, "Loopholes Let Iran off the Hook," *New York Times,* August 3, 2010. Hersh, "Iran and the Bomb."

27. Hersh, "Iran and the Bomb."

28. "Israeli Strike Would 'Ensure' Iran Seeks Bomb, Warns Blix," Agence France Presse, November 12, 2011. Matthew Lee, "AP Sources: U.S. Sees Iran's Leaders Split on Nukes," Associated Press, February 17, 2011.

29. Josh Rogin, "Bush's CIA Director: We Determined Attacking Iran Was a Bad Idea," *Foreign Policy,* February 19, 2012. Interview with senior White House official, September 8, 2015. Interview with Chris Backemeyer, December 3, 2015.

30. "Obama Accepts Nobel Prize," *Financial Times,* December 10, 2009. Interview with EU diplomat, June 21, 2010. Interview with senior State Department official, September 12, 2010. "Codel Skelton's Meeting with Prime Minister Netanyahu," classified U.S. State Department cable, December 23, 2009. "U/S Tauscher's December 1–2 Visit to Israel," classified U.S. State Department cable, December 22, 2009. Dan Williams, "Israel Urges Iran Oil Embargo Even Without U.N. Okay," Reuters, February 22, 2010. Roshanak Taghavi, "Iran, Bracing for Sanctions, Presses Its Parliament for Gas Money," *Christian Science Monitor,* January 5, 2010.

31. Kevin Bogardus, "House Readies Iran Sanctions on Gas Imports," *Hill,* December 15, 2009. Interview with senior Senate staffer, August 20, 2010. Laura Rozen, "Berman: Iran Sanctions Bill Empowers Obama," *Politico,* December 15, 2009, http://www.politico.com/blogs/laurarozen/1209/Berman_says_Iran_sanctions_bill _empowers_Obama_Iran_policy.html. Howard Berman, speech given at Center for Strategic and International Studies, Washington, DC, September 21, 2010. With J Street supporting the sanctions, Americans for Peace Now became the sole major Jewish organization opposing the sanctions measure. Ron Kampeas, "As Zero Hour Nears, Differences Emerge on Sanctions," Jewish Telegraphic Agency, January 5, 2010.

32. Josh Rogin, "Iran Sanctions Bill Update: Full Speed Ahead," *Foreign Policy,* January 19, 2010. Interview with senior Senate staffer, August 20, 2010. Josh Rogin, "Senators Pressure Obama on Iran Sanctions," *Foreign Policy,* January 27, 2010, and "Iran Sanctions Bill Benefits from Joe-mentum," *Foreign Policy,* January 29, 2010. Congressman Howard Berman (D-CA), Chairman, U.S. House Committee on Foreign Affairs, "Iran: Addressing the Nuclear Threat," St. Regis Hotel, Washington, DC, September 21, 2010. Interview with senior Senate staffer, September 2, 2010. Interview with Gerard Araud.

33. Arshad Mohammed, "China to Send Lower-Level Envoy to Talks on Iran," Reuters, January 14, 2010. Flynt Leverett and Hillary Mann Leverett, "'Narrow Stripes of Rationality' on the Iranian Nuclear Issue," Race for Iran, January 19, 2010, http://www.raceforiran.com/%E2%80%9Cnarrow-stripes-of-rationality%E2%80%9D-on-the-nuclear-issue. "Russia: Moving Beyond Bilateral Issues, Miliband Reopened Dialogue," classified U.S. State Department cable, November 5, 2009.

34. "Iran to U.N.: We Will Increase Uranium Enrichment," Fox News, February 8, 2010.

35. The letter to the IAEA can be found at http://graphics8.nytimes.com/packages/pdf/world/2009/IAEA-Letter.pdf. Helene Cooper, "U.S. Encounters Limits of Iran Engagement Policy," New York Times, February 16, 2010. Interview with Gary Samore, February 5, 2016.

36. "Saudi Foreign Ministry Pressing China to Stop Iranian Proliferation, Concerned About TSA Regulations," classified U.S. State Department cable, January 26, 2010. "Scenesetter for Secretary Clinton's Feb 15–16 Visit to Saudi Arabia," classified U.S. State Department cable, February 11, 2010. Kate Mackenzie, "Oil at the Heart of Latest Iranian Sanction Efforts," Financial Times, March 8, 2010. Interview with Rayed Krimly, November 25, 2010. Interview with Gerard Araud. Interview with Xavier Chatel, June 15, 2010.

37. Chris Strathmann and Kate McCarthy, "Netanyahu Calls for 'Crippling Sanctions' Against Iran," ABC News, April 19, 2010. "Russia, China Push Iran to Change Nuclear Stance," Reuters, March 24, 2010. "Iran's Top Nuclear Negotiator Heads to China," Associated Press, March 31, 2010. Julian Borger and Ewen MacAskill, "China Supports Barack Obama's Call for New Iran Sanctions," Guardian, March 31, 2010. Colum Lynch, "U.S. Urges U.N. Security Council to Impose Arms Embargo, Other Measures on Iran," Washington Post, April 15, 2010.

38. Louis Charbonneau, "Obama, Medvedev Discuss 'Progress' on Iran Sanctions," Reuters, May 13, 2010. "Brazil's Lula Arrives in Iran for Key Nuclear Talks," Agence France Presse, May 15, 2010. Viola Gienger, "Clinton Urges Action from Turkey, Brazil on Iran," Bloomberg, April 13, 2010.

39. Interview with State Department official, August 3, 2015.

40. Classified briefing for the Brazilian diplomatic corps by Celso Amorim, May 18, 2010. Interview with Celso Amorim, July 15, 2010. Interview with senior advisor to Lula, July 15, 2010. Şahin Alpay, "Ahmadinejad's Visit to Turkey Is Welcome," Today's Zaman, August 11, 2008. Sabrina Tavernise, "Turkish Leader Volunteers to Be U.S.-Iran Mediator," New York Times, November 11, 2008. Borzou Daragahi and Ramin Mostaghim, "Visit Raises Speculation over Turkish-Mediated U.S.-Iran Talks," Los Angeles Times, March 10, 2009. Interview with Cengiz Candar, June 18, 2010. "Turkey Chastises the West on Iran," BBC, October 26, 2009. "We watch the relations between Iran and U.S. with great concern," Mr. Erdogan said. "We expect such issues to be resolved at the table. Wars are never solutions in this age" (Tavernise, "Turkish Leader Volunteers to Be U.S.-Iran Mediator"). "Turkey-Iran Relations: Motivations, Limitations, and Implications," classified U.S. State Department cable, December 4, 2009.

A senior Turkish diplomat argued that war with Iran would have catastrophic consequences that would not even be comparable to Iraq (interview with senior Turkish diplomat, July 13, 2010). Interview with senior Turkish diplomat, August 15, 2010.

41. "Staffdel Kessler Engages the French on Iran, Sanctions and Afghanistan," classified U.S. State Department cable, January 22, 2010. "Amb. Rice's Meeting with Brazilian PermRep," February 16, 2010. "Brazil: Ambassador's Meetings with MRE Under Secretaries for Political Affairs," classified U.S. State Department cable, February 19, 2010. Interview with senior Brazilian diplomat, June 21, 2010.

42. Interview with senior advisor to Lula. Interview with Celso Amorim. Interview with Iranian nuclear negotiator. Interview with senior Turkish diplomat, July 13, 2010. State Department, "Background Briefing on Nuclear Nonproliferation Efforts with Regard to Iran and the Brazil/Turkey Agreement," May 28, 2010, http://www.state .gov/r/pa/prs/ps/2010/05/142375.htm. Viola Gienger, "Clinton Urges Action from Turkey, Brazil on Iran," Bloomberg, April 13, 2010. Charbonneau, "Obama, Medvedev Discuss 'Progress.'" Ilhan Tanir, "Turkey: 'There Is No Deadline for Iran,'" Hurriyet Daily News, April 16, 2010.

43. Laura Rozen, "Obama WMD Czar Discusses Iran Nuclear Program," Politico, May 11, 2010.

44. "Erdogan Calls a Trip to Iran 'Unlikely,'" BBC Persian, May 14, 2010. Interview with Celso Amorim.

45. Celso Amorim, presentation at Carnegie Endowment for International Peace 2011, Carnegie International Nuclear Policy Conference, Washington DC, March 28, 2011. Interview with Celso Amorim. Interview with Iranian nuclear negotiator.

46. Parisa Hafezi and Fernando Exman, "Iran Agrees to Atom Fuel Deal with Turkey, Brazil," Reuters, May 17, 2010. "Brazil's FM to G5+1: Study Contents of Deal Carefully," Islamic Republic News Agency, May 17, 2010. Stefan Simanowitz, "ElBaradei: To Dismiss Iranian Nuclear Agreement Would Be 'a Dead End Street,'" Payvand, May 18, 2010, http://www.payvand.com/news/10/may/1209.html. Daren Butler, "U.N.'s Ban Hopes Iran Deal May Bring Atom Settlement," Reuters, May 21, 2010. "The Decisive Support of 234 MPs for the Nuclear Swap Deal," Islamic Republic News Agency, May 18, 2010. "Iranian Political Activists Support Nuclear Swap Agreement," Radio Zamaneh, May 17, 2010. Interview with former Iranian lawmaker and pro-democracy activist, September 17, 2010. Interview with Ataollah Mohajerani, September 18, 2010.

47. "Timeline: Brazil-Iranian Relations," Al Jazeera, May 16, 2010. Peter Baker and David E. Sanger, "U.S. Makes Concessions to Russia for Iran Sanctions," New York Times, May 21, 2010. Interview with European diplomat, July 7, 2010. Interview with Russian diplomat, August 26, 2010. Conversation with senior U.S. diplomat, November 9, 2010.

48. Dan Robinson, "U.S.: Iran Nuclear Deal Will Not Slow UN Sanctions Drive," Voice of America, May 17, 2010. "U.S. Eyes Sanctions as Iran, Turkey Forge Nuclear Fuel Swap," PBS, May 17, 2010. Peter Baker, "Major Powers Have a Deal on Sanctions for Iran, U.S. Says," New York Times, May 18, 2010. "Clinton Blasts Brazil-Turkey Approach to Iran," Radio Free Europe/Radio Liberty, May 28, 2010. "Obama Talks Iran Sanctions, Israel with Jewish Lawmakers," Agence France Presse, May 19, 2010.

49. Interview with State Department official, September 17, 2010. Interview with former Iran Desk officer at the State Department. Interview with William D. Wunderle.

50. Hafezi and Exman, "Iran Agrees to Atom Fuel Deal with Turkey, Brazil." Interview with senior EU diplomat, May 27, 2010. Interview with French diplomat. Interview with senior EU official, June 14, 2010. Interview with Danny Ayalon, October 4, 2010. Gareth Porter, "Fuel Swap Shakes Sanctions Draft, Prods U.S. on New Iran Talks," Inter Press Service, May 29, 2010. Interview with EU diplomat, June 21, 2010. Interview with Russian diplomat. Interview with senior EU diplomat, September 15, 2010. Interview with senior EU official, September 10, 2010.

51. Conversation with senior State Department official, November 9, 2010. Interview with State Department official, September 17, 2010. Interview with State Department official, October 7, 2010. Interview with senior EU official, June 14, 2010. Interview with senior State Department official, July 21, 2010. Interview with Pierre Vimont. Nathan Hodge, "Iran's Nuke Fuel Deal: Breakthrough or Bogus?," *Wired,* May 17, 2010.

52. Interview with senior Turkish diplomat, July 13, 2010. Interview with senior Brazilian diplomat, June 21, 2010. Interview with Brazilian diplomat, July 7, 2010. Interview with Celso Amorim. Interview with senior advisor to Lula. "Turkey Chides U.S. in Iran Row, Urges Support for Swap Deal," Agence France Presse, May 27, 2010. "Turkey to Withdraw from Nuclear Fuel Deal If West Imposes Sanctions on Iran," Bernama, May 18, 2010. Scott Peterson, "U.S. Answer to Iran Nuclear Swap: Overnight Deal on Sanctions," *Christian Science Monitor,* May 18, 2010. Ahmet Davutoglu and Celso Amorim, "Giving Diplomacy a Chance," *New York Times,* May 26, 2010. Interview with senior Turkish diplomat, July 13, 2010.

53. Letter from Barack Obama to Lula da Silva, Politica Externa Brasileira, April 20, 2010, http://www.politicaexterna.com/11023/brazil-iran-turkey-nuclear-negotiations -obamas-letter-to-lula.

54. "Erdogan Joins Tehran Nuclear Talks," Agence France Presse, May 16, 2010. Ladane Nasseri and Steve Bryant, "Erdogan Heads to Tehran for Nuclear Talks with Ahmadinejad, Brazil's Lula," Bloomberg, May 16, 2010. "Iran Will Never Agree to Fuel Exchange," *Jerusalem Post,* April 30, 2010. Interview with Celso Amorim. Interview with Iranian nuclear negotiator. Interview with senior Turkish diplomat, July 13, 2010. Interview with Mohammad Khazaee.

55. Interview with Celso Amorim. Glenn Kessler, "U.S., Brazilian Officials at Odds over Letter on Iranian Uranium," *Washington Post,* May 28, 2010. For some of the Europeans, the letter became a problem as questions began to arise about the wisdom of rejecting the Tehran Declaration. "Even German parliamentarians asked why we didn't agree to it," an EU diplomat explained to me. "It was difficult not to appear irresponsible" (interview with senior EU diplomat, September 15, 2010).

56. Interview with former senior State Department official, September 2015.

57. Interview with former Iran Desk officer at the State Department. Interview with State Department official, September 17, 2010.

58. Interview with State Department official, September 17, 2010. Interview with former Iran Desk officer at the State Department. Interview with State Department official, September 2015. Interview with William D. Wunderle. Interview with senior Obama administration official, October 27, 2010. Interview with French diplomat. Interview with senior advisor to Lula.

59. Trita Parsi, "Analysis: Iran's Nuke Deal Irritates Washington," ABCnews .com, May 18, 2010. Interview with senior State Department official, September 10, 2010.

SEVEN All-Out Escalation

1. Months later, the story broke that a sophisticated U.S.-Israel cyberattack against Iran's nuclear program had destroyed many of its centrifuges: only 3,800 centrifuges were operating at Natanz, at only about 60 percent of their design capacity. While Obama believed this had slowed down Iran's nuclear program and added time to the diplomacy clock, it did not reduce Iran's LEU count. Since the cyberattack was a covert operation, the Obama administration publicly credited sanctions and technical problems for the slowdown. "Iran's ability to produce a nuclear weapon has been delayed by sanctions," Secretary of State Hillary Rodham Clinton said in a televised town hall meeting. "Iran has had technological problems that have made it slow down its timetable." David Ignatius, "Obama Offers Iran an Opening," *Washington Post,* August 5, 2010, and "Buying Time with Iran," *Washington Post,* January 9, 2011. Mark Landler, "Clinton Says Sanctions Have Stalled Iran's Effort to Make Nuclear Weapons," *New York Times,* January 11, 2011.

2. Interview with Ben Rhodes, deputy national security advisor to President Obama, October 27, 2015. Interview with Gary Samore, February 5, 2016. Interview with Ambassador Gerard Araud, September 17, 2015.

3. Interview with Bob Einhorn, November 24, 2015. Interview with senior Pentagon official, September 18, 2015.

4. Interview with Ben Rhodes. Interview with White House official, July 31, 2015. Interview with Mohammad Nahavandian, September 24, 2015.

5. Ed Pilkington, "U.S. Has Plan to Attack Iran If Needed, Military Chief Admits," *Guardian,* August 1, 2010.

6. Interview with Ben Rhodes. Interview with senior Pentagon official. Interview with White House official, July 31, 2015.

7. Interview with Jake Sullivan, September 23, 2015. Interview with Gerard Araud. Interview with senior White House official, January 12, 2016. Interview with Ambassador Peter Wittig, November 30, 2015.

8. "Britain, Germany, UAE Airports 'Refused Fuel' to Iran Planes," *Haaretz,* July 5, 2010. "EU, Canada Hit Iran with New Sanctions, Urge Nuclear Talks," Agence France Presse, July 26, 2010. Edward Cody, "European Union Imposes New Economic Sanctions Against Iran," *Washington Post,* July 27, 2010. "Iran Feels Sanctions Heat at UAE Ports—Sources," Reuters, August 3, 2010. Chip Cummins and Jay Solomon,

"U.A.E. Banks Cut Ties to Iranian Banks Blacklisted by U.S," *Wall Street Journal,* October 5, 2010.

9. Jay Solomon, *The Iran Wars: Spy Games, Bank Battles, and the Secret Deals That Reshaped the Middle East* (New York: Random House), 197. Chang Jae-Soon, "South Korea in Dilemma amid U.S. Pressure over Iran Sanctions," *Yonhap,* August 4, 2010. Christian Oliver, "U.S. Puts Seoul Under Pressure on Iran," *Financial Times,* August 4, 2010. "U.S. Urges Japan to Get Tough on Iran," Agence France Presse, August 4, 2010. "Japan Pulls Out of Iran's Biggest Onshore Oil Project," Agence France Presse, October 15, 2010.

10. Daniel Dombey and Jonathan Soble, "Energy Groups Agree to End Iran Operations," *Financial Times,* October 1, 2010. Interview with senior White House official, January 12, 2016. Russia and China opposed the unilateral sanctions Washington pushed its allies to adopt and even expanded their economic cooperation with Iran in areas not prohibited by the UN (Andrew Kramer, "Russia Plan to Help Iran Challenges Sanctions," *New York Times,* July 31, 2010). "China Disagrees with EU's Unilateral Sanctions on Iran," *Xinhua,* July 30, 2010.

11. "Lawmaker Stresses Iranian Nation's Resolve to Continue Nuclear Progress," Fars News, August 1, 2010. "Iran's Khamenei Vows to Circumvent Nuclear Sanctions," Agence France Presse, September 7, 2010. "President Says Sanctions Against Iran Political Game," Fars News, August 1, 2010. Howard Lafranchi, "Dissidents Say Iran Nuclear Sanctions Are Helping Ahmadinejad," *Christian Science Monitor,* August 12, 2010. Cody, "European Union Imposes New Economic Sanctions Against Iran." "Iran to Boycott Sanctions Sponsors—Minister," Press TV, August 3, 2010. "President Criticizes USA over Publishing 'Lies' on Iran," BBC, August 3, 2010.

12. "Rafsanjani Slates West's Hostile Approach Toward Iran," Fars News, August 1, 2010. "Iran Ready for Talks at Highest Level: Ahmadinejad," *Tehran Times,* August 2, 2010.

13. "Khamenei: Iran Won't Talk with U.S. in Current Climate," Reuters, August 18, 2010.

14. "Ahmadinejad Taunts West to Put More Pressure on Iran," Agence France Presse, October 5, 2010.

15. David Sanger, "Obama Set to Offer Stricter Nuclear Deal to Iran, Officials Say," *New York Times,* October 28, 2010.

16. "Secretary Clinton on Afghanistan, Iran," BBC, December 3, 2010. Robert Burns, "Clinton Hopes for Iranian Turnaround on Nukes," Associated Press, December 4, 2010.

17. Interview with former White House official, July 31, 2015. Steven Erlanger, "Direct Talks Concerning Iran's Nuclear Program Begin," *New York Times,* December 7, 2010.

18. In Geneva, the head of the Iranian delegation, Saeed Jalili, devoted much of his opening statement condemning the assassination in Tehran a week earlier of a physicist, Majid Shahriari, and a similar attack that same day on another nuclear scientist, Fereydoon Abbasi. The Obama administration distanced itself from the

assassinations and later leaked that they were conducted by the Israelis. See Richard Engel and Robert Windrem, "Israel Teams with Terror Group to Kill Iran's Nuclear Scientists, U.S. Officials Tell NBC News," NBC, February 9, 2012. Steven Erlanger, "Talks on Iran's Nuclear Program Close with No Progress," *New York Times,* January 23, 2011. Laura Rozen, "U.S., Europe Lukewarm About New Iran Proposals for Nuclear Talks," *Envoy,* May 10, 2011.

19. Interview with Robert Einhorn, November 24, 2011. Erlanger, "Talks on Iran's Nuclear Program." Rozen, "U.S., Europe Lukewarm."

20. Seymour Hersh, "Iran and the Bomb: How Real Is the Nuclear Threat?" *New Yorker,* June 6, 2011.

21. Julie Borger, "Covert Operations War Has Already Begun—In Secret," *Guardian,* November 4, 2011.

22. Yossi Melman, "Another Iranian Nuclear Scientist Murdered in Tehran," *Haaretz,* July 24, 2011. Hiedeh Farmani, "Blast 'Kills Top Iran Nuclear Scientist, Israel Blamed,'" Agence France Presse, November 29, 2011. Ali Akbar Dareini, "Gunmen Kill Iranian Nuclear Scientist in Tehran," Associated Press, July 23, 2011. Tom Burgis, "Timeline: Assassinated Iranian Scientists," *Financial Times,* January 11, 2012. Laura Rozen, "U.S. Condemns Car Bomb Attack on Iran Nuclear Scientist," *Al Monitor,* January 11, 2012.

23. Yossi Melman, "The War Against Iran's Nuclear Program Has Already Begun," *Haaretz,* December 2, 2011.

24. Richard Sale, "Stuxnet Loaded by Iran Double Agents," *Industrial Safety and Security Source,* April 11, 2012. Yossi Melman, "The Iran Deal's Bad for Israel? Netanyahu's to Blame," *Huffington Post,* August 3, 2015. David Sanger, "Diplomacy and Sanctions, Yes. Left Unspoken on Iran? Sabotage," *New York Times,* January 19, 2016. Melman, "War Against Iran's Nuclear Program." "Furious Iran Wants Action over Scientist's Killing," Agence France Presse, January 12, 2012. "Iran Buries Scientist Slain by 'CIA and Mossad,'" Agence France Presse, January 13, 2012. Melman, "War Against Iran's Nuclear Program."

25. "Iran: Murder of Nuclear Scientist Is Israeli-American 'Act of Terror,'" *Haaretz,* July 24, 2011. Ali Akbar Dareini, "Iran Blames Israel After Nuclear Scientist Killed," Associated Press, November 29, 2011. "Iran Foreign Minister Says West Hosting Scientists' Killers," BBC, February 28, 2012. Richard Engel, "Exclusive: Iran's Supreme Leader Personally Set Conditions for Nuclear Deal: Negotiator," NBC, January 28, 2012. Gareth Porter, "Behind the Scenes: How the U.S. and Iran Reached Their Landmark Deal," *Nation,* September 5, 2015.

26. Dareini, "Iran Blames Israel." Rozen, "U.S. Condemns Car Bomb Attack."

27. "Furious Iran Wants Action." Ethan Bronner, "Israel Says Iran Is Behind Bombs," *New York Times,* February 14, 2012. "Attacks Deepen Iran Nuclear Puzzle," Agence France Presse, February 17, 2012. Herb Keinon, "No Certainty New Delhi Attack Will Alter Indian-Iranian Ties," *Jerusalem Post,* February 17, 2012.

28. Trita Parsi, "From Iran to Bulgaria," *Daily Beast,* July 18, 2012. Jason Burke, "Iran Plotted to Bomb Israeli Diplomats," *Guardian,* June 18, 2012. Nicholas Kulish,

Eric Schmitt, and Matthew Brunwasser, "Bulgaria Implicates Hezbollah in July Attack on Israelis," *New York Times,* February 5, 2013.

29. Yossi Melman, "Exclusive: Israel's Rash Behavior Blew Operation to Sabotage Iran's Computers, U.S. Officials Say," *Jerusalem Post,* February 16, 2016. Yaakov Katz, "Iran's Centrifuges Again Enriching Uranium at Full Speed," *Jerusalem Post,* February 9, 2011. "Report: Iran Recovered Quickly from Cyber-Attack on Nuclear Plant," *Haaretz,* February 16, 2011. David Sanger, "Document Reveals Growth of Cyberwarfare Between the U.S. and Iran," *New York Times,* February 23, 2015. Bruce Riedel, "In Saudi Arabia and Israel, Signals That Iran Has Retaliation in Works," *Daily Beast,* October 26, 2012.

30. A NATO study argued that the Stuxnet virus qualified as an "illegal act of force." Patrick Meehan, "Iranian Cyber Threat Cannot Be Underestimated," *Hill,* April 26, 2012. Kim Zetter, "Legal Experts: Stuxnet Attack on Iran Was Illegal 'Act of Force,'" Wired .com, March 25, 2013. Siobhan Gorman and Julian Barnes, "Cyber Combat: Act of War," *Wall Street Journal,* May 31, 2011. In testimony, General Keith Alexander, commander of the United States Cyber Command, told the U.S. Senate that whether a cyberattack on the United States would be considered an act of war depended on the "impact of such an attack" (U.S. Senate Hearing, Committee on Armed Services, March 12, 2013).

31. Scott Peterson, "Used-Car Salesman as Iran Proxy? Why Assassination Plot Doesn't Add Up for Experts," *Christian Science Monitor,* October 12, 2011. Robert Mackey, "Some Experts Question Iran's Role in Bungled Plot," *New York Times,* October 12, 2011. "Obama Demands Plot Answers from Top Iranian Leaders," Agence France Presse, October 13, 2011.

32. "Obama Demands Plot Answers." Helene Cooper, "Obama Pledging Tough Sanctions for Iran in Plot," *New York Times,* October 14, 2011. Margaret Besheer, "UN Members Condemn Alleged Iranian Plot on Saudi Official," Voice of America, November 17, 2011.

33. "Iran Says False U.S. Plot Claim Aims to Distract, Divide," Agence France Presse, October 12, 2011. Ali Akbar Dareini, "Iran's Khamenei Warns U.S. over Assassination Claims," Associated Press, October 16, 2011.

34. Joby Warrick and Thomas Erdbrink, "U.S. First Unsure of Iran's Role in Plot," *New York Times,* October 13, 2011. Greg Miller, "U.S. Spy Agencies See New Iran Risk," *Washington Post,* February 2, 2012. "Iran Says 'Ready to Examine' U.S. Plot Accusations," Agence France Presse, October 17, 2011.

35. Julian Borger, "Nuclear Wikileaks: Cables Show Cosy U.S. Relationship with IAEA Chief," *Guardian,* November 30, 2010. "Iran Rejects IAEA Report on Nuclear Work," Agence France Presse, May 25, 2011.

36. Robert Worth and Rick Gladstone, "Iran Frames U.N. Nuclear Report as U.S. Bullying," *New York Times,* November 10, 2011. "Netanyahu: IAEA Report Confirms Israel's Suspicions on Nuclear Iran," *Haaretz,* November 11, 2011.

37. "Russia: UN Report on Iran Nuclear Program Is Biased, Unprofessional," *Haaretz,* November 20, 2011. "Iran News Agency Publishes Full Text of Non-Aligned Movement's Statement," BBC, November 19, 2011.

38. Julian Borger, "Nuclear Watchdog Chief Accused of Pro-Western Bias over Iran," *Guardian,* March 22, 2012.

39. Michael Slackman, "As Arab World Shakes, Iran's Influence Grows," *New York Times,* February 24, 2011. William Young, "Iran Views Arab Protests Through Lens of '79 Revolt," *New York Times,* January 29, 2011. William Young, "Across the Region, Wild Jubilation, with Pockets of Trepidation: Ahmadinejad Cheers Exit of Mubarak," *New York Times,* February 12, 2011.

40. Brian Murphy, "Iran on Edge as Ally Syria Fights for Survival," Associated Press, April 23, 2011. Simon Tisdall, "World Briefing: Arab Spring Has Changed the Game for Iran," *Guardian,* May 18, 2011. "Egypt Fuels U.S.-Iran Fight for Regional Influence: Analysts," Agence France Presse, February 16, 2011.

41. Slackman, "As Arab World Shakes." "Obama Calls for Peaceful Response in Middle East," Associated Press, February 15, 2011. Iran was not alone in pursuing a policy plagued by inconsistency. Iran supported the uprisings in Libya, Tunisia, Bahrain, and Egypt, while opposing it in Syria. Washington, in turn, praised the people's revolutions and even provided military support for the revolutionaries in Libya, while it stayed mum about the Bahraini regime's brutal repression of its demonstrators. The only consistency was that all regional powers pursued inconsistent policies in the wake of the Arab spring. Mark Landler and David Sanger, "U.S. Follows Two Paths on Unrest in Iran and Bahrain," *New York Times,* February 16, 2011. Murphy, "Iran on Edge."

42. "Syria Unrest Embarrasses Iran," Agence France Presse, April 28, 2011. Tisdall, "World Briefing." Slackman, "As Arab World Shakes." Helene Cooper and Mark Landler, "Interests of Saudi Arabia and Iran Collide, with the U.S. in the Middle," *New York Times,* March 18, 2011.

43. Ethan Bronner and Michael Slackman, "Saudis, Fearful of Iran, Send Troops to Bahrain to Quell Protests," *New York Times,* March 15, 2011. Conversation with senior Iranian official, November 2013. Cooper and Landler, "Interests of Saudi Arabia and Iran Collide."

44. Interview with former White House official, September 2015. Interview with Richard Nephew, August 3, 2015.

45. Mark Landler, "Iran Face-Off Testing Obama the Candidate," *New York Times,* January 17, 2012. Julie Pace, "U.S. Levies New Sanctions on Iran's Central Bank," Associated Press, February 6, 2012. Interview with Richard Nephew. Interview with former State Department official, September 21, 2015.

46. Thijs Van de Graaf, "The 'Oil Weapon' Reversed? Sanctions Against Iran and U.S.-EU Structural Power," *Middle East Policy Council* 20, no. 3 (2013). Interview with Richard Nephew.

47. Ali Akbar Dareini, "Iranian Diplomats Leave UK After Expulsion," Associated Press, December 2, 2011. Thomas Erdbrink and Joby Warrick, "Iran Facing Increased Isolation After Embassy Rampage," *New York Times,* December 1, 2011.

48. Barak Ravid, "Netanyahu: EU Oil Embargo Will Not Stop Iran Nukes," *Haaretz,* January 24, 2012. "Iran Further Isolated After British Embassy Storming," Agence France Presse, December 2, 2011. Van de Graaf, "'Oil Weapon' Reversed?" "EU

Squeezes Iran with New Oil Sanctions," NPR, January 23, 2012. Barak Ravid, "Top Israeli Official: Move to Cut Iran from SWIFT Network Is 'Mortal Blow' to Tehran," *Haaretz*, March 15, 2012.

49. Roshanak Taghavi, "Why Iran's Currency Dropped to Worst Low in Two Decades," *Christian Science Monitor*, January 3, 2012. "Iran's Rial Drops 10 Pct as EU Bans Oil Imports," Reuters, January 23, 2012. J. David Goodman, "Iran Responds with Anger to Proposals by Europe," *New York Times*, January 6, 2012. "Khamenei: Iran Can Withstand Global Diplomatic, Economic Pressure," *Haaretz*, March 20, 2012. "Iran Digs in with Oil Warning to Saudi Arabia," Agence France Presse, January 17, 2012. Ali Akbar Dareini, "Ahmadinejad Says Iran Ready for Nuclear Talks," Associated Press, January 26, 2012.

50. Goodman, "Iran Responds with Anger." Philip Inman, "Iranian Warning to U.S. over Gulf Sends Oil Price Soaring," *Guardian*, January 4, 2012. Interview with Gary Samore.

51. Siamak Namazi, "Sanctions and Medical Supply Shortages in Iran," *Woodrow Wilson Center Viewpoints* no. 20 (February 2013). Rick Gladstone, "A New Sign of Distress as Iran's Currency Falls," *New York Times*, October 1, 2012. Thomas Erdbrink and Rick Gladstone, "Violence and Protest in Iran as Currency Drops in Value," *New York Times*, October 3, 2012. Interview with Richard Nephew. Richard Gladstone, "Iranian Oil Minister Concedes Sanctions Have Hurt Exports," *New York Times*, January 7, 2013. Bijan Khajehpour, Reza Marashi, and Trita Parsi, "Never Give In and Never Give Up—The Impact of Sanctions on Tehran's Nuclear Calculations," National Iranian American Council, March 2013. James Ball, "Amid Sanctions, Tensions over Currency Spark Clashes in Iran," *Washington Post*, October 4, 2012. Joby Warrick and James Ball, "Iran's Economy May Offer Opening," *Washington Post*, October 5, 2012.

52. Khajehpour, Marashi, and Parsi, "Never Give In and Never Give Up," 26. Joby Warrick, "Iran's Nuclear Program Speeding Up, Report Says," *Washington Post*, September 3, 2011. Jonathan Tirone and Indira Lakshmanan, "IAEA: Iran Doubles Its Stockpile of Enriched Uranium in Three Months," Bloomberg, May 28, 2012. William Broad, "Iran's High Card at the Nuclear Table," *New York Times*, June 17, 2012.

53. Khajehpour, Marashi, and Parsi, "Never Give In and Never Give Up," 28.

54. Interview with Farideh Farhi, February 1, 2015. "[Sanctions] will create hate and discontent at the street level so that the Iranian leaders realize that they need to change their ways," a senior U.S. intelligence official told the *Washington Post* (Karen DeYoung and Scott Wilson, "Public Ire Is One Goal of Sanctions Against Iran, U.S. Official Says," *Washington Post*, January 11, 2012).

55. Matthew Lee, "AP Sources: U.S. Sees Iran's Leaders Split on Nukes," Associated Press, February 17, 2012. Miller, "U.S. Spy Agencies."

56. Anne Gearan, "New U.S. Sanctions on Iran Aim to Head off Israel," Associated Press, February 7, 2012. "Iran, Undeterred," *Washington Post*, July 22, 2011.

57. Interview with Kelsey Davenport, November 30, 2015. "Iran: Stumbling into War," *Guardian*, February 19, 2012. Simon Jenkins, "This Coward's Diplomacy with Iran Humiliates Britain," *Guardian*, January 4, 2012.

58. "China Opposes Unilateral Sanctions Against Iran, Says FM Spokesman," *Xinhau,* October 16, 2012. "Nuclear Sanctions Won't Affect Iran Economy, Russia Official Says," *Haaretz,* December 2, 2011. "Iran Buries Scientist." Interview with Ambassador Sergei Ryabkov, November 30, 2015.

59. Julian Borger and Chris Mcgreal, "Tehran Raises Hopes of Nuclear Trade-Off to Halt Oil Sanctions," *Guardian,* January 20, 2012. Laura Rozen, "How Iran Talks Were Saved from Verge of Collapse," *Al Monitor,* April 14, 2012. George Janh, "Exclusive: Iran Letter Shows 'Charm Offensive,'" Associated Press, September 13, 2011. "Iran, World Powers Hold Tough Talks," Agence France Presse, April 14, 2012. U.S. and EU officials described the talks as "constructive and useful." Jalili called the talks a "success," praising the "positive approach" of the P5+1. "For Iranian people, the language of threats and pressure don't work. But the approach of cooperation and talk could be fruitful" (Laura Rozen, "Are the Iran Nuclear Talks Finally Headed in the Right Direction?," *Al Monitor,* April 14, 2012). George Janh, "Iran, Western Powers Hail Latest Nuclear Talks," Associated Press, April 14, 2012. Joby Warrick, "U.S. Officials Encouraged by Talks with Iran," *Washington Post,* April 15, 2012. "U.S. Official Says Netanyahu Was Fully Briefed on Iran Talks," *Haaretz,* April 18, 2012.

60. Statement by High Representative Catherine Ashton on behalf of the E3+3 following the talks with Iran, Istanbul, April 14, 2012. "Iran Media See Nuclear 'Rights' Endorsed by Talks," Agence France Presse, April 15, 2012. Conversations with EU and Iranian diplomats after the Istanbul session, early May 2012. The Fars News Agency said "the talks were based on respecting Iran's nuclear rights under the NPT" ("Iran Media See Nuclear 'Rights'").

61. Rozen, "How Iran Talks Were Saved."

62. Ibid. Interview with former White House official, July 31, 2015. Reza Marashi and Trita Parsi, "How to Strike a Win-Win Deal with Iran," CNN.com, May 13, 2014. Statement by Catherine Ashton.

63. Herb Keinon, "Netanyahu Says Iran Talks Give Tehran a Five-Week 'Freebie,'" *Jerusalem Post,* April 16, 2012. "U.S. Official Says Netanyahu Was Fully Briefed."

64. Mark Landler, "U.S. Officials See Promising Signs for Iran Meeting," *New York Times,* May 19, 2012. Ali Akbar Dareini and Lara Jakes, "Iran Seeks Concessions in Baghdad Nuclear Talks," Associated Press, May 22, 2012.

65. Laura Rozen, "Iran Nuclear Talks in Baghdad Almost Foundered in Final Hours," *Al Monitor,* May 26, 2012. Landler, "U.S. Officials See Promising Signs." Liz Sly and Jodi Warrick, "Western Proposals 'Unbalanced,' Iran Says," *Washington Post,* May 24, 2012. Julian Borger, "Analysis: Moscow Talks Give Diplomacy a Small Chance," *Guardian,* June 18, 2012.

66. Sly and Warrick, "Western Proposals 'Unbalanced.'" "Iran: Baghdad Talks Should Result in Removal of Western Sanctions," Fars News, May 20, 2012.

67. Laura Rozen, "International Negotiators to Offer Detailed Confidence-Building Proposal to Iran," *Al Monitor,* May 22, 2012. Rozen, "Iran Nuclear Talks in Baghdad." Barak Ravid, "World Powers Want to Talk Nuclear, Iran Wants to Talk Syria," *Haaretz,* May 24, 2012.

68. "World Powers in Raw Over Proposals to Iran," *Fars News*, May 22, 2012.

69. Ellen Barry, "No One Budges in Tense Iran Nuclear Talks in Moscow," *New York Times*, June 19, 2012. Laura Rozen, "On to the Next Round of Iran Nuclear Talks," *Al Monitor*, June 19, 2012. Ellen Barry and Rick Gladstone, "Setback in Talks on Iran's Nuclear Program in a 'Gulf of Mistrust,'" *New York Times*, June 20, 2012. Laura Rozen, "U.S. Hardens Stance in Iran Nuclear Talks," *Al Monitor*, June 27, 2012, and "Iran's UN Envoy: We Will Not Initiate Confrontation," *Al Monitor*, July 11, 2012.

70. Julian Borger, "Iran Nuclear Talks Postponed to July Summit in Turkey," *Guardian*, June 20, 2012. Barry and Gladstone, "Setback in Talks." Julian Borger, "Global Powers Launch New Push to End Iran Nuclear Crisis," *Guardian*, October 12, 2012.

71. "Staggering to a Halt: Iran Nuclear Talks," *Guardian*, June 21, 2012. Jasmin Ramsey, "Worrying Development Ahead of Resumed Talks with Iran," *Lobe Log*, December 11, 2012.

72. Natasha Mozgovaya, "As Nuclear Talks Fail, U.S. Experts Urge Obama to Weigh Military Option on Iran," *Haaretz*, June 21, 2012. Herb Keinon and Lahav Harkov, "Israeli Official: Iran Must Feel That It's Under Threat," *Jerusalem Post*, June 7, 2012.

73. Trita Parsi, "The Blame Game," *Daily Beast*, June 29, 2012.

EIGHT Obama and the Mossad Against Netanyahu

1. See for instance Chris Hedges, "Iran May Be Able to Build an Atomic Bomb in 5 Years, U.S. and Israeli Officials Fear," *New York Times*, January 5, 1995.

2. Jeffrey Goldberg, "The Point of No Return," *Atlantic*, September 2010.

3. Laura Rozen, "Why Did Obama Give Bunker-Buster Bombs to Israel?," *Al Monitor*, September 26, 2011. "Report: U.K. Preparing for Military Strike on Iran Nuclear Facilities," *Haaretz*, November 2, 2011.

4. Barak Ravid, "Israeli Threats of Attack Sparked New Wave of Iran Sanctions, Officials Say," *Haaretz*, March 16, 2012. Interview with Tal Shalev, November 24, 2015. Interview with Ambassador Alon Pinkas, January 5, 2016. Interview with Chemi Shalev, February 3, 2016. Interview with Dalia Dassa Kaye, November 16, 2015.

5. "Barak: If Iran Sanctions Don't Work, Military Action Must Be Considered," *Haaretz*, February 2, 2012.

6. "Exclusive: Israel's Rash Behavior Blew Operation to Sabotage Iran's Computers, U.S. Officials Say," *Jerusalem Post*, February 16, 2016. David Sanger, "Diplomacy and Sanctions, Yes. Left Unspoken on Iran? Sabotage," *New York Times*, January 19, 2016. Interview with Amir Tibon, November 25, 2015.

7. David Ignatius, "An Interview with Iran's President Mahmoud Ahmadinejad," *Washington Post*, September 23, 2012. Saeed Kamaili Dehghan, "Iran Says It Has Missiles Trained on Israel and U.S. Bases in Gulf," *Guardian*, July 5, 2012. "Iran Says United and 'Ready for War' with Israel," *Haaretz*, November 3, 2011. "Hezbollah Chief: Israeli-U.S. Strike on Iran Will Lead to Regional War," *Haaretz*, November 11, 2011. Herb Keinon, "Jerusalem Dismisses Russian Warning Against Attack on Iran," *Jerusalem Post*, February 23, 2012. Amir Oren, "Israel's Plan to Attack Iran Put on Hold Until

Next Year at the Earliest," *Haaretz,* March 7, 2012. Interview with Ambassador Peter Wittig, November 30, 2015. Interview with Dr. Vitaly Naumkin, January 19, 2016.

8. Interview with former White House official, July 31, 2015. Conversation with senior Pentagon officials, January 2013. Interview with Ben Rhodes, October 27, 2015.

9. Barak Ravid, "U.S. Army Chief Heads to Israel as Fears over Attack on Iran Mount," *Haaretz,* January 15, 2012. Amos Harel, "U.S. Concerned That Barak Is Pushing for Israeli Attack on Iran," *Haaretz,* February 20, 2012. Barak Ravid, "Israel: Public U.S. Objections to Military Attack Serve Iran's Interests," *Haaretz,* February 21, 2012. Both Russian and EU officials joined the U.S. in pressing Israel not to start a war. British Foreign Secretary William Hague said he did not think "the wise thing at the moment" would be for Israel to launch a military attack on Iran (Herb Keinon, "British FM Joins Appeal to Israel: 'Don't Hit Iran,'" *Jerusalem Post,* February 20, 2012. Interview with Robert Einhorn, November 24, 2015).

10. Aron Heller, "Barak Says Israel Never Ruled out Attacking Iran," Associated Press, April 17, 2012. Barak Ravid, "U.S. Officials: Israel Refused to Commit to Withhold Surprise Attack on Iran," *Haaretz,* November 6, 2011.

11. Prime Minister Netanyahu's address at the AIPAC Policy Conference in Washington, March 7, 2012.

12. Jackie Calmes and Mark Landler, "Obama Scolds G.O.P. Critics of Iran Policy," *New York Times,* March 7, 2012. Obama's Super Tuesday press conference, March 6, 2012.

13. "Iran 'Zone of Immunity' Resonating with World," *Jerusalem Post,* March 19, 2012.

14. Ronen Bergman, "Will Israel Attack Iran?," *New York Times Magazine,* January 25, 2012. Barak Ravid, "U.S. Believes Israel Sees Iran Nuclear Problem 'Too Narrowly,'" *Haaretz,* February 9, 2012. Mark Landler and David Sanger, "U.S. and Israel Split on Speed of Iran Threat," *New York Times,* February 9, 2012.

15. Barak Ravid, "Mossad Chief: Nuclear Iran Not Necessarily Existential Threat to Israel," *Haaretz,* December 29, 2011. Peter Beinart, "Iran Is Not an 'Existential' Threat to Israel—No Matter What Netanyahu Claims," *Haaretz,* August 7, 2015. Gabe Kahn, "Dagan: No Existential Threat," *Arutz Sheva,* August 2, 2012. Eli Clifton, "Former Israeli Spy Chief: 'I Don't Think There Is an Existential Threat' to Israel," Thinkprogress .org, February 8, 2012. Yoav Zitun, "Iran Far from Posing Existential Threat," *Yedioth,* April 11, 2011.

16. Laura Rozen, "'The Regime in Iran Is a Very Rational One' Former Israeli Intelligence Chief Tells CBS," *Al Monitor,* March 8, 2012. Karin Brulliard and Joby Warrick, "On Iran, Key Israeli Cools Tone of Debate," *Washington Post,* April 26, 2012.

17. Seymour Hersh, "Iran and the Bomb: How Real Is the Nuclear Threat?" *New Yorker,* June 6, 2011. Brulliard and Warrick, "On Iran, Key Israeli Cools Tone." A similar divide between the intelligence and political establishment existed on the American side. Whereas Director of National Intelligence James Clapper testified at a closed Senate hearing that he had a high level of confidence that Iran did not have an active nuclear weapons program, Senator Joe Lieberman, a close ally of Netanyahu in the Senate, addressed the media after the closed hearing and conveyed the opposite message.

"I can't say much in detail," Lieberman said, "but it's pretty clear that they're continuing to work seriously on a nuclear-weapons program" (Hersch, "Iran and the Bomb").

18. Amir Tibon, "Netanyahu vs. the Generals," *Politico*, July 6, 2016. "Former Mossad Chief Slams Netanyahu: 'The Problem Is Iran, Not President Obama,'" *Jerusalem Post*, September 7, 2015.

19. Gili Cohen, "Israel Won't Withstand War in Wake of Strike on Iran, Ex-Mossad Chief Says," *Haaretz*, June 1, 2011. "Ex-Israeli Spymaster: Iran Response to Israeli Attack Would Be Devastating," *Haaretz*, March 12, 2012. Herb Keinon, "Ya'alon: Iran Is Laughing All the Way to a Bomb," *Jerusalem Post*, May 31, 2012. Amos Harel, "Former Mossad Chief: Israeli Attack on Iran Must Be Stopped to Avert Catastrophe," *Haaretz*, December 1, 2011. Cohen, "Israel Won't Withstand War." Dagan's preferred solution was to give Obama's sanctions and diplomacy a chance while continuing Israel's sabotage and assassination campaign. Dagan also believed that Iran's many ethnic minorities could be driven to revolt against the central government in Tehran. Economic pressure could produce internal instability and ethnic tensions that eventually would lead to regime change, he told U.S. officials. See Tibon, "Netanyahu vs. the Generals." Yaakov Katz, "Dagan Urged Support for Iranian Minorities to Overthrow Regime," *Jerusalem Post*, November 29, 2011. Ehud Barak, "Steinitz, Ya'alon Got Cold Feet Just Before Israel Was About to Attack Iran," *Jerusalem Post*, August 21, 2015.

20. Sanger, "Diplomacy and Sanctions." Tibon, "Netanyahu vs. the Generals."

21. Ari Shavit, "How Shimon Peres Stopped Israel from Bombing Iran," *Haaretz*, October 31, 2013. Jodi Rudoren, "Israeli Report Cites a Thwarted 2010 Move on Iran," *New York Times*, November 5, 2012. Three ministers also attended the meeting: Moshe Ya'alon, Dan Meridor, and Benny Begin (Ben Caspit, "Why Didn't Netanyahu Attack Iran?," *Al Monitor*, June 8, 2015. Interview with Alon Pinkas).

22. Yossi Melman, "Netanyahu Sought to Provoke, Not Attack, Iran in 2010," *Haaretz*, November 7, 2012. Caspit, "Why Didn't Netanyahu Attack Iran?" Brulliard and Warrick, "On Iran, Key Israeli Cools Tone." Anne Barnard, "Former Israeli Premier Assails Netanyahu on Iran," *New York Times*, April 30, 2012. Interview with Alon Pinkas. Tibon, "Netanyahu vs. the Generals."

23. Amir Tibon and Tal Shalev, "Scenes from a Failed Marriage," *Huffington Post*, November 12, 2015. Interview with former Pentagon official, September 18, 2015.

24. Interview with former White House official.

NINE The Arabs Who Brought Iran and the United States Together

1. Conversation with official involved in the Omani channel, October 2, 2015.

2. Richard J. Schmierer, "The Sultanate of Oman and the Iran Nuclear Deal," *Middle East Policy Council Journal* 22, no. 4 (2015). Saeed Kamali Dehghan, "Iranians Release American Hikers After $1M Bail Deal," *Guardian*, September 22, 2011. "U.S. Hikers: 'Iran Took Us as Hostages,'" Agence France Presse, September 26, 2011. Interview with Gary Samore, February 5, 2015.

3. Ana Echagüe, "Oman: The Outlier," *Fride,* October 29, 2015. Schmierer, "Sultanate of Oman." Interview with senior Iranian diplomat, October 4, 2015. Interview with former White House official, January 12, 2016.

4. Interview with former White House official, July 31, 2015. Saeed Kamali Dehghan, "Khamenei Squashes Hope of Negotiations with the U.S.," *Guardian,* February 8, 2013.

5. Conversation with official involved in the Omani channel. Julian Borger, "Keep Clear of West's Plan to Isolate Us, Iran Tells Gulf States," *Guardian,* January 20, 2012. David Ignatius, "Obama Sends Iran a Message on Nukes," *Washington Post,* April 6, 2012.

6. Interview with White House official, December 8, 2015. Interview with former Senate staffer serving John Kerry, September 21, 2015. Mark Landler, "For Hillary Clinton and John Kerry, Divergent Paths to Iran Nuclear Talks," *New York Times,* May 2, 2016. Mark Landler, *Alter Egos: Hillary Clinton, Barack Obama, and the Twilight Struggle over American Power* (New York: Penguin Random House, 2016).

7. Interview with Deputy National Security Advisor Ben Rhodes, October 27, 2015. Interview with former Senate staffer serving John Kerry. Shohini Gupta, "Oman: The Unsung Hero of the Iranian Nuclear Deal," *Foreign Policy,* July 23, 2015. Matt Viser, "An Inside Look at How the Iran Talks Unfolded," *Boston Globe,* July 14, 2015. Conversation with official involved in the Omani channel. A month before Kerry's visit to Oman, Puneet Talwar and Dennis Ross from the White House met with the sultan to assess the strength of the Omani channel. Landler, *Alter Egos.*

8. Conversation with official involved in the Omani channel.

9. Interview with former White House official, July 31, 2015. Landler, *Alter Egos.* Daniel Dombey, "Transcript: John Kerry Interview," *Financial Times,* June 10, 2009.

10. David Ignatius, "How the Iran Deal Became the Most Strategic Success of Obama's Presidency," *Washington Post,* September 15, 2016. Landler, *Alter Egos.* Hillary Clinton, *Hard Choices* (New York: Simon and Schuster, 2014), 471. Interview with Jake Sullivan, September 23, 2015. Interview with former White House official, July 31, 2015.

11. Landler, *Alter Egos.* Interview with Ben Rhodes.

12. Interview with head of the Iranian Atomic Energy Agency, Dr. Ali Akbar Salehi, April 15, 2016. Mohammad Ali Shabani, "Salehi Reveals New Details of Secret U.S., Iran Back Channel," *Al Monitor,* December 23, 2015.

13. Jay Solomon, "Secret Dealings with Iran Led to Nuclear Talks," *Wall Street Journal,* June 29, 2015. Interview with Dr. Ali Akbar Salehi. Shabani, "Salehi Reveals New Details." Richard Engel, "Exclusive: Iran's Supreme Leader Personally Set Conditions for Nuclear Deal: Negotiator," NBC, January 28, 2016.

14. Shabani, "Salehi Reveals New Details." Engel, "Exclusive." Interview with Dr. Ali Akbar Salehi.

15. Conversation with well-connected Iranian member of think tank, December 2011. There was an exception, however: direct talks with the United States about Iraq had been held, per the request of the Iraqi government. Shabani, "Salehi Reveals

New Details." Interview with Dr. Ali Akbar Salehi. Interview with Iran's foreign minister, Javad Zarif, July 1, 2015.

16. Engel, "Exclusive." Shabani, "Salehi Reveals New Details." Interview with Dr. Ali Akbar Salehi. Interview with Gary Samore.

17. Eric Schmitt, Thom Shanker, and David Sanger, "U.S. Adds Forces in Persian Gulf, a Signal to Iran," *New York Times,* July 3, 2012.

18. Indira Lakshmanan, "If You Can't Do This Deal . . . Go Back to Tehran," *Politico,* September 25, 2015.

19. Puneet Talwar, "Iran in the Balance," *Foreign Affairs,* July/August 2001. Jay Solomon and Carol Lee, "U.S.-Iran Thaw Grew from Years of Behind-the-Scenes Talks," *Wall Street Journal,* November 7, 2013. Conversation with official involved in the Omani channel.

20. Landler, *Alter Egos.* Conversation with official involved in the Omani channel. Conversation with senior Iranian official, July 1, 2015.

21. Laura Rozen, "Inside the Secret U.S.-Iran Diplomacy That Sealed Nuke Deal," *Al Monitor,* August 11, 2015. Interview with Jake Sullivan. Landler, *Alter Egos.* Shabani, "Salehi Reveals New Details."

22. Interview with Jake Sullivan. Landler, *Alter Egos.* Interview with former White House official, January 6, 2015.

23. Interview with Gary Samore. Interview with Phil Gordon, September 8, 2015. Interview with former White House official, January 6, 2015. Interview with Richard Nephew, August 3, 2015. Interview with Ben Rhodes. Interview with Dr. Ali Akbar Salehi.

24. Interview with Gary Samore. Interview with Jake Sullivan. Landler, *Alter Egos.* Interview with former White House official, January 6, 2015.

25. Interview with Jake Sullivan. Landler, *Alter Egos.* Conversation with official involved in the Omani channel. Interview with Dr. Ali Akbar Salehi. Washington's ambassador to Oman at the time pointed out that "if Iran is approached in an atmosphere of mutual respect, and Iranian interlocutors are given evidence and information which help dispel misplaced fears and establish trust, Iran is prepared to act pragmatically and on the basis of enlightened self-interest" (Schmierer, "Sultanate of Oman"). Interview with Ben Rhodes.

26. Interview with State Department official, December 3, 2015. Interview with Gary Samore.

TEN The "Concession"

1. Interview with senior member of the EU negotiating team, December 16, 2015. Interview with Ben Rhodes, October 27, 2015. See also Trita Parsi, *A Single Roll of the Dice: Obama's Diplomacy with Iran* (New Haven, CT: Yale, 2012), ch. 8. Jay Solomon, *The Iran Wars: Spy Games, Bank Battles, and the Secret Deals That Reshaped the Middle East* (New York: Random House, 2016), 264.

2. Barak Ravid, "In Ice-Cold Kazakhstan, World Powers Try to Thaw Nuclear Talks with Iran," *Haaretz,* February 26, 2013. Lara Jakes and Peter Leonard, "World

Powers Coax Iran into Saving Nuclear Talks," Associated Press, February 27, 2013. Laura Rozen, "'Robust' Iran Nuclear Talks Reveal Gulf Between Sides," *Al Monitor,* April 6, 2013. David Herszenhorn, "Nuclear Talks with Iran End Without Accord or Plans for Another Round," *New York Times,* April 7, 2013. "West Made 'Huge Demands' from Iran in Almaty Nuclear Talks—Analyst," BBC, April 9, 2013.

3. Interview with Robert Einhorn, November 24, 2015. Interview with Ben Rhodes.

4. Interview with Jake Sullivan, September 23, 2015. Interview with Ambassador Sergey Ryabkov, November 20, 2015. Interview with Robert Einhorn.

5. Thomas Erdbrink, "Nonaligned Nations Back Iran's Nuclear Bid, but Not Syria," *New York Times,* August 31, 2012. "Putin: Iran Nuclear Issue Must Be Settled Peacefully," CNN, February 27, 2012. Interview with Vitaly Naumkin, director of the Institute of Oriental Studies of the Russian Academy of Sciences, January 19, 2016. Interview with Russian expert close to the Putin government, September 22, 2015.

6. Interview with Ambassador Peter Westmacott, November 12, 2015. Interview with Helga Schmid, December 15, 2015. Interview with Wendy Sherman, November 12, 2015. Interview with key member of the EU negotiating team. Interview with former EU foreign policy chief Javier Solana, February 25, 2016. Interview with Ambassador Gerard Araud, September 17, 2015. Interview with senior German diplomat, November 30, 2015.

7. Interview with Gary Samore, February 5, 2016. Interview with Richard Nephew, August 3, 2015. Interview with Jake Sullivan. Interview with Javier Solana, February 25, 2016.

8. Interview with Richard Nephew. Interview with former White House official, July 31, 2015.

9. Interview with former senior Pentagon official, September 18, 2015.

10. Richard J. Schmierer, "The Sultanate of Oman and the Iran Nuclear Deal," *Middle East Policy Council Journal* 22, no. 4 (2015). Interview with former White House official, January 12, 2016. Interview with White House official, October 10, 2015. Conversation with official involved in the Omani channel, October 2, 2015. Interview with Gary Samore.

11. "We at no moment could imagine a nuclear weapon in Iran being located that close to our borders," Russia's Deputy Foreign Minister Sergey Ryabkov told me. "Having said that, we have never been able to agree to what our U.S. and our European friends declared as credible information of possible existence of so-called previously military dimensions or alleged studies" (interview with Sergey Ryabkov). Moreover, Russia opposed Iran's acquiring nuclear weapons, but rejected claims that Iran had engaged in weapons activities prior to 2003. Nor did the Russians share the United States' assessment of Iran as a threat. Moscow has "no grounds to suspect Iran of seeking to possess nuclear weapons," Russian Prime Minister Vladimir Putin told CNN in December 2010. Interview with Russian expert close to the Putin government. Interview with Vitaly Naumkin. Interview with Russian Prime Minister Putin, *Larry King Live,* CNN, December 1, 2010.

12. Jasmin Ramsey, "Experts Urge Obama to Revamp Iran Diplomacy," *Lobe Log,* December 20, 2012. The letter was organized by the National Iranian American Council and the Arms Control Association. Laura Rozen, "Obama Urged to Step Up Iran Diplomacy," *Al Monitor,* January 18, 2013.

13. Interview with Jake Sullivan.

14. Interview with White House staffer Chris Backemeyer, December 3, 2015. Interview with Kelsey Davenport, November 30, 2015.

15. Interview with former deputy secretary of state William (Bill) Burns, December 21, 2015. Interview with White House staffer, December 8, 2015. Interview with former senior State Department official, September 21, 2015. Interview with former senior White House official, September 2015.

16. Interview with Wendy Sherman, April 11, 2016.

17. "Panetta: Iran Is One Year Away from Producing Nuclear Weapon," *Haaretz,* January 30, 2012. Interview with White House staffer, December 8, 2012. Interview with Jake Sullivan. Event at the Center for the National Interest, July 17, 2015.

18. "Sanctions on Iran May Not Be Enough: Netanyahu," Agence France Presse, April 16, 2013. Another minister in Netanyahu's cabinet, Yuval Steinitz, said it's "high time" for the international community to issue Iran "a deadline or a timetable, or even a military threat" (Isabel Kershner, "Officials in Israel Stress Readiness for a Lone Strike on Iran," *New York Times,* April 19, 2013). Ian Black and Simon Tisdall, "Saudi King Told U.S.: You Must Bomb Iran," *Guardian,* January 29, 2011.

19. David E. Sanger, "Diplomacy and Sanctions, Yes. Left Unspoken on Iran? Sabotage," *New York Times,* January 19, 2016. Interview with Gary Samore. Interview with Sergey Ryabkov.

20. Interview with Sergey Ryabkov. Interview with Chris Backemeyer. Interview with Russian expert close to the Putin government. Interview with German Ambassador to the United States Peter Wittig, November 30, 2015.

21. Interview with former White House official, January 6, 2016.

22. Bijan Khajehpour, Reza Marashi, and Trita Parsi, "Never Give In and Never Give Up: The Impact of Sanctions on Tehran's Nuclear Calculations," National Iranian American Council, March 2013, 28.

23. Edward Henniker-Major, "Nationalisation: The Anglo-Iranian Oil Company, 1951, Britain vs. Iran," Seven Pillars Institute, *Moral Cents* 2, no. 2 (2013): 22.

24. Khajehpour, Marashi, and Parsi, "Never Give In and Never Give Up," 29.

25. Ibid., 17.

26. Interview with Foreign Minister Javad Zarif, July 2, 2015.

27. Khajehpour, Marashi, and Parsi, "Never Give In and Never Give Up," 18.

28. Ibid., 30.

29. Interview with Mohammad Nahavandian, chief of staff to President Hassan Rouhani, September 24, 2015.

30. Interview with former White House official, July 31, 2015. Conversation with official involved in the Omani channel.

31. Iranian officials from various factions referenced the "limping giant" argument in several conversations I had with them in this time period.

32. The report in question was Khajehpour, Marashi, and Parsi, "Never Give In and Never Give Up."

33. Meeting with senior White House official, July 9, 2015.

34. Statement by President Barack Obama, April 2, 2015.

35. Interview with former White House official, July 31, 2015.

36. Interview with White House official, December 8, 2015. Interview with Robert Einhorn. Interview with key member of the EU negotiating team. Interview with former White House official, July 31, 2015. Interview with Wendy Sherman, April 11, 2016. Iran also made a big concession: it agreed to a bilateral channel after having rejected any direct negotiations with the United States since 2010. However, that was arguably a procedural, not a substantive, concession. Interview with Bill Burns. Interview with Jake Sullivan. Interview with Richard Nephew.

37. Interview with Ben Rhodes.

38. Interview with Professor Nasser Hadian, a member of the Iranian foreign minister's inner circle, September 14, 2015. Interview with White House official, December 8, 2015. Mehdi Khalaji, "Domestic Issues Trump Foreign Policy in Iran," Washington Institute, Policy No. 1330, January 18, 2008.

39. Interview with Professor Farideh Farhi, February 1, 2016. Interview with Javad Zarif, July 1, 2015.

40. Interview with Nasser Hadian. Interview with Farideh Farhi.

41. Interview with Iran's former foreign minister and current head of Iran's Atomic Energy Program, Dr. Ali Akbar Salehi, April 15, 2016. Interview with Javad Zarif, July 2, 2015.

42. In the view of well-respected Iran expert Farideh Farhi, these were some of the factors that ultimately "pressured" Khamenei into green lighting the secret channel (interview with Farideh Farhi).

43. Laura Rozen, "Three Days in March: New Details on How U.S., Iran Opened Direct Talks," Envoy, January 8, 2014. Mark Landler, Alter Egos: Hillary Clinton, Barack Obama, and the Twilight Struggle over American Power (New York Penguin Random House, 2016). Conversation with official involved in the Omani channel.

44. Interview with Bill Burns. Interview with Robert Einhorn.

45. Interview with Wendy Sherman, April 11, 2016.

46. Interview with Gary Samore. Interview with former White House official, July 31, 2015. Interview with Wendy Sherman, April 11, 2016. Interview with Chris Backemeyer. Landler, Alter Egos. Interview with Richard Nephew. Interview with Bill Burns. In fact, some U.S. officials argue that the formulation was so vague and couched that it did not amount to an offer to accept enrichment. That account, however, was categorically rejected by all others involved in the secret channel from all sides. Interview with White House official, October 9, 2015.

47. Interview with Richard Nephew. Interview with Bill Burns. Interview with Ben Rhodes.

48. Conversation with official involved in the Omani channel. Interview with Dr. Ali Akbar Salehi. Interview with Javad Zarif, July 2, 2015. Interview with Bill Burns. Interview with Robert Einhorn. Interview with Ben Rhodes.

49. Conversation with official involved in the Omani channel. Interview with Dr. Ali Akbar Salehi. Interview with Bill Burns. Interview with Robert Einhorn. Interview with Ben Rhodes.

50. Interview with Dr. Ali Akbar Salehi. Conversation with official involved in the Omani channel. Interview with Robert Einhorn. Interview with Ben Rhodes.

51. Conversation with official involved in the Omani channel. Interview with Dr. Ali Akbar Salehi. Interview with Jake Sullivan. Interview with Deputy Foreign Minister Majid Ravanchi, October 4, 2015.

ELEVEN The Sheikh of Diplomacy

1. Trita Parsi, "Can the Iranian Regime Survive Yet More Political Cannibalism?," *New Statesman,* June 13, 2013.

2. Thomas Erdbrink, "Prospect of Iran's Election Stirs Little Hope This Time Around," *New York Times,* May 9, 2013.

3. Saeed Kamali Dehghan, "Iran Election: Rafsanjani Blocked from Running for President," *Guardian,* May 21, 2013. Thomas Erdbrink, "Trying Unlikely Comeback, Ex-Iran President Strikes Chord with Public," *New York Times,* May 18, 2013. Trita Parsi, "Iran's March to Naked Dictatorship?," *Huffington Post,* May 22, 2013. "Don't Let Them Run!: Iran's Presidential Election," *Economist,* May 22, 2013.

4. Interview with senior advisor to the Rouhani campaign and government, September 14, 2015. Conversation with official involved in the Omani channel, October 2, 2015. Interview with former advisor to President Rouhani, January 16, 2016.

5. Holly Yan Aad Talia Kayali, "686 Presidential Candidates Try to Succeed Ahmadinejad in Iran," CNN, May 28, 2013. Dehghan, "Iran Election." Iran Election Third TV Debate on Foreign, Domestic Policy: Velayati, BBC, June 9, 2013. Thomas Erdbrink, "President-Elect Stirs Optimism in Iran and West," *New York Times,* July 27, 2013.

6. Thomas Erdbrink, "In Iran Race, All 8 Candidates Toe Hard Line on Nuclear Might," *New York Times,* June 10, 2013. Interview with Ben Rhodes, October 27, 2015. "Iran Leader Not Backing Presidential Candidate," Associated Press, May 29, 2013.

7. Thomas Erdbrink, "From Inner Circle of Iran, a Pragmatic Victory," *New York Times,* June 17, 2013. Ali Akbar Dareini, "Iranian Candidates Quarrel over Nuclear Talks," Associated Press, June 6, 2013. Interview with independent journalist Hooman Majd, February 2, 2016.

8. Iran Election Third TV Debate.

9. Interview with former advisor to President Rouhani. Interview with senior advisor to the Rouhani campaign and government.

10. Interview with senior advisor to the Rouhani campaign and government. Interview with former advisor to President Rouhani. Interview with regime insider close to the Rouhani government, November 13, 2015.

11. Trita Parsi, "No, Sanctions Didn't Force Iran to Make a Deal," *Foreign Policy*, May 14, 2014.

12. Interview with senior advisor to the Rouhani campaign and government. Interview with Hooman Majd.

13. Interview with former advisor to President Rouhani. Interview with regime insider close to the Rouhani government. Polling numbers for the 2013 elections can be found at https://www.ipos.me/ (in Persian). Max Fisher, "A Rare Iran Presidential Poll Shows Tehran Mayor Ghalibaf as Runaway Favorite," *Washington Post*, June 10, 2013.

14. Thomas Erdbrink, "Iran Moderate Wins Presidency by Large Margin," *New York Times*, June 16, 2013. "UAE Leaders Greet Iran's New President, Offer Cooperation," Fars News, June 16, 2013.

15. Brian Murphy and Nasser Karimi, "Iran's Voters Show Fervor in Showdown Atmosphere," Associated Press, June 14, 2016. Erdbrink, "Iran Moderate Wins." Interview with senior advisor to the Rouhani campaign and government. Interview with Hooman Majd. Interview with regime insider close to the Rouhani government.

16. Parsi, "No, Sanctions Didn't Force Iran."

17. Interview with White House official, October 9, 2015. Interview with Richard Nephew, August 3, 2015. Interview with White House staffer Chris Backemeyer, December 3, 2015. Interview with former undersecretary Bill Burns, December 21, 2015. Interview with Ben Rhodes. Interview with senior advisor to the Rouhani campaign and government. Interview with former advisor to President Rouhani. Interview with Gary Samore, February 5, 2016. Interview with former White House official, July 31, 2015. Interview with former senior State Department official, September 21, 2015.

18. Interview with German ambassador to the United States Peter Wittig, November 30, 2015. Interview with former senior Pentagon official, September 18, 2015. Interview with White House official, December 8, 2015.

19. Conversation with official involved in the Omani channel. Interview with Professor Farideh Farhi, February 1, 2016. Parsi, "No, Sanctions Didn't Force Iran." Interview with former advisor to President Rouhani.

20. Interview with former White House official, July 31, 2015. Interview with White House official, October 9, 2015. Amir Paivar, "Iran: Rouhani's First 100 Days," BBC Persian, November 12, 2013. Interview with Chris Backemeyer. Interview with Bill Burns. Interview with Ben Rhodes. Laura Rozen, "P5+1 Consider Strategy for Meeting New Iran Team in NY," *Al Monitor*, September 12, 2013.

21. "UAE Leaders Greet Iran's New President." Erdbrink, "From Inner Circle of Iran," and "President-Elect Stirs Optimism."

22. Erdbrink, "President-Elect Stirs Optimism," and "From Inner Circle of Iran."

23. Laura Rozen, "Top Iran, EU Diplomats Agree to Meet to Plan New Nuclear Talks," *Al Monitor*, August 19, 2013. Thomas Erdbrink, "Once an Outcast, Iranian Minister Carries Hope of Easing Tensions," *New York Times*, August 27, 2013. David Ignatius, "Both Opportunity and Peril over Iran," *Washington Post*, September 20, 2013.

24. Erdbrink, "Once an Outcast."

25. Ariel Ben Solomon, "The Good and the Bad of Rohani's Election," *Jerusalem Post,* June 17, 2013. Gil Hoffman, "Steinitz Urges World to Downplay Iranian Election," *Jerusalem Post,* May 29, 2013. Barak Ravid, "Israel Is Sanctifying the Status Quo and Ignoring the Possibility of a New Iran," *Haaretz,* June 16, 2013.

26. Solomon, "Good and the Bad." Barak Ravid, "Israel Responds Coolly to Outcome of Iranian Presidential Election," *Haaretz,* June 15, 2013. Barak Ravid, "Washington Promises Israel: More Pressure on Iran, Not Less," *Haaretz,* July 14, 2013. Amos Harel, "With a Moderate as Iran's New Face, Netanyahu Will Struggle to Draw Up Support for an Attack," *Haaretz,* June 16, 2013.

27. Chemi Shalev, "Netanyahu: 'I Won't Wait Until It's Too Late' to Decide on Israeli Attack on Iran," *Haaretz,* July 14, 2013. Interview with Tal Shalev, November 24, 2015. Barak Ravid, "Netanyahu: Israel Won't Accept Less than Total Halt of Iran's Nuclear Enrichment," *Haaretz,* June 18, 2013.

28. Jim Lobe, "U.S. Congress Moves Toward Full Trade Embargo on Iran," *Lobe Log,* May 22, 2013. Michael Wilner, "U.S. Will Back Israeli Force Against Iran, Senate Resolution Declares," *Jerusalem Post,* May 24, 2013. "U.S. House Backs New Sanctions Before Iran Inauguration," Agence France Presse, July 31, 2013. Rick Gladstone, "Sending Message to Iran, House Approves Tougher Sanctions," *New York Times,* August 1, 2013. Michael Wilner, "U.S. Congressmen Say Rouhani Brings Little Change to Iran," *Jerusalem Post,* July 3, 2013.

29. "U.S. Sanctions Aimed at Economic Suffocation of Iran: Russian Diplomat," *Xinhau,* August 1, 2013. Joby Warrick and Anne Gearan, "Despite Sanctions' Toll on Iran, U.S. Sees No Shift in Nuclear Behavior," *Washington Post,* June 18, 2013.

30. Saeed Kamali Deghan, " 'We Have to Build Trust': Rouhani Pledges Return to Moderation in Iranian Politics," *Guardian,* June 18, 2013. Thomas Erdbrink, "Iran President-Elect Wants to Ease Strains with U.S., but Sees No Direct Talk," *New York Times,* June 18, 2013. Brian Murphy, "Iran's New President Looks Westward for Nuke Talks," Associated Press, June 26, 2013. Hassan Rouhani, "President of Iran Hassan Rouhani: Time to Engage," *Washington Post,* September 19, 2013. Ali Akbar Dareini, "Iran State TV Lauds New President's Nuke Stance," Associated Press, June 21, 2013.

31. Laura Rozen, "Iran's Rosh Hashana Twitter Diplomacy Stirs Amazement, Disbelief," *Al Monitor,* September 5, 2013. Erin Delmore, "Iran's Rouhani Tweets Rosh Hashanah Blessing," MSNBC, September 4, 2013. Laura Rozen, "Rouhani Says Nuclear Issue Can Be Resolved," *Al Monitor,* September 25, 2013. The Rouhani and Zarif team recognized that Iran's public diplomacy was abysmal under Ahmadinejad. The previous foreign minister, Ali Akbar Salehi, had planned to beef up Iran's media profile by launching an English and Arabic language website presenting Iran's perspective on the conflict, but it never came to fruition. Once Rouhani and Zarif took power, those plans were revitalized and enhanced with a social media strategy. Their public diplomacy team consisted of a group of young, Western-educated Iranians who handled among other things Rouhani's Twitter account. (Zarif manages his own account.) Interview with regime insider close to the Rouhani government.

32. Interview with Dylan Williams of J Street, November 16, 2015.

33. Interview with president of J Street, Jeremy Ben Ami, January 7, 2016. Interview with Stephen Miles, director at Win Without War, February 17, 2016. Interview with Congresswoman Jan Schakowsky (D-IL), January 8, 2016. "Unprecedented: 131 in Congress Call for New Iran Diplomacy," National Iranian American Council press release, July 19, 2013. Ehsan Abtahi, "Iran Paper Analyzes U.S., EU Stances on Nuclear Talks," BBC, July 27, 2013.

34. Interview with Congressman David Price (D-NC), December 1, 2015. Interview with Congressman Keith Ellison (D-MN), April 27, 2016.

35. Thomas Erdbrink and Rick Gladstone, "Iran's Next President Faults Ahmadinejad on Economy," *New York Times,* July 16, 2013. Michael Wilner, "U.S.-Iranian Group Calls on Obama to Negotiate with Rouhani," *Jerusalem Post,* July 17, 2013.

36. Saeed Kamali Dehghan, "Plea for West to Embrace Iran's New President," *Guardian,* September 24, 2013.

TWELVE From Muscat to Geneva

1. Thomas Erdbrink and Mark Landler, "Iran Said to Seek a Nuclear Accord to End Sanctions," *New York Times,* September 20, 2013.

2. Conversation with official involved in the Omani channel, October 2, 2015. Laura Rozen, "Exclusive: Burns Led Secret U.S. Back Channel to Iran," *Al Monitor,* November 25, 2013. Erdbrink and Landler, "Iran Said to Seek a Nuclear Accord to End Sanctions." Lauren Rozen, "Obama Corresponds with Iran's Rouhani, Holds out Hope for Nuclear Deal," *Al Monitor,* September 15, 2013. Interview with Ben Rhodes, October 27, 2015. "Leader Meets with Sultan of Oman," Khamenei.ir, August 26, 2013.

3. Interview with Iranian Foreign Minister Javad Zarif, July 1, 2015. It was Ambassador Ali Asghar Khaji himself—the lead Iranian diplomat in the Oman channel—who briefed Zarif on the talks with the United States.

4. Laura Rozen, "Iran's Rosh Hashana Twitter Diplomacy Stirs Amazement, Disbelief," *Al Monitor,* September 5, 2013. Interview with senior Iranian advisor to Foreign Minister Javad Zarif, September 24, 2015. Interview with Chris Backemeyer, Iran director at the National Security Council, December 3, 2015.

5. Interview with Robert Einhorn, November 24, 2015. Interview with Deputy Foreign Minister Majid Ravanchi, October 4, 2015. Interview with White House official, October 9, 2015.

6. Interview with former White House official, July 31, 2015. Barak Ravid, "Overcoming Past Pains, West Begins to Imagine Possible Nuclear Deal with Iran," *Haaretz,* October 18, 2013.

7. Laura Rozen, "Inside the Secret U.S.-Iran Diplomacy That Sealed Nuke Deal," *Al Monitor,* August 11, 2015. Interview with Jake Sullivan, September 23, 2015. Interview with Richard Nephew, August 3, 2015. Interview with Chris Backemeyer.

8. Interview with Foreign Minister Javad Zarif, July 1, 2015.

9. Interview with former White House official.

10. Interview with Rouhani's chief of staff, Mohammad Nahavandian, September 24, 2015. Interview with Majid Ravanchi. Interview with former White House official.

11. Bijan Khajehpour, Reza Marashi, and Trita Parsi, "Extending Hands and Un-clenching Fists: Reorienting Iran's Outlook Beyond the Nuclear Deal," National Iranian American Council, December 2013.

12. Arash Karami, "Ayatollah Khamenei's 'Heroic Flexibility,'" *Al Monitor*, September 19, 2013. Khajehpour, Marashi, and Parsi, "Extending Hands and Unclenching Fists."

13. Amos Harel, "With an Attack on Iran Less Likely, Israel's Leaders Add Fuel to the Media's Fire," *Haaretz*, August 16, 2012. Ari Shavit, "Former Israeli Intelligence Chief Breaks His Silence on Iran," *Haaretz*, September 13, 2012.

14. Ben Caspit, "Israeli Minister Lapid Hears 'New Music' in Iran," *Al Monitor*, September 20, 2013. Barak Ravid, "PM Calls Iran's Gestures a 'Smoke Screen' as He Orders Boycott of Rohani's Speech," *Haaretz*, September 24, 2013. Interview with Brigadier General Shlomo Brom, February 25, 2016. Interview with Dalia Dassa Kaye, November 16, 2015.

15. Barak Ravid, "Obama's Package Deal: Nuke-Free Iran for Palestinian State," *Haaretz*, September 24, 2013. Ben Caspit, "Netanyahu Swimming Upstream After Iran's Diplomatic Flurry," *Al Monitor*, September 27, 2013.

16. Edith Lederer, "Netanyahu: Israel Won't Let Iran Get Nuclear Arms," Associated Press, October 1, 2013. Somini Sengupta and Rick Gladstone, "Netanyahu Excoriates Iran's Leader and His 'Charm Offensive,'" *New York Times*, October 1, 2013.

17. Interview with former Israeli diplomat Alon Pinkas, January 5, 2016. Interview with Israeli journalist Tal Shalev, November 24, 2015.

18. Mark Landler, *Alter Egos: Hillary Clinton, Barack Obama, and the Twilight Struggle over American Power* (New York: Penguin Random House, 2016).

19. Laura Rozen, "Rouhani Says Nuclear Issue Can Be Resolved," *Al Monitor*, September 24, 2013. Scott Wilson, "Obama Vows to Pursue Better Relations with Iran," *Washington Post*, September 25, 2013. Landler, *Alter Egos*. Laura Rozen, "Obama Calls Iran's Rouhani," *Al Monitor*, September 27, 2013. Interview with a regime insider close to the Rouhani government, November 13, 2015.

20. Laura Rozen, "Why No Obama Rouhani Meeting: White House Offered, Iran Declined," *Al Monitor*, September 24, 2013. Landler, *Alter Egos*. Interview with a regime insider.

21. Rozen, "Obama Calls Iran's Rouhani." Landler, *Alter Egos*. Interview with a regime insider. Interview with former senior White House official, January 12, 2016.

22. Laura Rozen, "Iran's Zarif Meets Kerry to 'Jump Start' Nuclear Talks," *Al Monitor*, September 26, 2013. Conversation with Foreign Minister Javad Zarif, November 20, 2013. Interview with Iranian American author Hooman Majd, February 2, 2016.

23. Interview with Majid Ravanchi. Rozen, "Iran's Zarif Meets Kerry." A few days after the Zarif-Kerry meeting, Wendy Sherman was confronted about the enrichment issue in a Senate hearing. When asked by Senator Marco Rubio (R-FL) if Obama would allow Iran to continue to enrich on its own soil, Sherman avoided the question: "I am not going to negotiate in public, with all due respect," Sherman said. "I can only repeat what the President of the United States has said." Laura Rozen, "Top U.S. Negotiator: Onus Is on Iran to Propose Nuclear Plan," *Al Monitor*, October 3, 2013.

24. "There's a Chink of Hope: Iran and Its Nuclear Plans," *Economist,* October 19, 2013. Interview with Majid Ravanchi. Ravid, "Overcoming Past Pains." George Janh, "Iran Nuke Overture: More a Promise than an Offer," Associated Press, October 22, 2013.

25. James Blitz, "U.S. Signals Possible Agreement with Iran After Geneva Talks," *Financial Times,* October 16, 2013. Barak Ravid, "Iran and Powers Divided over Sanctions, U.S. Officials Say," *Haaretz,* October 17, 2013.

26. Ravid, "Iran and Powers Divided." Interview with Ben Rhodes. Interview with Robert Einhorn.

27. Conversation with official involved in the Omani channel. Bradley Klapper, "Senators Seek More Iran Sanctions After Nuke Talks," Associated Press, October 16, 2013.

28. Amir Tibon and Tal Shalev, "Scenes from a Failed Marriage," *Huffington Post,* November 12, 2015. Joby Warrick, "Rift on Iran Nuclear Deal as Israel, Arabs Warn Against Enrichment," *Washington Post,* October 24, 2013. Tovah Lazaroff, Yaakov Lappin, and Michael Wilner, "Netanyahu to Kerry: A Bad Iran Deal Is Worse than No Deal," *Jerusalem Post,* October 24, 2013.

29. Warrick, "Rift on Iran Nuclear Deal." Lazaroff, Lappin, and Wilner, "Netanyahu to Kerry." Jim Lobe, "U.S. Jews Less Hawkish on Iran," *Lobe Log,* October 29, 2013.

30. Interview with Richard Nephew. Interview with former White House official.

31. Conversation with White House official, December 2013.

32. Interview with Jake Sullivan.

33. Conversation with White House official.

34. Interview with Wendy Sherman, April 11, 2016. Interview with Richard Nephew. Interview with a senior EU negotiator, December 16, 2015.

35. Interview with senior German diplomat, November 2015. Interview with Ambassador Gerard Araud, September 17, 2015. Jonathan Leslie, Reza Marashi, and Trita Parsi, "Losing Billions: The Cost of Iran Sanctions to the U.S. Economy," National Iranian American Council, July 2014. Interview with a senior EU negotiator.

36. Interview with Chris Backemeyer. Interview with Russian Deputy Foreign Minister Sergey Ryabkov, November 20, 2015. Interview with Vitaly Naumkin, January 19, 2016.

37. Interview with a senior EU negotiator. Interview with Helga Schmid, December 15, 2015.

38. Interview with Jake Sullivan. Interview with Richard Nephew.

39. Interview with senior European diplomat, June 22, 2016. Interview with Majid Ravanchi. Laura Rozen, "Progress, but No Deal Yet, as Iran Talks Conclude," *Al Monitor,* November 10, 2013. Interview with NSC official, October 9, 2015. Interview with Chris Backemeyer. Interview with Ambassador Kazem Sajjadpour, senior advisor to Foreign Minister Javad Zarif, September 24, 2015. Scott Peterson, "Tweets Put a Twist on Diplomacy at Iran Nuclear Talks," *Christian Science Monitor,* November 26, 2013.

40. Trita Parsi, "Enrichment Dispute Between Iran and P5+1 Getting Resolved," *Huffington Post,* November 22, 2013. Interview with Hooman Majd, February 2, 2016.

Interview with former senior White House official. Interview with senior European diplomat.

41. Interview with senior administration official, August 16, 2016. "'A Fool's Game': France Skeptical About Possible Iran Deal," RT.com, November 9, 2013. Rozen, "Progress, But No Deal Yet." Interview with Majid Ravanchi.

42. Laura Rozen, "Diplomat Says P5+1 Divided over Draft Iran Accord," *Al Monitor,* November 9, 2013.

43. Interview with White House staffer, December 8, 2015. Interview with senior EU diplomat, December 16, 2015. Barak Ravid, "France's Hollande to Visit Israel, Reap Reward for Stance on Iran," *Haaretz,* November 16, 2013.

44. Ravid, "France's Hollande to Visit Israel." "Ian Deitch, French President Vows Tough Iran Stance in Israel," Associated Press, November 17, 2013.

45. Interview with Ben Rhodes. Dennis Ross, "How Obama Got to 'Yes' on Iran: The Inside Story," *Politico,* October 8, 2015. Michael Gordon, "West and Iran Seen as Nearing a Nuclear Deal," *New York Times,* November 8, 2013. Jodi Rudoren, "On Iran, Netanyahu Can Only Fume," *New York Times,* November 9, 2013. Barak Ravid, "Israeli Intel Revealed Secret U.S.-Iran Talks, Months Before Obama Briefed Netanyahu," *Haaretz,* November 24, 2013. Tibon and Shalev, "Scenes from a Failed Marriage."

46. Rozen, "Progress, but No Deal Yet." Paul Richter, "U.S., Iran Bicker over Talks Blame," *Baltimore Sun,* November 12, 2013.

47. Interview with senior administration official.

48. Karen Deyoung, "Kerry: Obama Not Bluffing with Iran," *Washington Post,* November 12, 2013.

49. "Iran Says Next Nuclear Talks Will Be 'Difficult,'" Agence France Presse, November 17, 2013. George Janh, "Deal Closer: Iran Concedes on 'Right' to Enrich," Associated Press, November 19, 2013.

50. Rozen, "Exclusive: Burns Led Secret U.S. Back Channel to Iran." Joby Warrick and Anne Gearan, "Kerry in Geneva, Raising Hopes for Historic Nuclear Deal with Iran," *Washington Post,* November 23, 2013.

51. Interview with Hooman Majd.

52. The YouTube video can be accessed at https://www.youtube.com/watch?v =Ao2WH6GDWz4.

53. "Iran Foreign Minister Discusses Nuclear Deal, Lauds Leader for Support," BBC, November 27, 2013. Interview with Majid Ravanchi.

54. Interview with Majid Ravanchi.

55. Interview with Richard Nephew.

56. Interview with former deputy secretary of state Bill Burns, December 21, 2015. "Iran Foreign Minister Discusses Nuclear Deal."

THIRTEEN The Pressure Paradox

1. Joby Warrick, "Key Terms of the Deal with Iran," *Washington Post,* November 25, 2013.

2. "Iran Foreign Minister Discusses Nuclear Deal, Lauds Leader for Support," BBC, November 27, 2013.

3. Interview with Robert Einhorn, November 24, 2015.

4. Brian Murphy and Adam Lee, "Anatomy of Iranian Nuclear Deal," Associated Press, November 24, 2013. Debb Reichmann and George Janh, "Kerry Tells Iran: Prove Peaceful Nuke Intentions," Associated Press, November 24, 2013. "EU Hails P5+1 Agreement with Iran," *Xinahu,* November 24, 2013.

5. "Rouhani Congratulates Supreme Leader on Nuclear Deal: TV," *Xinhau,* November 24, 2013. Thomas Erdbrink, "Praise in Iran All the Way to the Top, Where Efforts Reportedly Preceded a President," *New York Times,* November 25, 2013. "Iran Supreme Leader Welcomes Nuclear Agreement," *Xinhau,* November 24, 2013. "Iran Hard-Liners Call Nuclear Deal 'Poisoned Chalice,'" *Haaretz,* November 27, 2013.

6. Murphy and Lee, "Anatomy of Iranian Nuclear Deal." "Israel Minister: Iran Deal Based on 'Deceit,'" Associated Press, November 24, 2013. "Israel's Ex-Security Chiefs Stand with the International Community on Iran Deal," *Haaretz,* November 26, 2013. Amir Tibon and Tal Shalev, "Scenes from a Failed Marriage," *Huffington Post,* November 12, 2015. Barak Ravid, "U.S. Rejects Israeli Criticism, Says Not Avoiding Confrontation with Iran at Any Cost," *Haaretz,* December 3, 2013. Interview with former Israeli deputy national security advisor Brigadier General Shlomo Brom, February 25, 2016.

7. Tibon and Shalev, "Scenes from a Failed Marriage." Ravid, "U.S. Rejects Israeli Criticism."

8. Interview with Ben Rhodes, October 27, 2015. Interview with Robert Einhorn. "Israel's Ex-Security Chiefs." Barak Ravid, "World Powers to Israel: Stop Griping, Work with Us Toward Final Iran Deal," *Haaretz,* November 26, 2013. Interview with Israeli journalist Tal Shalev, November 24, 2015.

9. Ravid, "U.S. Rejects Israeli Criticism."

10. Interview with administration official, March 2016.

11. Interview with Ben Rhodes. "Barack, Bibi and Iran," *Economist,* November 16, 2013.

12. Adam Entous and Danny Yadron, "U.S. Spy Net on Israel Snares Congress," *Wall Street Journal,* December 29, 2015.

13. Jim Lobe, "Stakes over Iran Talks on the Rise," *Lobe Log,* November 23, 2013. Ravid, "U.S. Rejects Israeli Criticism."

14. Anshel Pfeffer, "As Israel's Allies Soften Stance on Iran, Netanyahu Scrambles to Regain Control," *Haaretz,* November 20, 2013.

15. Tibon and Shalev, "Scenes from a Failed Marriage." Allison Hoffman, "Bibi's Brain: Meet Ron Dermer, Israel's New Ambassador to the U.S.," *Tablet Magazine,* September 20, 2013. Ron Kampeas, "'Bibi's Brain' Comes to Washington," Politico.com, December 2, 2013.

16. "White House Steps Up Bid to Thwart New Iran Sanctions," Agence France Presse, December 4, 2013.

17. Ariel Ben Solomon, "Iran: Nuke Deal Dead If Congress Passes New Sanctions," *Jerusalem Post,* December 3, 2013. Bradley Klapper, "Kerry, Congress Spar over Iran Nuclear Deal," Associated Press, December 10, 2013.

18. Joby Warrick and Karen Deyoung, "On Iran, Senators Defy White House, Threaten New Sanctions," *Washington Post,* December 20, 2013. Jim Lobe, "Iran Sanctions Bill Big Test of Israel Lobby Power," *Lobe Log,* December 21, 2013. Mark Landler and Jonathan Weisman, "Obama Fights a Push to Add Iran Sanctions," *New York Times,* January 14, 2014. Mark Landler, "A Bill Stokes Debate, and Doubt, on Iran Deal," *New York Times,* January 17, 2014.

19. President Obama's State of the Union Address, January 28, 2014.

20. Ed O'Keefe, "Iran Sanctions Bill Nears Threshold for Senate Vote," *Washington Post,* January 11, 2014. Landler and Weisman, "Obama Fights a Push." Ryan Grim, "White House Dares Democratic Senators Pushing Iran Sanctions to Admit They Want War," *Huffington Post,* January 9, 2014. Interview with senior National Security Council official, October 9, 2015.

21. Interview with former National Security Council official, March 23, 2016. Landler and Weisman, "Obama Fights a Push to Add Iran Sanctions." Robert Menendez, "Diplomatic Insurance Against Iran," *Washington Post,* January 10, 2014.

22. Interview with former National Security Council official. Warrick and Deyoung, "On Iran, Senators Defy White House."

23. Conversation with senior White House official, April 15, 2015. Interview with former National Security Council official.

24. Michael Wilner, "AIPAC Conference to Focus More on Iran than U.S. Peace Efforts Between Israel, PA," *Jerusalem Post,* March 2, 2014. Jim Lobe, "Menendez, AIPAC Beat Tactical Retreat," *Lobe Log,* February 6, 2014. Douglas Bloomfield, "What's AIPAC's Plan B for Iran?," *Jerusalem Post,* February 13, 2014.

25. "Iran Nuclear Deal Comes into Force as U.S. Sanctions Loom," Agence France Presse, January 20, 2014. Jason Rezaian and Anne Gearan, "World Powers Lift Some Sanctions in Response to Action by Iran," *Washington Post,* January 21, 2014. "Uranium Stockpile Shrinks in Iran," *Washington Post,* February 21, 2014. Interview with White House staffer, December 8, 2015. Interview with Richard Nephew, August 3, 2015.

26. "Powers Seek to Forget Crimea for Iran Nuclear Talks," Agence France Presse, March 18, 2014. George Janh and Vladimir Isachenkov, "Russia: Iran Nuke Talks May Suffer over Ukraine," Associated Press, March 19, 2014.

27. Michael Gordon, "On Tour of Mideast, Kerry Says Iran Might Play Role in Syria Peace Talk," *New York Times,* January 6, 2014. Thomas Erdbrink, "U.S. and Iran Face Common Enemies in Mideast Strife," *New York Times,* January 7, 2014. "Ban Boots Iran Out of Syria Peace Talks," Agence France Presse, January 20, 2014. "Iran Says Will Attend Syria Talks, Rejects Conditions," Agence France Presse, January 20, 2014. Michael Gordon and Somini Sengupta, "U.N. Invites Iran to Syria Talks, Raising Objections from the U.S.," *New York Times,* January 20, 2014. Liz Sly and

Anne Gearan, "U.N. Rescinds Iran Invitation to Syria Talk," *Washington Post,* January 21, 2014.

28. "Syria Peace Talks Hit Hurdle After Iran Invite," Agence France Presse, January 20, 2014. Sly and Gearan, "U.N. Rescinds Iran Invitation." Jason Rezaian, "Iran Blames U.S. for Blocking It from Syria Peace Talks in Geneva," *Washington Post,* January 22, 2014. Thomas Erdbrink, "As Sunni Militants Threaten Its Allies in Baghdad, Iran Weighs Options," *New York Times,* June 12, 2014.

29. Interview with senior Iraqi defense official, July 22, 2016. "Ambassador in Tehran Thanks Iran for Saving Iraq from ISIS," *Rudaw,* July 31, 2016. Michael Gordon and Eric Schmitt, "Iran Aids Iraq with Drones and Military Gear," *New York Times,* June 26, 2014.

30. Jason Rezaian and Anne Gearan, "Iran, U.S. Signal Openness to Cooperation on Iraq," *Washington Post,* June 17, 2014. David Sanger, "Conflict in Iraq Adds New Angle to U.S.-Iran Nuclear Talks," *New York Times,* June 18, 2014. Eric Schmitt and Helene Cooper, "ISIS Fighters Seized Advantage in Iraq Attack by Striking During Sandstorm," *New York Times,* May 18, 2015. Jason Rezaian, "Iran's Leader Says Tehran and Washington Not Aligned on Iraq," *Washington Post,* June 24, 2014.

31. Interview with Ambassador Peter Wittig, November 30, 2015. Jeffrey Goldberg, "Obama to Israel—Time Is Running Out," Bloomberg, March 2, 2014.

32. Eliza Collins, "Obama Aide: Saudi Arabia Paid 'Insufficient Attention' to Extremist Funding," *Politico,* April 18, 2016. Interview with White House staffer, March 2016.

33. Interview with Professor Nasser Hadian, a member of the Iranian foreign minister's inner circle, September 14, 2015. Rezaian, "Iran's Leader Says."

34. Rezaian, "Iran's Leader Says." Interview with Iranian Foreign Minister Javad Zarif, October 4, 2015.

35. Interview with Javad Zarif, October 4, 2015.

36. Mohammad Javad Zarif, "Zarif: Iran Is Committed to a Peaceful Nuclear Program," *Washington Post,* July 14, 2014. "U.S., Iran Trade Barbs in Nuclear Talks Finale," Agence France Presse, July 2, 2014. Interview with former White House official, September 8, 2015.

37. Interview with senior administration official, January 28, 2016. Interview with Javad Zarif, April 20, 2016. Interview with National Security Council official Rob Malley, October 10, 2015. Interview with senior administration official, December 2015.

38. Interview with Javad Zarif, April 20, 2016. "Iran's Supreme Leader Reveals Demands in Nuclear Talks," Agence France Presse, July 8, 2014. George Janh, "Iran Wants to Greatly Expand Uranium Enrichment," Associated Press, July 9, 2014. Interview with Rob Malley.

39. Interview with Richard Nephew.

40. Trita Parsi, "The False Gospels That Threaten the Iran Nuke Talks," *National Interest,* January 30, 2015.

41. Ibid.

42. Ibid.

43. Laura Rozen, "Iran's UN Demand Emerges as Hitch in Nuclear Talks," *Al Monitor,* September 23, 2014. Laurence Norman, "Iran Nuclear Deal Remains in Doubt," *Wall Street Journal,* November 17, 2014. Michael Gordon and David Sanger, "Brinkmanship Heightens as Deadline for a Nuclear Deal Looms," *New York Times,* November 21, 2014.

44. David Sanger, Michael Gordon, and Peter Baker, "A Nuclear Deal for the U.S. and Iran Slips Away Again," *New York Times,* November 24, 2014.

45. "Time Is Not on His Side," *Economist,* November 24, 2014. Sanger, Gordon, and Baker, "A Nuclear Deal." David Sanger, Steven Erlanger, and Jodi Rudoren, "Iran Nuclear Pact Faces an Array of Opposing Forces," *New York Times,* November 16, 2014. Ali Akbar Dareini, "Iran Responds to Obama Letters, Says Won't Accept 'Decorative' Nuke Program," Associated Press, November 12, 2014.

46. Laura Rozen, "Last Days of Iran Talks Showed Signs of Promise," *Al Monitor,* November 25, 2014.

47. Interview with Javad Zarif, April 20, 2016. Conversations with Javad Zarif and other members of the Iranian negotiating team, November 24, 2014. Interview with Deputy Foreign Minister Majid Ravanchi, October 4, 2015.

48. Interview with Rob Malley. Interview with senior administration official, August 16, 2016.

49. David Sanger and Michael Gordon, "U.S. and Allies Extend Iran Nuclear Talks by 7 Months," *New York Times,* November 24, 2014. Laura Rozen, "'Progress Made' but Deadline Extended in Iran Nuclear Talks," *Al Monitor,* November 24, 2014.

50. William Booth, "Israel Greets Extension of Iran Nuclear Talks with Relief," *Washington Post,* November 24, 2014. Ben Caspit, "Israel Satisfied with Delay on Iran Nuke Deal," *Al Monitor,* November 28, 2014. "Time Is Not on His Side." "Israel Played Key Role to Stop 'Bad' Iran Nuclear Deal: PM," *Daily Mail,* December 7, 2014. Interview with Robert Einhorn.

FOURTEEN "Our Eyes Were Bleeding"

1. Statement by the president on Cuba policy changes, December 17, 2014.

2. Peter Kornbluh and William Leogrande, "Inside the Crazy Back-Channel Negotiations That Revolutionized Our Relationship with Cuba," *Mother Jones,* September/October 2015.

3. Thomas Erdbrink, "Iran Leader Suggests Direct Votes on Issues," *New York Times,* January 5, 2015. Mehrdad Balali, Stephanie Nebehay, and Fredrik Dahl, "Iranian President Upbeat About Nuclear Talks," *Haaretz,* December 15, 2014. "Rouhani: To Hell with Critics of Diplomacy," *Iran Primer,* August 11, 2014.

4. "U.S. Senator Tells Netanyahu Congress Will Follow His Lead on Iran Sanctions," *Jerusalem Post,* December 29, 2014. "Obama Urges Congress to Hold Off on Iran Sanctions, Threatens Veto," Agence France Presse, January 16, 2015. Josh Lederman, "Obama Comes out Swinging Against New Iran Sanctions," Associated Press, January 16, 2015.

5. Nicole Revise, "Obama Administration Eager to Prevent New Sanctions Against Iran," Agence France Presse, December 4, 2014. Michael Shear, "Obama and Senator Spar on How to Handle Iran," *New York Times,* January 16, 2015. Ellen Nakashima, "Administration, Lawmakers Clash over Iran Policy," *Washington Post,* January 22, 2015.

6. Lederman, "Obama Comes out Swinging." Michael Wilner, "Germany, France, UK Tell Congress to Hold Back on Iran Bill," *Jerusalem Post,* January 23, 2015.

7. Jeremy Peters, "Boehner's Invitation Is Aiding Obama's Cause on Iran," *New York Times,* January 29, 2015. Interview with Congresswoman Nancy Pelosi (D-CA), February 25, 2016. Donna Cassata, "Boehner Invites Israeli Leader to Address Congress on Iran," Associated Press, January 21, 2015. Adam Entous and Danny Yadron, "U.S. Spy Net on Israel Snares Congress," *Wall Street Journal,* December 29, 2015.

8. Amir Tibon and Tal Shalev, "Scenes from a Failed Marriage," *Huffington Post,* November 12, 2015. Entous and Yadron, "U.S. Spy Net." Interview with Congresswoman Jan Schakowsky (D-IL), January 8, 2016. Michael Gordan, "Kerry Cautions Critics of Nuclear Talks with Iran," *New York Times,* February 25, 2015.

9. Interview with Peter Beinart, December 10, 2015. Interview with Shlomo Brom, February 25, 2016.

10. Alexandra Jaffe, "58 Members of Congress Skipped Netanyahu's Speech," CNN, March 3, 2015. Rebecca Shimoni Stoil, "Obama Approves $225 Million in Iron Dome Funding," *Times of Israel,* August 5, 2014. Interview with Senator Dick Durbin (D-IL), March 8, 2016. Interview with Jan Schakowsky.

11. See transcript of Netanyahu's address to Congress at https://www .washingtonpost.com/news/post-politics/wp/2015/03/03/full-text-netanyahus-address -to-congress/.

12. Herb Keinon, "The New and the Omitted in Netanyahu's Address," *Jerusalem Post,* March 6, 2015. See transcript of Netanyahu's address to Congress.

13. Interview with Deputy National Security Advisor Ben Rhodes, October 27, 2015. Michael Wilner, "Rice Says PM's Stance on Iranian Nukes Is 'Not a Viable Negotiating Position,'" *Jerusalem Post,* March 4, 2015.

14. Interview with Amir Tibon, November 25, 2015. "Netanyahu Denounces Obama Push for Iran Nuclear Deal," Agence France Presse, March 3, 2015. Interview with Congressman Keith Ellison (D-MN), April 27, 2016. Interview with Nancy Pelosi.

15. "Netanyahu Denounces Obama Push." Tibon and Shalev, "Scenes from a Failed Marriage." Hamed Aleaziz, "FLASHBACK: Netanyahu Said Iraq War Would Benefit the Middle East," ThinkProgress, October 31, 2012.

16. Michael Gordon and Steven Erlanger, "Iran Presses for Progress on Nuclear Agreement," *New York Times,* February 9, 2015. Carol Morello, "Kerry Rules out Extending Iran Nuclear Talks Without an Outline of Deal Soon," *Washington Post,* February 9, 2015. Interview with former deputy secretary of state Wendy Sherman, April 11, 2016. Interview with Chris Backemeyer, December 3, 2015. Interview with Foreign Minister Javad Zarif, April 20, 2016.

17. Interview with senior administration official, January 2016. Interview with Gary Samore, February 5, 2016.

18. Interview with Colin Kahl, January 28, 2016. Gordon Michael and Steven Erlanger, "Negotiators Weigh Plan to Phase out Nuclear Limits on Iran," *New York Times,* February 24, 2015.

19. Interview with Wendy Sherman. Interview with Javad Zarif, April 20, 2016. George Janh and Bradley Klapper, "Top U.S., Iranian Nuke Officials Joining Iran Talks," Associated Press, February 21, 2015. Interview with Ali Akbar Salehi, April 15, 2016. Richard Stone, "Exclusive: Iran's Atomic Czar Explains How He Helped Seal the Iran Nuclear Agreement," *Science Magazine,* August 12, 2015.

20. Interview with Rob Malley, October 10, 2010. Interview with Ben Rhodes. Briefing at the White House, June 17, 2015.

21. Fred Thys, "For 2 Key Iran Deal Negotiators, MIT Experiences Created a Helpful Connection," WBUR, July 27, 2015. Kristin Toussaint, "How MIT Swag Helped Win an Iranian Nukes Deal," *Boston Globe,* July 16, 2015. Stone, "Exclusive." Matt Viser, "An Inside Look at How the Iran Talks Unfolded," *Boston Globe,* July 14, 2015.

22. Alan Yuhas, "Senate Democrats Denounce Republican Letter to Iran as Call for War," *Guardian,* March 11, 2015.

23. Interview with senior German diplomat, November 2015. Laura Koran and Deena Zaru, "Cotton, Iranian Leader Tangle Again on Social Media," CNN, April 30, 2015.

24. Interview with Secretary of State John Kerry, September 8, 2016. Bradley Klapper and George Janh, "Official: Iran Confronts U.S. at Nuke Talks over GOP Letter," Associated Press, March 16, 2015. Interview with senior administration official, August 16, 2016.

25. Interview with senior EU diplomat, December 16, 2015. Interview with senior White House official, January 28, 2016. Interview with Federica Mogherini, December 15, 2015.

26. Conversation with Javad Zarif, March 29, 2015. Interview with Federica Mogherini.

27. David McCabe, "Kerry Mourns Death of Iranian President's Mom," *Hill,* March 20, 2015.

28. Ali Watkins, Ryan Grim, and Akbar Shahid Ahmed, "Iran Warned Houthis Against Yemen Takeover," *Huffington Post,* April 20, 2015. "Guarded Optimism as Iran Nuclear Talks Enter 'Endgame,'" Agence France Presse, March 28, 2015. Michael Crowley, "As Yemen Escalates, White House Doubles Down on Iran Diplomacy," *Politico,* April 20, 2015.

29. David Kirkpatrick, "Saudis Make Own Moves as U.S. and Iran Talk," *New York Times,* March 31, 2015. Carol Morello, "A Make-or-Break Moment for Iran Nuclear Talks," *Washington Post,* March 27, 2015. Herb Keinon and Yaakov Lappin, "As Iran Deal Nears, PM Steps Up Criticism," *Jerusalem Post,* March 30, 2015.

30. Interview with Rob Malley.

31. Conversation with senior Iranian official, June 30, 2015. Interview with Rob Malley.

32. Interview with Chris Backemeyer.

33. Interview with Ali Akbar Salehi. Interview with Mohammad Nahavandian, September 24, 2015. "Once they accepted Moniz's logic and framework, it didn't matter how many centrifuges they had," Malley said. "There was no real difference between 5,000 and 6,000. It became symbolic. It made no difference" (interview with Rob Malley). Beyond that, the agreement was historic in Salehi's view because it was one of "very few occasions in which science came to settle a major political dispute."

34. "Deadline Abandoned in Marathon Iran Nuclear Talks," Agence France Presse, March 31, 2015. Interview with White House official, December 8, 2015.

35. John Goldman, "Inspector's Report to U.N. Cites Lack of Iraqi Cooperation," *Los Angeles Times,* December 16, 1998.

36. Amin Tarzi, "Contradictions in U.S. Policy on Iraq and Its Consequences," *Middle East Review of International Affairs* 4, no. 1 (2000). I partook in the UN Security Council deliberations at the time and was present at this specific meeting.

37. Interview with Chris Backemeyer. Interview with senior EU diplomat, June 22, 2016. Interview with Federica Mogherini.

38. Interview with White House official. Interview with senior administration official, December 2015. Interview with Bernadette Meehan, October 9, 2015.

FIFTEEN The Unclenched Fist

1. Interview with White House staffer, February 4, 2016. Interview with former State Department official Joy Drucker, March 2, 2016.

2. David Ignatius, "Israel's Side of the Iran Dispute," *Washington Post,* February 20, 2015. "Parameters for a Joint Comprehensive Plan of Action Regarding the Islamic Republic of Iran's Nuclear Program," State Department Media Note, April 2, 2015. Interview with administration official, December 8, 2015.

3. "Parameters for a Joint Comprehensive Plan." Interview with Rob Malley, October 10, 2010.

4. Interview with White House staffer, March 23, 2016.

5. Interview with Congresswoman Jan Schakowsky (D-IL), January 8, 2016. Jim Lobe, "150 House Democrats Bolster Obama's Position on Iran Deal," *Lobe Log,* May 7, 2015.

6. Lobe, "150 House Democrats."

7. Ellen Nakashima, "Administration, Lawmakers Clash over Iran Policy," *Washington Post,* January 22, 2015.

8. Michael Memoli, "Obama Compromise with Congress on Iran Deal Signals Shift in Approach," *Nation,* April 18, 2015. Douglas Bloomfield, "AIPAC Opposes Bibi's Amendment—For Now," *Jewish Week,* April 24, 2015.

9. "The Fate of the Iran Deal in Congress," *New York Times,* May 7, 2015. Interview with Senator Tim Kaine (D-VA), December 22, 2015.

10. Massimo Calabresi, "Exclusive: Netanyahu Canceled Intel Briefing for U.S. Senators on Iran Dangers," *Time,* March 14, 2015. Interview with Tim Kaine.

11. Bloomfield, "AIPAC Opposes Bibi's Amendment." Interview with Tim Kaine.

12. Interview with Tim Kaine.

13. The Senate can overturn a presidential veto if it has the support of two-thirds of the body. Interview with Tim Kaine.

14. Josh Rogin, "Senators Challenge Obama with New Iran Bill," *Bloomberg View,* February 27, 2015. Interview with Tim Kaine.

15. Interview with Tim Kaine.

16. John Bennett, "Iran Bill Sets Up Political Tests," Defense One, April 13, 2015. Interview with Tim Kaine.

17. Jennifer Steinhauer, "Senate Easily Passes Bill for a Voice on the Iran Nuclear Accord," *New York Times,* May 7, 2015. Interview with senior administration official, January 28, 2016. Ron Kampeas, "With House Set to Approve Iran Deal, Options to Shape Outcome Remote," Jewish Telegraphic Agency, May 12, 2015.

18. Amir Tibon and Tal Shalev, "Scenes from a Failed Marriage," *Huffington Post,* November 12, 2015. Interview with senior administration official, January 28, 2016.

19. Interview with Chris Backemeyer, December 3, 2015. Interview with National Security Council staffer, October 2015.

20. Interview with National Security Council staffer, October 9, 2015. Interview with senior administration official, January 28, 2016.

21. Interview with Rob Malley. Interview with Chris Backemeyer. Interview with senior EU diplomat, December 16, 2015. Michael Crowley, "Key Iranian Negotiator Sidelined by Illness," *Politico,* June 25, 2015. Briefing with Deputy Foreign Minister Majid Ravanchi, July 2, 2015.

22. Interview with Foreign Minister Javad Zarif, April 20, 2016. Interview with administration official. Interview with Rob Malley.

23. Interview with Rob Malley. Interview with Javad Zarif, April 20, 2016.

24. Closed briefing at the White House, June 17, 2016. Conversation with Javad Zarif, June 27, 2015.

25. Address by Vice President Joe Biden at the Washington Institute for Near East Policy, April 30, 2014. Parisa Hafezi, "Iran's Khamenei Rules out Freezing Sensitive Nuclear Work for Long Period," Reuters, June 23, 2015.

26. Conversation with Javad Zarif and Majid Ravanchi, June 27, 2015. Trita Parsi, "P5+1 and Iran Have Settled Framework for Sanctions Relief Timing, Say Iranian Sources," *Huffington Post,* June 28, 2016. Gareth Porter, "Behind the Scenes: How the U.S. and Iran Reached Their Landmark Deal," *Nation,* September 5, 2015.

27. Closed briefing at the White House, June 17, 2016.

28. Interview with Robert Einhorn, November 24, 2015. Porter, "Behind the Scenes."

29. Porter, "Behind the Scenes."

30. John Follain, Indira A. R. Lakshmanan, and Kambiz Foroohar, "Keep It Quiet, Aide Tells Shouting Kerry and Iran Minister," Bloomberg, July 8, 2015. Robin Wright, "Tehran's Promise," *New Yorker,* July 27, 2015. Porter, "Behind the Scenes." Conversation with Javad Zarif.

31. Wright, "Tehran's Promise." Interview with administration official.

32. Porter, "Behind the Scenes." Interview with Rob Malley. Interview with Federica Mogherini, December 15, 2015.

33. Matt Viser, "An Inside Look at How the Iran Talks Unfolded," *Boston Globe,* July 14, 2015. Wright, "Tehran's Promise." Arshad Mohammed and Warren Strobel, "For Kerry, Iran Deal Would Be a Legacy Hit After Many Misses," Reuters, June 23, 2015.

34. Background briefing by Majid Ravanchi, July 2, 2015. Interview with Federica Mogherini. Porter, "Behind the Scenes."

35. Interview with senior EU diplomat.

36. Interview with Secretary of State John Kerry, September 8, 2016. Laura Rozen, "Iranian Nuclear Talks Go on Even If Clock Strikes Midnight," *Al Monitor,* July 9, 2015. Interview with senior administration official, August 16, 2016. Interview with Foreign Minister Javad Zarif, April 20, 2016.

37. State Department briefing to the press on the Iran nuclear deal, July 16, 2015.

38. Interview with administration official. Porter, "Behind the Scenes."

39. "Revealed: Iran's 15 Deal Secrets," IranWire, August 3, 2015.

40. Najmeh Bozorgmehr, "Hurdle in Iran Nuclear Talks Harks Back to 1980s War with Iraq," *Financial Times,* June 24, 2015.

41. Background briefing by Iranian official, July 2, 2015. Bozorgmehr, "Hurdle in Iran Nuclear Talks." Conversation with Iranian diplomat, June 29, 2015. Closed briefing at the White House, June 17, 2016.

42. Background briefing by Iranian official. Porter, "Behind the Scenes." Closed briefing at the White House, June 17, 2016.

43. Closed briefing at the White House, June 17, 2015. Porter, "Behind the Scenes." Closed briefing at the White House, July 30, 2015.

44. Interview with Rob Malley. Carol Morello, "On the Verge of a Breakthrough Nuclear Deal with Iran, *Washington Post,* July 12, 2015.

45. Morello, "On the Verge." State Department briefing, July 16, 2015. Wright, "Tehran's Promise." Interview with Helga Schmid, December 15, 2015.

46. Viser, "Inside Look." Interview with Federica Mogherini. Interview with Helga Schmid.

47. Interview with Chris Backemeyer. Interview with Rob Malley. Interview with senior administration official, December 2015.

48. Interview with Federica Mogherini. Nicole Revise, "France, U.S. Uneasy Bedfellows as They Seek Iran Deal," Agence France Presse, December 13, 2014. Michael Wilner, "Powers Stiffen Postures Ahead of Critical Hour with Iran," *Jerusalem Post,* March 23, 2015. Conversation with Javad Zarif. Interview with senior administration official, August 16, 2016.

49. The final deal added detail and a schedule for many aspects, but primarily concerned the sanctions relief. Iran's implementation of the Additional Protocol (AP) would begin on implementation day—which would occur once the IAEA had certified that Iran had completed its initial steps and sanctions would start being lifted. But

Iran would not ratify the Additional Protocol to the NPT until year eight of the agreement, at which point the United States would lift its sanctions through congressional action. Prior to that, the United States would only waive the sanctions. Iran also agreed to permit the IAEA to monitor Iran's entire nuclear supply chain, including uranium mines for twenty-five years and all centrifuge production facilities for twenty years. It would also work with the IAEA on a road map to close the file with regard to past possible military dimensions (PMD) to its nuclear activities—though the judgment of the report would be inconsequential. These steps, combined with the IAEA's use of the most modern technologies, would make this the most rigorous inspections regime in the world.

On sanctions relief, the parties agreed that the UN Security Council would adopt a new resolution endorsing the JCPOA and terminating all provisions of the previous UN Security Council resolutions relating to Iran, while incorporating certain restrictions, such as the sale of arms to or from Iran for five years and Iran's development of ballistic missile technologies for eight years. The United States would lift all nuclear-related sanctions, including those on banking, energy, and trade, on implementation day—that is, very early on in the process. U.S. sanctions focused exclusively on Iran's support for terrorism, its human rights abuses, and its missile activities would remain, as would the U.S. trade ban on Iran, though certain items would be licensed or otherwise exempted from the ban. The EU, in turn, would terminate all nuclear-related sanctions, including those on banking, energy, and trade, on implementation day.

Regarding the schedule, it had to be adjusted to the congressional review process. Thus, "Adoption Day"—the date when Iran would begin to dismantle its centrifuges and the United States and the EU would make a legally binding decision to lift sanctions once Iran's steps had been fulfilled—would take place ninety days after the endorsement of the JCPOA by the UN Security Council. This would allow enough time for Congress to review the agreement. Once this process was completed and the IAEA certified it, "Implementation Day" would arrive. Then, either eight years after Adoption Day or the date on which the IAEA concludes Iran's nuclear program is peaceful, Iran will seek to ratify the Additional Protocol while the U.S. Congress will repeal its nuclear-related sanctions legislation. That day will be referred to as "Transition Day."

The parties also settled on an elaborate dispute resolution mechanism. A joint commission would be formed consisting of representatives of the P5+1 and Iran. Any state could file a complaint to the commission. There would also be a three-person advisory board for issuance of nonbinding opinions on compliance issues. If any matter could not be resolved by the commission, any state could refer the matter to the UN Security Council. The UN Security Council would need unanimous consent among the P5 to continue the lifting of sanctions or else all the provisions of the previous Security Council resolutions would kick back into place. As a result, all permanent members of the Security Council would be able to unilaterally move to reimpose UN Security Council sanctions on Iran.

50. Wright, "Tehran's Promise." Interview with John Kerry, September 8, 2016. Interview with Sergey Ryabkov, November 20, 2015. Interview with Federica Mogherini.

51. Interview with Chris Backemeyer. Interview with National Security Council Deputy Spokesperson Bernadette Meehan, October 9, 2015. Interview with senior White House staffer, April 11, 2016.

52. Thomas Erdbrink, "Ayatollah Khamenei, Backing Iran Negotiators, Endorses Nuclear Deal," New York Times, July 18, 2015.

53. "Revealed: Iran's 15 Deal Secrets."

54. Ibid.

55. Scott Peterson, "Why Iran's Revolutionary Guard Backs a Nuclear Deal: It's Just Business," Christian Science Monitor, June 3, 2015. Najmeh Bozorgmehr, "Iran's Revolutionary Guards Wary of Threat to Business Interests," Financial Times, July 2, 2015. Thomas Erdbrink, "Iran's Hard-Liners Sharpen Attacks on U.S. as Nuclear Talks Continue," New York Times, July 9, 2015.

56. Press conference by the president, White House, July 15, 2015. Press conference by John Kerry, U.S. Department of State, July 14, 2015.

57. Thomas Friedman, "Obama Makes His Case on Iran Nuclear Deal," New York Times, July 15, 2015.

SIXTEEN The War Zone in Washington

1. Ben Caspit, "Is Israel in Cahoots with Saudi Arabia?," Al Monitor, May 14, 2015. Baz Ratner, "Israel Military Cautiously Upbeat on Iran Nuclear Deal," Reuters, June 4, 2015. Chaim Levinson, "Israel's Nuclear Advisory Panel Endorses Iran Deal," Haaretz, October 22, 2015. Joshua Mitnick, "Is Iran Deal a Threat To Israel? New Signs Military Is at Odds with Netanyahu," Christian Science Monitor, August 3, 2015. J. J. Goldberg, "Israel's Top General Praises Iran Deal as 'Strategic Turning Point' in Slap at Bibi," Forward, January 26, 2016. Graham Allison, "Is Iran Still Israel's Top Threat?," Atlantic, March 8, 2016. Uzi Eilam, the former director of Israel's Atomic Energy Commission, even quietly lobbied the U.S. Congress to embrace the deal during the summer of 2015 (Uzi Eilam, "I Ran Israel's Atomic Energy Commission. I Know the Iran Deal Is Working," J Street Blog, July 12, 2016).

2. Efraim Halevy, "Why Israel Must Bury Hatchet with U.S. over Iran—Now," Forward, September 17, 2015. Carol Giacomo, "In Israel, Some Support the Iran Deal," New York Times, July 23, 2015. Interview with Tal Shalev, November 24, 2015. Interview with president of J Street, Jeremy Ben-Ami, January 7, 2016.

3. Giacomo, "In Israel." Interview with Israeli journalist Amir Tibon, November 25, 2015.

4. Barak Ravid, "Netanyahu, U.K.'s Hammond Spar Publicly over Iran Deal," Haaretz, July 16, 2015.

5. Ibid.

6. Laly Waymouth, "Israeli Defense Minister: Iranian Nuclear Deal 'a Very Bad One,'" Washington Post, June 2, 2015. Moshe Ya'alon, "Israeli Defense Minister: Don't Be Fooled by Iran's 'Charm Offensive,'" Defense News, December 13, 2015.

7. Jonathan Adler, "Ex-Intel Chief: Iran Deal Good for Israel," *Daily Beast,* July 21, 2015. David Ignatius, "Israel's Side of the Iran Dispute," *Washington Post,* February 20, 2015.

8. Ignatius, "Israel's Side." Michael Wilner, "Rice Says PM's Stance on Iranian Nukes Is 'Not a Viable Negotiating Position,'" *Jerusalem Post,* March 4, 2015.

9. Rob Kampeas, "How Bibi Alienated All His Jewish Allies at the White House," *Forward,* June 3, 2015. "Israeli Minister Steinitz: We Can 'Sway' U.S. Public Opinion on Iran Nuclear Deal," *Algemeiner Journal,* July 13, 2015. Dennis Ross, "How Obama Got to 'Yes' on Iran: The Inside Story," *Politico,* October 8, 2015.

10. Uri Savir, "Netanyahu, the Great Pretender," *Al Monitor,* November 22, 2015. Interview with Dalia Dassa Kaye of the RAND Corporation, November 16, 2015. Interview with Dylan Williams, vice president of Government Affairs at J Street, November 16, 2015. Interview with Peter Beinart, December 10, 2015. Kampeas, "How Bibi Alienated." It should not be forgotten that Netanyahu may have felt that he had no choice but to fight Obama on the deal. After all, for the past two decades, no Israeli politician had pushed the argument that Iran constituted an existential threat more than Netanyahu. "It's 1938, and Iran is Germany, and Ahmadinejad is Hitler," he repeatedly warned. After having personified the notion of Iran as an existential threat, what maneuverability did he have to turn around and tell the Israeli public that he had no choice but to succumb to Obama's compromise with Iran? How could he politically sell a compromise with an existential threat? Netanyahu might have simply painted himself in a corner.

11. Eli Lake, "Israelis and Saudis Reveal Secret Talks to Thwart Iran," Bloomberg, June 4, 2015. Barak Ravid, "Thaw Between Washington and Tehran Brings Israel and Gulf States Closer," *Haaretz,* September 29, 2013. Ben Caspit, "Is Israel in Cahoots with Saudi Arabia?," *Al Monitor,* May 14, 2015. Waymouth, "Israeli Defense Minister."

12. David Sanger, "Saudi Arabia Promises to Match Iran in Nuclear Capability," *New York Times,* May 13, 2015. Interview with Colin Kahl, January 28, 2016. Anne Barnard, "Saudi Arabia Cuts Billions of Aid to Lebanon, Opening Door for Iran," *New York Times,* March 2, 2016.

13. On-the-record White House conference call on the Gulf Cooperation Council summit, May 11, 2015.

14. Alisa Chang, "Lobbyists Spending Millions to Sway the Undecided on Iran Deal," NPR, August 6, 2015. Chuck Freilich, "Opposing the Iran Deal Has Done Great Damage to AIPAC," *Newsweek,* October 13, 2015. Nathan Guttman, "Was Battle Against Iran Deal a Noble Crusade—Or Epic Flop?," *Forward,* September 2, 2015. Interview with Peter Beinart. Interview with Chevi Shalem, February 3, 2016. Jim Lobe, "Former AIPAC Official on Iran's Importance to AIPAC," *Lobe Log,* July 24, 2015. Interview with retired Brigadier General Shlomo Brom, February 25, 2016.

15. Adam Entous and Danny Yadron, "U.S. Spy Net on Israel Snares Congress," *Wall Street Journal,* December 29, 2015. Interview with senior administration official, January 28, 2016.

16. Interview with senior administration official, January 2016. Interview with Senator Dick Durbin (D-IL), March 8, 2016.

17. Interview with Bob Creamer, February 22, 2016. Interview with Congresswoman Jan Schakowsky (D-IL), January 8, 2016.

18. Bernard Avishai, "How Chuck Schumer Lost on Iran," *New Yorker,* September 9, 2015.

19. Alexander Bolton, "GOP Crafts Iran Deal Attack Plan," *Hill,* July 14, 2015.

20. Interview with White House staffer, February 4, 2016.

21. Interview with Joe Cirincione, February 29, 2016.

22. Michelle Dover, "Grants on Steroids," *Huffington Post,* February 25, 2016.

23. Eli Clifton, "Anti-Iran Deal Groups Better Funded than Pro-Deal Groups by Nearly Five to One," *Lobe Log,* July 27, 2015. Eli Clifton, "Why the Hawks Are Winning the Iran Debate," *Nation,* July 24, 2015.

24. Interview with Stephen Heintz, February 27, 2016. Interview with Suzanne DiMaggio, March 16, 2016. Interview with Ambassador Bill Luers, March 15, 2016.

25. Interview with former undersecretary of state Tom Pickering, December 7, 2015. Interview with Stephen Heintz. Interview with Suzanne DiMaggio. Interview with Bill Luers.

26. Interview with Joe Cirincione.

27. Amy Davidson, "Crocodiles and Pontius Pilate: The Iran Debate's Descent," *New Yorker,* July 29, 2015. Sabrina Sidiqqui, "John Kerry Pushes Back as Republicans Attack Iran Deal at Senate Hearing," *Guardian,* July 23, 2015.

28. Nathan Guttman, "Meet Barack Obama's Jewish Flack Catcher," *Forward,* December 7, 2015. Interview with National Security Council staffer, October 9, 2015. Interview with senior administration official, January 28, 2016. Interview with White House staffer, December 8, 2015. Interview with Congressman David Price (D-NC), December 1, 2015. Interview with White House staffer, February 4, 2016.

29. Interview with Dick Durbin. Interview with White House staffer, February 4, 2016.

30. Interview with Dick Durbin. Mike DeBonis, "How Sen. Durbin Spent His Summer Saving the Iran Deal," *Washington Post,* September 11, 2015.

31. Interview with Ambassador Gerard Araud, September 17, 2015. Interview with Ambassador Peter Wittig, November 30, 2015. Interview with Ambassador Peter Westmacott, November 12, 2015.

32. Interview with Jan Schakowsky. Interview with Congresswoman Nancy Pelosi (D-CA), February 25, 2016. Ruth Sherlock, "British Ambassador to Washington: I Had a Hard Time over the Iran Deal," *Telegraph*, February 14, 2016. Jennifer Steinhauer, "Republicans Have Minds Made Up as Debate Begins on Iran Nuclear Deal," *New York Times*, July 23, 2015.

33. Interview with Nancy Pelosi, February 25, 2016. Interview with White House staffer, February 4, 2016. Julian Hattem, "How Obama Won on Iran," *Hill,* September 9, 2015.

34. Interview with Jan Schakowsky. Interview with Nancy Pelosi.

35. Interview with White House staffer, February 4, 2016.

36. Interview with Jan Schakowsky. Interview with Nancy Pelosi.

37. DeBonis, "How Sen. Durbin Spent His Summer." Interview with Dick Durbin.

38. Michael Crowley, "Nuclear Experts Fall in Behind Obama," *Politico,* August 18, 2015. William Broad, "Top Scientists Back Iran Deal in Letter," *New York Times,* August 8, 2015. Interview with Kelsey Davenport of the Arms Control Association, November 30, 2015.

39. Hattem, "How Obama Won." Jacob Kornbluh, "Obama Implores Supporters to Lobby Congress in Favor of Iran Nuclear Deal," *Haaretz,* July 31, 2015.

40. Rick Gladstone, "On Youtube, Iran Activists Urge America to Back Nuclear Deal," *New York Times,* August 25, 2015. "Iran Reformists Implore U.S. Congress: Approve Nuclear Deal to Boost Human Rights," *Jerusalem Post,* August 26, 2015. Nahal Toosi, "Scholars: Iran Deal Will Stabilize Mideast," *Politico,* August 27, 2015. Philip Elliott, "Jewish Leaders Urge Congress to OK Deal with Iran," *Time,* August 20, 2015.

41. Pamela Constable, "Iranian Exiles Respond in Unexpected Ways to Idea of U.S.-Iran Nuclear Talks," *Washington Post,* May 21, 2015.

42. Eli Clifton, "AIPAC Bristles at Obama's Reminder of Iraq War Lobbying," *Lobe Log,* August 5, 2015. Jeffrey M. Jones, "Among Religious Groups, Jewish Americans Most Strongly Oppose War," Gallup News Service, February 23, 2007. Laurie Goodstein, "Threats and Responses: American Jews; Divide Among Jews Leads to Silence on Iraq War," *New York Times,* March 15, 2003.

43. MJ Rosenberg, "AIPAC Spent Millions of Dollars to Defeat the Iran Deal. Instead, It May Have Destroyed Itself," *Nation,* September 11, 2015.

44. Interview with Bob Creamer. Daniel Kurtzer, "Why Iran Deal Is Good for Israel," CNN, August 5, 2015.

45. Jonathan Weisman and Alexander Burns, "Iran Deal Opens a Vitriolic Divide Among American Jews," *New York Times,* August 28, 2015. Chemi Shalev, "Obama Accused of Using 'Dark, Nasty Stuff' Against Jewish Critics like Schumer," *Haaretz,* August 8, 2015. Ellen Nakashima, "Administration, Lawmakers Clash over Iran Policy," *Washington Post,* January 22, 2015.

46. Julie Hirschfeld Davis, "Fears of Lasting Rift as Obama Battles Pro-Israel Group on Iran," *New York Times,* August 7, 2015. Interview with White House staffer, March 23, 2016.

47. Private briefing at the White House, July 30, 2015. Interview with White House staffer, March 23, 2016. Hirschfeld Davis, "Fears of Lasting Rift."

48. Interview with White House staffer, March 23, 2016. Hirschfeld Davis, "Fears of Lasting Rift."

49. Kevin Liptak, Deirdre Walsh, and Jim Acosta, "Obama Tries to Reassure American Jewish Leaders on Iran," CNN, August 5, 2015. Interview with Jeremy Ben Ami, January 7, 2016.

50. "Obama to U.S. Jews: On Iran, Keep in Mind We're All Pro-Israel," *Haaretz,* August 28, 2015. Liptak, Walsh, and Acosta, "Obama Tries to Reassure." Interview with

White House staffer, March 23, 2016. Weisman and Burns, "Iran Deal Opens a Vitriolic Divide."

51. "Obama to U.S. Jews." Liptak, Walsh, and Acosta, "Obama Tries to Reassure."
Interview with White House staffer, March 23, 2016. Hirschfeld Davis, "Fears of Lasting Rift." Interview with Jeremy Ben Ami. Weisman and Burns, "Iran Deal Opens
a Vitriolic Divide." Kevin Liptak and Hilary Krieger, "Obama's Iran Nuclear Deal
Rhetoric Troubles American Jews," CNN, August 10, 2015.

52. Remarks by the president on the Iran nuclear deal, August 5, 2015.

53. "Polling: American Jews Strongly Support the Iran Deal & Obama, July 2015,"
Jewishdatabank.org, July 28, 2015. Todd Gitlin and Steven Cohen, "On the Iran Deal,
American Jewish 'Leaders' Don't Speak for Most Jews," Washington Post, August 14,
2015. Interview with Jeremy Ben Ami.

54. Julian Hattem, "Schumer Comes out Against Iran Deal," Hill, August 6, 2015.
Interview with National Security Council staffer, December 8, 2015. Interview with
White House staffer, March 2, 2015. Interview with White House staffer, February 2, 2015.

55. Hirschfeld Davis, "Fears of Lasting Rift." Dan Roberts, "White House
Warns Chuck Schumer: Disapprove of Iran Deal at Your Own Peril," Guardian,
August 7, 2015.

56. Interview with Dick Durbin. Roberts, "White House Warns Chuck Schumer."
Brian Stewart, "More than 185,000 Join Democratic Party Donor Strike, Pledging to
Withhold $43 Million to Democrats Who Scuttle Diplomacy with Iran," MoveOn.org,
August 20, 2015.

57. Interview with White House staffer, February 2, 2015. Roberts, "White House
Warns Chuck Schumer." Interview with Bob Creamer. Interview with Jeremy Ben
Ami. Interview with White House staffer, February 4, 2016. Kristina Peterson and
Carol Lee, "Obama Secures 34 Senators' Support for Iran Nuclear Deal," Wall Street
Journal, September 2, 2015. Interview with White House staffer, December 8, 2015.

58. Interview with White House staffer, December 8, 2015. Karoun Demirjian,
"Senate Rejects Attempt to Derail Iran Deal in Victory for Obama," Washington Post,
September 10, 2015. Erin Kelly, "Democrats Block Senate Vote to Reject Iran Nuclear
Deal for Second Time," USA Today, September 15, 2015.

59. Julie Hirschfeld Davis, "Influential Pro-Israel Group Suffers Stinging Political Defeat," New York Times, September 10, 2015. Rosenberg, "AIPAC Spent Millions."
Chuck Freilich, "Opposing the Iran Deal Has Done Great Damage to AIPAC," Newsweek, October 13, 2015. Amir Tibon and Tal Shalev, "Scenes from a Failed Marriage,"
Huffington Post, November 12, 2015. Interview with Bob Creamer.

60. Interview with Amir Tibon. Guttman, "Was Battle Against Iran Deal a
Noble Crusade?"

61. Interview with Jan Schakowsky. Interview with Congressman Keith Ellison
(D-MN), April 27, 2016. Ellison believes that had it not been for the groups that pushed
for diplomacy early on, such as the Friends Committee on National Legislation and
the National Iranian American Council, the victory on the Hill could not have been
secured. "The truth is NIAC was indispensable to this whole thing," he said. "I don't

think it would have happened without you guys because the people who wanted to push for the pro-diplomacy position wouldn't have had the information, wouldn't have had the support, wouldn't have had the writing ability."

62. Interview with White House staffer, February 4, 2016.

63. Interview with Nancy Pelosi. Interview with Joe Cirincione.

64. John Hudson, "Kerry: There Is No 'Better' Iran Deal," *Foreign Policy,* August 11, 2015.

65. AIPAC Statement on Proposed Iran Nuclear Agreement, July 15, 2015. Closed briefing at the White House, July 30, 2015. Interview with Nancy Pelosi.

66. AIPAC Statement on Proposed Iran Nuclear Agreement. Doug Bloomfield, "Chuck Schumer—The Canary in the Coalmine," *Jewish Week,* July 15, 2015.

67. Interview with Ben Rhodes, October 27, 2015. Interview with former National Security Council official, October 9, 2015.

68. Interview with Bob Creamer. Interview with Tom Pickering. Interview with Stephen Miles, February 17, 2016.

69. Karoun Demirjian and Carol Morello, "How AIPAC Lost the Iran Deal Fight," *Washington Post,* September 3, 2015. Jeffrey Goldberg, "Netanyahu's Victory over Iran," *Atlantic,* September 11, 2015.

70. Avishai, "How Chuck Schumer Lost on Iran." Interview with Bob Creamer. Eli Lake and Josh Rogin, "How Obama Out-Muscled AIPAC," Bloomberg, September 17, 2015. Guttman, "Was Battle Against Iran Deal a Noble Crusade?" Interview with Joe Cirincione.

71. Interview with John Bisognano of the White House, March 2, 2015.

72. Goldberg, "Netanyahu's Victory."

73. Freilich, "Opposing the Iran Deal." Lake and Rogin, "How Obama Out-Muscled AIPAC."

SEVENTEEN Conclusion

1. Daniel Levy, "Israel's Iran Deal Enthusiasts," *Foreign Affairs,* August 12, 2015.

2. Jeffrey Goldberg, "The Obama Doctrine," *Atlantic,* March 10, 2016.

3. Ibid.

4. "Britain Says Iran Too Powerful to Leave in Isolation," *Washington Post,* August 24, 2015. Interview with Ambassador Peter Wittig, November 30, 2015.

5. Robin Wright, "Obama on War and Peace," *New Yorker,* August 6, 2015. Dan De Luce, "After Iran Deal, U.S. Bids to Revive Peace Talks on Syria," *Foreign Policy,* August 10, 2015. "Kerry: Movement on Syria Not Possible Without Iran Deal," *Charlie Rose,* April 6, 2016. Interview with Federica Mogherini, December 12, 2015. Tim Arango and Ahmed Azam, "U.S. and Iran Unlikely Allies in Iraq Battle," *New York Times,* September 1, 2014. John Kerry's remarks at the Aspen Ideas Festival and conversation with Walter Isaacson, June 28, 2016.

6. Wright, "Obama on War and Peace." Interview with Ambassador Peter Westmacott, November 12, 2015. The hope was for shifts not just in Iran's foreign policy, but

also its domestic orientation. "The deal carried a lot of potential for what this means for Iran and for the region, but also what it will mean for Iran internally," Ambassador Wittig told me. "This is a tremendously important aspect of this deal that is underappreciated in the United States. But it won't happen overnight" (interview with Peter Wittig).

7. Jeffrey Goldberg, "How Obama Views the Men and Women Who (Also) Rule the World," *Atlantic*, March 18, 2016, and "Obama Doctrine."

8. Nawaf Obaid, "The Salman Doctrine: The Saudi Reply to Obama's Weakness," *National Interest*, March 30, 2016. Goldberg, "Obama Doctrine."

9. Obaid, "Salman Doctrine." Colum Lynch, "Syria Crisis Tests Newfound Détente Between Washington and Tehran," *Foreign Policy*, November 4, 2015.

10. Interview with Stephen Heinz of the Rockefeller Brothers Fund, February 27, 2016. Admiral Mike Mullen, "Why I Like the Iran Deal (Sort Of)," *Politico*, April 16, 2015.

11. Yaroslav Trofimov, "Saudi Arabia Reluctantly Finds Common Ground with Israel About Iran," *Wall Street Journal*, June 18, 2016. Shibley Telhami, "On Iran, the GCC Is Paying the Price of Relying on Benjamin Netanyahu," Brookings, May 19, 2015. Interview with Jake Sullivan, September 23, 2015. Levy, "Israel's Iran Deal Enthusiasts." Efraim Halevy, "Before We Storm Capitol Hill," Ynetnews, August 20, 2015.

12. Payam Mohseni, "Tipping the Balance?: Implications of the Iran Nuclear Deal on Israeli Security," Belfer Center at Harvard University, December 2015. Moshe Ya'alon, "Why Iran Is More Dangerous than Islamic State," *Los Angeles Times*, September 29, 2016. David E. Sanger, "ISIS Fight Raises Fears That Efforts to Curb Iran Will Slip," *New York Times*, September 12, 2014. Ben Norton, "Israeli Think Tank: Don't Destroy ISIS; It's a 'Useful Tool' Against Iran, Hezbollah, Syria," Salon, August 23, 2016. Adam Taylor, "Israeli Defense Minister: If I Had to Choose Between Iran and ISIS, I'd Choose ISIS," *Washington Post*, January 19, 2016.

13. Interview with senior administration official, January 2016. Ariel Whitman, "Ex Mossad Chief: Israel's Biggest Threat Is Potential Civil War, Not Iran," *Jerusalem Post*, August 30, 2016. Ben Rhodes also rejects the idea that more dialogue with Israel would have impacted the outcome. The conversations between Obama and Netanyahu confirmed "that there was never going to be a deal they supported. We could have talked to them a hundred times, and they still wouldn't have supported the deal" (interview with Ben Rhodes, October 27, 2015).

14. Rob Kampeas, "How Bibi Alienated All His Jewish Allies at the White House," *Forward*, June 3, 2015.

15. "Netanyahu Brought About Iran Nuke Deal, Says Ex-Mossad Head in Last Interview," *Times of Israel*, May 6, 2016. Interview with Shlomo Brom, February 25, 2016. Amir Tibon and Tal Shalev, "Scenes from a Failed Marriage," *Huffington Post*, November 20, 2015. Yossi Melman, "The Iran Deal's Bad for Israel? Netanyahu's to Blame," *Huffington Post*, August 3, 2015.

16. Interview with Javad Zarif, April 20, 2016.

17. Patrick Goodenough, "Kerry: 'Successful' Iran Nuclear Deal a 'Model' for How to Deal with North Korea," *CBS News*, June 7, 2016. Thomas Friedman, "Obama

Makes His Case on Iran Nuclear Deal," *New York Times,* July 15, 2015. In fact, Russia's role in the negotiations was extremely constructive by all accounts. Russian Foreign Minister Sergey Lavrov and Zarif were old colleagues from their time as UN ambassadors. They both knew the UN system "by heart," and the United States often turned to Lavrov to make clear to Zarif that "there was no more arguing space" on any specific variable in the negotiations. Sergey Ryabkov, the Russian deputy foreign minister who led the negotiations from the Russian side, was even more instrumental. Not only did he ensure that the worsening U.S.-Russia bilateral relations didn't impact the nuclear talks, but his creativity and diligence saved the talks on more than one occasion. Interview with Federica Mogherini, December 15, 2015. Laura Rozen, "Russian Envoy Helps Advance Iranian Nuclear Deal," *Al Monitor,* December 4, 2014.

18. Obama's address at the American University, August 5, 2015. Interview with Mohammad Nahavandian, chief of staff to President Hassan Rouhani, September 24, 2015.

19. Interview with former White House official, July 31, 2015. Interview with Deputy Foreign Minister Sergey Ryabkov, November 20, 2015.

20. Discussion with Secretary of State John Kerry at the Council on Foreign Relations, July 24, 2015.

21. Obama's address at the American University.

22. Jay Solomon, *The Iran Wars* (New York: Random House, 2016), 7.

23. Philip Ewing, "Why the Pentagon Wants an Iran Deal," *Politico,* July 9, 2015.

24. "Netanyahu Brought About Iran Nuke Deal." Shibley Telhami, "Netanyahu Steered U.S. Toward War with Iran—The Result Is a Deal He Hates," *Jerusalem Post,* July 25, 2015.

25. Interview with former National Security Council official, October 2015.

26. Interview with Mohammad Nahavandian. Interview with Deputy Foreign Minister Majid Ravanchi, October 4, 2015. Interview with Professor Mohsen Milani, February 8, 2016. Interview with senior European diplomat, June 22, 2016.

27. Interview with senior administration official, August 16, 2016. Interview with Ben Rhodes. Carol Morello, "U.S., E.U. Hold Grueling Talks with Iran About Its Nuclear Program," *Washington Post,* October 16, 2014.

28. Ya'alon, "Why Iran Is More Dangerous." Interview with senior National Security Council director, October 2015. Interview with senior EU diplomat, December 16, 2015.

29. "Iran Unveils Monument to Jewish Soldiers Killed in War with Iraq," *Haaretz,* December 18, 2014. Ben Caspit, "Israeli Security Officials Recognize Change in Iran," *Al Monitor,* February 2, 2014.

30. Interview with senior State Department official, September 21, 2015. Interview with former White House official. Interview with senior administration official, August 16, 2016. Interview with White House staffer, December 8, 2015. Interview with former senior National Security Council director, September 2015.

31. Interview with an informal advisor to Foreign Minister Javad Zarif, September 14, 2015. Interview with former White House official.

32. Arash Karami, "Araghchi: Iran's Nuclear Achievements Led to Agreement," *Al Monitor,* August 17, 2015. In the same recording, Araghchi acknowledges that Iran could have paid a lesser price had it pursued different tactics, but rejects the idea that Iran could ultimately have become a nuclear threshold state without paying a price. "During the last 10–12 years, the principle of our nuclear policy has been constant. However, I do not deny that if someone says that had we behaved in a different way—in tactics, not in principle—it was possible that our costs would have been less." He continued, "It's possible to say that had we pursued a certain method earlier or later, had we done more or done less, we would have paid fewer costs or we would have gotten better results. This discussion is always there. But could we have become nuclear without costs? Certainly not. We had to pay the costs. Everything has a cost."

33. Interview with former senior National Security Council director. David Morrison and Peter Oborne, "U.S. Scuppered Deal with Iran in 2005, Says Then–British Foreign Minister," *Open Democracy,* September 23, 2013.

34. Morrison and Oborne, "U.S. Scuppered Deal."

35. Interview with Javier Solana, February 25, 2016. Conversation with Javad Zarif, March 27, 2015. Closed briefing at the White House, November 2013. Interview with former State Department official, September 2015.

36. John Kerry, "Remarks on Nuclear Agreement with Iran," Department of State, September 2, 2015.

37. Sabrina Sidiqqui, "John Kerry Pushes Back as Republicans Attack Iran Deal at Senate Hearing," *Guardian,* July 23, 2015.

38. "Iran Lawmakers Curtailed on Power to Veto Nuclear Deal," Ynetnews, July 21, 2015. Thomas Erdbrink and Somini Sengupta, "Iran's Supreme Leader Orders Parliament to Vote on Nuclear Deal," *New York Times,* September 3, 2015. Farideh Farhi, "Whatever Happened to the Iranian Parliament's JCPOA's Review?," *Lobe Log,* September 25, 2015.

39. "Iran's Rouhani Blasts Critics as 'Political Cowards,'" Agence France Presse, August 11, 2015.

40. Interview with Ben Rhodes. Interview with Joe Cirincione, February 29, 2016. Interview with Stephen Heintz, February 27, 2016.

41. Interview with senior administration official, August 16, 2016.

42. Interview with White House staffer. Interview with senior National Security Council official, October 10, 2015. Friedman, "Obama Makes His Case."

43. Interview with Farideh Farhi, February 1, 2015.

44. Ben Rhodes, comments at the Aspen Ideas Festival, June 29, 2015.

45. "Obama on Iran Deal: 'Attitudes Will Change,'" NPR, August 11, 2015. Gardiner Harris, "Deeper Mideast Aspirations Seen in Nuclear Deal with Iran," *New York Times,* July 31, 2015. Interview with Senator Dick Durbin (D-IL), April 3, 2016.

46. Interview with Reza Marashi, April 2, 2016. Stephen Heintz and Ben Rhodes Discuss American-Iranian Relations, Atlantic Council, June 16, 2016.

47. Discussion with Iranian diplomats, June 28, 2015.

48. Background briefing by senior Iranian diplomat, July 2, 2015. Jeffrey Goldberg, "John Kerry on the Risk of Congress 'Screwing' the Ayatollah," *Atlantic*, August 5, 2015. De Luce, "After Iran Deal." Interview with President Hassan Rouhani, *60 Minutes*, September 20, 2015.

49. Interview with Farideh Farhi. Thomas Erdbrink, "Iran's Hard-Liners Sharpen Attacks on U.S. as Nuclear Talks Continue," *New York Times,* July 9, 2015. Seyed Mohammad Marandi, "Ayatollah Khamenei and a Principled Foreign Policy," Renovation and Intellectual Ijtihad in Imam Khamenei, Beirut, June 6–7, 2011. Ellie Geranmayeh, "Khamenei on Negotiations with U.S.," *Lobe Log*, June 7, 2016. Scott Peterson, "Is Iran Ready to Improve U.S. Ties? Leader's Tough Talk Masks Debate," *Christian Science Monitor,* July 21, 2015.

50. Ibid.

51. Trita Parsi, "Trump Hasn't Mastered the Art of Killing the Iran Deal," *Foreign Policy*, November 11, 2016.

52. Ibid.

53. Interview with Dalia Dassa Kaye, November 16, 2015. Mullen, "Why I Like the Iran Deal." Daniel Levy, "Israel's Iran Deal Enthusiasts," *Foreign Affairs,* August 12, 2015.

54. Interview with Ambassador Gerard Araud, September 17, 2015.

55. Matthew Rosenberg, Mark Mazzetti, and Eric Schmitt, "In Trump's Security Pick, Michael Flynn, 'Sharp Elbows' and No Dissent," *New York Times,* December 3, 2016. Mark Perry, "James Mattis' 33-Year Grudge Against Iran," *Politico,* December 4, 2016. James Carden, "With Mattis, Trump Adds Another Iran Hawk to His Cabinet," *Nation,* December 7, 2016. Paul Armstrong, "Iran: 'Ramadan Terror Plot' on Tehran Foiled," CNN, June 20, 2016. Jack Moore, "Iran Dismantles Foreign ISIS Cell Plotting to Bomb Ashura Mourners," *Newsweek,* October 13, 2016.

56. Interview with Secretary of State John Kerry, September 7, 2016. Interview with Rob Malley, October 10, 2015.

57. Trita Parsi, "The Iran Deal Proves That Peace Is Possible," *Foreign Policy*, June 24, 2015.

Index